Eloquenc

Electronic Age

ELOQUENCE IN AN ELECTRONIC AGE

The Transformation of Political Speechmaking

Kathleen Hall Jamieson

OXFORD UNIVERSITY PRESS
New York   Oxford

Oxford University Press

Oxford   New York   Toronto
Delhi   Bombay   Calcutta   Madras   Karachi
Petaling Jaya   Singapore   Hong Kong   Tokyo
Nairobi   Dar es Salaam   Cape Town
Melbourne   Auckland

and associated companies in
Berlin   Ibadan

Copyright © 1988 by Oxford University Press, Inc.

First published in 1988 by Oxford University Press, Inc.,
200 Madison Avenue, New York, New York 10016

First issued as an Oxford University Press paperback, 1990

Library of Congress Cataloging-in-Publication Data

Jamieson, Kathleen Hall.
Eloquence in an electronic age/Kathleen Hall Jamieson.
p.   cm.
Bibliography: p.
Includes index.
1. Public speaking.   2. Eloquence.   I. Title.
PN4121.J327   1988
808.5'1—dc19   87-23057
                                                CIP
ISBN 0-19-503826-6 (alk. paper)
ISBN 0-19-506317-1 (pbk.)

4   6   8   10   9   7   5   3

Printed in the United States of America

To K. B.

Preface

On October 14, 1912, Theodore Roosevelt's life was saved by a scripted speech when the folded text in his coat pocket slowed the bullet of a would-be assassin. Had the former president been more concise or had the advent of TelePrompTers eliminated the need for his typed version, he might not have lived to declare to the stunned audience, "I will make this speech or die!"

This book is not about speakers who outlived their speeches but about speeches whose power gives them a life of their own. So, for example, FDR's words transformed December 7 into a day that will live in infamy, and Lincoln's words continue to commit us to the belief that ours is a "government of the people, by the people and for the people." The statements that shaped history include: "Go ye therefore and teach all nations," "Land, Peace and Bread," "entangling alliances with none," "war to make the world safe for democracy," "we have nothing to fear but fear itself," "we shall fight them on the beaches," and "I have a dream."

From Rome's Cicero to New York's Mario Cuomo, speechmaking is powerful. Cicero's orations drove the tyrant Cataline from Rome; a single speech at the 1984 Democratic convention by Cuomo catapulted him into contention for a nomination he repeatedly disclaimed.

My interest in eloquence is prompted by a desire to understand how we elect and whom we elect. Penetrating public speech is increasingly important in a time when voters are searching behind promises for

> Under these circumstances, it has been a matter of
> genuine regret to me that Senator LaFollette, who has done
> so much for the Progressive Cause, has felt that because of
> his antagonism to me he was obliged to range himself against
> the Progressive Movement in this campaign, thereby giving to
> his old-time enemies, the reactionaries, a much needed support
> which they have acknowledged by the first praise they have
> given him in twenty years.   It has been asserted that I did
> not take sides with the LaFollette people in their campaign
> in Wisconsin in 1904. This is an error. On October 16th,
> of that year, I made my position clear in a letter to Mr. Cor-
> telyou, Chairman of the National Republican Committee, which ran
> in part as follows:
>
>   "I think Babcock and his people should
>   be told that, especially in view of the decision
>   of the Supreme Court, there must not be any kind

For more than a millennium, students of public address have speculated about the effects of speeches and the criteria that properly determine whether a speech is noteworthy. This speech text gained prominence for slowing a bullet shot at Theodore Roosevelt on October 14, 1912, by an anti-third term fanatic. Its significance resides as well in TRs insistence that he was willing to die to deliver it. Although the bullet had lodged in his chest, TR declared, "I will make this speech or die. It is one thing or the other." (Courtesy Political History Division, Smithsonian)

clues about whether or not a candidate is honest, knowledgeable, high principled, and temperamentally suited to lead the nation. In voter decisions, the candidate's character is now more central than his or her stands on issues and party identification. In the interstices of sentences and the intersections between speech and behavior, voters find data they consider decisive. In spring 1987, these data discredited presidential hopeful Gary Hart. Hart had countered rumors about womanizing by challenging reporters to "go ahead" and "put a tail on me," prophesying that "They'd be very bored."[1] His words established a test of his personal credibility that reporters for the *Miami Herald* accepted. The married candidate's subsequent weekend with attractive, young Donna Rice and his protestations about the innocence of the encounter undid his presidential aspirations. The contradiction between his words and his actions called into doubt his honesty and at the same time raised questions about whether he was disposed to take risks and to believe that he was not bound by conventional moral codes. Here was a candidacy dramatically unhinged not by a position on foreign or domestic policy but by concerns about the person who would be president.

The news stories confirmed two dramatic changes in the political climate. Where reporters' observations of President John Kennedy's trysts went unreported, Hart was "staked out." The barrier that once shielded the private lives of politicians from public view has crumbled. At the same time, a photo of Donna Rice on Hart's lap provided a form of evidence more damning than any words. The relationships between public speech and private self, self-disclosure, and visual cues are the subjects of later chapters.

What we traditionally knew as eloquence cannot survive this new environment intact. This book searches out eloquence's new incarnations and ultimately asks whether they can and should mesh with the ancient art.

At a time in which the word rhetoric more often than not is said with a sneer and meant as a slur, eloquence retains its respectability. Yet, if not used promiscuously, the word at least is employed with an enervating casualness. Any political speech by a prominent person that elicits the enthusiasm of a large audience is quickly peppered by commentators with the label eloquent. This is true even if the speech produced only applause where it sought action and even when applause was prompted by predispositions, not freshly forged conviction.

Ironically, these same pundits pine for those halcyon days beyond recall when audiences were interested and candidates eloquent. The lament is a long-lived one. In 80 A.D., Tacitus attributed the decline of oratory to inattentive parents, incompetent teachers, dissolute young men and neglect of the "ancient discipline."[2] In the mid-nineteenth century, Charles Dickens complained that newspapers were groaning "heavily under a pressure of orations, each vying with the other . . . in having little or nothing to do with the matter at hand."[3] "Today," wrote Lance Morrow in *Time* in August 1980, "oratory seems in serious, possibly terminal decline."[4] In Tacitus' time, a politically sterile environment repressed free speech and, with it, public eloquence. But the nineteenth century produced Disraeli and Gladstone, Lincoln, Webster and Calhoun, Douglass, Stanton, and the Grimke sisters. In our own century, the speeches of Gandhi, Churchill, and FDR stand out. And Ronald Reagan's speech at Normandy holds up well as do speeches delivered on a number of occasions by Mario Cuomo.

This book is about political eloquence—what it is and isn't, how our concept of it has changed and how it has remained the same,.the talents and techniques that differentiate those who are eloquent from those who wish they were but aren't, the ways and means of speakers from Demosthenes to Reagan, and the work and wiles of speechwriters, Republican and Democrat, ancient and modern. Throughout, the book asks: "Has television changed our concept of eloquence, altered its audience's receptivity to eloquence, or functioned as the scapegoat blamed for destroying something it never laid electrons on?"

In pursuit of this illusive yet alluring phenomenon, I will argue that the old eloquence of fire and sword has given way to an intimate disclosive art bent on conciliation, not conquest; that the eloquent person whose ideas are refined by the process of writing and rethinking is increasingly not the speaker but the speechwriter; that speakers' successes can sow the seeds of their failures: that those factors accounting for the eloquence of speakers from Cicero to Churchill are now largely missing from education; and that, in the age of television, dramatic, digestive, visual moments are replacing memorable words, making Carter's walk down Pennsylvania Avenue the rhetorical equivalent of FDR's "nothing to fear but fear itself." Accordingly, televised scenes of death in Vietnam were more potent than any antiwar speech. More eloquent than any rhetoric advocating civil rights were the televised images of police setting guard dogs and fire hoses against peacefully protesting black citizens.

This work hinges on its ability to explain why for so long Ronald Reagan remained more popular than his policies and why he was considered a "Great Communicator." Specifically, I will demonstrate that Ronald Reagan's success as a communicator was at least partially attributable to his embrace of a style once condemned as effeminate, that his use of self-disclosive stories immunized him from political assaults to which he otherwise was vulnerable, and that his knack for visual assertion enabled him to make claims that defied traditional logic and our usual tests of evidence. Reagan's performance also displayed the dangers in divorcing thought from the act of speaking it. Finally, I will argue for a concept of eloquence that unites pictures and verbal propositions, argumentative substance, illustrative stories, and the conception and delivery of ideas.

I wish to thank Herb Simons, Jane Blankenship, Robert Hopper, George Kennedy, Steve Lucas, Gerry Hauser, Curtis Church, and Karlyn Campbell for their midwivery of early chapters; Seamus Neary for research and photographic assistance; Kevin Dean for tracking elusive bibliographic material; Maura Clancey for research support; Roger Mudd for asking the questions this book tries to answer; and the staff of the East-West Center for providing an ocean, mountains, and a collegial environment in which to write. The book would not have gotten from prospectus to completed project were it not for the support of Mimi Melek who saw the work into production, Rosemary Wellner who again suffered through my Latinate constructions to edit with good humor and precision, and Susan Rabiner, an astute critic, talented editor, and good friend. At the University of Texas, Deanna Matthews and Charlotte Richards translated my cryptic handwriting into typed pages and Margaret Surratt and Robert Risher made it possible to chair a department and retain a semblance of sanity. Dean Bob Jeffrey protected my writing time from assault by memo and administrative detail and Vice President Gerry Fonken made me glad that I lost his $1.00 bet that he could lure me to UT. Without the generous research and travel support provided by the G. B. Dealey professorship this book would still be an outline. Through it all, Roderick P. Hart, in his Puritan Irish way, made my world safe for absurdity and Robert Hopper, recreating a role pioneered in grad school, made my world safe from bureaucracy. Beth Macom (bless her) "proofread."

I am grateful as well to the three men who add laundry and love to my life: Robert, Jr., and Patrick, who supplied hugs and the insistence that more people would read the book if it were called *Elephants in an Electronic Age*, and my husband Robert, who gave up the Navy to be landlocked with us in Austin. Finally, I am indebted to Kenneth Burke, to whom this book is gratefully dedicated, for enriching the academic scene and my life with puns, poetry, and perspective by incongruity.

Austin, Texas   K. H. J.
September, 1987

Contents

1. Educating the Eloquent Speaker   3

2. Incapacitating the Eloquent Speaker   31

3. The Flame of Oratory, The Fireside Chat   43

4. The "Effeminate" Style   67

5. The Memorable Phrase, The Memorable Picture   90

6. Dramatizing and Storytelling   118

7. Conversation and Self-Revelation   165

8. The Divorce Between Speech and Thought   201

9. Mating the Best of the Old and the New   238

   Notes   257

   Bibliography   269

   Index   293

*Eloquence in an
Electronic Age*

1

Educating the Eloquent Speaker

The early efforts of the classical world's greatest orator were derided for their "strange and uncouth style, which was cumbered with long sentences and tortured with formal arguments to a most harsh and disagreeable excess." To complicate his problems, he had "a weakness in his voice, a perplexed and indistinct utterance and a shortness of breath, which, by breaking and disjointing his sentences much obscured the sense and meaning of what he spoke." So, "in the end, being quite disheartened, he forsook the assembly."

When Demosthenes complained to Satyrus that "drunken sots, mariners, and illiterate fellows were heard, and had the hustings for their own, while he himself was despised," the actor encouraged him to practice his delivery. "Hereupon," Plutarch continues, "he built himself a place to study under ground . . . and hither he would come constantly every day to form his action and to exercise his voice; and here he would continue, oftentimes without intermission, two or three months together, shaving one half of his head, that so for shame he might not go abroad, though he desired it ever so much." In the privacy of his study, he also formulated arguments for and against the matters that had crossed his path that day and reworked the speeches he had heard others deliver. "Hence, it was that he was looked upon as a person of no great natural genius, but one who owed all the power and ability he had in speaking to labour and industry." [1]

Those who doubt that eloquence can be learned need only guess

3

which more recent but still revered speaker delivered this passage in his youth:

> I know the great volcano at Washington, aroused and directed by the evil spirit that reigns there, is belching forth the lava of political corruption in a current, broad and deep, which is sweeping with frightful velocity over the whole length and breadth of the land, bidding fair to leave unscathed no green spot of living thing; while on its bosom are riding, like demons on the waves of Hell, the imps of that evil spirit, and fiendishly taunting all those who dare resist its destroying course with the hopelessness of their effort; and, knowing this, I cannot deny that all may be swept away. Broken by it, I, too, may be; bow to it I never will. . . . If ever I feel the soul within me elevate and expand to those dimensions not wholly unworthy of its Almighty Architect, it is when I contemplate the cause of my country, deserted by all the world beside, and I standing up boldly and alone and hurling defiance at her victorious oppressors. Here, without contemplating consequences, before High Heaven, and in face of the world, I swear eternal fidelity to the just cause, as I deem it, of the land of my life, my liberty, and my love.[2]

Less than two and a half decades later, that speaker would deliver the Gettysburg Address. The transformation is not as astonishing as it at first may seem—few are eloquent from childhood.

Early in his career, another orator "found himself on his feet, with his mind a complete blank, while the awful silence was broken only by friendly, encouraging noises; he stood his ground until at last he could bear it no longer; back in his seat, he could only bury his head in his hands. After his breakdown in the House of Commons he dreaded getting up to speak more than ever. Sometimes he would persuade himself that what he was about to say had already been said, or that the time to say it was past. Any excuse served to keep him in his seat."[3] In 1953, that speaker received the Nobel Prize in literature in part for his "scintillating oratory." In the dark years of World War II he had rallied his country with ringing speeches. In the most often quoted, he said:

> We shall go on to the end. We shall fight in France, we shall fight on the seas and oceans, we shall fight with growing confidence and growing strength in the air, we shall defend our island, whatever the cost may be. We shall fight on the beaches, we shall fight on the landing grounds, we shall fight in the fields and in the streets, we shall fight in the hills; we shall never surrender, and even if, which I do not for a moment believe, this island or a large part of it were subjugated and starving, then our Empire beyond the seas, armed and guarded by the British Fleet, would carry on the

struggle, until, in God's good time, the new world, with all its power and might, steps forth to the rescue and the liberation of the old.[4]

In 1950, Winston Churchill confided to his physician, "Speaking to five thousand people through a microphone is no more tiring than talking to a hundred. It doesn't bother me. I'm not overawed by them. I've got used to it."[5]

In the lessons left us by our eloquent ancestors, there is good news and bad. The good news is that, by engaging in certain activities, our innate oratorical talents can be refined. The bad news is that these activities have been lost, stolen, or have strayed from our schools. When speaking held the central role in the conduct of public affairs, the disposition toward eloquence was cultivated. It no longer is.

Eloquence Flourishes Where Public Speaking Is an Honored Art

Ancient oratory was considered "a fine art, an art regarded by its cultivators, and by the public, as analogous to sculpture, to poetry, to painting, to music and to acting. This character is common to Greek and Roman oratory."[6] So, for example, Isocrates notes that listeners broke into loud applause when antitheses, symmetrical clauses, or other striking rhetorical figures were skillfully presented.[7]

Because it was the only way to reach a mass public, speech was not *a* means of influence but *the* means. Accordingly, as Whately noted, "the character of Orator, Author, and Politician, almost entirely coincided; he who would communicate his ideas to the world, or would gain political power, and carry his legislative schemes into effect, was necessarily a Speaker; since, as Pericles is made to remark by Thucydides, 'one who forms a judgment on any point, but cannot explain himself clearly to the people, might as well have never thought at all on the subject.' "[8]

Evidence of the importance of speech can be seen in its choice as the form in which significant ideas would be preserved. A number of Isocrates' undelivered works take the form of speeches as do the Second Philippic of Cicero[9] and Milton's stirring defense of freedom of the press.

When the world of entertainment, persuasion, and politics was in the main an oral one, listeners were drawn together in large numbers to experience a piece of communication. The speeches of Demosthenes and Cicero drew large audiences. So too in the nineteenth century did the speeches of Webster, Sumner, and Clay.

Not so today. Nearly four out of ten viewers will watch reruns or alternative programming rather than a speech by Ronald Reagan. Indeed, the Nielsen numbers reveal a decade-long decline in the share of the audience attracted to a presidential speech and a corresponding decline in the total number of viewers. While few would deny that Reagan is a better speaker than either of his two immediate predecessors, more Americans watched Gerald Ford's speeches than Jimmy Carter's and more tuned in to hear Carter than Reagan. Where televised presidential speeches once drew a larger audience than the programming they replaced, the prospect of listening to the president now drives viewers away. By contrast, in the nineteenth century, families would walk for miles to spend two hours standing in a field listening to a speech on national affairs.

"Charles Sumner was an aristocrat," recalled James Burton Pond a century ago. "He was my father's ideal. After I had got back from Kansas and visited my father's home in Wisconsin, father said to me: 'James, the Honorable Charles Sumner is going to speak at R——. We must hear him.' So we arranged to go. We walked nine miles to hear him speak. My father never spoke of him without giving him his title. He had enjoyed that speech intensely. I do not know whether I did or not. Father occupied a front seat with the intention of rushing up to the platform and greeting him by the hand when he was finished, but the Honorable Charles was too quick for him. He disappeared, got to his hotel, and nobody saw him."[10]

In the nineteenth century Charles Sumner was accorded the sort of attention now reserved for Charles Kuralt or Charley Pride.

Some symptomatic evidence of the lowly position that public address holds in our society comes in the lack of seriousness accorded it by the mass media. There are no major newspaper or TV critics of oratory as there are of films, television shows, art, music, and theatrical performances. Few reporters would pretend to be critics of any of these arts without special training, yet they routinely categorize a speech as good, effective, memorable, or eloquent. The impulse to assume the role of critic of oratory is a natural one. While few of us act, draw, or play an instrument without special training, most of us speak. That ability prompts the inference I speak therefore I critique.

Knowledgeable critics of film, plays, and television educate the public in their respective arts and in the standards by which these arts should be assessed. The absence of such evaluation of public speech denies the mass audience comparable assistance in evaluating an art that plays a direct role in the affairs of state.

News coverage also devalues the speech. Newspapers once routinely reprinted the texts of important speeches; now, with the exception of *The New York Times*, few regularly do. Newspapers justified the change on the same grounds used by politicians to explain why hour-long radio speeches gave way to thirty- and sixty-second spot ads: the public wasn't paying attention to the full-length speech. In 1913, the Earl of Roseberg voiced the relief with which speakers and newspaper readers greeted a paper filled with "matters of greater interest." "No conscientious speaker ever rose in the morning and read his morning newspaper without having a feeling of pain, to see in it, reported verbatim, with agonizing conscientiousness, things which he would rather not have said, and things which he thought ought not to bear repetition." As for readers, "I never could find anybody who read my speeches. It was quite different in the time when I was young, when practically the whole family sat down after breakfast and read the whole debate through. But the present age is in too great a hurry for that. . . . [N]ot one man in a hundred ever read the speeches which were so largely reported in the Press. Their removal from the Press gave space to other matters of greater interest, and is one of the greatest reliefs the newspaper reader ever experienced."

The low regard in which the network news organizations hold the speech is evident in their coverage of the Democratic and Republican national conventions. With the exception of the keynote address, the addresses of major contenders, and the party's nominees, other speeches are routinely intercut with interviews from the floor or commentary from the booth. So, for example, speeches by likely 1988 candidates Robert Dole and Howard Baker were not heard in their entirety on CBS. Former President Ford's speech to the Republican convention was picked up midway through by NBC; Dole's speech also was given abbreviated coverage. NBC excerpted Andrew Young's speech to the Democrats; CBS ignored it. CBS cut in and out of 1984 contender and 1972 nominee George McGovern's speech and ignored the speech by Democratic House leader Tip O'Neill. Shirley Chisholm's speech did not appear on NBC; Marion Barry and Tom Bradley's nominating speeches were heard there but not on CBS.

If past is prophet, abbreviated coverage of the 1984 conventions meant that the networks denied the public the privilege of assessing the substance and political potential of some important speakers. Hubert Humphrey first caught national attention with his stirring speech on civil rights at the 1948 Democratic convention. John Kennedy gained public notice by narrating the convention film in 1956, visibility that preceded his dash for the vice presidency when Stevenson threw selection of that nominee open to the floor. One of the most eloquent convention speeches given in modern history was the speech with which Eugene McCarthy nominated Adlai Stevenson in 1960. Had these

SPEECH

OF

SENATOR DOUGLAS,
OF ILLINOIS,

AGAINST THE

ADMISSION OF KANSAS

UNDER

THE LECOMPTON CONSTITUTION.

DELIVERED

IN THE SENATE OF THE UNITED STATES,

MARCH 22, 1858.

WASHINGTON:
PRINTED BY LEMUEL TOWERS.
1858.

speeches been delivered in 1984, none would have occurred during the times scheduled for regular network coverage. Abbreviated coverage also meant that the public was denied the right to hear articulate presenters debate the alternative sides of important platform planks. The network's decision to minimize coverage meant that the number of speakers given access to a national audience declined. As a result, the national audience has no way of knowing whether a Humphrey, a McCarthy, or a Kennedy debuted on the convention stage. At the same time, blacking out seconding speeches denied the audience the ability to assess the bases of support on which each candidate relied and would depend as president. These speeches also reveal the constituencies a presidential candidate feels indebted to.

By cluttering the convention floor with reporters, technicians, and minicams, and by conducting interviews from the floor, the news media make it nearly impossible for convention delegates to listen to the speakers. At the 1984 Democratic convention, some delegates carried pocket radios to be able to hear the speeches.

Television's news broadcasts also devalue the speech. The way in which we get·most of our news means that we hear snippets instead of speeches. George Washington University's Media Analysis Project found, for example, that the average number of seconds a candidate for president was shown speaking on a network news segment in the 1984 campaign was 14.79 seconds.

Aware that at best they will receive less than a minute of speaking time in network evening news and anxious to jet from media market to media market to capture time on as many local news shows as possible, presidential candidates deliver speeches that are as short as possible—less than twenty minutes on the average, with part of that time preempted by applause.

Speeches delivered on purchased radio and TV time have been compressed as well. In the early days of radio the hour-long speech was the norm. By the 1940s the half-hour speech had emerged as the standard. As entertainment was added to lure and retain audiences, speech time shrank. With the advent of television, the half-hour speech reappeared but held its own only in 1952. Just as the full speech text was

---

Today, a voter is hard-pressed to locate a complete text of any important non-presidential speech; in the nineteenth century, such speeches were reprinted routinely and distributed widely (Courtesy Political History Division, Smithsonian)

replaced in newspapers by the brief excerpt or the abstract until that
too was supplanted by the occasional quote within news stories, the
amount of time devoted to political speaking first on radio and then on
television declined. As the media evolved, the shortest speech became
the fittest for survival. By 1956 the cost of air time and the dwindling
attention of the public prompted politicians to purchase five-minute
blocks of speaking time. In the 1970s the five-minute speech gave way
to the sixty-second ad.

Assessing responsibility for the shift is difficult. When politicians paid
for half-hour time slots, as a general rule the public fled in droves to
other channels. The most astonishing instance of this occurred in 1964
when the viewing public chose "Peyton Place" and "Petticoat Junction"
overwhelmingly over Eisenhower's conversation with Goldwater at Gettysburg. It made financial and political sense to give the public what it
was willing to watch.

Those pointing the finger claim that politicians should share the blame.
The short attention span of the public was invited, they reason, in part,
by political sloganeering. By 1964 the public had been conditioned by
spot political ads to expect its political information in twenty-, thirty-,
and sixty-second bites.

The widespread assumption that spots are not as nourishing as longer
speeches is amply justified. When limited to sixty seconds, complex ideas
must either be ignored or treated simplistically. Except in unusual instances, argument will be replaced by assertion. Where a half-hour speech
can be a mural, a thirty-second ad can be little more than a collage.

Spot ads are well equipped to telegraph a candidate's position on an
issue and to associatively link that position with things we value; they
are ill equipped to build a convincing case for a nuanced position. So,
for example, in 1984, Mondale's televised ads told us that he was fighting for our future without revealing the nature either of that future or
of the fight he was waging. Reagan's ads asserted that Mondale would
raise taxes to pay for promises made to special interests. Instead, Mondale had claimed that he would apply the increased revenue to balanc-
ing the budget. To build the case for the incumbent, Reagan's ads visually allied his presidency with flag raisings, small-town parades, a
wedding, and smiling people at work.

The format featured in each of the presidential debates from
Kennedy-Nixon through Mondale-Reagan also forced the candidates
to capsulize. In the second Mondale-Reagan debate of 1984, for example, answers to panelists' questions were either two and a half or
one minute long; each candidate was alloted four minutes for a closing
statement. By contrast, in each of their seven senatorial debates of 1858,

Lincoln and Douglas spoke for ninety minutes each on a single topic: the future of slavery in the territories.

Whatever the cause and whoever the culprit, the result of this compression is changed political discourse. Speakers of earlier ages routinely traced the history of the matter under discussion. In the process, they revealed how they saw the world. By contrast, history has little place in contemporary discourse except when selectively marshalled to argue that a proposed policy is a mistake.

In the golden ages, speakers spent time defining their terms, a process that forces assumptions into the open. It made a great deal of difference whether speakers in 1967 saw the Vietnam war as a civil war or as an act of self-defense by the South against invaders from the North. Whether the "Communists" were viewed as a monolithic block composed of China, Russia, and North Vietnam or as dissimilar countries with divergent political systems and interests also made a difference. At the point of definition, such conflicting assumptions are made plain. Without this stage of discourse, we can talk past each other unaware that our primal premises are at odds. The problem is an important one. Few of the recent presidential statements on arms limitation, for instance, have assumed the burden of understanding and explaining the definitions each side brings to the discussion.

Speakers in the golden ages of American, British, Roman, and Greek oratory routinely laid out the range of policy alternatives for examination, scrutinizing each in turn. Only after showing the flaws in the alternative options, weighing the objections to their proposals, and arguing the comparative advantages of the course they favored did they conclude. Such speeches demonstrated that the speaker commanded the facts of the situation, understood the alternatives, and could defend the choice of one over the others.

These speeches engaged the ideas of the opposing sides in a way that moved the argument forward. When the bulk of the available evidence favored one side, such speeches helped audiences toward consensus. By contrast, contemporary political discourse tends to reduce the universe to two sides—one good, one evil—when in fact there may be four or five sides, each with its own advantages and disadvantages. After drawing simplistic and often false dichotomies, contemporary speech tends to canonize one side and anathematize the other.

In the golden ages, speakers lovingly explored the range of available evidence. Today, speeches argue by hitting and running. A single supposedly telling statistic, report, or anecdote is slung under a claim before the speaker moves on.

Then, as now, speakers dramatized their points. Then as now, con-

In the last century, important presidential pronouncements such as Washington's Farewell, Jackson's Veto of the Bank, and Lincoln's second inaugural were permanently printed on cloth and displayed in homes. This silk broadside preserves a proclamation by President Andrew Jackson. (Courtesy Political History Division, Smithsonian)

crete description of the problem was a powerful move. Then, as now, narrative about victims was the stuff of poignant, powerful speech. Such dramatization was formerly *an* element in a speech, often one that amplified a point already made in other ways. Dramatically illustrated discursive argument has given way to dramatically bodied assertion.

Politicians view exposure on television as a testament to their accomplishments and a warning to their potential opponents. Since drama is to television what honey is to bears, skilled dramatists find themselves on network news more often than skilled speakers who lack dramatic flair. And since television will at most abstract a clip, why bother building a carefully crafted case to a convincing conclusion?

Because television is a visual medium whose natural grammar is associative, a person adept at visualizing claims in dramatic capsules will be able to use television to short-circuit the audience's demand that those claims be dignified with evidence. As I will argue in a later chapter, part of Ronald Reagan's success as a communicator is a function of his ability to use visual vignettes to make unstated arguments.

In the golden ages, as now, speeches revealed the speaker's position. In short ads and in news clips little else is now done. As a result citizens are invited to take one of two postures. They can embrace a position either because it is already theirs and the political statement functions to show that they and the politician are like-minded or they can adopt it because they endorse the politician and hence are willing to take on faith the legitimacy of his or her conclusions. Neither alternative encourages contemplation; neither produces conversion; neither is conducive to long-term commitment.

An audience that accepts a speaker's interpretation of the history of a question, grants the definitions offered, weighs the alternatives and with the speaker finds them wanting, sees the problem in memorable, dramatized human terms, and then reaches the speaker's conclusion is a person likely to retain a commitment to that position. The much discussed volatility of public opinion may be, in part, a by-product of politicians' reliance on granulized forms of communication.

When the public is unwilling or unable to evaluate the reasoned exposition of candidates, it cannot know whether the candidates have examined alternatives to the policies they espouse. Nor can it know whether the would-be leader has understood the lessons of the past. In the absence of the information that can only be provided in longer speech forms, the public cannot scrutinize the reasons that impel the convictions of their leaders. In longer communicative forms, we are better able to see a mind at work.

None of this means that a thirty-second spot is necessarily simple-minded or that a thirty-minute speech is usually substantive. It does mean that it is impossible to adequately warrant complex claims in sixty, thirty, twenty, or fourteen seconds.

The limited amount of time available for network news coverage has exacerbated a second negative tendency in political discourse. While hyperbole has always been with us, until recently nothing in the system has invited it as a norm. Now 435 members of the House and 100 members of the Senate compete for the crumbs of network time left after the president has gotten his share. By dramatizing, kernalizing, and shouting wolf, they bid against each other for that time. In the process, complex ideas are transformed into parodies of their former selves and the capacity of language to express outrage is exhausted.

Whatever its useful commercial and social purposes, product advertising has numbed our ability to appreciate the cost of this compression of political discourse. Day after day radio and TV ads bombard us with messages that argue from unwarranted associations to hyperbolic claims. An audience accustomed to the form and content of such messages is unlikely to do what former White House speechwriter Bill Safire asked when he wrote, "I think we have to send a message to the podium from the audience. We're ready for more Q. and A. We're ready for five or ten minutes of sustained explication. A 'fireside chat' will not turn out our fires. On the contrary—if a speaker will take the time to prepare, we are prepared to pay in the coin of our attention."[11] Having sent such a message, we might show our good faith by choosing Roger Mudd's award-winning documentary "Teddy" over "Jaws" or Eisenhower and Goldwater over "Peyton Place" the next time such a choice confronts us.

By relying on an associative grammar to imply causality, product ads also have dulled our analytic acuity. Unaccustomed to questioning the relationship between the gleeful kids or the sexy model and the products they tout, we docilely draw the inference that the actors appearing in the soft-filtered nostalgia of a reconstructed town are smiling not at the thought of the residuals they will earn but because Ronald Reagan has "brought America back." So pervasive is this associative logic that no outcry emerged when a still at the end of one set of 1984 ads showed a picture of Ronald Reagan actually wrapped in a flag.

Television did not single-handedly evict eloquence from the assembly and tie it to the railroad track. A number of accomplices polished the tracks, purchased the rope, and then condemned the train for being punctual.

Decline in the Occasions that Nurture Speakers

Every major rhetorical theorist has noted the important role practice plays in perfecting the reflexes of a speaker. Yet ours is an age in which occasions calling for speechmaking rapidly are going the way of the dinosaur. The decline in the number of civic occasions on which an aspiring speaker can practice is paralleled by the decline of public speaking in the classroom.

Many students can now enter high school and eight years later exit from college without ever having had to deliver a formal public speech. If a requirement that students take a course in speech has survived, it can often be met with classes such as "Interpersonal Communication" or "Group Discussion" that require no public speaking. The number of universities requiring a speech course declined in the 1960s. Competitive contest speaking also has declined as has university support for intercollegiate debate. Where previously colleges used oral exams to test students' mastery of individual subjects, written exams and term papers are now the rule. On many campuses and high schools, the valedictorian and salutatorian no longer deliver addresses at commencement. What this means in practical terms is that those who aspire to speak well have few ready-made occasions in which to test their talents.

The American colonists brought with them a sense of the importance of public address. The Boston Massacre was yearly commemorated with speeches on the meaning and misfortune of that act, speeches that fueled the revolution. In 1783, the city of Boston declared that the Boston Massacre address would thereafter be replaced by commemoration of Independence Day. On this day, an orator would deliver a public address "in which the Orator shall consider the feelings, manners and principles which led to this great National Event as well as the important and happy effects whether general or domestic which already have and will forever continue to flow from the Auspicious Epoch."[12] These speeches revivified the principles for which the country had fought and on which it was founded.

The Fourth of July address survived in towns and cities into the 1960s when the Vietnam war undercut the common values on which it was predicated. No longer could the country's mission be defended without causing division. No longer could patriotism, the justness of the causes for which we fought, and the glories of past wars be rehearsed without underscoring schisms within the community. Unable to build from commonly shared premises, the speech was widely abandoned.

With it went a forum that from the country's first murmurings of nationhood had nurtured its young orators. Traditionally, the town's best speakers were those called on to speak on the Fourth of July. The occasion set role models of rhetorical excellence and gave those who aspired to the public life the chance to learn by doing.

Other such forums disappeared as well. Throughout the nineteenth century, communities routinely gathered to commemorate the anniversaries of the deaths of famous statesmen. So the deaths of the founders were commemorated at regular intervals. That form of address disappeared with our sense that we walk among great persons. Anniversaries also were commemorated. The beginning and completion of the Bunker Hill monument prompted speeches, for example, as did the second centennial of the landing of the Pilgrims. Nothing comparable to the Lyceum and the Chautauqua platforms survives either. The after-dinner speech has all but disappeared. Even the number of Jefferson-Jackson day dinners, with their complement of political speeches, has declined.

History tells us that a suitable education and adequate practice will facilitate the production of eloquence. At the moment, neither is easily attained in the United States. With the loss of occasions requiring speech, the aspiring speaker's ability to polish individual skills is minimized. The likelihood that one would have something to say if the occasion arose is also undercut by an educational system that, at every turn, defies the recommendations of the past.

Eloquence and an Education in the Liberal Arts

The importance of training in rhetoric was heightened by the fact that the Greek citizen was expected to be able to speak in public in the exercise of citizenship. The presumption that the citizen would be a citizen-orator is reflected in the use of the word rhetor, orator, to designate the politician. In the Greek city-state all male citizens were presumed to be able to speak on their own behalf in the law courts, the assembly, and on ceremonial occasions. About 390 B.C., Isocrates, whom Cicero regarded as the father of eloquence, founded a school in which "speaking or writing on large political topics was inculcated as a practical training for the active duties of a citizen."[13] In both Greek and Roman education, training in rhetoric played a pivotal role. The centrality of rhetoric in the curriculum persisted into the Middle Ages where, with grammar and dialectic, rhetoric formed the Trivium.

In classical times, training in rhetoric was part of educating the whole person. So in his oration for A. Licinus Archias, Cicero confesses to the judges that at no time in his life has he been averse to the study of the best of the liberal arts since an understanding of the science *(ratio)* of speaking begins with them. Later, in the same address, he expresses his conviction that all the arts related to culture *(humanitatem)* have a common bond and are interrelated.

The program of learning outlined by Quintilian in the *Institutes of Oratory* included the study of philosophy, logic, history, religion, law, and oratory. Its goal was education of the orator-statesman-philosopher, the citizen-orator, the "good man speaking well." The ideal persevered. In the seventeenth century Rene Rapin identified poetry, history, philosophy, and eloquence as a vehicle capable of educating the whole person. The ideal gained expression on American soil with the founding of Harvard. In 1643 the college publicized the graduation of its first class, an event that occurred when nine men had completed their schooling the year before. The publicity about the class and curriculum, which took the form of a work titled *New England's First Fruits*, was published in London.

From it, we learn that the first criterion for admission to Harvard required that a student be able to speak Latin, decline nouns and verbs in Greek, and demonstrate an understanding of "Tullius (Cicero) or such like classical Latin author *extempore*." In addition to reading Scripture, the curriculum called for study of logic, physics, ethics, politics, Greek, etymology, syntax, prosodia, dialects, poesy, style, composition, imitation, epitome, Hebrew, grammar, and rhetoric. The précis notes that "every scholar may declaim once a month." [14]

By contrast, a 1984 report on undergraduate education in the United States found that "most of our college graduates . . . remained short-changed in the humanities—history, literature, philosophy, and the ideals and practices of the past that have shaped the society they enter."

A student can earn a B.A. "from 75 percent of all American colleges and universities without having studied European history; from 72 percent without having studied American literature or history; and from 86 percent without having studied the civilizations of classical Greece and Rome." [15] At the high school level, research for the National Commission on Excellence in Education found that, from 1969 to 1981, credits in Western civilization declined 50 percent, in U.S. history, 20 percent, and in U.S. government, 70 percent. [16] A 1987 study funded by the National Endowment for the Humanities documented the presumed results: "[M]ore than two-thirds of the nation's seventeen-year-olds are unable to locate the Civil War within the correct half-century. More than two-thirds cannot identify the Reformation or Magna Carta.

By vast majorities, students demonstrate unfamiliarity with writers whose works are regarded as classics: Dante, Chaucer, Dostoevsky, Austen, Whitman, Hawthorne, Melville, and Cather."[17]

The philosophy of education championed by Cicero, Quintilian, and Rapin produced students knowledgeable about their country's history and traditions. It exposed them to the ideas and practices that constituted their culture. In the process, it made it possible for speakers to assume that they and their audiences shared a body of knowledge. In short, it facilitated the creation of enthymemes.

In his treatise on *Rhetoric*, Aristotle had termed the enthymeme the soul of persuasion. A speaker creates an enthymeme by suppressing premises in an argument on the assumption that the audience will invest the argument with them. Enthymemes gain their power from their reliance on unexpressed beliefs and information. As the amount of shared cultural information—history, literature, mythology, theology, philosophy, common experience—decreases, so too does the speaker's ability to construct enthymemes. By stripping enthymemes of their ability to rely on unstated premises, the increasing specialization of education in the United States limits the ability of a political speaker to persuade the body politic. Specialized vocabularies shrink the means of persuasion available to a speaker required to find a language capable of bridging disciplines.

At the same time, dismissing philosophy from the educational core separated rhetoric from a companion who had been faithful since their births in Athens. Although many would dispute Plato's belief that philosophy would teach the true, the good, and the just, few doubt that the study of philosophy engenders habits of thought and an understanding of the nature of evidence useful in the construction of arguments.

Meanwhile, although signs of a resurgence are on the horizon, the study of foreign languages declined. The Modern Language Association notes that in 1983 only 14 percent of all colleges and universities in the United States listed some foreign language as a requirement for admission. Where in 1966, 89 percent of all institutions required some foreign language study for the B.A. degree, in 1983 that percentage had dropped to 47.[18]

The 1987 NEH report *American Memory: A Report on the Humanities in the Nation's Public Schools* saw a hopeful turnaround, however. Some states are now requiring that their school districts offer foreign language instruction from kindergarten through high school. And nationwide the percent of high school students enrolled in a foreign language has increased since 1978.[19]

The study of a foreign language helps students appreciate and communicate with those from other cultures, the standard justifications for such learning. But it also provides the advantage Cicero saw in translation. Translating refines the translator's understanding of and facility in the native tongue.

In the Roman model, the study of poetry preceded the study of rhetoric. Virgil set the stage for Cicero. "The object of the poetry was to develop the linguistic sense, impart general culture, quicken the imagination, and especially to enlarge the vocabulary," notes Shorey.[20] Literary critic Northrop Frye agrees that the study of poetry contributes to a "good prose style in both speech and writing."[21] "[T]here is the sense of wit and heightened intelligence, resulting from seeing disciplined words marching along in metrical patterns and in their inevitably right order," Frye adds. "And there is the sense of concreteness that we can get only from the poet's use of metaphor, and of visualized imagery. Literary education of this kind, its rhythm and leisure slowly soaking into the body and its wit and concreteness into the mind, can do something to develop a speaking and writing prose style that comes out of the depths of personality and is a genuine expression of it." These values were lost as the study of literature and poetry waned.

Although tying effect to cause is risky, if the great speakers are correct that the study of poetry and of other languages refines verbal facility, then the erosion of both should carry with it a decline in verbal skill. That decline has occurred. Between 1964 and 1982 the performance of students on eleven of the fifteen major Subject Area Tests of the Graduate Record Exam declined; the steepest declines were registered in subjects requiring high verbal skills.[22]

In addition to studying history, philosophy, literature, and language, the well-educated students of the past also studied great speeches, an activity that expanded their awareness of the available means of persuasion and helped them ingest models of excellence. The value of these activities is confirmed in Lucian's ridicule of them in his satire on public speaking where he urges his pupil to avoid the speeches of "that twaddling Isocrates or that uncouth Demosthenes"[23] and to scorn those who display "dead men of a bygone age to serve as patterns, and [expect] you to dig up long-buried speeches as if they were something tremendously helpful."[24]

Lucian's advice runs counter to the practice of the eloquent speakers of the past. Cicero studied the speeches of the Greek masters, particularly Demosthenes. The elder William Pitt (Lord Chatham) "wrote out again and again carefully-prepared translations of some of the great models of ancient oratory, and . . . in this way he acquired his easy command of a forcible and expressive style."[25] The younger Pitt, the second son of Lord Chatham, memorized the finest passages from Shakespeare, studied the writings of Bolingbroke, and translated Greek and Latin works.[26] Edmund Burke read the orators of antiquity as well as the speeches and writings of Bolingbroke.[27] As a young man, Lincoln studied excerpts from Cicero, Demosthenes, and the Earl of Chatham as well as the speeches of Hamlet, Falstaff, and Henry V. His speeches provide ample evidence of familiarity with the Bible and with the speeches of Webster, Calhoun, and Clay.[28] Winston Churchill studied Chatham's speeches.[29] Like the students of his day, he also memorized passages for declaiming. In 1953, five days after his stroke, he recited an 86-line poem for his physician to prove that his memory was unaffected.[30]

In addition to ingesting speeches, students studied the principles of rhetoric. "[T]he qualities, good and bad, of Lysias, Isocrates, and the other Attic orators, were analyzed, classified, and technically named by the contemporaries of Demosthenes and still more by those later Greek schools of rhetoric which taught, imitated, and commented on his orations for seven hundred years," recalled classical scholar Paul Shorey. "This together with the Philosophic rhetoric that began with Plato, which was carried on by Aristotle and the Stoics, and was more or less blended with the other in the writings of Cicero and Quintilian, constitutes a huge body of rhetorical theory and criticism."[31] Now that body of knowledge, studied for seven centuries by all educated ancients, reexamined by most of those educated in the Renaissance, "is forgotten by all but specialists." The loss is unfortunate for, as Shorey concludes, "if we are to study and analyze oratorical expression and prose style at all, there is much both in its substance and its terminology that would save us from intellectual confusion and futile logomachy."

The broad-based education recommended by Cicero and Quintilian not only increased the available means of persuasion, fine-tuned the reasoning powers, and refined the use of one's native tongue but also created what British theorist and practitioner Henry Brougham in his *Dissertation on the Eloquence of the Ancients* called "a delicate sense of rhetorical excellence."[32] This audience listened not merely to weigh deliberative matters but also "to enjoy a critical repast." What the audience expected was a well-wrought, artistically satisfying, moving oration. There are speeches of Demosthenes, observes Macaulay in the *History*, that are so perfect that to alter a word is to change the speech for the worse.[33]

Today, television's tendency to reduce the speech to the thirty-five-second clip has accustomed us to the notion that we should be satisfied with a few moving passages; in ancient Greece the discourse was judged as a whole and critiqued by the high standards and with the discerning tastes of a rhetorically literate audience.

By training speakers to choose the best from among the available means of persuasion, classical education also enabled listeners to detect "sophistry." The student familiar with history, literature, and the law knew when they were being misappropriated. The student who knew how to appeal to an audience also was empowered to unmask inappropriate appeals. In addition to teaching about the enthymeme and example, Aristotle's *Rhetoric* treated fallacies. A task of contemporary education in rhetoric, too seldom accomplished, is creating "in every audience a resisting minority that cannot be stampeded by plausible sophistry and emotional volubility."[34] Instead of training audiences in "the habits of logical analysis and suspense of judgment that would enable [them] to resist . . . hypnotization," we too often are interested "in the 'psychology' of 'putting it over' and 'getting it across.'" That focus is reflected in the titles of best selling texts that promise to teach the purchaser to win friends, influence people, sell, or persuade.

In the process of trying to allay the student's fear of public speaking, texts promising that speaking is "easy" have also done the art of rhetoric a disservice.

Eloquence and the Cultivation of the Art of Memory

The oral nature of Greek and Roman society resulted in the cultivation of an appreciation for the artfully wrought speech, the subtle argument, the telling phrase, the suitable word. Audiences relished oral communication. The masterful speech was an art form to be appreciated as an aesthetic work as well as an applied appeal.

Where orality is central so too will be the art of memory. Although he did not treat it in detail, Aristotle considered memory to be one of the canons of rhetoric, along with the invention of arguments, arrangement, style, and delivery. From the fifth century B.C., theorists and practitioners were concerned with aiding the orator's ability both to recall ideas in their appropriate order and to retrieve the arguments of preceding speeches for rebuttal. "What can I say of that repository for all things, the memory, which, unless it be the keeper of the matter and words that are the fruits of thought and invention, all the talents of the orator, we see, though they be of the highest degree of excellence, will be of no avail?" Cicero asked in *De Oratore*.[35]

In answer, he recalls the story of Simonides who in the middle of a party was called outside to speak with two youths. During his absence, the building collapsed, killing his companions. Their bodies were crushed beyond recognition. By recalling where each had been standing, Simonides was able to identify the remains for proper burial. This led him to discover, says Cicero, that "it is chiefly order that gives distinctness to memory; and that by those, therefore, who would improve this part of the understanding, certain places must be fixed upon, and that of the things which they desire to keep in memory, symbols must be conceived in the mind, and ranged, as it were, in those places; thus the order of places would preserve the order of things, and the symbols of the things would denote the things themselves; so that we should use the places as waxen tablets, and the symbols as letters."[36]

In the *Rhetorica ad Herennium*, written around 85 B.C., memory receives careful treatment. That work, for centuries misattributed to Cicero, instructs students in the placement of images against a familiar background, usually a physical place the student is familiar with. Each image stands for an idea in the speech. These image-ideas are organized in the background in the order in which they will be delivered. Memory also receives treatment in Quintilian. By the eighteenth century the canon had all but disappeared from the rhetoric texts, a fact that led to its identification as the "lost canon."

The great orators, those ready to respond appropriately to an opponent on any important matter of state, have, by whatever means, cultivated a retentive memory. Wendell Phillips "would listen to an elaborate speech for hours, and, without a single note of what had been said, in writing, reply to every part of it as fully and completely as if the speech were written out before him."[37] By contrast, poor orators too often find themselves in the position of an opponent of Cicero's, previewing three points, developing four, and midway through the exposition losing their lines of thought. But unlike that speaker, few would have the nerve to argue that the amnesia had been induced by the witchcraft and sorcery of the opponent! Instead, our inability to sustain an extemporaneous line of argument should be blamed on lack of training.

In his closing statement at the second Reagan-Mondale debate of 1984, Reagan demonstrated the perils in losing one's train of thought. After taking the audience on a trip down a California highway, Reagan meditated on the message one should leave future generations. Had the rambling narrative occurred before Reagan's deft dismissal of the so-called age issue, its lack of coherence would have magnified public concerns about his command of the presidency. So entangled did Reagan get in his tangent that by the time he regrasped the thread of his thought, his time was up:

Several years ago, I was given an assignment to write a letter. It was to go into a time capsule and would be read in 100 years when that time capsule was opened. I remember driving down the California coast one day, my mind was full of what I was going to put into that letter about the problems and issues that confront us in our time and what we did about them.

But I couldn't completely neglect the beauty around me, the Pacific out there on one side, the highway shining on the other side. And I found myself wondering what it would be like for someone, wondering if someone 100 years from now would be driving down that highway and if they would see the same thing.

And, with that thought I realized what a job I had with that letter. I would be writing a letter to people who know everything there is to know about us. We know nothing about them. They would know all about our problems, they would know how we solved them and whether our solution was beneficial to them down through the years or whether it hurt them.

They would also know they live in a world with terrible weapons, nuclear weapons, terrible destructive power aimed at each other, capable of crossing the ocean in a matter of minutes and destroying civilization as we knew it.

And then, I thought to myself, what, what are they going to say about us? What are those people 100 years from now going to think? They will know whether we used those weapons or not.

Well, what they will say about us 100 years from now depends on how we keep our rendezvous with destiny. Will we do the things that we know must be done and know that one day down in history 100 years or perhaps before, someone will say, thank God for those people back in the 1980s for preserving our freedom? For saving for us this blessed planet called Earth with all its grandeur and its beauty.

You know, I'm grateful to all of you for giving me the opportunity to serve you for these four years, and I seek reelection because I want more than anything else to try to complete the new beginning that we charted four years ago.

George Bush, who I think is one of the finest vice presidents this country has ever had, George Bush and I have crisscrossed the country and we've had in these last few months a wonderful experience. We have met young America. We have met your sons and daughters.

Newman *(moderator):* Mr. President, I am obliged to cut you off there under the rules of the debate. I'm sorry.

Apart from the training that enables musicians to commit scores of scores to memory, little in contemporary education cultivates memory. Formerly, tradition was perpetuated and memory polished by an educational system that insisted that students commit to memory sections of great plays, passages from great pieces of literature, great poems, and eloquent orations. I remember surprise when my grandmother answered a question I had about Daniel Webster by reciting a long passage from his Bunker Hill oration, an address she had memorized in high school. She also could recite Washington's farewell address and the Gettysburg Address, the preamble to the Constitution, and a large portion of the Declaration of Independence. Her husband courted her, she recalled, by reciting "by heart" great love poetry. The dissimilar metaphors embedded in "I learned it by heart" and "I learned it by rote" reflect antithetical views of the nature and value of committing materials to memory.

The Resources Provided by Memory and Knowledge

When the material committed to memory was of value, the educational idealization of *ars memoriae* enabled the speaker to draw on an individual repertoire of knowledge to argue a claim. We see that facility used dexterously by the great orators. Demosthenes reportedly transcribed the history of Thucydides six times[38] and drew comfortably on it and on the classic poets; Cicero notes that Lysias and Critias gained their eloquence from imitation of "the vigorous style of Pericles"[39] and himself drew on the speeches of Demosthenes. Lincoln mines the Bible with a sure hand; indeed one of his most famous claims is taken directly from it: "A House Divided Against Itself Cannot Stand." Edmund Burke uses Cicero as one would draw on the wisdom of an old friend.

We know that Burke's recollections of passages from the past are being summoned from memory because the quotations are often paraphrases. So, for example, he notes in a reissue of his *Reflections on the Revolution in France* that Aristotle's observation that a democracy has striking resemblance with a tyranny had been "quoted from memory." But he adds, "after many years had elapsed from my reading the passage." Subsequently, "A learned friend has found it, and it is as follows."[40] In the same work we see Burke slightly modifying a passage from Cicero, again because he is recalling it from memory.[41]

Commanding the classics is not an empty phrase when used to describe such speakers, for they could summon the masterpieces of the past and bid them speak on their behalf. Having such capacity at one's disposal gave the orator access not only to the wisdom and authority of the past but also to models of style. By making the words their own, orators began the process of assimilating a sense of style, an ear for language effectively used. Persons "of quick intellect and glowing temperament find it easier to become eloquent by reading and listening to eloquent speakers than by following rules for eloquence," noted Augustine, the rhetoric professor turned bishop.[42]

Once committed to memory, the masterpieces were presented orally, a practice that polished delivery. This ability was so valued that Archias' recitation of "a great number of excellent verses" pertinent to a matter under discussion is cited by Cicero as grounds for granting him his citizenship.[43]

A sense of the value of such ability persisted. Milton recommended that pupils read "the choice Histories, Heroic Poems, and Attic Tragedies of stateliest and most regal argument, with all the famous Political Orations." Some should be memorized, he added, and "solemnly pronounced with right accent, and grace, as might be taught, would endue them even with the spirit and vigor of Demosthenes or Cicero, Euripides, or Sophocles."[44]

Through the centuries, theorists have believed that listening to the delivery of eloquence disposed one to eloquence. Accordingly, in one of the speeches delivered as part of his education at Harvard in the mid-seventeenth century, Michael Wigglesworth said that "after the hearing of a well-composed speech, lively expressed, the understanding of the auditor is so framed into the mould of eloquence, that he could almost go away and compose the like himself, either upon the same or another subject. And what's the reason of this? Why, his mind is transported with a kind of rapture, and inspired with a certain oratoric fury, as if the orator together with his words had breathed his soul and spirit into those that hear him."[45]

The great teachers of rhetoric went beyond mere memorization and recitation to help students see the strengths and weaknesses of the models they were studying. So, although he recommends copying that "which has been invented with success" so that the student could make what is excellent in each speaker "his own," Quintilian wanted his students to add excellence of their own to compensate for the deficiencies of their models so that the students would surpass those who preceded them and would be able to instruct those who followed.[46] That model was perpetuated by John Ward who published *System of Oratory* in 1759.[47] In his system, students enlarged on the expression of a masterpiece, drew from parts of a masterpiece as Cicero in his speeches against Mark Anthony drew on Demosthenes against Philip of Macedon, retained the idea but applied it to a new subject, or altered the order of the original thoughts. Ward defends this method by noting that those we recognize as masters imitated and expanded on the master works of their predecessors as Virgil imitated Homer and Terence, Menander.

Speech as Thought vs. The Speech as Text

Plato forecast problems should the written word become the means of conserving information. Because writing discourages memory, reliance on it would drain the vitality from speech. For Plato, forgetfulness draws us from the true, the good, and the just and is as a result harmful.[48] Telling the story of the invention of writing by the Egyptian God, Theuth, Plato observes that writing prompted students to trust the writing rather than themselves.

When Theuth offered the Egyptian king writing, the ruler replied: "If men learn this, it will implant forgetfulness in their souls: they will cease to exercise memory because they rely on that which is written, calling things to remembrance no longer from within themselves, but by means of external marks; what you have discovered is a recipe not for memory, but for reminder. And it is no true wisdom that you offer your disciples, but only its semblance; for by telling them of many things without teaching them you will make them seem to know much, while for the most part they know nothing; and as men filled, not with wisdom, but with the conceit of wisdom, they will be a burden to their fellows."

Writing is freighted with other problems. Once a speech is reduced to writing it loses its ability to respond, to speak. So Socrates remarks that written words "seem to talk to you as though they were intelligent, but if you ask them anything about what they say, from a desire to be instructed, they go on telling you just the same thing for ever." Plato illustrates this claim when Phaedrus presents a written speech by Lysias and then proves unable to defend it.

In one sense contemporary classicist George Kennedy is correct when he suggests that "The relative importance of the spoken as contrasted with the written word steadily decreased until the twentieth century, when the process began to be reversed by radio and television."[49] The broadcast media increased the amount of information that we receive through an oral channel, displacing the newspaper as our prime means of political information gathering. But in another sense, Kennedy's claim requires qualification, for much of what appears on television is the oral delivery of the printed word. The sitcoms, dramas, and commercials that predominate in prime-time programming are all scripted as are the words that the network anchors speak on the evening news. The political speeches excerpted for evening news are, in the main, delivered from scripts as are the televised speeches of the president to the nation and the Congress. As those who learned to spell "antidisestablishmentarianism" by watching "The $64,000 Question" were shocked to learn, for a time the game shows were scripted as well.

With the speech as text came the speechwriter as unseen and unannounced author. Speaking could now be divorced from the act of thinking, and feeling from the act of speaking. No longer was the speaker required to be a thinker, only an artful reader. With the sundering of thinking from speaking came problems I will address in a later chapter.

In many ways we are a less oral age than those periods prior to Gutenberg. Because television is an audiovisual, not a print medium, and since the question "Why Can't Johnny Read?" is one that plagues us, this claim at first may seem surprising. But where the ancient orators rarely read an entire speech to an audience, today's TelePrompTer-bred American politicians routinely do.

Striking testimony of the textbound nature of modern politics can be found in the gaffes of Ronald Reagan. The meaning that he is communicating on formal occasions resides not in his memory but in the text crawling before his eyes on the prompter or enshrined on cards before him. This bondage to the printed word entrapped him in his acceptance speech at the convention in 1984, in his second inaugural, and in his welcome to the Pope in fall 1987. In his acceptance speech the president did not see the period separating two lines. As a result he indicted his own administration instead of that of Carter-Mondale.

The second inaugural suffered when at the last minute the speech was moved from outdoors, where it would have been delivered with the help of the prompter, to indoors where it was delivered from cards. Apparently unable to read the cards clearly, Reagan seemed momentarily to commit the nation to filling the world with beaches, a welcome thought to those suffering subzero weather but hardly the sort of action likely to help balance the budget. Reagan said: "For all our problems, our differences, we are together as of old. We raise our voices to the God who is the author of this most tender music." And may "He continue to hold us close as we fill the world with our sand, sound—in unity, affection and love."

The divorce between knowledgeable thought and the speech act was demonstrated anew when Reagan mangled the name of noted philosopher Jacques Maritain in his speech welcoming the Pope (September 10, 1987). By citing "Ma *Ree* Ten," Reagan seemed to posit a new nationality for the Frenchman and at the same time revealed his own ignorance of the philosophy to which he was paying tribute and his unfamiliarity with the text from which he was reading.

The command of the classics, the cultivation of a private mental li-

brary, is reflected in the practice current from ancient Greece through
nineteenth-century America of backing or illustrating one's claims with
quotations from or allusions to the classics, poetry, or revered religious
sources. Accordingly, William Jennings Bryan advised orators that
"classical allusions ornament a speech, their value being greater of course
when addressed to those who are familiar with their sources. Poetry
can often be used to advantage, especially when the sentiment is appropriate and is set forth in graceful language. By far the most useful
quotations for an orator, however, are those from Holy Writ. The people are more familiar with the Bible than with any other single book,
and lessons drawn from it reinforce a speech."[50]

As educational institutions turned from required reading of such
sources; as memorization, imitation, and recitation gave way to a focus
on the present and on original composition; speakers lost the ability to
summon the past to their purposes. When the past masters were cited,
parenthetical information was included to situate them in a time and
place lest the audience misunderstand or stare uncomprehendingly.
When so little past information resides in the audience that a brief history lesson must be appended to any allusion, the skillful speaker rec-
ognizes a digression in the making and a didactic tone in the offing
and abandons the reference.

We can hear the speakers' confidence in their audiences' command
of the past slipping away in speeches by John Hamilton (Lord Belhaven) in the eighteenth century, Daniel Webster in the nineteenth,
and Edward R. Murrow in the twentieth. Hamilton was comfortable
with the assumption that his audience knew who Hannibal was, what
he had done, and what relevance those actions had to the Scottish Parliament when in November 1706 he pleaded:

> Hannibal, my Lord, is at our gates—Hannibal is come within our gates—
> Hannibal is come the length of this table—he is at the foot of the throne.
> He will demolish the throne if we take not notice. He will seize upon these
> regalia. He will take them as our *spolia opima*, and whip us out of this
> House, never to return again.[51]

By contrast, the peroration of his speech in the Dartmouth College
case reveals that Daniel Webster feels the need to ensure that his audience is familiar with some of the particulars of Caesar's death before
analogizing present to past. Unlike Hamilton, Webster assumes that the
audience requires that Latin be translated, as well.

> It is, sir, as I have said, a small college, and yet there are those who love
> it.
>   Sir, I know not how others may feel but for myself, when I see my Alma

Mater surrounded, like Caesar in the Senate house, by those who are re-iterating stab after stab, I would not, for this right hand, have her turn to me and say, *Et tu quoque, mi fili!* And thou too, my son![52]

Where familiarity with the major works of Shakespeare once could be comfortably assumed, Edward R. Murrow felt it necessary, in his televised attack on Joseph McCarthy in March 1954, to identify Shakespeare's *Julius Caesar* as the source of his closing statement about the Senator. "See It Now" showed McCarthy addressing the Secretary of the Army with the question, "Upon what meat does this our Caesar feed?" Murrow rephrased the line to preview his analysis of McCarthy, "And upon what meat does Senator McCarthy feed?" His answer: "the investigations, protected by immunity, and the half-truth. . . ." In closing, Murrow noted, "Had he looked three lines earlier in Shakespeare's *Caesar*, he would have found this line, which is not altogether inappropriate: 'The fault, dear Brutus, is not in our stars, but in ourselves.' "[53]

Now a speaker risks blank stares by assuming audience familiarity with Shakespeare, the stories of Cain and Abel, the strategies or importance of Trafalgar, Tripoli, or Dien Bien Phu or the memorable phrases of Demosthenes, Burke, Jefferson, or Churchill. Such collective amnesia means that one can safely bet that most will be unable to account for the effect of General Garfield's words to a mob assembling in New York in City Park Hall on the night of Lincoln's assassination. Although the mob was inclined to storm an anti-Lincoln newspaper, Garfield calmed it by proclaiming:

"Clouds and darkness are round about him;
Righteousness and judgment are the habitations of his throne"
Fellow citizens, God reigns and the government at Washington still lives!

The crowd dispersed. Psalms 97:2 had a power then that it now lacks. To a contemporary audience, the statement speaks only its literal meaning, a meaning inadequate to account for the reported effect.[54]

The central claims of Madison Avenue, of prime-time television, and of widely viewed films have replaced those of the Bible, Shakespeare, and the great speeches as the *lingua franca* of contemporary oratory. John Kennedy showed awareness of the change when he said that "he was reading more now but enjoying it less," a rephrasing of a cigarette ad's slogan. Similarly, the slogan of a hamburger chain, "Where's the beef?" became a pivotal political question in the 1984 primaries. In spring 1985 Reagan answered a press conference question with the Clint Eastwood phrase "Make my day." And in summer 1987 Oliver North certified his desire to be candid with the Select Committee of the Senate and House and with the American people by averring, in the words of another Eastwood film, that he was committed to revealing "the good, the bad and the ugly." Reporters who share the culture from which the statement is drawn did not need to ask for a clarifying context.

Neither the delivery nor the study of speeches is a routine part of education anymore. Dismissed in the classroom, devalued by the media, divorced from the disciplines that develop the habits of mind that are its mainstay, eloquence is orphaned. But the prospects for eloquence are not as bleak as they were a decade ago. Although those calling for a return to the study of the liberal arts and a reemphasis on foreign language skill seem unaware of it, their proposed course of study would prepare students to appreciate and perhaps produce eloquence.

Meanwhile, the U.S. government is exporting a commodity that is scarce at home. Where Quintilian idealized the "good man speaking well," intelligence agents envision the "good guerrilla." In the early 1980s, a CIA manual enjoining the Contras to make both rhetoric and war was distributed by U.S. operatives in Nicaragua. Titled *Psychological Operations in Guerrilla Warfare,* the guidebook enunciated "many of the literary devices in frequent use in oratory." "We recommend," said the pseudonymous Tayacan, "that those interested use them in moderation, since an orator who overuses literary devices loses credibility."

In addition to guns and butter, the United States has supplied the Contras with apostrophe, paralipsis, litotes, and interrogation. Tayacan wrote:

> *Apostrophe* consists of addressing something supernatural or inanimate as if it were a living being. For example, "Mountains of Nicaragua, make the seed of freedom grow."
>
> *Paralipsis* involves the pretense of discretion. For example, "If I were not obligated to keep military secrets, I would tell you about all the armaments we have, so you would feel even more confident that our victory is assured."
>
> *Litotes* is a way of conveying a lot by saying little. For example, "The nine commanders haven't stolen much, just the whole country."
>
> *Interrogation* consists of asking a question of oneself. For example, "if they have already murdered the members of my family, my friends, my peasant brothers, do I have any path other than brandishing a weapon?"[55]

A century or so from now, when archeologists uncover a moldering copy of Tayacan's treatise amid the signs of a military camp on a Nicaraguan hillside, they may marvel at a guerrilla movement that apparently taught its illiterate followers to read by illustrating the classical Roman figures of speech with propagandistic claims about its cause.

2

Incapacitating the Eloquent Speaker

"Nothing succeeds like success" may be true in business but, for the speaker, success carries with it a deadly tendency to transplant what worked well in the past into a new and sometimes unsympathetic environment. Success can undercut speakers by limiting their ability to choose the best from among the available means of persuasion. The eloquent person sees new occasions on their own terms not as repeats of past occasions. Reflexively resurrecting arguments, evidence, and types of discourse that worked before can cripple a speaker. In the first chapter we examined the ways in which eloquent individuals can increase their awareness of the available means of persuasion. We also noted how they can refine their ability to choose the best from among those means. Here we examine factors that blind the speaker and encourage the choice of inappropriate styles and strategies.

William Jennings Bryan was among the finer speakers of his age. Yet he was ultimately the victim of his own rhetorical success. He saw a new situation through the lens provided by past triumphs. Because the lens distorted, the means of persuasion he marshalled from his past were inadequate for the new occasion. Success had also overpolished his confidence in his own abilities as a speaker. For Bryan, this signalled an inability to appreciate that he was master of the monologue but unskilled in interrogation. Hubris combined with habit to dictate that he choose to speak in a forum in which he could not succeed.

William Jennings Bryan at the Scopes Trial[1]

William Jennings Bryan called it a "duel to death";[2] Clarence Darrow characterized it "as brazen and bold [an] attempt to destroy liberty as was ever seen in the Middle Ages."[3] By its conclusion, "Bryan was broken, if ever a man was broken. Darrow never spared him. It was masterly, but it was pitiful," wrote Pulitzer Prize-winning reporter Paul Y. Anderson.[4] "To see this wonderful man . . . this man whose silver voice and majestic mien had stirred millions, to see him humbled and humiliated before the vast crowd which had come to adore him, was sheer tragedy, nothing less." "The whole world has been made familiar with the issues," commented the acerbic H. L. Mencken, "and the nature of the menace that fundamentalism offers to civilization is now familiar to every schoolboy. And Bryan was duly scotched."[5] "When Clarence Darrow got him on the witness stand," observed *The Nation*, "he revealed himself as a pathetically sincere and pitifully ignorant old man."[6]

The Scopes Trial *(State of Tennessee* v. *John Thomas Scopes)*, played out in Dayton, Tennessee, from July 10 through July 21, 1925, pitted a noted trial attorney against a noted orator. At issue was whether John T. Scopes had violated a Tennessee statute making it unlawful to teach any theory that "denies the story of Divine creation of man as taught in the Bible and teach instead that man descended from a lower order of animals."[7] Although Darrow was Scopes' defender and Bryan his prosecutor, both sought Scopes' conviction: Bryan to vindicate the law and its fundamentalist underpinnings, Darrow to appeal the case to the higher courts.

So, in a superficial sense, the outcome of the trial represented a victory for both sides. In reality, however, Darrow's hour and a half interrogation of Bryan marked the rhetorical denouement of the three-time candidate for the presidency who was for a short period Woodrow Wilson's Secretary of State, the man who captured the American political stage and his party's nomination for president with a speech declaring "you shall not crucify mankind upon a cross of gold."

Bryan's rhetorical demise in this famous trial cannot be explained either as the victory of "sense" over "bigotry, ignorance, hatred, [and] superstition" as Mencken claimed[8] or as Bryan "caught and ground" beneath Darrow's "massive erudition" and "ruthless logic" as Anderson contended.[9] Equally unsatisfying is Scopes' explanation that Bryan's "inability to adjust to courtroom conditions was a strong symptom of his mental deterioration."[10] Missing in these explanations is the realization that Bryan was a tragic figure propelled by his own past rhetoric into entering a rhetorical forum that magnified Darrow's rhetorical strengths and his own weaknesses. A self-defining basic premise in Bryan's earlier rhetoric mandated that he spring the trap that the defense set for him when inviting him to take the stand in fundamentalism's defense. Once ensnared in the alien interrogatory genre, Bryan's rhetorical defeat was ordained.

Bryan's Self-Definition

In the speech "Moses vs. Darwin," delivered at Moody Church in Chicago, January 8, 1923,[11] Bryan seems to be prophesying the confrontation with Darrow in the Dayton trial. That speech closes with an autobiographical claim that tells the audience what Bryan perceives to be his role, his mission: "I am for the Bible against all those that oppose it."[12] This position, an echo of Bryan's weekly syndicated commentaries on Scripture, entails that he take the stand in the Scopes Trial. "But when I want to defend something I always attack the enemy who attacks the thing I defend, and fight the enemy on his territory."[13] Throughout "Moses vs. Darwin" Bryan poses questions for the Darwinians and then responds in their name. In each hypothetical exchange, fundamentalism triumphs. The speech also posits a trial of Darwinism in which Bryan vanquishes the opposition.

> I want to tell you that if Darwin's descendants ever sue me for slandering their ancestors, there will be a great trial. And if the case is called for trial, and the sheriff goes to the door and says, "Oh, yes, oh, yes, all the witnesses of Darwin will come into court," and not a one will come. And the judge will say, "Mr. Bryan, as the burden of proof is on the plaintiff, and as they have presented no evidence, you need not call your witnesses." But I tell him I want to call them anyway. Then I will take an alphabetical list of all the species, a million of them. I will bring them all into court, and I will ask them one question and they will answer in concert. I will say, "Do any of you species know of any change in your family?" And every one will say, "Not in my family." With no witnesses on one side and a million on the other, that is the way the case will stand.[14]

So Bryan publicly defines himself as a defender of the Bible eager to meet its opponents on their own territory and projects that in a head-on clash his views will triumph. By defining Bryan as the leader of the opposition and by crediting him with responsibility for the existence of this case, Darrow, in his opening speech, casts Bryan in the same role he has claimed to assume in the past.

After reminding the audience of his oft-repeated claim that there has been no observable change within species, Bryan, in his opening speech

In the courtroom, where he was master, Darrow lured Bryan into that style and away from the expository genre that was Bryan's forte. Bryan's humiliation at the trial is, in part, a function of his retreat to the public monologue in a forum that demanded response to the specific questions put to him by Darrow. (Courtesy Library of Congress)

at the trial, extends his self-definition from defender of the Bible to expert defender of the faith. "I suppose this distinguished scholar who came here shamed them all by his number of degrees—he did not shame me, for I have more than he has, but I can understand how my friends felt when he unrolled degree after degree. . . . Did he tell you how life began? Not a word; and not one of them can tell you how life began."[15] This parenthetical exhibition of hubris is fatal, for by positioning himself as more expert than the defense's experts, Bryan closes the escape route that might have saved him from Darrow's interrogation.[16]

In a subsequent exchange (before the request that Bryan take the stand), Darrow polishes Bryan's credentials: "this case has been made a case where it is to be the Bible or evolution, and we have been informed by Mr. Bryan, who, [is] himself, a profound Bible student and has an essay every Sunday as to what it means."[17] Bryan's affirmative response to Darrow's first question "You have given considerable study to the Bible, haven't you, Mr. Bryan?" embeds in their exchange the premise that spells Bryan's downfall. After the trial, Darrow will concede that Bryan was "very likely" not "an expert on the meaning of the Bible."[18] However, after his own glorification of his credentials, after tacitly accepting the prosecution's repeated characterization of him as an expert, after Darrow's public reminder that Bryan syndicates his preaching on the Bible, and after sermons such as that delivered in Moody Church in which he challenged Darwinians to engage him and prophesied victory for fundamentalism, claiming insufficient expertise in the Bible is no longer a viable position for Bryan in the trial.

The following statements from his testimony as witness confirm that Bryan's self-definition as a defender of the Bible motivated him to take the stand.

> These gentlemen . . . did not come here to try this case. They came here to try revealed religion. I am here to defend it, and they can ask me any question they please.[19]

> I am simply trying to protect the word of God against the greatest atheist or agnostic in the United States *(prolonged applause)*. I want the papers to know I am not afraid to get on the stand in front of him and let him do his worst. I want the world to know *(prolonged applause)*.[20]

> The reason I am answering is not for the benefit of the superior court. It is to keep these gentlemen from saying I was afraid to meet them and let them question me and I want the Christian world to know that any atheist, agnostic, unbeliever, can question me any time as to my belief in God, and I will answer him.[21]

> The only purpose Mr. Darrow has is to slur at the Bible, but I will answer his question.[22]

Bryan's repeated public self-definition as a knowledgeable defender of the Bible who would vanquish Darwinism in any confrontation with it propelled him to take the stand in the Scopes Trial. In so doing he entered a rhetorical arena in which he was vulnerable and of which Darrow was master.

Bryan's Self-Immobilization

In the first part of this section we examined the haunting presence of Bryan's past arguments in his decision to confront Darrow from the witness stand. Here we analyze the numbing influence of ancestral form. It is my claim that Bryan had developed facility in and dependence on a rhetorical genre alien to that demanded of a witness. Consequently, the outcome of the clash between Bryan and Darrow was ordained once Bryan agreed to assume the witness chair.

William Jennings Bryan's performance as a witness can be viewed as a study in self-immobilization. While Bryan had developed his rhetorical reflexes on the Chautauqua circuit, Darrow's were formed in the courtroom. Bryan's strength lay in polished exposition; Darrow's in interrogation. Bryan had perfected his lectures over years until they embodied his true sentiments and inspired the desired response. His most popular lecture, "The Prince of Peace," which had been delivered throughout the world, evolved in this way. By contrast, Darrow's rhetorical environment demanded immediate response to constantly changing rhetorical challenges. When Bryan had faced interrogation it was, as we have seen in "Moses vs. Darwin," of his own making.

Although Bryan was by education a lawyer, at the time of the Scopes Trial he had, by his own admission, not practiced law for twenty-eight years.[23] In his first major statement to the court, Bryan betrays both his discomfort with courtroom rhetorical conventions and also the perservering power of the rhetorical conventions of the lecture circuit when he says, "Now, my friends—I beg pardon, if the court please, I have been so in the habit of talking to an audience instead of a court, that I will sometimes say 'my friends' although I happen to know not all of them are my friends."[24]

Long accustomed to building arguments from premises embraced by his audience, Bryan was rhetorically ill equipped to cope with an adversary and a rhetorical form bent on probing each premise. Consequently, the exchanges between Darrow and Bryan reveal a relentless interrogator pursuing a prey desperately searching for the shelter of a monologic form. Indeed, whenever possible, Bryan not only interposes the sort of speech that elsewhere was his strength but also transports whole chunks of past speeches and essays into his answers, regardless of their relevance to Darrow's line of inquiry. In the process Bryan creates the impression that he is either a poor defender of the Bible or that the Bible, as interpreted by the fundamentalists, is indefensible.

So, for example, when Darrow attempts to reduce literal interpretation of the Bible to absurdity by questioning the plausibility of the sun standing still for Joshua, Bryan, retreating from the unfamiliar interrogatory genre, responds not by answering the question but by drawing on a portion of his lecture "The Prince of Peace":

> I can take a glass of water that would fall to the ground without the strength of my hand and to the extent of the glass of water I can overcome the law of gravitation and lift it up, whereas without my hand it would fall to the ground. If my puny hand can overcome the law of gravitation, the most

universally understood, to that extent, I would not set a limit to the power of the hand of the Almighty God that made the universe.

An illustration that had drawn applause from Chautauqua audiences could not satisfy the demands of either the interrogatory genre or of Darrow:

> I read that years ago. Can you answer my question directly? If the day was lengthened by stopping either the earth or the sun, it must have been the earth?
>
> [Bryan]: Well, I should say so.[25]

This line of inquiry culminates in Darrow's observation that if the earth stood still, it would be converted to a molten mass. Bryan's assurances that God could cope with such difficulties ultimately are replaced by his admission that he has not thought about the alternatives posed by Darrow. The image of Bryan that Darrow implants in the audience is one of a person who has not tested his assumed premises.

A preacher addressing believers does not expect his premises to be challenged. But when, in the Scopes Trial, Bryan accepted the forensic role of defender of the Bible, his rhetorical accountability changed. His answers betray his desire to spurn that accountability for the comfort of a genre he commands.

This pattern emerges again when Darrow attempts to trap Bryan into accepting Bishop Ussher's calculation that 4,262 years have passed since the flood. Bryan admits that he "only" accepts it "because I have no reason to doubt it."[26] Darrow then asks a series of questions that presuppose that civilizations existed before that period. "Don't you know that the ancient civilizations of China are 6,000 or 7,000 years old, at the very least?" Bryan denies that any civilization can antedate creation, which he sets at 6,000 years ago. To question after question, Bryan responds that he either doesn't know the answer or has not studied the matter. On the defensive, Bryan admits that he has not found it necessary to investigate how long man has been on earth, has not studied how old those ancient civilizations were, does not know how old either the Chinese or the Egyptian civilization is, is unaware that other "old religions" describe the flood.

Finally, Darrow asks a question to which Bryan can give an affirmative answer. Yes, he has examined other religions but he has not determined whether they describe the flood: "The Christian religion has satisfied me, and I have never felt it necessary to look up some competing religion." Here Darrow makes a tactical error by straying into a line of questions about competing religions that culminates in an open-ended question: "What about the religion of Buddha?"

Bryan sees the opportunity to shift to the genre at which he excels. He insists that Darrow permit him to answer the question.

[Bryan]:   I can tell you something about that, if you want to know . . .
[Darrow]:   What about the religion of Confucius or Buddha?
[Bryan]:   Well, I can tell you something about that, if you would like to know.
[Darrow]:   Did you ever investigate them?
[Bryan]:   Somewhat.
[Darrow]:   Do you regard them as competitive?
[Bryan]:   No, I think they are very inferior. Would you like for me to tell you what I know about it?[27]

Realizing that Bryan is about to shift to delivery of a speech, Darrow responds "no." But Bryan will not relinquish his opportunity: "Well, I shall insist on giving it to you." Aware that Bryan will shift to ground on which he is more comfortable, Darrow tries to forestall the shift with sarcasm that reveals more than Darrow intended. "You won't talk about free silver, will you?" Bryan responds, "Not at all."

By recalling the speech about free silver that Bryan stampeded the Democratic nominating convention with in 1896, Darrow's question breathes both his awareness that the oration is a form that Bryan wields deftly and his desire to foreclose Bryan's exercise of that genre. What Darrow is asking is: will you deliver a speech of such power that it will obscure the weaknesses in you and your positions that I have just demonstrated in interrogation? Will you deliver another "Cross of Gold" speech? In this context, Bryan's "Not at all" is a tragically prophetic admission. No, he will not succeed in wresting the forum from Darrow. No, he will not duplicate the great oratorical triumph of 1896. "Not at all."

One of Bryan's partners tries to stop the examination, but Bryan insists on making his statement: "But I think when the gentleman asked me about Confucius I ought to be allowed to answer his question." Bryan then delivers a 219-word statement drawn argument by argument from his essay titled "Christianity versus Confuciansm"[28] originally published in 1906. Darrow responds that Bryan has evaded his question, "I haven't asked you that."[29] In a vain attempt to continue his monologue Bryan previews a second point: "That is one of the differences between the two." But Darrow, intent on not being sidetracked again, returns to his original line of inquiry: "Do you know how old the Confucian religion is?" Again Bryan is forced into a series of admissions of ignorance. But Bryan attempts to turn the tables on Darrow by asking him to provide the information of which Bryan has admitted ignorance. Because the ploy violates the rules governing the interrogatory courtroom genre, Darrow is able to sidestep the question with the promise that Bryan will have his turn to act as questioner. Indeed, Bryan has taken the witness stand on the assumption that he will then be able to interrogate Darrow, an opportunity he is not given.

[Bryan]:   When you display my ignorance, could you not give me the facts so I would not be ignorant any longer? Can you tell me how many people there were when Christ was born?

[Darrow]:   You know, some of us might get the facts and still be ignorant.

[Bryan]:   Will you please give me that? You ought not to ask me a question when you don't know the answer to it.

[Darrow]:   I can make an estimate.

[Bryan]:   What is your estimate? [If Darrow responds to this question, Bryan will have reversed roles and grasped hold of the interrogatory genre but Darrow is too skilled in this genre to fall victim to such a maneuver.]

[Darrow]:   Wait until you get to me. Do you know anything about how many people there were in Egypt 3,500 years ago?

[Bryan]:   No.[30]

Finally, after another set of questions yields confessions of disinterest or ignorance, Darrow asks two synoptic questions.

[Darrow]:   You don't care how old the earth is, how old man is and how long the animals have been here?

[Bryan]:   I am not so much interested in that.

[Darrow]:   You have never made any investigation to find out?

[Bryan]:   No, sir, I have never.[31]

Sensing a transition, Bryan interjects, "Now, will you let me finish the question?" Darrow is momentarily taken back.

[Darrow]:   What question was that. If there is anything more you want to say about Confucius I won't object.

[Bryan]:   Oh, yes, I have got two more things.

[Darrow]:   If your honor please I don't object, but his speeches are not germane to my questions.

One of Bryan's colleagues objects that Darrow's questions aren't germane either. Again the door has been opened for Bryan to retreat to a genre he is comfortable with. He proceeds to deliver a paraphrase of the remaining section from his essay on Confucius. Then, in a second effort to transform a transition into a speech, Bryan notes, "Now, Mr. Darrow, you asked me if I knew anything about Buddha."

Darrow does not intend to be trapped a second time. Again he implies that Bryan is dodging behind an inappropriate genre: "You want to make a speech on Buddha, too?" Darrow has asked a question. Bryan is entitled to respond. His response indicates that he is finally warming to the interrogatory genre: "No, sir; I want to answer your question on Buddha."

In an attempt to box Bryan back into the interrogatory genre, Darrow rephrases the question.

> [Darrow]: I asked if you knew anything about him.
> [Bryan]: I do.
> [Darrow]: Well, that's answered then.

Bryan is saved by the judge.

> [Bryan]: Buddha—
> [Darrow]: Well, wait a minute, you answered the question—
> [The Court]: I will let him tell what he knows.[32]

Bryan launches into an extended anecdote. Darrow unsuccessfully protests: "If your honor please, instead of answering plain specific questions we are permitting the witness to regale the crowd with what some black man said to him when he was traveling in Rang-who, India." Bryan continues the story. Again Darrow objects: "I object to Mr. Bryan making a speech every time I ask him a question." At the end of Bryan's disquisition on Buddhism, Darrow reasserts the interrogatory genre and secures three more transcribed pages of self-damaging answers.

In this context, one filled with answer after answer of "I am not sure" and "I couldn't say about that" Bryan backs into the damning admission that not all of the Bible is to be interpreted literally.

> [Darrow]: Do you think the earth was made in six days?
> [Bryan]: Not six days of twenty-four hours.[33]

There were gasps from the fundamentalists in the courtroom.[34] Realizing that Bryan has blundered, his colleague Gen. Stewart interposes another objection asking, "What is the purpose of this examination?" Bryan's response, delivered "pale and trembling" and in a hoarse voice betrays his awareness both that he has been ridiculed and that he has blundered: "The purpose is to cast ridicule on everybody who believes in the Bible."[35]

The concession that the days of creation were not literally twenty-four hours discredited Bryan on the very terms specified in his definition of role, the role that had lured him to the witness stand in the first place. In their interchange after the trial, Darrow twisted the knife with relish: "He [Bryan] did say he believed the literal days of creation mentioned in the first book of Genesis were probably not literal days, but were vast periods of time, which would seem to warrant the inference that if Mr. Bryan could place his interpretation of a day which opened in the morning and closed in the evening, it might not be an evidence of original sin if someone else placed an interpretation on the method by which God made man."[36]

Bryan's credibility had been shattered. Even his devoted wife, with a less than felicitous turn of phrase, admitted that "his answers made him appear more ignorant than he is."[37]

Bryan was the victim of a definition of himself that propelled him into a forum and a rhetorical form he could not control. At the same time, circumstances he could not foresee deprived him of the right to deliver the sermonic lecture he had prepared for the trial's summation. Aware of his power as a platform orator, Darrow planned to frustrate Bryan's chances for giving his carefully created summation. After the first summation by the prosecution, the defense planned to rest the case, thereby prohibiting Bryan from speaking. This strategy went unimplemented when motions by the judge accomplished the same objective.

Unfamiliar with the legal maneuvers that could limit him, unaware that he would be called as a witness, Bryan undoubtedly viewed the rhetorical situation as essentially similar to those he had successfully dealt with for decades. The scenario was uncomplicated: the trial would not pivot on the facts of the case, for the facts were simple. If Scopes admitted teaching evolution, he had violated the law. The summations would function as the fulcrum of the trial. And in summation, Bryan, a person whose reputation was tied to his eloquence, a person who had lectured throughout the world, would vanquish the forces of Darwinism with a speech rivalling the "Cross of Gold" and "Prince of Peace" speeches. Copies of the intended summation awaited distribution to the press. When denied the right to deliver a summation, Bryan's scenario crumbled.

History has judged Bryan harshly, unaware that he was the victim of a rhetorical variable he did not control. Lured by a self-defining premise into a mode of communication Darrow commanded, deprived of a forum in which to capitalize on his own strengths as a speaker, Bryan's rhetorical defeat was ordained. He died days after the trial. His undelivered summation was published posthumously.

The "Cross of Gold" speech survives in William Jennings Bryan's own voice because, years after its original delivery, he recreated it for a phonograph record. By listening to it now, we can imagine what it must have been like to hear old-style stump speaking crackling through a radio into one's living room for the first time. William Jennings Bryan was one of the last masters of fiery oratory.

Even as Bryan stormed the Democratic national convention of 1896 with the "Cross of Gold" speech, the wherewithal to make such speeches sound quaint was on the horizon. The year before, Marconi had demonstrated the wireless telegraph. As Bryan toured the world perfecting the "Prince of Peace" speech, Sir John Flemming was testing the first vacuum electron tube. That invention made it possible to electronically detect radio waves. By 1904 music and speech could be transmitted. Two years later, as Bryan was writing his columns in defense of Christianity, Lee De Forest tested the audion that would detect and amplify radio waves. The patenting of the regenerative receiver had made long-range radio reception possible by the time Woodrow Wilson named Bryan his Secretary of State in 1913. As Bryan was fighting unsuccessfully for the Democrats to embrace prohibition in 1920, the first commercial radio station in the country carried the news. Radio transmitted word of the "Great Commoner's" death in 1925.

Radio and then television changed the rules for speakers of public words and for their listeners. A liberal education, a quick intellect, a dexterous command of the available means of persuasion, and a talent for adapting to new situations would remain valuable for the good person aspiring to speak well. But unless complemented by the skills required by the electronic media, those trusted old friends of eloquence would produce fiery oratory where the new medium invited instead the fireside chat.

3

The Flame of Oratory, The Fireside Chat

John Kennedy had been shot in Dallas. Before the first newspaper could carry the news to street corners and doorsteps, television viewers had learned that the president of the United States was dead.

In the National Cathedral and on the floor of Congress, eulogists spoke movingly of the meaning of John Kennedy's life and the tragedy of his death. Senators, ministers, and friends offered words of comfort to the Kennedy family and to the nation. Kennedy would live, they said, in our hearts, in history, and in our efforts to create the world he had envisioned. Two and a half decades later, their words are lost to memory.

Television's images survive indelibly. In them we experienced a eulogy neither Pericles nor Lincoln could have delivered. Yet both would have recognized it, for, like traditional eulogies spoken in churches and at grave sites, it acknowledged the death, recalled and interpreted the meaning of the life, said farewell, reassured that the community would survive, and asserted that the deceased would live on in his effects on our lives and in our memories of him.

What Pericles and Lincoln could only say in words, television's eulogy for Kennedy conveyed in pictures. The film of an amateur photographer showed the president arching back into the seat of the limousine and then slumping into his wife's arms. The blood-splattered suit of the widow and the flag-draped coffin confirmed the death. His life was recalled and memorialized in photos of him as bridegroom, brother, husband, father, candidate, president, in replayings of vignettes from his inaugural address, his press conferences, and his speech on the Cuban Missile Crisis. The citizens who paid final tribute as Kennedy's body lay in state said farewell for us as did Caroline as she kissed the coffin and John John as he saluted. Throughout, symbols of communal survival projected the future: of the office—through a photo of Johnson swearing the oath aboard the presidential plane; of the family—through the black-veiled widow and her two small children; of the country—in the citizens massed along the route to Arlington Cemetery; of the world—in the presence of the heads of state from other countries. Pictures also consigned Kennedy to history and memory: the black stallion, its stirrups carrying empty boots, the cortege framed by the Lincoln Memorial, the slow pan from the cemetery back to Lincoln. Finally, the cameras cut from a still of Kennedy captioned by the dates of his birth and death to the eternal flame at his gravesite. Mortality had been displaced by immortality.

The storehouse from which we retrieve these images commingles who and where we were then with our memories of the eulogy: mention of Kennedy's death calls up the otherwise forgotten places in which we learned of it, the people we were with, the way we felt. This collage of ourselves and the remembered moments of the eulogy gives John Kennedy an immortality denied Franklin Roosevelt. FDR's death was a private act, privately mourned by individuals alone with their radios.

During those four days in 1963, television delivered the contemporary equivalent of the Gettysburg Address. But where Lincoln's words were long remembered, the pictures from the Kennedy eulogy survive. Where Lincoln's eulogy was heard only by those crowding a Pennsylvania field, Kennedy's was seen by over ninety percent of the homes in the United States and by the citizens of twenty-two other nations. Where the Gettysburg Address was inaccessible to those not fluent in English, the visual images of the Kennedy eulogy spoke a universal language.

Television has changed public discourse dramatically. Increasingly, eloquence is visual, not verbal. Where once we expected messages laced with impassioned appeals, now we respond positively to a cooler, more conversational art; where once audiences expected to be conquered by an art bent on battle, today's television viewer expects instead an intimate rhetoric of conciliation. Not only must the successful politicians of today speak softly, they must also avoid the appearance of carrying a big stick.

Public discourse is now more personalized, self-disclosive, and autobiographical; today's public speech comfortably includes Fala, Checkers, Amy, and Nancy. Audiences too have changed. Crowds once gave thunderous applause in open fields, now we nod our tacit approval in living rooms. Private conversation between a leader and the public has replaced public address by a public speaker to a crowd. The compartments into which our world was parsed have collapsed. Public address now seems a collaborative and intimate act that enmeshes speaker and audience. We can start to detect the similarities and differences between speechmaking as it once was and as it now is by looking at the metaphors in which theorists and practitioners have captured their experience of public address. '

The Old Eloquence

The old eloquence, which spoke in metaphors of battle and fire, was contentious, passionate, and intense. Today, speakers who still try to conquer and inflame are as anachronistic as the amphitheater and the aqueduct. Fiery words of combat have no place on the intimate media of radio and television; fire metaphors and the style they signal have given way to metaphors of electricity and a cooler conversational style. Just as obsolete is the view that wordfare is warfare.

Eloquence as Flame

Until recently, Western eloquence was a form of spontaneous combustion that sparked, inflamed, and burned. "Your burning words, ferocious Trojan, do not frighten me," Turnus tells Aeneas, "it is the gods alone who terrify me."[1] "Great eloquence, like fire, grows with the material," observed Tacitus, "it becomes fiercer with movement, and brighter as it burns."[2] "I have read a fiery gospel writ in burnished rows of steel," wrote Julia Ward Howe in the "Battle Hymn of the Republic."[3]

From Cicero to Grover Cleveland, fire sparked the images of Western eloquence. The association was a natural one. "The symbolic affinities between words and fire, between the live twist of flame and the darting tongue, are immemorially archaic and firmly entrenched in the subconscious," notes George Steiner. "Thus it may be that there is a language-factor in the Prometheus myth, an association between man's mastery over fire and his new conception of speech. Prometheus was the first to hold Nemesis at bay by silence, by refusing to disclose to his otherwise omnipotent tormenter the words which pulse and blaze in his own visionary intellect."[4] The cliché "tongues of fire" speaks the affinities between speech and flame.

Fire embodied the beliefs that eloquence was powerful but not always predictable, valued but nonetheless feared, potentially destructive but also productive of good. At the same time, the metaphor captured eloquence's disposition to quicken the convictions of a crowd.

In early Western uses of the fire metaphor, eloquence inflamed the mind. Greece was "fired with a passion for eloquence," wrote Cicero. If a speaker lacked the ability "to inflame the minds of his hearers,"[5] he missed the most essential attribute of an orator.[6] Yet, early in the history of rhetoric, theorists concluded that rhetoric worked in different ways on the mind and on the will, a realization we hear in Augustine's counsel that "The eloquent divine, then, when he is urging a practical truth, must not only teach so as to give instruction, and please so as to keep up the attention, but he must also sway the mind so as to subdue the will. For if a man be not moved by the force of truth, though it is demonstrated to his own confession, and clothed in beauty of style, nothing remains but to subdue him by the power of eloquence."[7] Gradually, "inflaming" came to be associated with appeals to the will or the passions and "enlightening" with the intellect, the mind. The assumption lodged in this distinction was that appeals to the intellect were superior.

So, a nineteenth-century critic praises Lincoln for "he has always addressed the intelligence of men, never their prejudice, their passion, or their ignorance."[8] Similarly, Woodrow Wilson recoiled from the tone of passion in a protest by a group of blacks who objected to racial segregation of federal employees:

> [Wilson]: If this organization is ever to have another hearing before me it must have another spokesman. Your manner offends me. . . . Your tone, with its background of passion.
>
> [Mr. Trotter]: But I have no passion in me, Mr. President, you are entirely mistaken; you misinterpret my earnestness for passion.[9]

No major rhetorical theorist has argued that eloquence either does or should work on the emotions alone. Yet appeal to what have at various times been called passions, emotions, inclinations, motives, and the will is necessary, for, as theorists have always recognized, truth alone does not persuade. By tying the rational to the emotional, what eloquence can do is make what a speaker considers true palatable to the audience. Nineteenth-century Presbyterian clergyman Lyman Beecher explains that "Eloquence is logic on fire."[10] Oliver Wendell Holmes used the same metaphor to express a related idea when he said, "Eloquence may set fire to reason."[11] As the view that eloquence works in different ways on the mind and the will took hold, the metaphor was refined to argue that its heat inflamed the passions of the audience, its light illumined the intellect. The dark underside of eloquence was that it could be used to circumvent reason and prompt audiences to act on impulses better kept in check.

As the twentieth century dawned, to inflame an audience became a mark of demagoguery. Henry Adams observed in 1885: "To a new society, ignorant and semi-barbarous, a mass of demagogues insisted on applying every stimulant that could inflame its worst appetites, while at the same instant taking away every influence that had hitherto helped to restrain its passions."[12]

Increasingly, inflaming the passions became the legitimate goal of the lover, not the leader. And those passions were unleashed in private, not in public. Fire metaphors become vehicles with which to damn the demagogue or demonstrate the ardor of the suitor and seducer. In the process, the metaphor used by theorists from Cicero to Webster shifted disciplines. Its home was now sex education, not public communication.

Eloquence as War by Other Means

The rhetoric of fire and of battle are allies. Until the twentieth century "fire and sword" cohabited as a synonym for war. Both metaphors depict the audience as an object to be overcome. Both predicate persuasion on the superior power or capacity of the speaker. Both depict persuasion as a less than rational process.

The sources of the alliance between rhetoric and battle are many. In the Iron Age of seventh- and eighth-century Greece, the right to fight with words was earned along with the capacity for service in one of the heavily armed phalanxes of citizen-soldiers known as hoplites. Unless the phalanx moved as a single cooperative body, it failed. Where horse-mounted aristocrats once had dominated the arts of war and statecraft, now farmers and the middle class stood at their side. Equals in war became equals in deciding whether to war. From this change in warfare was born the hoplite franchise: by equipping himself for war and functioning in a phalanx, a citizen-soldier gained a voice in the conduct of public affairs.

In Sicily too, the art of rhetoric arose from conflict. When a flood destroyed all records in 467 B.C., citizens required a means of establishing the ownership of contested property. Two skilled public speakers, Corax and Tisias, formalized an art that argued from probability and for pay that one claimant and not another was the rightful possessor of the contested pigs, pots, and pomegranates. Of conquest and legal clash was Western rhetoric fashioned. From a Greek word for war comes the English "polemic."

Unsurprisingly, rhetoric was defined in a language appropriated from war. "If it is a disgrace to a man when he cannot defend himself in a bodily way," wrote Aristotle in the West's first major rhetoric treatise, "it would be odd not to think him disgraced when he cannot defend himself with reason."[13] So too he wrote of "fighting the case with the facts alone."[14] Accordingly, persuasion is an act of compelling compliance or obedience.[15] In the passive voice the Greek word for persuade means obey.

Rome followed suit. The *Ad Herrenium* likened arguments to "the arraying of soldiers in battle,"[16] an image compatible with Quintilian's discussion of metaphors, arguments, evidence, and figures of speech as "weapons."[17] In Martianus Capella's fifth-century treatise, eloquence held weapons readied "for defense or attack." Her weaponry gleamed "with the flash of lightening."[18] The imagery persisted. In the eighteenth century, theorist George Campbell recommended discourse that fused the lofty and the vehement. Such a fusion enabled the orator to "fight with weapons which are at once sharp, massive, and refulgent, which, like heaven's artillery, dazzle while they strike, which overpower the sight and the heart at the same instant."[19]

The disputations that characterized Roman and Medieval rhetorical training carried the adversarial assumptions of the ancient world into modern times. Students required to "defend" an M.A. thesis or doctoral dissertation are the legatees of these assumptions.

Reliance on battle metaphors survived the Medieval period. Throughout the nineteenth century, masterful speeches were described as a "public armory," from which other speakers drew weapons.[20] By "captivating" and "enchaining" audiences, speakers reduced them to prisoners of war.

Battle images continued to cling to the cooler, more conversational art that supplanted fiery oratory. They persevere in part because our system of government invites a confrontational concept of public discourse. In the fifty-first *Federalist*, for example, Publius argues for "fortifying" the office of the executive, guarding against "dangerous encroachments," and ensuring the equal power of "self-defense" among branches of government by using the principle of "opposite and rival interests." In Madison's scheme, checks and balances would frustrate faction.

The notion of party also was steeped in the desire to deal with conflict. Recognizing that the nature of "man" would produce "violent dissensions and discords," Jefferson concluded that "Perhaps this party division is necessary to induce each to watch and relate to the people the proceedings of the other."[21] In the same spirit, South Carolina

Congressman Robert Goodloe Harper defended the two parties as "combatants" with the public as judge.[22]

The process by which we still elect representatives invites a rhetoric of contest and campaign. Ours is not a system designed to foster governing coalitions, an outcome inviting conciliatory campaign discourse, but is instead one in which a single person holds a single office. A system that fosters a winner is conducive to the combative discourse of contest, victory, and defeat.

By disposing candidates to the claim that since birth their opponents have not had an idea of value, the resulting campaign discourse does a disservice to the candidates, the electorate, and the body politic. Areas of disagreement are stressed, areas of agreement ignored. Conceding that the incumbent had voted the right way once in a while, might, after all, invite the audience to reelect rather than repudiate. In simplistic, Manichean discourse, both sides take credit for blessings not of their own creating. Blame is indiscriminately assigned as well. Every imaginable social ill is dropped at the opponent's door. Campaign discourse becomes a caricature of its better self.

Conventional language conspires with our history and system of government to dispose contemporary political discourse to the language of scourge, siege, and surrender. Routinely, we speak of engaging our audiences and rhetorical adversaries in combat whose outcome is capitulation, not contemplation. On the battleground bequeathed to us by Greco-Roman rhetoric, speakers, "armed" with "forceful," "compelling" argumentative "strategies," "muster" cases, "marshal" arguments, "attack" and "defend," "outmaneuver" their "opponents," "combat" errors, "take," "hold" or "yield" ground, and "battle" their "adversaries" with "weapons" of evidence and logic. "Overpowered," "overwhelmed," and "overcome," audiences and adversaries alike "yield" to an "onslaught" of evidence.

While our daily speech is rich with the words describing discourse as an act of war, the corresponding vocabulary of conciliation is impoverished. The rhetoric of courtship offers one alternative. Such discourse would both stress the worth and centrality of the audience and have co-creative action as a desired end. The "courted" audience can choose either to spurn or embrace the suitor.

Once past the hearts and flowers, however, the rhetoric of the suitor quickly veers into talk of seduction, a frequent barrack-mate of such words of war as "succumb to advances," "overcome," and "surrender." The rhetoric of courtship does open one useful question: Will the politician still respect the electorate in the morning? But what of the audience disposed to entertain the proposals of more than one suitor? The rhetoric of partnership offers another alternative. But none of these has the range and popularity of war metaphors. As I will argue, the currency of these combative metaphors baits a sometimes deadly trap for unsuspecting politicians.

The New Eloquence of Conciliation and Conversation

Recognizing the costs of a rhetoric of assault and surrender, contemporary theorists recommend beating the sword of eloquence into a plowshare. The old rhetoric, noted twentieth-century theorist I. A. Richards, "was the theory of the battle of words and has always been itself dominated by the combative impulse. Perhaps what it has most to teach us is the narrowing and blinding influence of that preoccupation, the debaters' interest."[23] In place of the old rhetoric, Richards envisioned a rhetoric that would be "a study of misunderstanding and its remedies."[24] Similarly, Kenneth Burke rejected the old rhetoric of contention for the new rhetoric of identification.[25] Where the old rhetoric sought to "overcome resistance, to a course of action, an idea, a judgment," the new seeks "cooperation, mutuality, social harmony."

Nonetheless, many modern presidents have persisted in reducing politics and political discourse to words of war or its domesticated kin— sports. This was as true of FDR who declared that he loved "a good fight"[26] as of JFK who awarded Winston Churchill honorary American citizenship by proclaiming that he had "mobilized the English language and sent it into battle." For some, the presidency itself seemed to be a battleground. Lyndon Johnson viewed building the Great Society as a process of "conquering thousands of enemies and hurdling hundreds of obstacles." "I was determined to turn those lordly men into good soldiers," he vowed.[27]

Those who have pledged to make verbal war no more often carry the electorate to the peace table with them. By viewing it as a "debate," Nixon "lost" the first Kennedy-Nixon joint appearance. His varsity debate instincts at the ready, the vice president marshalled his facts against Kennedy's, contested points, and defended his ground. He instead should have showcased himself against the backdrop Kennedy provided. By combatting Kennedy's arguments, Nixon legitimized the less experienced senator and ignored an opportunity to appear presidential.

Two decades later, another Republican demonstrated that he understood that television was more hospitable to lovers than fighters. As the debate of October 28, 1980, was about to begin, a smiling Ronald Reagan strode comfortably across the stage to shake the incumbent president's hand. Carter's look of surprise suggested that he thought he was about to be knifed. The handshake was as lethal. How could Carter then cast a smiling hand-shaker as a mad bomber who would destroy Social Security, the environment, and perhaps the world?

Throughout the debate, as Carter pummelled him with detail after detail, Reagan retained that amiable posture. Reagan's decisive dismissal of Carter with "There you go again" was the verbal equivalent of a smile and a shrug.

Reagan appeared "relaxed, smiling, robust," wrote Carter aide Hamilton Jordan, while President Carter was "erect, lips tight, looking like a coiled spring, ready to pounce, an overtrained boxer, too ready for the bout."[28] Guided by the ghosts of Corax, Tisias, Cicero, and Quintilian and grounded in a history of attracting broadcast news bites by attacking their opponents, Carter and Nixon assumed that televised "debate" was a two-sided, adversarial form in which the goal was to conquer your opponent. Theirs was the old rhetoric in a time demanding the new.

From Fire to the Electrified Fireside Chat

By 1905, electricity had been captured in light bulbs that could be used safely in the home. As electricity transformed our homes and lives, electrical metaphors displaced fiery ones. "The eloquence of one [speaker] stimulates all the rest," wrote Emerson, "some up to the speaking-point, and all others to a degree that makes them good receivers and conductors, and they avenge themselves for their enforced silence by increased loquacity."[29] "A capacity for electrifying an audience, to use a modern phrase, is valuable in a speaker, in the case of some it is indispensable," wrote one anthologist in 1903.[30]

Where orators "dampened" the enthusiasm "sparked" by their opponents, now speakers "defused" their opponents' arguments. Groups were "fused" together.[31] Both figuratively and literally, speakers and their audiences were "on the same wavelength." Discourse still "sparked" new ideas, interest and enthusiasm, but increasingly ideas were "conveyed," "relayed," and "channeled." Channel now communicated not only canals but avenues through which messages travelled. The Latin derivative transmitted now echoed a world of transmitters; audiences' attitudes were "transformed." Before it was appropriated by the drug culture, "turned on" described an excited audience just as "tuned in" bespoke an attentive one. Ideas that formerly had been "conceived," a primal metaphor, were instead "generated." This network of language reminds us of the extent to which communication is now technologi-

Prior to the advent of the broadcast media, speakers could alter their speeches to accommodate feedback from their audiences. Here William Jennings Bryan addresses a group of loggers. (Courtesy Political History Division, Smithsonian)

cally mediated. William Jennings Bryan could inflame an audience only by direct contact with it. Ronald Reagan electrifies his audience with the cooperation of NBC, CBS, ABC, and the local power company.

In the old universe of fire, the orator was inflamed. In the new universe of electricity, the audience, not the speaker, is electrified. The shift in metaphors marked a shift in the locus of energy from the orator to the idea. "Condense some daily experience into a glowing symbol," wrote Emerson, "and an audience is electrified."[32] This shift was accompanied by a move away from impassioned delivery and strong direct pathetic appeals.

As discourse was cast in electrical metaphors, theories premised on conservation of energy took hold. So, for example, nineteenth-century

British philosopher Herbert Spencer argued that audiences have a finite amount of energy to expend on grasping a speech. Predicating "economy of attention" as a principle, he claimed that a speaker should do all possible to interest the audience because energy spent on holding one's attention on a dull speech could not be used to reflect on its content.

This confluence of factors produced three of the changes in public speechmaking on which later chapters will focus; conversational delivery and natural gesture replaced impassioned speech. With the advent of television, words functioned more readily to caption pictures than to create them and the speaker emerged autobiographically in the speech.

The Advent of Conversational Delivery

For well over a century before electricity entered our homes, a more controlled notion of the human communication process, one centered on reason not emotion, had been on the horizon. In 1783, Hugh Blair noted in his *Lectures on Rhetoric and Belles Lettres*[33] that "the Greeks and Romans aspired to a more sublime species of Eloquence, than is aimed at by the Moderns. Theirs was of the vehement and passionate kind, by which they endeavored to inflame the minds of their hearers, and hurry their imaginations away." By contrast, he concluded, "Modern Eloquence is much more cool and temperate."

Whatever the cause, audience members report much more emotive responses to the oratory of early days than to our own. So, for example, Sir Gilbert reported that "there was not a dry eye in the assembly during Sheridan's great Begum Speech, [and] that he himself never cried so on a public occasion."[34] Earlier audiences clearly had reactions that we would now find aberrant. Professor Ticknor's reaction to Daniel Webster's Plymouth Address might have caused his physician consternation: "Three or four times I thought my temples would burst with the gush of blood. . . . When I came out, I was almost afraid to come near to him. It seemed to me that he was like the mount that might not be touched, and that burned with fire."[35]

As William Jennings Bryan gave way to Woodrow Wilson, Calvin Coolidge, and Herbert Hoover, the emergence of cooler, more controlled communication required a changed metaphor. The rise of radio in the United States accelerated the trend away from impassioned oratory and toward public conversation between speaker and audience. The electric metaphor captured the changed practices it had helped produce.

By the second decade of the twentieth century the subtle, plain style had become the norm. "We read," wrote James Winans in 1917, "that the ancients would endure the most direct assaults upon their feelings. Pleaders in court might dramatically bare their scars; and the young children of a defendant might be exhibited with the open intent of winning sympathy. These methods have not entirely lost vogue, but they can rarely be used so openly with good effect. The modern man, and especially the American and Englishman, though emotional enough, dislikes direct appeals to his feelings. He may hang his head or he may jeer; but he is in all cases likely to resist when he is conscious that an assault upon his feelings is being made."[36]

With the changed style came a changed mode of delivery. The slapping of the thigh and the foot stamping that in the Roman forum accentuated strong appeals now survived only on the stage. Still, until the advent of amplified sound, speakers needed to project their voices great distances. "Many public speakers have not the advantage of enjoying lungs and other organs of speech always adequate to the constant emission of that volume of sound, which is necessary to fill those buildings, commonly devoted to the purposes of oratory," noted John Quincy Adams.[37] "To them the soundest advice perhaps would be to devote themselves to some occupation more compatible with their tenderness of constitution."

Having a voice like a pipe organ, as Daniel Webster did, carried an advantage as long as the unamplified human voice was required to reach each member of the audience. So Macaulay was praising Pitt when he wrote of his delivery, "the sound rose like the swell of the organ of a cathedral, shook the House with its peal, and was heard through lobbies and down the staircases, to the Court of Requests and the precincts of Westminster Hall."[38] Before the broadcast media, when you said a person spoke "forcefully," you were probably referring to delivery; in the broadcast age such statements usually describe content, not delivery.

Rarely did women have voices like pipe organs. Although many noteworthy female orators in the abolition and suffrage movements overcame the obstacle, the articulatory volume required to project a message to thousands of listeners made it more difficult for women to speak effectively in such an environment. The intimate nature of broadcast communication altered not only the volume but the tone of discourse. "Before electronic amplification, the very size of an audience could build up the agonistic temper of discourse," notes cultural theorist Walter Ong. "It is hard to project irenic gentleness in roaring vocalization, which lends itself readily to combative situations."[39]

When the fire metaphor was extinguished, so too were the related notions that the orator commanded lightning and thunder or could storm the audience. More frequently, electrical metaphors came to describe the cooler rhetoric that Hume and Blair saw as native to the modern forum. Scholars began to conceive the universe of discourse in terms of this newly domesticated force. Writing near the turn of the century, William James introduced *The Will to Believe* by noting, "Let us give the name of hypothesis to anything that may be proposed to our belief; and just as the electricians speak of live and dead wires, let us speak of any hypothesis as either live or dead. A live hypothesis is one which appeals as a real possibility to him to whom it is proposed. If I ask you to believe in Mahdi, the notion makes no electric connection with your nature—it refuses to scintillate with any credibility at all. As an hypothesis it is completely dead."[40]

Electricity transported communication into an intimate environment. Radio and television deliver their messages to family units of twos and threes. By contrast, the torch parade drew hundreds and occasionally thousands to hear a speaker. In the quiet of our living rooms we are less likely to be roused to a frenzy than when we are surrounded by a swarming, sweating mass of partisans.

From Cicero's *De Oratore* through the nineteenth-century treatise *Orators and Oratory*, the word orator was an honorable one. In the electronic age, that word lost currency. Just as inflaming a public became the province of the demagogue, orating came to signal speaking in "an elevated and often pompous manner."[41] Departments and professorships of oratory gave way to "public address."

FDR's fireside chats suggested a new model of communication: one person in the private space of his living room chatting with millions of other individuals in theirs. Could such discourse properly be labelled public address? Some argued that the mass media's small families and solitary viewers were not a public in any traditional sense. Moreover, conversing privately with families through publicly accessible channels did not seem to approximate address. Its "public" turned private and its "address" turned conversation, "public address" joined bustles in the linguistic attic.

Correspondingly, instead of being called orators, those who addressed audiences were now called speakers. Where once they orated, now they spoke. Many noticed the differences. Dale Carnegie, whose Carnegie Clubs popularized nonacademic speech training, observed:

> [S]ome schoolboys are still being forced to recite the ornate "oratory" of Webster and Ingersoll—a thing that is as much out of style and as far removed from the spirit of the age as the hats worn by Mrs. Ingersoll and Mrs. Webster would be if they were resurrected today.

An entirely new school of speaking has sprung up since the Civil War. In keeping with the spirit of the times, it is as direct as a telegram. The verbal fireworks that were once the vogue would not longer be tolerated by an audience in this year of grace.

A modern audience, regardless of whether it is fifteen people at a business conference or a thousand people under a tent, wants the speaker to talk just as directly as he would in a chat, and in the same general manner that he would employ in speaking to one of them in conversation.[42] .

Speeches became talks. In the transition, the sacred slipped away. As fire came from Sinai and Olympus, the word orate whispered its kinship to prayer, a kinship forged in the Latin root *orare* meaning "to pray." Oratory was once the art of speaking; an oratory, a place of prayer. Fiery oratory now gave way to the fireside chat.

Televised Words Caption rather than Create Pictures

In intensity, style, tone, and even length, the new eloquence is more constrained than the old. The same tendency is reflected in the abandonment of another traditional metaphor: that of eloquence as a painting of thought. Here, the old rhetor is to the new as the muralist is to the minimalist.

For Pascal as for many of his predecessors, eloquence was a "painting of thought." "[T]hose who, after having painted it, add something more, make a picture instead of a portrait."[43] So central was this visualizing process that in *De augmentis* Francis Bacon argued that "it is the office of Rhetoric to make pictures of virtue and goodness, so that they may be seen."[44] Because man was the victim of original sin, argued Fenelon, he was enmeshed in "palpable things" and could not long attend to the "abstract." Accordingly, "lively portraiture" is the "soul" of eloquence.[45]

Theorists assumed that sight was the most powerful sense and probed appeals to "the visual imagination." Forms of demonstration that invited an audience to see a person or event were codified and enshrined in directories of figures of speech.

The belief that rhetoric should paint a picture produced detailed descriptive passages that we now find peculiar and excessive in nineteenth-century American public address. So, for example, in his eulogy of Abraham Lincoln, Charles Sumner found it necessary to describe the sixteenth president:

> In person he was tall and bony, with little resemblance to any historic portrait, unless he might seem in one respect to justify the epithet given to an early English king. As he stood, his form was angular, with something of

By incarnating an important idea in memorable language on a noteworthy occasion, Martin Luther King, Jr.'s "I Have a Dream" speech met the traditional
tests of eloquence. (Courtesy National Archives)

that straightness in lines so peculiar in the figure of Dante by Flaxman.
His countenance had more of rugged strength than his person, and while
in repose, inclined to sadness; yet it lighted easily. Perhaps the quality that
struck most at first was his constant simplicity of manner and conversation,
without form or ceremony beyond that among neighbors.[46]

Today such passages are unnecessary. Many of us could recognize
Ronald Reagan more readily than we could our own neighbors. Nor is
it necessary for President Reagan to capture the mortar of the Berlin
Wall when speaking before it on June 12, 1987. The news cameras
show the wall as Reagan notes, "Behind me stands a wall that encircles
the free sectors of this city." It is an image known even to those who
have never set foot in Germany for, as the president observes, "the
newsphoto and the television screen have imprinted this brutal division
of a continent upon the mind of the world." Where rhetoric once painted
murals, television now transports the actual landscape to the nation's
living rooms. The camera now shows as the speaker tells. In spot ads,
in television news, and in political documentaries, the spoken word is
attached to images almost like a caption.

The civil rights movement of the 1950s and 1960s was catalyzed not

The unprecedented size of the audience dramatically set the stage for King's speech. Its response to the speech telegraphed to the living rooms of America the conclusion that King's words had embodied the sentiments of the Civil Rights Movement. Prior to the delivery of that speech, King was *a* leader of the movement. After its delivery, he was *the* leader. (Courtesy National Archive)

by eloquent words but by eloquent pictures. The most moving words of spring 1963 were written by Martin Luther King, Jr., from a jail cell in Birmingham, Alabama: "[W]hen you take a cross-country drive and find it necessary to sleep night after night in the uncomfortable corners of your automobile because no motel will accept you; when you are humiliated day in and day out by nagging signs reading 'white' and 'colored'; when your first name becomes 'nigger,' your middle name becomes 'boy' (however old you are) and your last name becomes 'John,' and your wife and mother are never given the respected title 'Mrs.'; when you are harried by day and haunted by night by the fact that you are a Negro, living constantly at tiptoe stance, never quite knowing what to expect next, and are plagued with inner fears and outer resentments; when you are forever fighting a degenerating sense of 'nobodiness'—then you will understand why we find it difficult to wait." But pictures from Birmingham, not words, precipitated passage of the Civil Rights Act.

The power of the televised picture was illustrated dramatically when

Birmingham Police Commissioner "Bull" Connor used firehoses and police dogs to disperse peaceful blacks protesting the injustices of segregation. Movement leaders agreed that "the Kennedys were sensitive to the international impact of the Birmingham photos, and that the embarrassment, coupled with the domestic outpouring of support for the movement, might push the administration into more aggressive support of civil rights than it had been willing to risk."[47] "I don't think you should be totally harsh on Bull Connor," JFK told two civil rights leaders. "After all, he has done more for civil rights than almost anybody else."[48] Television made palpable the indignities of segregated schools and buses, lunch counters, restrooms, and water fountains. Millions for whom the civil rights movement had been an abstraction now empathized with Connor's victims.

A turning point came on the day in May 1963 when Connor unleashed dogs and firehoses on protesting black children. For three months, the civil rights bill had lain unnoticed in the committee hopper. Now the mounting public outcry demanded action. Congressional hearings were scheduled. The landmark Civil Rights Act began to move through Congress, its provisions toughened by legislators whose resolve was firmed by the conviction that the farmers of the Midwest and the factory workers of the Northeast would stand behind those who worked to alleviate the injustices that nightly were being conveyed to the nation's living rooms.

With the passage of the Civil Rights Act of 1964, the agenda of the Civil Rights Movement shifted to winning voting rights. Here too television's visual power played an important role. On March 7, 1965, six hundred unarmed men, women, and children lined up two by two to begin a peaceful, fifty-mile march for voting rights from Selma to Montgomery, Alabama. On the Edmund Pettus bridge in Selma the demonstrators were confronted by a phalanx of Alabama state troopers, gas masks on their belts, billy clubs in their hands. The major in charge of the police ordered the marchers to disperse. When the demonstrators held their ground, the troopers advanced. The networks interrupted their programming to carry pictures of the brutal assault to the nation. The thickening tear gas and the choking sounds of its victims suggested that here was a nation at war with its own people. At the bridge in Selma young children and elderly women were among those clubbed unconscious. ABC cut from its broadcast of the film *Judgment at Nuremberg* to carry the bloodbath. "When that beating happened at the foot of the bridge," recalls Selma's Mayor Joseph Smitherman, "it looked like war. That went all over the country. And the people, the wrath of the nation came down on us."[49] Ten days later in a nationally broadcast address to a joint session of Congress, President Lyndon Johnson urged adoption of his Voting Rights Act.

By delivering Bull Connor, George Wallace, and the troopers at Selma to homes in Minneapolis as well as Memphis, television united the nation behind civil rights legislation and in the process advanced Lyndon Johnson's political agenda. But as television's pictures crippled his conduct of the Vietnam war, Johnson learned that this medium's disposition toward the digestive, dramatic visual image could orphan actions incapable of speaking its language. The day after he announced that he would not seek reelection to the presidency, Johnson speculated that television "may be somewhat better suited to conveying the actions of conflict than to dramatizing the words that leaders use in trying and hoping to end the conflict. Certainly, it is more 'dramatic' to show policemen and rioters locked in combat than to show men trying to cooperate with one another. The face of hatred and of bigotry comes through much more clearly—no matter what its color. The face of tolerance, I seem to find, is rarely 'newsworthy.' Perhaps this is because tolerance and progress are not dynamic events—such as riots and conflicts are events. Peace, in the news sense, is a 'condition.' War is an 'event' " (April 1, 1968).

Recognizing the power of the visual image, politicians have become preoccupied with providing the lens with irresistible pictures. Pseudo-events abound. In the world of television, public leaders and reporters are only seen and heard selectively. When the visual and verbal dance in step, the power of each is magnified. But while the visual message is a flamenco dancer, its verbal partner is a wallflower.

This visual dominance makes it difficult for the words of a television correspondent to find fault effectively with a campaign's choreography of the news. During the 1984 campaign, for instance, CBS correspondent Lesley Stahl attempted to demonstrate the extent and expense to which the Reagan staff was willing to go to enwrap his speeches in a visually enticing context. "The orchestration of television coverage absorbs the White House," Stahl stated. "Their goal? To emphasize the president's greatest asset, which, his aides say, is his personality. They provide pictures of him looking like a leader. Confident, with his Marlboro Man walk. A good family man. They also aim to erase the negatives. Mr. Reagan tried to counter the memory of an unpopular issue with a carefully chosen backdrop that actually contradicts the President's policy. Look at the handicapped Olympics, or the opening ceremony of an old-age home. No hint that he tried to cut the budgets for the disabled and for federally subsidized housing for the elderly."[50]

Red, white, and blue balloons, the Olympic Torch, soaring jets, enthusiastic crowds, and waving flags documented her claim. Although it verbally eviscerated their visual manipulation, Reagan's staff loved the piece. So totally had the visual images worked their intended magic that the verbal debunking was lost in a red, white, and blue patriotic pro-Reagan blur.[51]

By contrast, the televised images of 1984 were problematic for the Democratic nominee. Where his first general election parade should have featured enthusiastic throngs, the network newscasts instead showed Mondale waving determinedly to store fronts, fire hydrants, parked cars, and only an occasional Democrat. The scene was symptomatic of the campaign's lack of sophistication in scheduling and packaging events. The image of a candidate whose message was not being heard was one that words could not readily dislodge.

So central are images to contemporary political communication that we can synopsize the rise and fall of entire presidencies wordlessly. Jimmy Carter visualized his victory by assembling his friends and former rivals on the podium at the end of the 1976 Democratic convention. A powerful message of reconciliation was telegraphed by the presence of both George Wallace, noted for barring to blacks the entrance of a Southern school, and Martin Luther King, Sr., the father of the slain civil rights leader. By walking back to the White House after being sworn in, Carter proclaimed his populism in a way unexpressible in an inaugural address. The image again spoke more than did a thousand words when Carter embraced Sadat and Begin at the end of the ceremony at which they signed the Camp David Accords. In each instance the visual moment capsulized the longer verbal message. The news media impressed the moment into public consciousness, reducing the convention speech to the image of unity, the inaugural to a presidential stroll, and the triumph of Camp David to a vignette of reconciliation.

Just as the triumphs of the Carter presidency were telegraphed in images, so too were its tragedies: Carter, supported by Secret Service agents, unable to finish a marathon; Carter engaged in a futile attempt to replicate the unity of 1976 by clasping Edward Kennedy's hand at the end of the 1980 convention.

The Rise of Autobiographical Speechmaking

The presidential speeches of Washington, Jefferson, and Lincoln contain no mentions of their wives, their children, or their pets. Until the intimacy of radio licensed such self-disclosure, presidents routinely suppressed their personal identity in their public speeches. By contrast, Gerald Ford's "beloved wife" figures in his first presidential speech, and Ronald Reagan's first post-summit speech to Congress contained a public valentine to Nancy. Many who cannot name the wives of any president before FDR can identify the breed, owner, and political history of Fala and Checkers.

This "interiorization" of public discourse finds parallels in the progression from the external to the internal that Kahler identified in Western fictional narratives and Ortega y Gasset documented in Western forms of art. The change produced in public discourse is profound. "A political leader running for office is spoken of as 'credible' or 'legitimate' in terms of what kind of man he is, rather than in terms of the actions or programs he espouses," noted Richard Sennett in *The Fall of Public Man*. "We are likely to describe as a 'credible' or 'charismatic' or 'believable' leader someone who can make appeals to groups whose interests are alien to his own beliefs, constituency, or ideology. . . . [W]e get excited when a conservative French President has dinner with a working-class family, even though he has raised taxes on industrial wages a few days before, or believe an American President is more 'genuine' and reliable than his disgraced predecessor because the new man cooks his own breakfast. This political 'credibility' is the superimposition of private upon public imagery."[52] Accordingly, in his resignation speech Richard Nixon defended the judgments that had caused his political demise by saying "they were made in what I believed at the time to be the best interest of the nation." "For more than a quarter of a century in public life," he declared, ". . . I have fought for what I believed in." And finally, "I have done my very best" to keep the pledge made when "I took the oath of office." Abuse of the powers of the presidency and complicity in illegal acts are swept aside in a speech awash in avowals of personal conviction and honorable intention.

Similarly, Ronald Reagan dismissed what others labeled a "lie" to the American people on the grounds that his "heart and his best intentions" told him that his statement was true (March 3, 1987). And in his bravura performance before the committee investigating the Iran-Contra affair, Lt. Colonel Oliver North converted questions about what he had done into exculpations rooted in explanations of why he had done it.

Television's close-ups give us a more detailed look at our leaders than we have of most of our friends. Here is a proximity otherwise reserved for infants, lovers, and actors in mouthwash ads. The words we ordinarily hear from such close-up faces are intimate and self-revelatory. The scrutiny possible at such range is intense. Because it simulates intimate spatial relationships between viewer and viewed and because it invites conversational speech, television is a medium conducive to autobiographical, self-disclosive discourse.

Early in television's history, two dramatic moments demonstrated the power of televised self-disclosure. On September 23, 1952, vice-presidential candidate Richard Nixon saved his place on the Republican ticket and eventually in the White House with a speech "baring his soul." The unprecedented look into the finances and family life of the candidate distracted audience attention from the fact that Nixon nowhere disclosed from whom he had gotten the money in the so-called slush fund. Instead, the speech told of what he owed his parents and the bank and what he owned in government bonds and insurance. Also featured in the speech were Pat's cloth coat, his daughters' dog, and a small check from a supporter. Here was a speech that could be spoken appropriately in a living room but not in a lecture hall.

Television's fondness for self-disclosure salvaged one prominent political career in the 1950s and savaged another. Joseph McCarthy's credibility as a Communist-hunter was destroyed not so much by his inability to produce the much sought-after list of names but rather by destructive moments of self-revelation in the thirty-six days of nationally broadcast Army-McCarthy hearings that occurred between April 22 and June 16, 1954. By repeatedly interrupting witnesses and intruding "points of order" when none legitimately was warranted, and by speaking to aides while questions were being addressed to him, McCarthy suggested to the viewing world that he was arrogant, obstructive, and opportunistic. His odd, loud, self-conscious laugh compounded the audience's discomfort with him as a person. This sensed audience unease increased his vulnerability to Joseph Welch, the down-home lawyer selected by the Army as its special counsel.

When McCarthy accused Welch of attempting to plant a pro-Communist lawyer on the committee, Welch, in the hearing's decisive moment, documented McCarthy's methods and dramatized the damage they had inflicted on innocent citizens.

> [Welch]: Senator, you won't need anything in the record when I finish telling you this. Until this moment, Senator, I think I never really gauged your cruelty or your recklessness. Fred Fisher is a young man who went to the Harvard Law School and came into my firm and is starting what looks to be a brilliant career with us. When I decided to work for this Committee, I asked Jim St. Clair, who sits on my right, to be my first assistant. I said to Jim, "Pick somebody in the firm to work under you that you would like." He chose Fred Fisher and they came down on an afternoon plane. That night, when we had taken a little stab at trying to

see what the case was about, Fred Fisher and Jim St. Clair and I went to dinner together. I then said to these two young men, "Boys, I don't know anything about you, except I've always liked you, but if there's anything funny in the life of either one of you that would hurt anybody in this case you speak up quick." And Fred Fisher said, "Mr. Welch, when I was in the law school, and for a period of months after, I belonged to the Lawyers' Guild," as you have suggested, Senator.

He went on to say, "I am Secretary of the Young Republican's League in Newton with the son of the Massachusetts governor, and I have the respect and admiration of my community, and I'm sure I have the respect and admiration of the twenty-five lawyers or so in Hale & Dorr." And I said, "Fred, I just don't think I'm going to ask you to work on the case. If I do, one of these days that will come out, and go over national television and it will just hurt like the dickens." And so, Senator, I asked him to go back to Boston. Little did I dream you could be so reckless and so cruel as to do an injury to that lad. It is true, he is still with Hale & Dorr. It is true that he will continue to be with Hale & Dorr. It is, I regret to say, equally true that I fear he shall always bear a scar needlessly inflicted by you. If it were in my power to forgive you for your reckless cruelty, I would do so. I like to think I'm a gentle man, but your forgiveness will have to come from someone other than me.[53]

In the thirty-six days of hearings, thirty-two witnesses had spoken over two million words. In collective memory, twenty-seven of those words have come to stand for the hearings. "A moment later," recalled McCarthy's aide Roy Cohn, Welch "uttered what is perhaps the most remembered line of the hearings: 'Let us not assassinate this lad further, Senator. You have done enough. Have you no decency, sir, at long last? Have you left no sense of decency?' "

Cohn's account continues:

> Mr. Welch, tears now glistening in his eyes, refused to discuss the subject further and took his seat. Suddenly the tension in the room snapped. Spectators and even newsmen burst into applause despite Chairman Mundt's frequent warnings against any demonstrations.
>
> No dramatist could hope to write a more eloquent and moving scene.[54]

The nation's twenty million viewers undoubtedly were unaware that they were witnessing a revolutionary communicative act. In ways more powerful and decisive than those open to the traditional speech, Welch's exchange with McCarthy discredited both the senator from Wisconsin and the tactics that would come to bear his name.

Viewing McCarthy and Welch in close-up enabled us to call on the resources we ordinarily use to assess the integrity and worth of the individuals who cross our lives. On these visceral intuitions, we decide whom to marry, to whom to entrust the care of our children, and from whom to buy a used car. At close range, Welch proved credible— McCarthy did not.

Part of Welch's ethos grew from his use of characteristics we have already identified with the new eloquence: his statement was powerfully self-disclosive; it was spoken as conversation with McCarthy and in an intimate tone. Welch's credibility also flowed from his use of features of the new eloquence we will explore in later chapters: he was speaking not through a scripted text but directly; his claim was grounded in personal experience and structured as a story; the story dramatized and personalized his central point; his message was capsulized in a digestive statement that could stand for the entire exchange.

In the hearings the worst of the old met the best of the new. McCarthy pivoted on misconstrued "fact" saying "I refer to the record . . . the news story." Instead, Welch offered firsthand experience, lived truth. "Senator, you won't need anything in the record when I finish telling you this." Where McCarthy asserted, "It seems that Mr. Welch is pained so deeply he thinks it's improper for me to give the record, the Communist front record of a man whom he wanted to foist upon this Committee," Welch responded with an appeal to basic human dignity. "Mr. McCarthy, I will not discuss this further with you. You have sat within six feet of me and could ask, could have asked me about Fred Fisher. You have seen fit to bring it out and if there is a God in heaven, it will do neither you nor your cause any good. I will not discuss it further."

McCarthy's model of communication is one of warfare. Welch's gestures of conciliation toward McCarthy's chief counsel Roy Cohn contrast with McCarthy's assault on Welch's protégé, Fred Fisher. The contrast between the two styles as well as the explicit content of McCarthy's claims legitimizes Welch's conclusion that McCarthy has assassinated "the lad."

> [McCarthy]: Mr. Chairman. Mr. Chairman. May I say that Mr. Welch talks about this being cruel and reckless. He was just baiting. He has been baiting Mr. Cohn here for hours, requesting that Mr. Cohn before sundown get out of any department of the government anyone who is serving the Communist cause. Now, I just give this man's record and I want to say, Mr. Welch, that it had been labeled long before he became a member, as early as 1944—
> [Welch]: Senator, may we not drop this? We know he belonged to the Lawyers' Guild. And Mr. Cohn nods his head at me. I did you, I think, no personal injury, Mr. Cohn.
> [Cohn]: No, sir.

[Welch]:   I meant to do you no personal injury, and if I did, I beg your pardon. Let us not assassinate this lad further, Senator. You've done enough. Have you no sense of decency, sir, at long last? Have you left no sense of decency?

[McCarthy]:   I know this hurts you, Mr. Welch.

[Welch]:   I'll say it hurts.

[McCarthy]:   Mr. Chairman, as a point of personal privilege, I'd like to finish this.

[Welch]:   Senator, I think it hurts you too, sir.

Although Welch's statement prefigured the new eloquence, the change he foreshadowed was still distant—not until more than two decades later would this new form of communication come into its own. By the time Ronald Reagan revealed the strengths and dangers of personal, dramatic, self-disclosive narrative, most had forgotten the soft-spoken lawyer who one afternoon in 1954 delivered the contemporary equivalent of Demosthenes' "On the Crown."

Where the old eloquence consisted in delivering cogent, compelling, verbal claims, the new entails an alliance among self-disclosure, conversation, visual dramatization and verbal distillation. Ironically, this "new" alliance reincarnates the "effeminate" style which for centuries was spurned by all who wished to speak credibly in the public forum.

4

The "Effeminate" Style

History has many themes. One of them is that women should be quiet. By the turn of the century when humorist Ambrose Bierce defined a woman as an "animal" which "can be taught not to talk,"[1] many of the instructional methods used to elicit her silence had been lost to memory. Among them were the ducking stool, the gag, and the gossip's bridle.

In seventeenth-century colonial America, the ducking stool held a place of honor near the Courthouse alongside the pillory and the stock. After being bound to the stool, the "scold," "nag," "brabling *(sic)*" or "unquiet" woman was submerged in the nearest body of water where she could choose between silence and drowning. When the stool was raised, the drenched, breathless woman was offered the chance to renounce her verbal past. If she repentently promised to control her speech, the dunkings would cease. Her submergence and submission invited silence from women who might otherwise be disposed to disrupt the social order with speech. An English ditty and the laughter it invited carried the warning of the ducking stool to the pubs and playgrounds:

> If noisy dames should once begin
> To drive the house with horrid din
> Away, you cry, you'll grace the stool
> We'll teach you how your tongue to rule

No brawling wives, no furious wenches
No fire so hot but water quenches.[2]

Less deadly but comparably humiliating was the public gagging of
women prone to disruptive speech. In Boston, in the century before
the signing of the Declaration of Independence, "scolds" were gagged
and publicly exhibited before their own doors. The humiliation hear-
kened back to branking, a Middle Ages practice aimed at silencing blas-
phemers and raucous women. Also known as the scold's bridle, the
branks consisted of a metal bit and muzzle that were strapped into the
victim's mouth. As a warning to others, the bridled person was either
tied to a post in the square or paraded through the town.[3]

Long after ducking stools and gossip's bridles had become curiosities
in museums, the silence they enforced and the warnings they imposed
continued to haunt women. Where few descriptors characterize the
maleness of male speech, the vocabulary exists to condemn female speech
with variety, color, and dispatch. Women are "scolds," "nags," "shrews,"
"fishwives," "harpies," "viragos," "bitches," "harridans," "magpies," and
"termagants." By condemning the expressive woman, these names en-
join her sisters to silence.

Where women's public speech traditionally has been suspect, their
silence has been golden. Abbé Fenelon was expressing a societal commonplace when in 1687 he wrote that "The good woman spins, con-
fines herself to her household, holds her tongue, believes and obeys."[4]
This chapter examines the exorcisms involved in unlearning silence and
relearning those forms of speech traditionally condemned as "effeminate," forms ideally suited to effectiveness in an electronic age.

By banning them from both education and citizenship and by barring them from the pulpit, the bench, the jurybox, and the floor of
Congress, society encouraged women to be seen but not heard. Silencing women proved a tricky business. Access to the reading public required a pen, a press, and the ability to write, all subject to institutional
control, but public speech simply needed a voice, a message, and an
audience.

The assumption that women are biologically unsuited for political
activity was legitimized by Aristotle who held that women's minds should
be kept free from exertion because "children evidently draw on the
mother who carries them in the womb, just as plants draw on the soil."[5]
The differences between males and females occurred in other species
as well. Where females expend much energy forming their ova, noted
Darwin, the male expends "much force in fierce contests with rivals, in
wandering about in search of the female, in exerting his voice."[6]

Whispered in the discussions of male discourse and implied in the treatment of female speech is the assumption that the energy expended by the male in coitus and by the female in conception, gestation, and birth robbed each of eloquence. For men whose voices are shrill and "womanly," Quintilian recommends sexual abstinence.[7] For women, the choice was more stark: barren brains or barren wombs. On this assumption, a seventeenth-century eulogist for the childless but intellectual Duchess of Newcastle praised her as one of the exceptions to her frail sex "who have Fruitful Wombs but Barren Brains."[8]

By risking their reproductive capacity through public speech, women supposedly sacrificed their womanhood. Effective female speakers, such as Maesia Sentia, a first-century Roman, were labelled androgynes by their admirers, in this case by Valerius Maximus.[9] The assumption that politics and progeny don't mix survived the assaults of the suffrage movement. In the early 1970s Representative Patricia Schroeder, a Colorado Democrat, told a hostile constituent, "Yes, I have a uterus and a brain, and they both work."[10]

In the eighteenth and nineteenth centuries, Aristotle's intellectual heirs would claim that if women persisted in speaking in public and other political activities, their uteruses would dry up. An opponent of women's rights who was confident in his conclusion that speech induced sterility should have invited feminists to speak. Had public speaking proved the powerful contraceptive they supposed, the species of feminist orator would have gone extinct, the victim of self-induced sterility.

Yet even after women were granted access to higher education, their right to present their own ideas in public was denied. Lucy Stone was admitted to Oberlin in 1837. Although permitted to attend classes with men, she was not allowed to read her own papers in class or participate in debates. When she fulfilled the requirements to graduate, she learned that she could write her own commencement address but not deliver it. As a leader of the woman's movement, Stone later helped establish women's competence as speakers.[11]

Though similar, the sexual ascriptions bound to speaking differ in important ways from those tied to authoring. By defaming and, when that failed, by damning female speakers, society aggressively moved to curb female speech.

To hold the speech of women in check, the clergy, the courts, and the keepers of the medical profession devised labels discrediting "womanly" speech. "Heretics!" said the clergy. "Hysterics!" yelled the doctors. "Witches!" decreed the judges. "Whores!" said a general chorus. "Harpies!" exclaimed those husbanding their power over women's names and property. These names invited the silence that in earlier times had been ensured by force. "If a woman speaks disrespectfully to a man," says an Urakaginan edict, "that woman's mouth" will be "crushed with a fired brick."[12] By falling silent or speaking submissively, women purchased protection.

In wielding such labels, opponents of women's rights exercised one of language's most powerful properties: the capacity to name. Each label identifies its object as a deviant to be shunned. Each deprives the speaker of those audiences disposed to listen to a woman but disinclined to hear a witch, a whore, a heretic, or an hysteric.

One way a woman could earn these labels was by engaging in forbidden or disapproved speech acts. In each instance some institutionalized male role was threatened. Where the clergy spoke in the name of the church, the judges in the name of the law, and the doctors in the name of science, those labelled whores, witches, heretics, and hysterics uttered individualized personal speech. The notion that an institution must credential public speech is challenged by the implicit personalized assumptions underlying the discourse of these condemned women. If God could speak through a woman, then the legitimacy of a male priesthood was suspect. By seeming to prefer speaking through women, the devil provided his fellow males with a consoling counterpoint.

Each indicting name specifies a nonrational genesis for female speech and hence underscores the assumption that male speech, based in the intellect, is the superior form. The heretic's speech was spun either from the devil or from a demented mind. The speech of the hysteric came from her ungoverned emotions. The whore purchased her public speech at the price of her uterus. The witch voiced the devil's sentiments.

In each case the threatened institution offered the threatening woman the opportunity to repent her public speech, an act reestablishing the power of male discourse. Only when women refused was their verbal defiance punished with the permanent silence of ostracism or death. Accordingly, both the heretic and the witch were invited to recant, a metaphor that suggests that they reclaim their speech from its public sphere and seal it within themselves. The hysteric was asked to return to the womb of the bed and, after disavowing her past patterns of speaking, to be reborn at male hands into the male-dominated household, a reformed woman. The whore was counselled to abjure her evil speech and public presentation of self and return to the plain dress and modest demeanor of a submissive home-bound woman.

Speaker as Whore

Just as public speech by a woman betokened promiscuity, so too her silence testified to her modesty. "For a silence and a chaste reserve is a woman's genuine praise and to· remain quiet in the home,"[13] wrote Euripides. Aristotle too saw silence and modesty as conjoined virtues befitting a woman.[14] The New Testament cast silence, salvation, and childbearing as confederates. The role of women was to be chaste, silent, subordinate to a male and fruitful. "Let a woman learn in silence with all submissiveness," wrote Paul.[15] "I permit no woman to teach or to have authority over men; she is to keep silent. For Adam was formed first, then Eve; and Adam was not deceived, but the woman was deceived and became a transgressor. Yet woman will be saved through bearing children, if she continues in faith and love and holiness with modesty."

As women edged through the classroom to the public forum, they employed speech to dispute the tie between modesty and silence. In her 1793 valedictory at the Young Ladies Academy of Philadelphia, Eliza Laskey claimed the "liberty to speak on any subject which is suitable" and distinguished modesty from "dull and rigid silence," warning that silence must not be mistaken for virtue.[16]

Her speech took issue with a long-lived alliance between loquacity and lasciviousness. "[B]y their wanton laughter, loquacity, insolence and scurrilous behavior," Castiglione had noted in his treatise on the Courtier, women who were "not unchaste" appeared to "be so."[17] Similarly, at the climax of Ben Jonson's play *The Silent Woman*, Morose links lewdness and female speech when he exclaims "[T]his is the worst of all worst worsts that hell could have devised! Marry a whore, and so much noise!"

These attitudes were translated into behavior when Abby Kelly, a nineteenth-century feminist, found herself the subject of a sermon delivered in church. "The Jezabel is come among us also," intoned the preacher. Using Scripture for their purpose, the congregation and those sympathetic to its sentiments jeered Kelly, pelted her with rotten eggs when she rose to speak, and threw stones at her.[18]

The institution threatened by the "harlot" was the family. Public speaking took women from the home, where, their opponents assumed, they should be bearing and raising children.

Speakers as Hysterics

If speech did not assign a woman to the streets, it could consign her to the sickbed or the insane asylum; expressive, emotional female speech was seen as a symptom of a diseased uterus or a distressed mind.

Meddling in the male world was sometimes more than the mind of woman could bear. So, for example, Puritan leader Jonathon Wintrop recorded the case of a woman who had lost "her understanding and

72 ELOQUENCE IN AN ELECTRONIC AGE

reason." She had given herself "wholly to reading and writing and had written many books." Her wits might have been spared had she "attended her household affairs and such things as belong to women and not gone out of her way and calling to meddle in such things as are proper for men whose minds are stronger."[19]

Hysteria, a disease peculiar to women, was first identified by Hippocrates who drew its name from the Greek word for uterus. Because a woman was dominated by her reproductive role, any signs of mental distress could readily be attributed to a malfunctioning womb.

The symptoms of an hysteric were partially speech-based: she paid too little attention to detail, expressed too much emotion, and was flamboyant. These displays of feeling supposedly weakened physical endurance and endangered a woman's ability to bear strong children. To combat hysteria and other kindred nervous disorders, Dr. S. Weir Mitchell pioneered "The Rest Cure" in the nineteenth century. The cure, which consisted in mandated rest and reprogramming, required that patients place their bodies and minds in Mitchell's care. During their convalescence, he instructed them in ways to control their urges to express their feelings to others.[20]

Charlotte Perkins Gilman, a respected nineteenth-century feminist, was among Mitchell's patients. In her novel *The Yellow Wallpaper*, she indicts the psychiatrist for collusion with the protagonist's husband in the destructive "cure." The room to which Gilman was confined for Mitchell's treatment was the nursery, a location that symbolized the cure's attempt to reduce the patient to childlike submissiveness.[21]

Women whose speech defied such cures risked being labelled crazy and institutionalized. Early feminists recognized the purposes served by such diagnoses. "Could the dark secrets of insane asylums be brought to light," wrote Elizabeth Cady Stanton in *Eighty Years and More* (1898), "we should be shocked to know the great number of rebellious wives, sisters, and daughters who are thus sacrificed to false customs and barbarous laws made by men for women."[22]

The disproportionate number of women who were lobotomized translates the same indictment into another form. A number of scholars have concluded that psychosurgery is not administered as much to cure an illness as to minimize behavior considered inappropriate in a woman. This behavior includes aggressive speech and action and overt sexuality.[23]

Social stereotypes aided Mitchell in his role as tongue-depressor. Aristotle sanctified the belief that women lack full deliberative capacity *(bouleutikon)*.[24] Accordingly, women are "more void of shame and self-respect, more false of speech [and] more deceptive than men."[25] That view persisted. In his sixteenth-century *Arte of Rhetorique* (1560)[26] Wilson illustrates the figure of description by citing "a woman babbling, inconstant, and ready to believe all that is told her." The assumption that women are more gullible than men was used both for and against them when they were charged with witchcraft in the sixteenth century.

What women supposedly lacked in the power of reasoning, they found in emotion and passion. In women, observed Aristotle, reason seems less able to control the appetites.[27]

Where Mitchell saw a plea for the "Rest Cure," some defenders of women's rights saw a potential asset. A woman's susceptibility to "a higher degree of excitement," "nervous temperament," and "spirit" are the material of great orators, argued John Stuart Mill.[28]

The widespread belief that women are driven by emotion prompted Margaret Fuller to caution nineteenth-century female speakers not to "speak in the heat of wild impulse," to lead lives "unstained by passionate error," and to "be severe lawgivers to themselves."[29] In 1843, Fuller considered it necessary to assure her readers that "those who had seen the great actresses, and heard the Quaker preachers of modern times, would not doubt, that women can express publicly the fullness of thought and emotion, without losing any of the peculiar beauty of her sex."[30]

Speakers as Heresiarchs

Since the times of myth and magic, men have chronicled their fears of the seductive powers and sinful purposes of women's speech. A popular seventeenth-century rhyme conjoined female preaching and fiendish glee: "When women preach and cobblers pray/ The fiends in hell make holiday."[31] Just as the songs of the Sirens lured men to physical death, Eve enticed Adam into spiritual demise. The sexuality simmering just below the surface in those seductions took explicit form in the witch trial's claim that the Devil spoke through a witch's vagina. Similarly, the Serpent spoke through Eve.

One of the "heresies" rooted out by the Inquisition gloried in the proclamation that not only was the Holy Spirit a woman but that she had been incarnated in Guglielma of Milan. Guglielma proclaimed a new church headed by a female pope and female cardinals. The Guglielmites were not alone in claiming privileged speech and actions for women. So concerned was Pope Boniface VIII about the rise of female prophetesses and heresiarchs that he issued the bull *Nuper ad audientiam* (1296) condemning women who proclaimed new dogma and revelled in immorality. By claiming to speak for and as God, Guglielma posed a profound threat to the papacy and clergy. Condemned by the inquisition, her remains were exhumed and burned.[32]

Female Lollards also threatened Medieval Christendom. These women taught followers in their homes, reinterpreted scripture, and affronted the clergy with claims to being as learned as they. They too were burned.

As part of the case building against heretics, sexual excess was routinely alleged. When the heretic was female these allegations discredited the speech acts. In fact, many of the heresiarchs were celibate. Still, the threat they posed to the male clergy was direct. By preaching and teaching, these women violated societal norms and usurped clerical functions.

As society became more civilized, ostracizing and institutionalizing replaced incinerating as a preferred response to the woman who claimed theologically suspect religious privileges. When Anne Hutchinson asserted leadership of the congregation of the Boston church in colonial America, she was banished. In 1860 a clergyman demonstrated his control over his "heretical" wife by having her committed to the Jacksonville State Hospital in Illinois. The dementia of Mrs. E. P. W. Packard was manifest in her disagreement with her husband on items of faith and religious observance. By filing a writ of habeas corpus, Mrs. Packard won release from the mental hospital. "Had I lived in the sixteenth instead of the nineteenth century," wrote Mrs. Packard, "my husband would have used the laws of the day to punish me as a heretic for this departure from the established creed—while under the influence of some intolerant spirit he now uses this autocratic institution as a means of torture to bring about the same result—namely *a recantation of my faith.*"[33]

Where some saw sin, others saw saintliness. If it was God not mammon who spoke through a woman's mouth, which man would dare silence her? A number of women found prophesying a powerful means of self-expression in the seventeenth century. Not only were the prophesies of Eleanor Davies, Mary Cary, and Anna Trapuel published, but they also delivered "oracular speeches" in such prominent places as Parliament.[34] Perhaps fearful that their own futures would be foretold and in the telling ordained, churchmen shied away from condemning the speech of those whose predictions came true.

Religions that preached spiritual equality permitted women to preach. In the seventeenth century, when secular authorities were ducking and gagging outspoken women, female Quaker preachers carried their religious convictions not only to London and Dublin but to the New World as well.

Speakers as Witches

In Essex County, Massachusetts, more "witches" were convicted of "assaultive speech" than any other crime including "lying."[35] Encompassed in such assaults were "slander," "defamation," "filthy speeches," and "scandalous speeches." An inability to control one's tongue was a sign of witchcraft.

Because women presumably were not governed by reason, they were susceptible to the seditious advances of the devil. As men use language for their purposes, the devil uses the weak woman. When the devil did not speak through the woman's vagina, an act that explicitly tied female speech and sexuality, he spoke in his own voice through her mouth. The Rev. John Whiting reports that one victim "said she knew nothing of those things that were spoken by her, but that her tongue was improved to express what was never in her mind, which was a matter of great affliction to her."[36]

Consistent with social stereotypes and societal needs, the abrasive, contentious woman was more likely than her soft-spoken sister to be labelled a witch. Since speech and reproduction supposedly were mutually exclusive, a woman was more likely to be identified as a witch if she had few children or none at all.

Not only did her speech threaten the established order but she challenged part of the institutional structure by appropriating its skills. Where the heretic threatened the clergy by claiming knowledge of scripture and access to God, the witch was likely to have practiced "doctoring."[37]

Witches and heretics died in ways that symbolized the extinction of their speech. At the stake, fire, a metaphor for speech, consumed the witch and her capacity to speak. Alternatively, fiery words were drenched permanently by drowning. Hanging simultaneously choked the ability to speak and the speaker.

Since in the course of normal household events speech was required from even the most docile woman, those who wielded the labels, whore, heretic, hysteric and witch defined a mode of appropriate female discourse. Whether the product of nature or nurture, choice or censorship, a distinct "feminine style" consistent with traditional notions of femininity emerged. "Structurally, 'feminine' rhetoric is inductive, even circuitous, moving from example to example, and is usually grounded in personal experience," notes rhetoric scholar Karlyn Kohrs Campbell. "Consistent with their allegedly poetic and emotional natures, women tend to adopt associative, dramatic, and narrative modes of development, as opposed to deductive forms of organization. The tone tends to be personal and somewhat tentative, rather than objective or author-itative."[38]

The Manly Speaker

For millennia, effectiveness and manliness were synonyms. To call a woman manly was to praise her. In 1843 Margaret Fuller noted that a friend meant the phrase "a manly woman" as a high compliment.[39] By deifying "manly" speech and devaluing "effeminate" or "womanly" speech, theorists implied that nature had privileged the speech of men.

The distinction between the manly and the effeminate was rooted in the conviction that because their minds govern their discourse, men and their speech are inherently superior. Its origin in the emotions meant that the speech of women was defective. The widespread notion that the man is the head of the family, the woman the heart, translated to the notion that men had the right and obligation to control female speech.

Because it was presumably driven by emotion, womanly speech was thought to be personal, excessive, disorganized, and unduly ornamental. Because it was presumably driven by reason, the manly style was thought to be factual, analytic, organized, and impersonal. Where womanly speech sowed disorder, manly speech planted order. Womanly speech corrupted an audience by inviting it to judge the case on spurious grounds; manly speech invited judicious judgment.

The view that public virtues are the by-products of the manly was underscored by the Queen who proclaimed that were she "turned out of the realm" in her petticoat, she would be able to live anywhere in Christendom. Elizabeth I told the troops braced for the assault by the Spanish Armada that "I have but the body of a weak and feeble woman; but I have the heart of a King, and of a king of England, too."[40] Since the heart not the head was presumed to control female speech, Elizabeth's kingly heart certified that her claims were trustworthy, not effeminate. Only a sovereign uttering manly speech could claim credibly that should Britain be invaded, "I myself will take up arms—I myself will be your general, judge and rewarder of every one of your virtues in the field."

Although some men deliver "effeminate" speech and some women master "manly" speech, theorists held that speakers generally stayed true to their gender. Those women willing to forego reproduction for the conception and delivery of ideas were presumed to aspire to be men. If a wife "still wants to appear educated and eloquent," noted

Juvenal, "let her dress as a man, sacrifice to men's gods, and bathe in the men's baths."[41] This aspiration was not taken to be the sincerest form of flattery because, said women's rights opponents, "when she unsexes herself, and puts on the habiliments and claims to exercise the masculine functions of man in society, she has lost the position which she should occupy. When woman violates the law which God has given her, she has no law, and is the creature of hateful anarchy."[42]

Under rare circumstances, a woman's "manly" speech won praise. But even then, it was male control that accounted for its success. The credit for their accomplishments was given to the men who had taught them, which was the case with Laela and Hortensia, the daughters of famous Roman orators. Like Elizabeth, whose "heart" was that of a king, the eloquence of these famous daughters was attributed to the bloodline that enabled them to transcend their gender.

If a woman spoke as a stand-in for an absent male and did so to "preserve her female nature," her chances for a favorable reception increased. So, for example, in 42 B.C., Hortensia delivered a widely acclaimed speech in which she argued: "You have already deprived us [women] of our fathers, our sons, our husbands, and our brothers on the pretext that they wronged you, but if, in addition, you take away our property, you will reduce us to a condition unsuitable to our birth, our way of life, and our female nature."[43]

The state was civilized by manly speech, corrupted by effeminate speech. Not only could speaking cost a woman her ability to bear children, it would cost the body politic its capacity to bear arms. Apparently believing that female speech would drain the nation of its testosterone, opponents of women's rights claimed that "the transfer of power from the military to the unmilitary sex involves national emasculation."[44] To save the country from the dustbins of history, women would have to return to their dustpans and aprons.

The distinction between manly and effeminate speech is long-lived. The Romans distinguished between a manly style, which was revered, and the effeminate style, which was reviled. However, what constituted manly and effeminate speech has varied from decade to decade and century to century. Some in Cicero's time thought his loose structure, high level of repetition, and general "tumidity" "effeminate," for example.[45]

By the late nineteenth century the scientific style was enshrined as manly. "The eloquence of Mr. Adams resembled his general character, and formed, indeed, a part of it," noted Daniel Webster. "It was bold, manly, and energetic."[46] Nineteenth-century textbooks lauded the "plain, manly, oratorical style."[47]

The Rational, Instrumental, Impersonal Style and Its Opposite

The "logical" manly style appealed to "reason." The eloquence used to address judges "is grave, composed, luminous, compact," nineteenth-century Boyleston chair holder Edward Channing told his students. "It is under such restraints as a man's good taste will impose, when he is in the presence of his acknowledged superiors, who are to decide upon the strength of his reasoning, and who have made such questions as he is investigating the serious study of their lives. The style of this eloquence is masculine, earnest and impressive."[48]

Manly discourse works in the service of "ambition, business, and power," noted eighteenth-century theorist Hugh Blair. Accordingly, it is impersonal, unemotional, and competitive. Where manly discourse persuades, effeminate discourse pleases. Manly discourse inhabits the public forum where it engages in debate about public affairs. The proper place for effeminate discourse is either the parlor or the corrupt government.

✳ ⌐The interchangeability among the terms rational, manly, and scien-⌐
  └tific discourse dictates the exclusion of women from the domain of each.⌐
According to "nineteenth-century stereotypes or rhetorical idealizations, a woman scientist was a contradiction in terms—such a person was unlikely to exist, and if she did (and more and more of them were coming into existence), she had to be 'unnatural' in some way."[49]

Where women were seen as "delicate, emotional, noncompetitive, and nurturing," science was viewed as "tough, rigorous, rational, impersonal, masculine, competitive, and unemotional."[50] The emphasis of the scientific method on objectivity contrasts with the supposed feminine focus on subjectivity. The scientist who aspired to distance himself from the subject, control the environment, and manipulate variables expressed his findings in impersonal, dispassionate prose. Within this frame of reference scientists were heirs of Descartes living in his world of extension and motion; women by contrast, were projected into the world of Pascal who held that the heart has reasons that reason could not know. Judged by the scientific standard, the behaviors and style supposedly native to women were considered defective; those native to scientific man were desirable.

Womanly Discourse Is Shrill; Manly Discourse Is Robust

For centuries, their opponents argued that women's fundamental irrationality and congenital emotionalism should disqualify them from public speaking and public office. The high pitch of the woman's voice was seen as symptomatic not of physiological differences in the vocal mechanism but of excessive emotionalism. "[H]igh-pitched vocalizations tend to be strongly associated with emotional or irrational outbursts," observes contemporary theorist Max Atkinson, "a deeply rooted cultural assumption that no doubt derives from, and is sustained by, the screams of each new generation of infants."[51]

Noting that shrillness characterized the voices of eunuchs, women, and invalids, Quintilian recommended that men increase the robustness of their voices by abstaining from sexual intercourse.[52] Later theorists were equally concerned that men not sound womanish. "Some have a womanish squeaking Tone," wrote John Mason in *An Essay on Elocution and Pronunciation* (1748) "which, Persons whose Voices are shrill and weak, and overtrained, are very apt to fall into."[53] Unlike Quintilian, Mason did not recommend sexual abstinence as a solution.

Eager to mute the inference that their voices signalled irrational or emotional natures, female politicians, Margaret Thatcher among them, have sought voice retraining. Under the supervision of a tutor from the National Theatre, Mrs. Thatcher lowered the natural pitch at which she spoke in public.[54]

Women's emotional natures supposedly accounted for their inability to either produce or understand rational discourse, and for their disposition to speak too much and too often, to employ a shrill tone, and finally to overdress discourse in ornamental language.

The Manly Style Is Perspicacious; the Effeminate, Ornamental

The belief that language is the dress of thought is a commonplace among rhetorical theorists. The cultural assumption that ornamental dress was appropriate only for Roman women disposed the Romans to identify the stylistic devices that ornament the dress of language as feminine. In drawings of Dame Rhetoric, the figures of speech beautify her garments.

As theorists grappled with the relationship between thought and language, the notion took hold that the figures of diction were soft, ornamental, dispensable, and feminine while figures of thought were vital and virile. "The figure of diction (*figura dictionis*) is a figure by which speech is formed from words resonating pleasingly and smoothly among themselves," noted Omer Talon, in 1567. "The figure of thought (*figura sententiae*) is a figure by which speech is fashioned from some kind of sententious statement affecting movement of the will." Figures of thought provide a "virile dignity, superior to a soft and delicate beauty *(venustate).*" Where figures of diction adorn and color an oration, figures of thought supply its vigor.[55]

Striking parallels ally effeminate discourse and the traditional role of women. Both are expected to please and soothe but not engage in the rigors of vigorous public debate. Both are soft and ornamental. Both flourish when their freedom is circumscribed. To prevent them from veering into excesses of one sort or another, both require control by men. In both, ambition and a desire for power are vices.

The scientific revolution argued that rhetoric's ornamental dress obscured the essentials of discourse. So, we hear Thomas Sprat dismissing "specious tropes and figures" because they cloud our knowledge with "mists and uncertainties."[56] The Royal Society, for which Sprat spoke, sought to disrobe rhetoric. The ideal of that Society was "a naked, natural way of speaking" that was "as near Mathematical plainness" as possible.[57] Ultimately, the debate over whether expression should be naked or clothed was rendered pointless when inorganic metaphors replaced organic ones. A naked engine is hardly the object of a voyeur's attentions or affections. Nor are the naked extension and motion that survived Descartes' skepticism.

In the aftermath of the scientific revolution, the notion that language was the dress of thought gave way to the belief that language expressed thought. Then that view too was displaced by the conviction that language and thought are indistinguishable.

From the late 1800s to the present, the woman's movement debunked pejorative uses of "womanly." These attacks drove the labels effeminate and manly from the vocabularies of theorists.

By embedding a condemnation of effeminate speech in the language in which eloquence was defined, theorists ensured that if a woman rose to speak she would embrace "manly" norms of discourse, thereby in some important sense counterfeiting her identity. Before the notion of a manly style lost currency, female speakers had absorbed its norms.

By embracing such "manly" norms, women created an ironic situation for their descendants. The age of television, not even envisioned as the Grimke sisters took to the circuit, would invite the style once spurned as "womanly." In the television age, men would have to learn and women recapture the "womanly" style. Unfolding that irony is my remaining task.

We judge discourse today by standards set by the "manly" style. Insofar as it was combatively argumentative and saw overcoming its audience as a desired end, the rhetoric of fire and sword was manly. In the scientific age, manly discourse took on additional meanings: it was impersonal, rational, direct, and data-based.

Whether men and women are naturally disposed to different communicative styles is difficult to ascertain. The task of separating stereotypes about male and female communication from actual behavior is complicated by our tendency to internalize the behaviors and attitudes approved by society. Incorporating societal expectations into our concept of self can transform stereotypes into behaviors.[58] Countering this tendency is the ability of stereotypes to warn against and hence minimize disapproved behavior. Also difficult to know is whether dissimilar communicative behaviors are the by-product of nature, nurture, or the biased perception of the observer. Additional complications arise because much research on the role of gender in communication is suggestive rather than conclusive. Nonetheless, one might conclude that women are neither irrational nor more talkative than men. Whatever their cause, and despite the fact that the assertiveness of female speakers is on the rise, gender-associated differences remain.

The Female Style and Television

The intimate medium of television requires that those who speak comfortably through it project a sense of private self, unself-consciously self-disclose, and engage the audience in completing messages that exist as mere dots and lines on television's screen. The traditional male style is, in McLuhan's terms, too hot for the cool medium of television. Where men see language as an instrument to accomplish goals, women regard it as a means of expressing internal states. In conversation, men focus on facts and information, women on feelings. In group settings, men focus on accomplishing the task, women on maintaining the harmony and well-being of the group.[59]

Once condemned as a liability, the ability to comfortably express feelings is an asset on television. Women are more inclined than men to verbally indicate emotion[60] This does not mean, however, that women respond to events more emotionally. Instead, it seems that women are more disposed to display their reactions in emotional terms.[61] Females are advantaged in conveying emotion by their more expressive faces and body movements and their general skill in deciphering the nonverbal cues of others.[62] Consistent with their harmonizing tendencies, women look more at the person they are conversing with than men do.[63] Overall, females are more empathic than males;[64] they tend to both give and receive more emotional support than men.[65]

The inability to disclose some sense of private self on an intimate mass medium has proven a barrier for most men in politics today. Here too the "manly" style is a noose. While "the speech of men is characterized by action and the projection of themselves as actors upon their environment; women are concerned with internal states and behaviors which would integrate other persons with themselves into the social situation."[66] The self-disclosure of men and women is consistent with their instrumental and expressive differences. Women reveal themselves in service of expressive or affiliative needs where men tend to disclose about goals related to instrumental needs.[67]

As I noted earlier, television favors a conciliatory style over a combative one. Here too the style once demeaned as effeminate is desirable.

Because girls identify positively with their mothers and then recreate the mothering role in their own lives, some psychologists believe that their capacities for nurturance and empathy are more developed than boys'. Accordingly, it is natural for a woman to define herself through her social relationships.[68] By contrast, male exposure to the military and to competitive sports may engender such traditional male values as aggressiveness.[69]

Whatever the cause, where women tend to cooperate, men tend to compete.[70] Whether in public or private communication, men are more comfortable than women in a combative "debate" style. Lecturing, arguing, pivoting on claims from reason or logic, and demanding or providing evidence are more typically male than female behaviors.[71] Consistent with these findings, women use less hostile verbs than men.[72] Men are more likely than women to engage in verbal dueling.[73]

Not only are the messages of women less verbally aggressive but they tend to be more pro-social, particularly in their stress on relationships rather than on autonomous action.[74] In their political ads, women usually stress their strengths rather than counteract their weaknesses.[75]

The Personal Female Style and Television

The impersonal nature of male speech is evident in a male disposition toward using numbers to describe.[76] By contrast, for women "[t]he implied relationship between the self and what one reads and writes" and presumably says "is personal and intense." Consequently, women's novels and critical essays are often autobiographical. "Because of the continual crossing of self and other, women's writing may blur the public and private."[77] Denied access to the public sphere, women developed facility in such private forms of communication as conversation and storytelling. Accordingly, the poems of the twelfth-century female troubadours employ "the more straightforward speech of conversation."[78] Since educated men spurned the oral form of the ballad for the prestige of learned written poetry, women became the custodians of the ballad tradition. "[B]allads are old-wives' tales which were able to develop and change in authentically feminine ways mainly because men left them alone."[79]

In the French salons of the Renaissance and seventeenth and eighteenth centuries, women perfected the art of conversation. Literary breakfasts and evening conversational parties performed the same function in Britain.

Because the mass media are fixated on differences between the private and public self of public figures, a comfort with expressing rather than camouflaging self, or at the minimum an ability to feign disclosure, is useful for a politician. That utility benefits females. And because the broadcast media invite an intimate style, their conversational and narrational skills also advantage women.

Womanly Narrative Is Well-Suited for Television

The cliché old-wives' tales remind us that traditionally women are a family's storytellers. So, for example, Goethe credits his father with engendering in him "the seriousness in life's pursuits" but praises his mother for transmitting "the enjoyment of life, and love of spinning fantasies."[80] When this skill is seen as a liability, its mistresses are condemned as gossips. Sixteenth-century critic Steven Guazzo noted that although gossip was a vice common to many, "it is most familiar with certain women."[81] Such gossips retell the misfortunes of their neighbors in "speeches." "Have you not hearde the hard hap of my unfortunate neighbor," they ask. "[A]nd thereupon making the storie, they rehearse howe the husbande by means of his servant, took her tardie in her hastie business. Then they tell (the details of) the wall, and the way whereby her lover got downe: next, how cruelly her husband beate her, and her maid, and thinke not that they leave anything behind untolde, but rather will put too somewhat of their own devise."[82] The indictment of the female gossip survived the centuries. "The second kind of female orator," writes Addison in the *Spectator*, "are those who deal in invectives, and who are commonly known by the name of the censorious. . . . With what a fluency of invention and copiousness of expression will they enlarge upon every little slip in the behavior of another! With how many different circumstances, and with what variety of phrases, will they tell over the same story!"[83] Television's bias prizes the narrative skills that once were pilloried.

It is a skill women retain. In both primitive and advanced cultures, women are the repositories of parable-like dramatic vignettes, concise stories that transmit the common wisdom from woman to woman and generation to generation.[84]

The talent for capturing ideas and lessons in brief dramatic narratives is one cultivated by mothers telling bedtime stories to their children. It is a talent of use as well to those who transmit the goings-on of the community. Because society has encouraged women to cultivate these dispositions to narrative, they are better able than men to respond to television's narrative demands.

Television invites a personal, self-disclosing style that draws public discourse out of a private self and comfortably reduces the complex world to dramatic narratives. Because it encompasses these characteristics, the once spurned womanly style is now the style of preference. The same characteristics comprise a mode of discourse well suited to television and much needed in times of social stress or in the aftermath of divisive events. By revivifying social values and ennobling the shared past, epideictic or ceremonial discourse helps sustain the state. In a later chapter I argue that the early 1980s required leaders to have a talent for the epideictic.

Politicians and the Manly and Womanly Style

Capitalizing on the newly recognized strengths of their once disdained style is not as simple for women as it at first seems. Before they can bring centuries of acculturation to television, women must overcome their socially reinforced fear of public speech; they must then abandon the "manly" style they adopted in order to deliver socially acceptable public discourse.

Such beliefs as "Little girls should be seen and not heard" couple with other means of devaluing women's speech to dispose women to avoid the public forum. Females report more difficulty than males in expressing themselves in public and in gaining either a hearing or respect for their ideas.[85] Consistent with social sanctions against aggressive speech by women, they are also less likely than men to speak on controversial topics.[86]

Although no one seriously credits the view that women pay in shrivelled uteruses for speaking in public, women's role as child bearer continues to affect perception of her public role. Because they have raised their families before entering public service, women seeking high public office for the first time are generally older than their male counterparts.[87] Being the married mother of young children is a political liability for a female politician because it reminds the public of a role that voters have been socialized to believe "makes women less suitable and available for public office."[88] The presumption that women bear responsibility for child rearing and maintenance of the family means that a mother of young children cannot as readily appeal to those family values that her presence on the public stages appears to violate.

Those who invade the linguistic domain of men must overcome their own sense of the inadequacies of a woman's speech. Unsurprisingly, then, political women are more "assertive, more venturesome, more imaginative and unconventional, and more liberal in their attitudes" than women in the population at large.[89] The pressures of deviating from expected social roles exact a price. Female politicians tend toward "a serious and dutiful manner and . . . a fretful uncertainty about themselves and their situation."[90]

In constructing campaign strategies, consultants are mindful of the existence of stereotypes. When Evelyn Gandy faced William Winter in the Mississippi Democratic gubernatorial primary in 1979, Winter's consultant Bob Squier redefined the governorship as a manly, military job. In spot ads Winter was shown confidently striding among armored tanks. The governor is the commander-in-chief of the National Guard argued Winter's ads. "The Guard is the first line of national defense," proclaimed the candidate. Since the federalized National Guard had played an important role in confrontations with Southern governors in the 1960s there was a certain remote plausibility to the claim. Meanwhile, by showing her looking feminine and sounding maternal, Gandy's ads played into Squier's hands. The woman portrayed in her ads did not seem able to fulfill the requirements of the role Squier had defined as central to the governorship. Winter won.

To disassociate the role of California state attorney general from that of tough, rugged, male policeman, consultant Michael Kaye dissolved from pictures of his candidate, Yvonne Braithewaite Burke, in a police uniform to a picture of her in a suit. Nonetheless, voters elected her male opponent.

Republican consultant Ed Blakely, whose firm has helped elect three female congressional candidates, advises women seeking public office to "stick to the facts and the issues. They should be tough without losing their femininity, smart but not in a threatening way." Whenever possible, he shows them holding their own against male bureaucrats.[91]

The belief that women speak from emotion grounded the assumption that females respond to political cues "irrationally," focusing on good looks, style, character, or personality rather than on candidates' stands on public policy. In fact, women are as issue-oriented as men.[92]

In her 1984 debate with Vice President George Bush, the first female vice-presidential nominee of a major party adopted communication cues traditionally identified as "masculine." (Courtesy League of Women Voters)

Even in campaigns in which issue distinctions are clear, men and women alike consider personal evaluations of candidates as important or more important than their stands on issues.[93]

The difference in our expectations of men and women was highlighted in the 1984 vice-presidential debate between George Bush and Geraldine Ferraro. There, Ferraro was asked a question that presupposed that, unlike a man, a woman might be unable to initiate an act of war. "How can you convince the American people and the potential enemy that you would know what to do to protect this nation's security, and do you think that in any way that the Soviets might be tempted to try to take advantage of you simply because you are a woman?" Three days later on "Meet the Press" Marvin Kalb asked Ferraro a question that had not been asked of Bush or the male presidential contenders: "Are you strong enough to push the button?"

Sex stereotypes about female leaders both advantage and disadvantage them. When a male attacks his male opponent, he is behaving in a culturally accepted way. But should a woman do likewise, she risks the perception that she is unfeminine, shrill, and nagging. "[T]he United Nations is an institution which specializes in talking," noted former UN

Ambassador Jeane Kirkpatrick. "It's a place where people make speeches and listen to speeches. But if I make a speech, particularly a substantial speech, it has been frequently described in the media as 'lecturing my colleagues,' as though it were somehow peculiarly inappropriate, like an ill-tempered schoolmarm might scold her children. When I have replied to criticisms of the United States (which is an important part of my job), I have frequently been described as 'confrontational.' . . . Terms like 'tough' and 'confrontational' express a certain very general surprise and disapproval at the presence of a woman in arenas in which it is necessary to be—what for males would be considered—normally assertive."[94]

In the vice-presidential debate, Bush too felt social constraints. We disapprove of men who bully, attack, or patronize women. The interplay of stereotypes and behavior was evident when Bush said, "Let me help you with the difference, Mrs. Ferraro, between Iran and the embassy in Lebanon." The patronizing edge in the offer would have been less noted had it been made to a male opponent. Although warned by his coaches of the hazards of patronizing, Bush had stumbled. Ferraro responded, "I almost resent, Vice President Bush, your patronizing attitude that you have to teach me about foreign policy." The response was widely replayed in news synopses of the debate.

Sex stereotypes were at play as well in Bush's identification of Ferraro as Mrs. Ferraro rather than Congresswoman Ferraro; subtly, the fact of her marriage invited hostility from those disposed to hear the founders' discussion of "domestic tranquility" as a claim that a woman's place is in the home.

Like members of other disenfranchised groups, women tended to adopt the socially approved style. Until recently, women who attained political power did so by adopting the manly approach.[95] Here Ferraro was a victim. Because her communicative style was forged in the clashes of law school and the courtroom, she reverted to a combative, impersonal, data-deluged form at key points in the debate. At the same time, reliance on the notes she took to rebut Bush led her to focus eye contact on the note cards rather than on the audience, a move that undercut her credibility.

Ferraro's style manifests the double bind in which television traps a female politician. The style traditionally considered credible is no longer suitable to television. But only a person whose credibility is firm can risk adopting a style traditionally considered weak. So a male candidate whose credibility is in part a function of presumptions made about those of his sex is more likely to succeed in the "womanly" style than is an equally competent but stereotypically disadvantaged female candidate.

Ronald Reagan can employ a female style, Geraldine Ferraro cannot. Only after Ronald Reagan and other credible male leaders have legitimized television's preferred style will females running for high office be able to reembrace the "womanly" style without risk. Meanwhile, females holding state and local offices can pave the way for the change in perception of the style appropriate to the nation's highest elective offices.

The natural compatibility between the "womanly" style and television is not the only factor propelling candidates toward that style. Two bodies of evidence invite the "womanly" style as the natural marriage of political substance and expression. Both favor female candidates over males.

The gender gap revealed that female voters differ from their husbands, brothers, and fathers on humanitarian issues and matters of war and peace.[96] Moreover, female candidates are more credible than males on those "human" issues that tie intuitively to a maternal role. These include nutrition for infants, food stamps, aid to the elderly, Social Security, and initiatives that would prevent sons from dying in war.[97]

Style and substance coalesced. Not only were women more inclined to personal speech but they were more inclined to favor issues that lent themselves to such speech. Not only were women inclined to oppose military intervention but they also were ill disposed to hostile verbs, aggressive verbal behavior, and clear refutative postures. Not only did women favor a nurturant, incorporative style but they also supported programs that nurtured.

At the same time, women's sense of political efficacy increased and with it their disposition to participate in politics. In 1960, the authors of *The American Voter* concluded that "Men are more likely than women to feel they can cope with the complexities of politics and to believe that their participation carries some weight in the political process."[98] By 1976 women and men of the same age had developed similar senses of political efficacy.[99]

Female candidates for local and statewide office responded to this convergence by returning to a more personal womanly style. Bella Abzug gave way to Barbara Jordan; Barbara Jordan to Geraldine Ferraro. What most clearly distinguishes the political ads for male and female candidates is the females' emphasis on their compassion and warmth. By contrast, men stress their toughness.[100]

Since society approved their use of the "manly" style in public but the "womanly" style in private, many women entered the televised age proficient in both. Increasingly, female candidates felt comfortable blending the strengths of each style. Barbara Mikulski, elected to the

→ MUTED
GROUP

Senate from Maryland in 1986, "fights" for humanitarian causes and comfortably combines data-giving and dramatizing.

The broadcast age has rendered the combative, data-driven, impersonal "male" style obsolete. Two ironies result: only to the extent that they employ a once spurned "womanly" style can male politicians prosper on radio and television; meanwhile, in their surge toward political equality, women abandoned and must now reclaim the "womanly" style. Later, I will argue that by employing a self-disclosive, narrative, personal, "womanly" style, Ronald Reagan, an ideological conservative, pioneered a revolution not only in televised communication but, implicitly, in women's participation in politics on their own terms. But his was not the quintessential art. Sacrificed in Reagan's preoccupation with pictures was the additional power his discourse might have drawn from a well-argued case capsulized in a memorable phrase.

5

The Memorable Phrase, The Memorable Picture

The cover of *The New Republic* of October 17, 1983, pictured the Reverend Jesse Jackson, his right hand raised, his left on the Bible, swearing the presidential oath of office. The headline read " 'I have a scheme . . .' President Jesse Jackson?" By playing on our associations with Martin Luther King's "I have a dream," "I have a scheme" telegraphs a powerful indictment. If Jackson would substitute a scheme for King's dream, then he is unworthy to be president. *The New Republic* is engaging here in the sort of concise, memorable phrasemaking that is now demanded of those who wish to speak to a mass audience. In this chapter we explore the form and function of memorable phrases and pictures in political eloquence.

Among the components that eloquent speeches have in common is the existence of a memorable statement that capsulizes the speech and serves as the hook on which we hang it in memory. Often, history titles the speech with its memorable phrase: Patrick Henry's "Liberty or Death" speech, FDR's "Arsenal of Democracy" speech, Martin Luther King, Jr.'s "I Have a Dream" speech, Churchill's "Finest Hour" and "Blood, Sweat and Tears" and DeGaulle's "Vive Quebec Libre" speeches are examples.

A talent for digesting a speech into a memorable phrase is a characteristic of eloquent persons. In our age of television where political speakers are more likely to be heard in news clips than in any other environment, the value of this talent is magnified. The person who can synopsize an issue in a clear, concise, dramatic statement that takes less than thirty-five seconds to deliver is more likely to be seen and heard on broadcast news than those who lack that talent. When that synoptic statement is spoken in a visual environment that dramatizes it, the visual-verbal moment will become the capsule in which television viewers store the event. By telling a perfervid audience of West Germans massed before the Berlin Wall that "Two thousand years ago the proudest boast was 'Civis Romanus Sum.' Today, in the world of freedom, the proudest boast is 'Ich bin ein Berliner'—Let them come to Berlin," John Kennedy created such a moment. The moment is stored in memory on the peg provided by the statement "Ich bin ein Berliner."

Some memorable phrases are more than signposts signalling the possibility of eloquence and lures beckoning news coverage. In addition to serving these functions, such phrases survive their generative contexts to define the past for us. "Give me liberty or give me death" and "War to make the world safe for democracy" are such phrases. Others, such as "I shall return" and "The lady's not for turning," characterize persons, specifically Douglas MacArthur and Margaret Thatcher. Similarly, "governments derive their just powers from the consent of the governed" defines a people and "nothing to fear but fear itself" and "segregation now, segregation tomorrow and segregation forever" summon memories of both persons and periods. "Are you better off now than you were four years ago?" synopsizes the central question framed by Reagan and asked of voters in the 1980 presidential campaign. Some statements, such as "I have a dream," stand for the discourse in which they originally were embedded. The digestive function served by "I have a dream" stands as a warning to speakers creating eloquent phrases. The central claim of King's speech was not "I have a dream" but now is the time to make real the promises of democracy. The eloquent phrase has led us to mistake the speech's central idea.

The ability of a small unit of discourse to stand for an entire piece and, occasionally, for a presidency or a period in history means that such phrases function as synecdoche. They are a part that stands for the whole from which they were drawn. Of the mountains of words uttered by public figures, these epitomizing phrases and sentences are most generative of collective assent.

Eloquent persons skillfully use synoptic phrases to ground discourse, forestall debate, and characterize themselves and the institutions for which they speak. In the process, such speakers increase the likelihood that their discourse will be considered eloquent and at the same time aid the chances that it will be covered on news broadcasts.

Synecdochic phrases serve useful rhetorical and social functions. By specifying grounds to which the community assents and by stipulating patterns of language whose use speaks the communal bond, they create a rhetorical community. Through synecdochic phrases, a community absorbs and transmits its interpretation of its own history. So, for example, the history of the United States can be captured in such phrases as "all men are created equal," "government derives its just powers from the consent of the governed," "government of the people, by the people, for the people," "Liberty and union, now and forever, one and inseparable." Presidencies also can be capsulized by synecdochic markers. "Make the world safe for democracy" is to Wilson's presidency what "Ask not what your country can do for you, ask what you can do for your country" is to Kennedy's.

The raw materials of which these statements are forged often preexist their memorable embodiment. Eloquent rhetors mine this material and fashion it to their purposes. So, for example, Jefferson's stature is enhanced by the felicitous phrases etched into the stone of the Jefferson Memorial and into the nation's consciousness even though the same ideas had been expressed, albeit in a more pedestrian form, by others before him. To appreciate Jefferson's genius we need only recall how incisively he reworked Mason's "Declaration of Rights" for Virginia. Mason had written: "all men are created equally free and independent, and have certain inherent natural rights, of which they cannot, by any compact, deprive or divest their posterity; among which are the enjoyment of life and liberty . . . happiness and safety . . . all power is by God and Nature vested in, and consequently derives from, the people."[1] Mason's cumbersome statements are transformed into grounding premises *(archai)* through the workings of Jefferson's pen.

Memorable phrases that serve as the premises from which other discourse is built often must wait for an eloquent rhetor to impress them in history and on the collective memory. When that occurs, they draw part of their stature as grounding premises precisely from the consent they merited before their felicitous expression. So John Adams' sharp-lipped observation that there were no ideas in the Declaration "but what had been hackneyed in Congress for two years before"[2] is to Jefferson's credit, not his shame. As Jefferson repeatedly noted, he had not intended to "invent new ideas" but rather to express "the American mind."[3] Similarly, we mistakenly attribute Jefferson's "entangling alliances with none" to the first president while forgetting Washington's similar admonition because, to borrow criteria from Cicero, Jefferson's formulation is more *accommodatus, aptus, congruens.*

But the existence of an eloquent spokesperson does not of itself assure that the raw material will be fashioned into a remembered phrase.

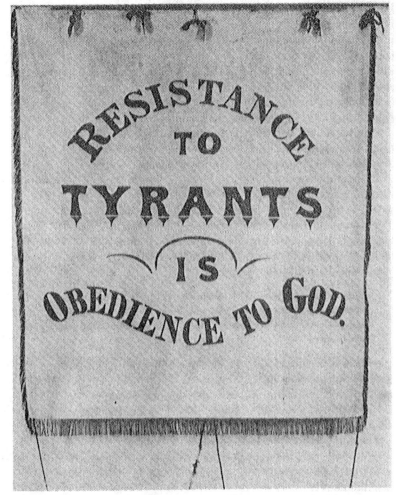

Because they are able to stand for entire constructions of reality, slogans are a powerful rhetorical device. This slogan has been used repeatedly by groups agitating for change. (Courtesy Political History Division, Smithsonian)

By lodging it in a founding document, tying it to an important event—a war, for example—or placing it in the mouth of an important rhetor who commands public attention, such as a president, its likelihood of survival increases. So, for instance, "of the people, by the people, for the people" is linked in the public mind to Abraham Lincoln's Gettysburg Address, not to Daniel Webster or Theodore Parker's earlier uses of the phrase because neither of these predecessors commanded the public and historical attention afforded a president and neither led the country into war upon itself. For the same reason, we hear "A house divided against itself cannot stand" either as a biblical expression, a statement of Lincoln's, or both but not as a remnant from a speech delivered by Daniel Webster in 1851.[4] Although the house was not divided when Lincoln made that statement, it would ultimately be at war during his tenure as president. That division, identified with the Lincoln presidency, fuses with Lincoln's stature as president to dictate that a commonplace phrase will be known as his, not Webster's.

The summative function performed by "house divided" contributes to our inclination to attribute it to Lincoln. We hear the "house divided" as a prophesy of war even though that was not Lincoln's intent. The statement was sundered from its context because it served so effectively to synopsize a growing popular conviction that war was inevitable and because in retrospect that unintended prophesy was accurate. What Lincoln had actually said was:

> A house divided against itself cannot stand. I believe this government cannot endure, permanently half *slave* and half *free*. I do not expect the Union to be *dissolved*—I do not expect the house to *fall*—but I *do* expect it will cease to be divided.[5]

Lincoln was bewildered by the conclusion that he was forecasting civil war. "I said no such thing," he insisted in a letter.[6] The sentence had assumed a life of its own. Lincoln was no longer its master.

Heads of established institutions inherit both a palimpsest on which their predecessors have inscribed the rhetorical history of the institution and the power but not necessarily the ability to augment that legacy. Spokespersons for an institution may ignore, underscore, or rewrite this rhetorical legacy but they cannot erase it. Some of these rhetors view themselves as acolytes whose rhetorical function is to display the rhetorical past as Moses displayed the tablets—for public edification. Others conceive themselves as stockbrokers who create fresh rhetorical capital by investing the rhetorical past. The first relishes epideictic, the second deliberative rhetoric.

Eloquent presidents not only write the characterizing phrases by which we come to judge their tenure but also embellish our sense of who we are as a people and forge shaping phrases that define the meaning of events. One test of a president's eloquence is whether he forged the statement or statements by which we remember and judge his presidency. Consequently, although we revere Washington as the father of our country, it is Jefferson among the founders whose eloquence we eulogize. Similarly, Lincoln who contributed "government of the people, by the people, and for the people" among other phrases to the national vocabulary is remembered as the most eloquent of the nineteenth-century presidents and Wilson, FDR, and John Kennedy are regarded as the rhetorical superiors of Warren Harding, Herbert Hoover, Harry Truman, Gerald Ford, and Jimmy Carter.

The presence of Wilson on this list serves as a reminder that the historical judgment accorded a president's defining rhetorical legacy may be condemnatory. When a situation proves sour, the eloquent phrase that characterized it can be resurrected as an indictment. So, for example, "war to make the world safe for democracy" is an epitaph on the grave of Wilson's greatness, not an enshrinement.

Eloquent presidents succeed in arranging our perception of major events and of their presidency under the canopy of phrases of their choosing. The synoptic phrases carved by JFK and FDR to define their presidencies illustrate the power that follows from this rhetorical facility.

Before Kennedy implanted his presidency in "Ask not what your country can do for you . . . ," he attempted to relegate the defining phrases of his two most eloquent immediate predecessors to a status as historical curios—phrases that no longer grip an audience's sense of itself but are rather the means by which an audience characterizes an historical person or event. He did this by insinuating that Wilson's and FDR's visions were based in an unbecoming, morally inferior self-preoccupation while his own was rooted in selflessness. Kennedy set his new moral order in place in his acceptance speech where he declared "Woodrow Wilson's New Freedom promised our nation a new political and economic framework. Franklin Roosevelt's New Deal promised security and succor to those in need. But the New Frontier of which I speak is not a set of promises—it is a set of challenges. It sums up not what I intend to offer the American people, but what I intend to ask of them. It appeals to their pride, not their pocketbook—it holds out the promise of more sacrifice instead of more security."[7]

From the Inaugural Address's "Ask not what your country can do for you . . ." to programs such as the Peace Corps and speeches such as that cornering big steel, that theme reverberated throughout the Kennedy presidency. The theme expressed in "Ask not . . ." forecast the philosophy and tone of the Kennedy administration and at the same time provided a prism through which the Kennedy presidency could be viewed and judged. Its power was magnified by its apparent congruence with the myth of the Broadway hit *Camelot*, an analogy tenderly massaged after Kennedy's death by his widow with the assistance of Arthur Schlesinger, Jr. The eagerness with which, two decades later, the press and public recall Kennedy as "the Camelot president" testifies to the success of that subalterned symbol and its synecdochic pontifex, "Ask not. . . ."

The ability of a phrase to stand for an entire construction of reality enables a rhetor to modify an antagonist's philosophy by controverting a single significant rhetorical fragment. Because Kennedy successfully reduced his presidency to "Ask not . . ." Richard Nixon could establish the difference between his philosophy and Kennedy's by declaring in his Second Inaugural, "Let each of us ask—not just what will government do for me but what can I do for myself?"[8] Daniel Webster made the same move when in his second reply to Hayne (1830) he transformed his opponent's claim "Liberty first and Union afterwards" into "Liberty and Union, now and forever, one and inseparable."[9]

Eloquent presidents also employ synecdochic phrases to fashion our perception of important events. Rhetoric's ability to distill whole philosophies into a phrase is manifest here too. Indeed, the synecdochic nature of such rhetoric means that whole debates can be written in headline form. The debate between Woodrow Wilson and Theodore Roosevelt over the nature and objectives of the First World War illustrates this and also illuminates the inventional resource digestive rhetoric creates.

Roosevelt gored Wilson's idealist objectives with transmutations of Wilson's defining phrases. "We did not go to war to make democracy safe," Roosevelt intoned, "and we did not go to war because we had a special grievance. We went to war, because, after two years, during which, with utter contempt of our protests, she had habitually and continually murdered our noncombatant men, women, and children on the high seas, Germany. . . ."[10]

For another of Wilson's grounding premises, "Peace without victory," Roosevelt substituted "the peace of overwhelming victory."[11] To Roosevelt "the peace of over-whelming victory" meant that "the peace that we win must guarantee full reparation for the awful cost of life and treasure which the Prussianized Germany . . . has inflicted on the entire world." Wilson's phrase "Peace without victory" expressed instead the likelihood that retributive victors would foment a second world war. Each phrase pinpointed the philosophy of its author. Each provided a text through which the war could be interpreted.

The task of journalists is eased by eloquent presidents who synopsize their presidencies and their interpretation of events in distilled phrases. When the White House is occupied by an eloquent president, headlines prefigure their corresponding essays in recast synecdochic statements originally of the president's making. So, for example, in a headline in *Outlook* (London, August 18, 1923)[12] war to end war becomes "Peace to End Peace." Peace without victory becomes "Peace only through Victory" in *The New York Times* in October 1918,[13] retains its phrasing "Peace without Victory" in a headline in the *New Republic* of December 23, 1916,[14] but becomes "Victory without Peace" in the *New Republic* of January 11, 1919.[15]

To this point we have noted an eloquent president's ability to impress memorable phrases on his presidency or on the events it encompasses; we have also examined the inventional possibilities opened for opposing rhetors by such synoptic discourse. So our focus has been on the legacy a president leaves, not on the legacy he inherits.

Eloquent presidents underscore or rewrite this rhetorical legacy; their pedestrian brothers ignore it, albeit at considerable risk. As the custodians of the nation's symbolic past, eloquent presidents perform four functions. First, they invigorate moribund phrases that have passed from an expression of conviction to cliché. Second, they redeem the repudiated statements of their predecessors. Third, they redefine grounding premises in the rhetorical legacy to encompass contemporary needs. Finally, they reconcile or recontextualize antagonistic premises in the rhetorical heritage of the institution.

The eloquent president is both historian and herald who has a talent for making concise, memorable phrases of the raw consensual stuff in the rhetorical environment. So Jefferson's phrasing and framing of "entangling alliances with none" bespeaks his eloquence as surely as Washington's clumsy expression of the same notion betrays his ineloquence. An eloquent president is also rhetorically self-reflective, a quality manifest in reworking principles until they are cast in an immortal form. So, for example, in his acceptance speech at the Democratic convention, we hear John Kennedy searching for the form that will enter the country's rhetorical heritage as "Ask not . . ." in the inaugural.

To some extent, all candidates for president rehearse grounding principles as a means of establishing rhetorically that they are qualified to lead. Eloquent presidents are differentiated by the clarity of their articulated sense of the principles they cherish, by the sensitivity of their reading of the threats to these principles, and by the skillful use they make of the rhetorical legacy.

Rhetorically instated *archai* ultimately define our past and tell us who we are as a people. In the short term, they ground action and, by telegraphing entire constructions of reality in a few words, create potent enthymemes. Consequently, leaders and their opponents engage in skirmishes, such as those fought by Theodore Roosevelt and Woodrow Wilson, to control the form and content of the grounding symbols. A president of the United States, like any institutional leader, inherits a palimpsest of symbols which, whether he wills it or not, will circumscribe the visions he is able to render credible for his audience. Even the most artful rhetor cannot wipe the slate clean. Skilled rhetors underscore the unchallenged premise, reformulate the challenged premise, and inscribe other compatible premises on the palimpsest. Their adversaries attempt to frustrate this process so as to inscribe premises suited to their own ends.

A skillful rhetor cultivates grounding principles in ways designed to immunize them to challenges. In the speech in which he advocated "peace without victory" Wilson allied his principles with respected opinion: "These are American principles, American policies. We could stand for no others. And they are also the principles and policies of forward looking men and women everywhere, of every modern nation, of every enlightened community. They are the principles of mankind and must prevail."[16] Leaders do not argue grounding premises, they proclaim them.

A rhetor who creates a compelling synoptic phrase is, in some senses, its prisoner. The phrase may stand, for example, as a standard by which to judge success or failure, as one test of Wilson's success was whether or not World War I did make the world safe for democracy. The synoptic phrase may also launch demands for action unintended by the rhetor as suffragists used Wilson's call to make the world safe for democracy as a lever to alter his opposition to woman suffrage. Finally, the rhetorical posture implied by the phrase may foreclose some rhetorical options and open others. Wilson could not defend World War I on selfish grounds after declaring that its intent was to make the world safe for democracy. Public acceptance of that synoptic phrase dictated that the war be defended in crusading, moralistic terms.

Redeeming Repudiated Premises

Eloquent presidents also salvage the worn synecdochic statements of their predecessors and reconstruct them to argue that they and we have learned the lessons of the past. Subsequent presidents' refashioning of the frayed statements of World War I illustrate this rhetorical function. The tendency of presidents to reformulate past phrases underscores our Darwinian sense that as a people we are progressing, learning from the past, not repeating past errors. By so doing, presidents affirm the viability of the "nation" and the "presidency."

Because of the president's unique role as custodian of the national vocabulary and because some presidents such as Washington, as founding father, and Jefferson, as author of a founding document, have special authority in their role as guardians, skilled rhetors misattribute would-be *archai* to them as we anachronistically credit Washington with Jefferson's ban on "entangling alliances" and ascribe to Jefferson a motto created in the Jackson era: "That government governs best which governs least." Our tendency to misremember also is manifest in our identification of "war to end war" with Wilson. Although he publicly employed H. G. Wells' phrase "war to end war" only once, we tend to recall that that phrase resided at the core of Wilson's vocabulary.

Wilson's reasons for fighting World War I functioned as grounding premises that were repudiated when that war failed to either end war or make the world safe for democracy. Those premises were later redeemed by his successors. Evidence that Wilson's call to "make the world safe for democracy" functioned as a guiding principle can be found in comparable expressions by one of Wilson's usual adversaries. Henry Cabot Lodge, an ardent Republican opponent of Wilson's, declared that "We enter this war to unite with those who are fighting the common foe in order to preserve human freedom, democracy, and world civilization."[17] And while Theodore Roosevelt's savaging of Wilson's premise betrays his envy of Wilson's ability to ground action in memorable phrases, it also reveals that even he does not dispute the ultimate legitimacy of Wilson's premise: "Until we make the world safe for America (and incidentally, until we make democracy safe in America), it is empty rhetoric to talk of making the world safe for democracy: and no one of these objects can be obtained merely by high sounding words."[18]

The extent to which Wilson's premise anchored the congressional decision to declare war is revealed also in the insistent disclaimer of a senator who feared that his vote for the declaration of war would be interpreted as endorsement of Wilson's premise. "I am not voting for war in the name of democracy," Senator Harding insisted. "I want to emphasize that fact for a moment, because much has been said upon that subject on the floor. . . . it is up to us to demonstrate the permanency of a republic before we enter upon a worldwide war to establish democracy."[19]

The power of Wilson's claim that the war was being fought to make the world safe for democracy was magnified by his vocabulary. He described the war's end as "the final triumph of justice," pledged that the League would contain no "selfish economic combinations," described the "covenants" of the League, declared that "Germany will have to redeem her character," called for "sacrifice and self-denial," and stated that the interest of the weak is "sacred." The language in which British leaders had cast the war prefigured Wilson's moralistic, crusading rhetoric and created in those Americans sympathetic to Britain a predisposition to embrace Wilson's rhetorical formulation of the war. British Prime Minister Herbert Asquith, for example, had depicted the war as a spiritual conflict involving the "sanctity" of international covenants and waged on behalf of mankind.

The afterlife of rallying calls to war illustrates well the persistence and power of decisive shaping statements. When World War II provided incontrovertible evidence that World War I had not ended war, rhetors stripped "war to end war" of its function as a grounding premise and asked what evidence had posited their original belief in the power of that prophecy. Acceptance of H. G. Wells' claim that World War I was a war to end war was predicated on the assumption that war *could* end war. Those betrayed by that belief generalized from their experience with one war to the premise "war cannot end war." Consequently, "war cannot end war" replaced "war can end war" as an unquestioned premise. In an address in Pittsburgh in 1950, for example, Dwight D. Eisenhower noted that "no one has yet explained how war prevents war. Nor has anyone been able to explain away the fact that war begets conditions that beget further war."[20] Similarly, Harry Truman wrote: "There is nothing more foolish than to think that war can be stopped by war. You don't 'prevent' anything by war except peace."[21] Neither Eisenhower nor Truman dignifies with evidence his dismissal of the notion that war can end war. Instead, the claim "war cannot end war" functions as an unchallenged premise. The burden of proof has shifted to those who would defend the discredited view.

The prospect that a third world war would signal nuclear annihilation added cogency to the contention that war cannot end war. When John Kennedy told the U.N., "Mankind must put an end to war—or war will put an end to mankind,"[22] he was reconstructing Wells' phrase to reflect the realities of an atomic age.

Wilson's success in embedding his grounding premises in the consciousness of the Allies is evident in the expressions of disillusionment that followed the realization that the allied victory had not created a world flowing with milk and honey. The public's belief that it had been gulled transformed the meaning of Wells' and Wilson's phrases. No longer did they define the country's mission; instead they symbolized self-deception. Skilled rhetors recognized the transformation. Richard Nixon, for example, observed, "Every wartime President since Woodrow Wilson has been tempted to describe the current war as the war to end wars. But they have not done so because of the derision that the phrase evoked, a reminder of lost dreams, of lights that failed, of hopes that were raised and dashed."[23]

Because grounding premises, like tenets of faith, presuppose belief, the vocabulary of religion is well suited to express the process by which they are transformed. Articles of faith had proven heretical. Apostles of Wilson's premises became apostates. Yet, just as an anathematized tenet dominates the bull that would extirpate it, Wilson's memorable phrases continued to shape public rhetoric.

The rhetoric that attempted to exorcise Wilson's symbols was penetential. Leaders confessed that they too had been duped by the "war to end wars" and war "to make the world safe for democracy." The vehemence with which they were anathematized suggests the original potency of these phrases. "One of the most impressive slogans ever invented to encourage flagging spirits during the War was that the purpose of the War was to 'make the world safe for Democracy'. . . . If we look across Europe today it is quite evident that the world has not in fact been 'made safe for Democracy' " declared Viscount Halifax in September 1934.[24] "How many of the lies you were told do you still believe?," American poet Langston Hughes asked an international conference of artists in Paris in 1934. "Does any Negro believe, for instance, that the world was actually saved for democracy?"[25]

After publicly repenting, leaders assured their constituents that the seductive statements had taught them a useful, albeit bitter, lesson. We are no longer vulnerable to such enticing claims, they argued. That rationalization translated into the antiwar posture of such leaders as Neville Chamberlain who justified the Munich Pact by invoking the lesson of the war's failed symbols. "Does the experience of the Great War and of the years that followed it give us reasonable hope that, if some new war started, that would end war any more than the last one did?," he asked. His answer was "No."[26] "We convinced ourselves that war would prove a solvent," observed Halifax, "and thought that the spectre of war might be exorcised for all time and not only for our generation. There we were wrong. . . . We have learnt by bitter experience that, however righteous the cause, war is likely to leave a legacy of greater difficulties than it can resolve."[27] Gradually, flagellation gave way to the search for the premises that could ground a more tenable faith. And here too, Wilson's statements were formative.

By adapting rather than adopting failed premises, leaders assure us that their vision of the country's future has profited from a study of the past, that they will neither repeat its errors nor reject its lessons. In the process, leaders can rehabilitate failed statements. The words in which leaders based World War I imposed inventional constraints on subsequent rhetors by circumscribing future summons to war. Yet at the same time, the repudiated statements created inventional capital by inviting reformulation.

The way in which sensitive rhetors capitalized on Wilson's failure illustrates that residual rhetoric is a rich inventional resource. FDR reconstructed one of Wilson's failed statements as a call to "an end to the beginning of all wars."[28] Kennedy also abstracted from the past the lesson that no single action can end war. After signing the test-ban treaty, he noted: "It will not put an end to war. It will not remove basic conflicts. It will not secure freedom for all. But it can be a lever."[29] An analysis of the afterlife of Wilson's calls to war suggests that rhetors and audiences do not discard memorable grounding phrases. Instead, subsequent rhetors refashion them.

In fact, Wilson's symbols are a rich resource for presidential rhetoric advocating detente. In what Sorensen terms "the single most important foreign-policy speech in the entire Kennedy legacy"[30] (the speech Khrushchev credited with paving the way for the test-ban treaty), Kennedy refashioned two failed symbols. Kennedy's speech at American University underscored its call for detente by transmuting Wilson's "The world must be made safe for democracy" and Neville Chamberlain's "Peace for our time."

The phrase "peace for our time" was contaminated by association with the disastrous aftermath of the Munich conference. Whether the rhetor intends it or not, the phrase summons the trauma of Hitler's conquest of Europe. Chamberlain's prophecy symbolizes misplaced trust, naive optimism, and foolish concession. In his speech at American University, Kennedy repudiated such a posture toward other nations by advocating "not merely peace in our time but peace for all time."[31]

By replacing Wilson's contention that "the world must be made safe for democracy" with the contention that "at least we can help make the world safe for diversity,"[32] Kennedy implied that war did not make the world safe and established our willingness to tolerate ideological differences in other political systems. That skeletal notion is fleshed out in a speech at Amherst in which Kennedy declared, "I look forward to a world which will be safe not only for democracy and diversity but also for personal distinction."[33]

Nixon too prefigured detente by fashioning new premises from the symbolic legacy of Wilson and Chamberlain.

> When we know one another we cannot hate one another.
>
> In this still imperfect world, I am convinced that realistic understanding is on the rise and mindless hatred is on the decline.

The strong likelihood exists that there will be no need for a war to end wars, that instead, by taking one careful step at a time, by making peace for one full generation, we will get this world into the habit of peace.

By his example, Woodrow Wilson helped make the world safe for idealism.

By following that example, by not fearing to be idealists ourselves, we shall make the world safe for free men to live in peace.[34]

It is ironic that a Republican president mired in a bitter war sanctified Wilson's idealism and attempted to redeem his failed premises. Yet it is no accident that both Kennedy and Nixon constructed their vision of detente on the failed symbols of Chamberlain and Wilson. Both men endorsed the ends toward which Wilson and Chamberlain strove but rejected their means. Nixon, in particular, held that the premises were noble, although naive. And both elevated American self-esteem by implying that the original statements were honorable ones honorably embraced and consequently ought to be reconstructed, not spurned.

The tenacious grip of Wilson's rallying cries on the political rhetoric of subsequent decades suggests that, by grounding national action, a digestive statement lodges itself in the memory of audiences and rhetors. Such statements are then bequeathed in oral and written history as a cultural legacy enabling children who cannot name the countries involved in the First World War to report that it was a war to end war and make the world safe for democracy. A skillful rhetor finds in this rhetorical legacy an inventional goldmine; a feckless rhetor finds only dross.

Redefining Revered Premises

Principles articulated in one time and place do not necessarily relocate comfortably into changed environments. The president's responsibility is to smooth the readjustment by rehearsing the principle in a way that effectively but not explicitly neutralizes it in the new environment. If the principle is the legacy of a founding father or a founding document or mistakenly attributed to either, it cannot be repudiated outright. Instead, strategies that I call contravention by delimitation and contravention by extension often come into play. FDR's encounter with "the best government is the least government" illustrates the first strategy, Woodrow Wilson's dance around the ban on "entangling alliances" manifests the second.

As I have noted earlier, both statements are misattributed. The first, actually the motto of a Jacksonian newspaper, is credited to Jefferson, in part because it parsimoniously synthesizes the contention of his first

inaugural that aside from restraining men from injuring one another
a wise government "shall leave them otherwise free to regulate their
own pursuits." In the case of "entangling alliances with none," Washington is given credit for Jefferson's more felicitous expression of a
concept in the first president's farewell address.

Contravention by Extension

Since Jefferson did not hold Washington in high regard, it is ironic
that Washington is associated with what Jefferson termed one of the
"essential principles of our Government."[35] The misattribution by such
knowledgeable historians as Woodrow Wilson is understandable. By at-
tributing the ban on "entangling alliances" to Washington, a rhetor is
able to identify it with the foreign policy of the United States from the
very inception of the presidency and to brand those opposing Washington's view with rhetorical parricide for assaulting a central belief entrusted to us by the "father of our country." In addition, since the public now mistakenly believes that the phrase was Washington's, a rhetor
who ascribes it instead to Jefferson risks being thought ignorant about
our genesis as a people. But why, if crediting the phrase to Washington
is freighted with advantage, has the actual statement of Washington's
not survived in the compendium of phrases that defines us as a people?
Because Jefferson's phrase more graphically digests the Washingtonian
principle into a concise, memorable form and consequently, unlike
Washington's, has survived as a statement summarizing our identity.

The ability of the phrase to survive was enhanced by the fact that it
is corroborated by the set of premises expressed as "the Monroe Doctrine." The phrase no "entangling alliances" is consistent with Monroe's
principle of American noninterference in European affairs and European noninterference in American affairs.

Yet World War I created pressure on Wilson to break with the principle underlying "Washington's" and Madison's admonitions. "In this
cause, and under the changed conditions," Harvard professor Charles
W. Eliot entreated Wilson, "would not the people of the United States
approve of the abandonment of Washington's advice that this country
keep out of European complications?"[36] So impressed was Wilson with
Eliot's letter that he read it to his Cabinet.

Nonetheless, even in war, a memorably phrased grounding premise
cannot be abandoned casually. As early as 1900, Wilson had begun the
process of converting Washington's abjuration to an adjuration. According to Wilson, the actual message of Washington's "Farewell" was:
"I want you to discipline yourselves and stay still and be good boys . . .

until you are big enough to go abroad in the world. Wait . . . until you
need not be afraid of foreign influence, and then you shall be ready to
take your part in the field of the world."[37] That time, Wilson concluded, had arrived. Even then Wilson did not repudiate Washington's
admonition. Instead, he reinterpreted the text of the "Farewell." That
strategy presages Wilson's strategic contravention of the principle by
extension. In a speech to the Senate on January 22, 1917, Wilson proposed that "the nations should with one accord adopt the doctrine of
President Monroe as the doctrine of the world: that no nation should
seek to extend its polity over any other nation or people, but that every
people should be left free to determine its own polity."[38] Under the
guise of implanting the Monroe Doctrine as a grounding premise in
world discourse, Wilson justified U.S. intervention in a European war.
Then, by proposing that "all nations henceforth avoid entangling alliances which would draw them into competitions of power . . . ," Wilson created the fiction that Washington's principle could be applied to
the dealings of countries throughout the world without nullifying that
principle. But doesn't U.S. cooperation with the Allies constitute an
entangling alliance? Wilson dismisses the suggestion: "There is no entangling alliance in a concert of power. When all unite to act . . . in
the common interest and are free to live their own lives under a common protection." (Wilson employed the same line of argument in an
address delivered September 27, 1918: "We still read Washington's immortal warning against 'entangling alliances' with full comprehension
and an answering purpose. But only special and limited alliances entan-
gle; and we recognize and accept the duty of a new day in which we
are permitted to hope for a general alliance which will avoid entangle-
ments and clear the air of the world for common understandings and
the maintenance of common rights.")

After implicitly overturning a principle that had governed American
foreign policy for over a century, Wilson quickly moved to bond the
revised principle to another primal premise. In the next sentence, he,
in effect, pits Washington's unrevised principle against a distilled phrase
from the Declaration of Independence: "I am proposing government
by the consent of the governed." To challenge Wilson's reformulation
of the principle proscribing foreign involvement is to challenge a premise handed down not by Washington, Jefferson, or Monroe but by a
founding document.

If one ignores the content of this passage and listens only to its form,
one would conclude that Wilson has endorsed both the Monroe Doctrine and "Washington's" proscription. Consequently, if challenged on
the grounds that he has repudiated a primal principle, Wilson ingen-

uously can uphold the premise and at the same time reduce the debate
to wrangling over Washington and Monroe's actual intent. Meanwhile,
Wilson's pro-war, pro-League claims, ostensibly grounded in premises
implanted by Washington and Monroe, are, in fact, based in audience
commitment to the consent of the governed.

Despite Wilson's linguistic acrobatics, the principle expressed by the
ban on "entangling alliances" persisted tenaciously. As a result, Wilson
was careful to describe the United States as an "associated" not an "allied" power in the war and the postwar battle over the United States'
entrance into the League of Nations would pivot, in part, on a dispute
over whether entrance constituted an entangling alliance. For instance,
in an eloquent address delivered moments before a crucial Senate vote
on the League (November 19, 1919), Senator William E. Borah argued
from the inviolability of the Washingtonian proscription: "[T]ell me
where is the reservation in these articles which protects us against entangling alliances with Europe," he asked. "[T]ell me what one of them
protects the doctrine laid down by the Father of his country." Borah
then argues that the premises embodied in the Monroe Doctrine are
themselves noted in Washington's principle. "We cannot protect the
Monroe Doctrine unless we protect the basic principle upon which it
rests and that is the Washington policy."[39] In both Wilson and Borah's
rhetoric the principles of Washington and Monroe are treated as if
they are mutually supportive. Indeed, for practical purposes Wilson
cannot extend one without extending the other or he will invite his
opponents to barricade themselves behind either the Monroe Doctrine
or the Washingtonian proscription and attack him for inconsistency with
a founding premise.

Yet the existence of strong counterargument means that for some in
the audience the challenged principle may no longer be able to anchor
arguments. So Borah too backstops the principles of Monroe and
Washington with an unchallenged premise. "Mr. President, there is another and even a more commanding reason why I shall record my vote
against this treaty. It imperils what I conceive to be the underlying, the
very first principles of this Republic. It is in conflict with the right of
our people to govern themselves free from all restraint, legal or moral,
of foreign powers." Both Borah and Wilson assume that an appeal to
the principles embodied in a founding document will re-anchor the
challenged principles of Washington and Monroe. Since a president
can only articulate his own view of who we are as a people, such views
are more fallible than the views of who we are as a people expressed
in a founding document. When a principle expressed by a president is

challenged, the constitution and the Declaration of Independence function as a supreme court of appeal.

By encasing the challenged principles of Monroe and Washington in a more primal premise, Borah gains the short-term advantage of employing all available means of persuasion with a crucial audience at the price of a long-term disadvantage—erosion of the principles of Monroe and Washington. Borah, in effect, concedes that the presumably unchallengeable principles of Washington and Monroe can no longer stand as primal premises. They themselves must now be situated in an antecedent premise. Borah simultaneously argues that a premise is an indisputable primal premise and acts as if it is not. Consequently, he denies the premise the ability to ground his discourse, thus weakening its power to ground discourse in the future and opening it to the sort of subtle reformulation Wilson is attempting.

The displacement of Monroe and Washington's principles as primal premises in both the speech of Wilson and the speech of Borah prophesies eventual collapse of these premises as granted first premises *(archai)*. But the process of disintegration was both labored and complex. Indeed, as late as October 1935, when faced with war between Ethiopia and Italy, FDR would argue from the assumption that the Washingtonian proscription constituted American foreign policy: "[D]espite what happens to continents overseas," he declared, "the United States of America shall and must remain, as long ago the Father of our Country prayed that it might remain—unentangled and free."[40] The longevity of Washington's proscription may have been partially a function of the perceived failure of the "entanglement" for which Wilson, in effect, had argued in leading the country through the First World War. Whatever the reason, FDR clearly felt the constraints of the Washingtonian proscription and the sort of behavior it entailed. The strategy he would employ to disentangle the country is evident in his juxtaposition of "freedom" and "entanglement." In 1935 "freedom" and the desire to remain "unentangled" were compatible. When they became incompatible in Roosevelt's rhetoric, the proscription would be jettisoned as it was when, in the name of defense of freedom in March 1941, Congress passed the Lend Lease Act. Confronted by this legislation, the isolationists again battled from behind the ban on "entangling alliances." When Lend Lease passed, Senator Arthur Vandenberg wrote in his diary: "We have torn up 150 years of traditional foreign policy. We have tossed Washington's Farewell Address into the discard."[41] Vandenberg's eulogy for "entangling alliances with none" was premature. So reluctant was FDR to become entangled in European affairs that only when Hitler declared war on the United States four days after the U. S. declaration of war against Japan did the United States finally issue a declaration of war against Germany.

Contravention by Delimitation

Before the New Deal could instate an economic bill of rights and corresponding governmental responsibility, FDR first had to clear the terrain of the philosophy rooted by Hoover that assumed that solutions lay with individuals, not with government. Standing as a bulwark buttressing that philosophy was the "Jeffersonian" claim that government that governs best, governs least. So, it was rhetorically expedient for FDR to banish the presence of Jefferson from the debate by severely circumscribing the meaning of the "Jeffersonian" phrase. Just as Wilson assaulted "entangling alliances with none" years before he bent it to his will as president, so too FDR engaged the Jeffersonian dictum years before he vanquished it to secure the New Deal on firm ground. In both instances these leaders reveal that they earned their reputations as eloquent not simply for being fine wordsmiths but for their sensitivity to the existence and function of a formative rhetorical legacy. In 1926 Roosevelt told the Democratic state convention in New York:

> If we accept the phrase "the best government is the least government" we must understand that it applies to the simplification of governmental machinery, and to the prevention of improper interference with the legitimate private acts of the citizens, but a nation or a State which is unwilling by governmental action to tackle the new problems, caused by immense increase of population and by the astounding strides of modern science, is headed for decline and ultimate death.[42]

In FDR's reinterpretation, the "Jeffersonian" claim retains relevance and meaning while no longer banning an enlarged governmental role. The reinterpretation has delimited the claim's original meaning.

Reconciling Contradictory Premises

Because the president is the spokesperson of the nation, he may also elect to either reconcile or reinterpret contradictory premises housed in the national vocabulary. Again, it is eloquent presidents such as Lincoln and Wilson who embrace this task—Lincoln with his focus on "all men are created equal" as a transcending phrase that envelops and mutes contradictory premises such as "slave is property" and Wilson with his redefinition of "entangling alliances."

Meanwhile, rhetors such as the poet Langston Hughes who do not speak for the "institution" are free to expose the failure of a phrase and do not in the process incur the obligation to refurbish it. Nor do pirates from unrelated movements incur that obligation. The prohibitionists "make the world safe for hypocrisy" intoned one opponent of the Volstead Act. "This nation cannot exist half license and half prohibition" declared another sober participant in the dialogue about national drinking.[43]

To this point we have focused on the ability of synoptic, memorably phrased premises to anchor calls for action. By serving as ultimate assertions from which there is no further appeal, these phrases and statements can also close debate. Some pre-empt further debate by signifying a compromise both sides can endorse. Such a case occurred at the National Governors' Conference in Washington, D. C., in February 1982. There the governors and Reagan agreed that they would suspend skirmishes over Reagan's proposal to return a number of federal programs to the states. The truce was reached under the rubric that was supposed to govern future deliberations, "No winners, no losers."

Other phrases summarize and seal debate by concisely articulating a conviction that blocks avenues for further discussion. The existence of mantras in the Indian rhetorical tradition invests synoptic phrases that seal debate with a special power. A mantra is a sacred counsel or formula that is repeated. In a speech in Bombay in August 1942 Gandhi offered the audience "a *mantra*, a short one . . . You may imprint it on your hearts and let every breath of yours give expression to it. The *mantra* is: 'Do or Die.' "[44] That *mantra* asserted that compromise with the British was impossible. For Gandhi, it meant "We shall either free India or die in the attempt; we shall not live to see the perpetuation of our slavery. . . . Let every man and woman live every moment of his or her life hereafter in the consciousness that he or she eats or lives for achieving freedom and will die, if need be, to attain that goal." "Take a pledge," Gandhi told his followers, "with God and your own conscience as witness, that you will no longer rest till freedom is achieved and will be prepared to lay down your lives in the attempt to achieve it. He who loses his life will gain it; he who will seek to save it shall lose it. Freedom is not for the coward or the faint-hearted." Having specified the meaning signified by the phrase, Gandhi develops the other arguments of his speech. Because the phrase synopsizes his position and forecloses all but the options he specifies, he can now conclude the speech by saying "I have pledged the Congress and the Congress will do or die."[45]

A culture that meditates on truths embedded in sacred phrases is particularly susceptible to use of synoptic phrases as goads to action. Yet, even in cultures that lack such a tradition, a well-crafted synoptic phrase can stifle debate. This occurred in the United States, at the close of the Civil War, when the phrase "the Negro's hour" joined with the phrase "The Negro once safe, the woman comes next" to close discussion among influential abolitionists on whether women and blacks should be enfranchised jointly or separately.

Blacks had been emancipated. The North had won the Civil War. The Fifteenth Amendment to the Constitution enfranchising black males had been submitted. In the wake of these triumphs, female leaders of the woman's movement who had labored for freedom for both women and blacks were stunned to find such influential abolitionists as William Lloyd Garrison and Wendell Phillips arguing that the enfranchisement of women should wait until the Negro had been given the vote.

Elizabeth Cady Stanton stated the premise of woman suffrage succinctly when she wrote to the editor of the *Standard*, "the disenfranchised all make the same demand, and the same logic and justice that secures suffrage to one class gives it to all."[46] In the same letter, Stanton summarized the case of those advocating a delay in female suffrage, "It is all very well for the privileged order to look down complacently and tell us, 'This is the Negro's hour; do not clog his way; do not embarrass the Republican party with any new issue; be generous and magnanimous; the Negro once safe, the woman comes next.' "[47] Their former allies averred that they had not abandoned the women; instead, the abolitionists argued "that while woman and negro suffrage were both just and logical, the nation would not accept two reforms at one time; therefore the question of suffrage must be divided and the first chance be given to the Negro."[48]

These arguments for delay were distilled in a synoptic phrase that signalled that, for those who employed it, debate on the issue was closed. The phrase constituted the conclusive argument, the unchallengeable statement. As " 'This is the Negro's hour' became the universal response to the woman's appeal," noted Catt and Shuler,[49] so, for example, when petitions for "universal suffrage were submitted for their signatures, abolitionists refused to sign them, saying, 'This is the Negro's hour.' "[50]

Leaders of the woman suffrage movement understood the rhetorical power of the phrase and realized too that it was the vehicle denying them suffrage. "Thinking is always a laborious and painful process for the average human being," Catt and Shuler wrote, "and the great leaders had simplified it for him by giving him an answer for every query— 'the Negro's hour.' "[51]

Stanton, Anthony, Catt, and other suffragists tried to suborn the phrase to their own ends by arguing that the Negro's hour also could be the woman's hour, but to no avail. Some abolitionists such as Stephen S. Foster joined them saying, "our demand for this hour is equal suffrage to all disenfranchised classes, for the one and the same reason—they are all human beings."[52] Henry Ward Beecher's words at the time were prophetic. He advocated "manhood and womanhood suffrage for all" with the rationale that "When the public mind is open, if you have anything to say, say it. If you have any radical principles to urge, any organizing wisdom to make known, don't wait until quiet times come. Don't wait until the public mind shuts up altogether. Progress comes by periods, by jumps and spurts. We are in the favored hour."[53]

Implied in "the Negro's hour" is the phrase that often accompanied it, "the woman comes next." The promise was explicit in the rhetoric of many. Horace Greeley, for instance, argued "It would be wise and magnanimous in you to hold your claims, though just and imperative I grant, in abeyance until the Negro is safe beyond peradventure, and your turn will come next."[54] When suffragists persisted, he withdrew his own support and the support of the *Tribune* from their cause.

So, under the promise of future suffrage, the enfranchisement of women was postponed for another day, a day long in coming; the premise implied in "the Negro's hour" was quickly forgotten once black males had secured the vote. "Appeals to party leaders who had faithfully pledged their help to women when the Negro's hour should have passed fell upon deaf ears and resisting minds."[55] Promises that the woman's hour would follow capsized in the backwash against reconstruction.

In their history of woman suffrage, Catt and Shuler controvert the phrase "the Negro's hour" to indict the long delay that followed. In their use of the phrase we hear the abandonment of their earlier argument that all humans are created equal. In its place is the assumption that "American" women are superior to those who have been enfranchised, an assumption previewed in Anthony's objection to seeing " 'Sambo' walk into the kingdom first."[56]

Catt and Shuler bitterly condemn use of newly enfranchised foreigners and of special interests against woman suffrage: "There had been hours for the Indian, the Russian, the German, the Chinese, the foreigner, the saloon, hours when each had decided the limits of woman's sphere, but no woman's hour had come."[57]

Memorable synoptic statements can function not only as the premises that ground and close debate but also as commentators on the character, conduct, or consciousness of a rhetor. Just as we inherit phrases that synopsize traumatic or significant historical events so too are we the bearers of phrases that signify lessons about individual temperament. Eloquent rhetors store such phrases for calculated use in attack and defense. Headline writers drew on our storehouse of such phrases when they characterized Ronald Reagan's 1982 budget with the statement "Let them eat cake." Use of such phrases implies an analogy between a contemporary and some memorable miscreant or saint. These phrases may whisper an analogic warning that a person possesses pernicious traits. Correlatively, such phrases may summon a sanctified act as "I regret that I have but one life to give for my country" bespeaks courage and patriotic sacrifice. Because such phrases carry a full-blown view of the character of an historical person, they are a rich resource for novelists, poets, and polemicists.

Synoptic statements can then characterize persons as well as policies and periods. To understand the power of a synecdochic statement one need only grasp its incarnating context, its reincarnations, and the assumptions that sustain it.

In an earlier chapter, I noted that the erosion of study of the past had minimized the ability of speakers to construct enthymemes. It has damaged the capacity of audiences to appreciate synecdochic statements as well. This is ironic because television news is predicated on synecdoche—the part, a clip from an event, stands for the whole event. Good reporters search for the news segment that reveals as much of the whole as possible. But where, in the past, the audience experienced the event or the whole speech and used the synecdochic statement as a memory-evoking digest, now the audience is often not exposed to the whole for which the part stands. When this occurs, the part simply stands for the part.

This means that the reporter not the speaker or the viewer now determines which moments in the speech will come to stand for the speech. In the process, reporters have assumed a role as custodians of our sense of our own present and past. When the audience is exposed to the whole event, as it is in the presidential debates, the reductive tendency of broadcast news to digest to the synecdochic means that moments after the completion of the event the audience is invited to see it not through the audience's own experience of it but rather through the dramatic, synthetic moment selected by the cameras to stand for the whole debate. Accordingly, the middle Ford-Carter debate was reduced to a moment initially unimportant to viewers who failed to recognize it as a blunder until television began casting the debate in terms of it— Ford's statement that Poland was not dominated by the Soviet Union.

The Bush-Ferraro debate was condensed to Ferraro's demand that Bush not patronize her. And the final Reagan-Mondale debate was digested to Reagan's dismissal of the age issue with his observation "I want you to know that also I will not make age an issue of this campaign. I am not going to exploit for political purposes my opponent's youth and inexperience."

One's view of the debate would be very different if it focused on moments provided by Reagan in his rambling wrap-up speech. What saves him from that possibility is the brevity of the light-hearted joke contrasted with the four-minute length of the final speech. The former lends itself to the news clip, the latter does not.

By selecting the moment that will come to stand for the event that is the debate, the media shape viewers' memories of an event they themselves have experienced, a fact that explains why Ford was the perceived winner of the "Poland" debate until the media defined the Poland remark as a gaffe and replayed it to the point that it was more memorable than any other moment.

This reductive function of the media places a new requirement on political speakers. The speaker able to offer irresistible characterizing statements that synopsize will see those blessed by the media as the characterizing moment of the event. Speakers who do not craft these statements carefully will hear themselves indicted by their own words. Richard Nixon's declaration that "I am not a crook," Spiro Agnew's observation that if you've seen one slum, you've seen them all, George Romney's claim that he had been brainwashed, and Goldwater's pronouncement that extremism in the defense of liberty is no vice are illustrative.

Both vice president Spiro Agnew and presidential nominee Barry Goldwater were cursed by their talent for coining memorable phrases. Goldwater's contributions to his opponents' repertoire included "Sometimes I think this country would be better off if we could just saw off the Eastern seaboard and let it float out to sea." Had Goldwater lacked this talent, his chances in the 1964 election would have improved greatly, for it was of the raw stuff of those statements that his opponents in the primaries and the general election fashioned their indictments of him.

A speaker can increase the chances that a statement will not become the clip from which a news story is built by muddling its syntax and increasing the length of sentences so that the idea cannot be edited into a brief clip without eliminating part of a sentence. One reason Ronald Reagan's 1976 statement that he would consider the use of troops in Rhodesia did his campaign little damage was that the idea was not expressed in an easily edited unit of thought.

As I noted earlier, the reductive nature of news and the lack of public access to entire political speeches means that the essential coherence of a politician's discourse is less likely now to be assessed by press or public than it once was. Knight-Ridder reporter Frank Greves reports, for example, that the incoherence of one of Reagan's statements during the 1984 primaries was not the subject of news coverage because without taking an inordinate amount of broadcast time or print space one could not document the absence of coherence.[58]

The speaker who is able to reduce situations and issues to synoptic statements, as Jesse Jackson repeatedly did in the primary debates of 1984, exercises the power that comes from helping to shape the media's definition of key events. The speaker unable to do this will cede control of the event to those who can or to the media. The capsulizing phrase or statement has always played a role in eloquent speeches; one of the facts that differentiates present from past is that that role is now central.

Television's audiovisual nature has produced a second profound change in the parts that stand for the whole discourse or event. Because visual images are more quickly comprehended and more readily retained than verbal ones, increasingly it is what television news elects to show visually, not what it says verbally, that stands for the events it reports. Consequently, as noted in an earlier chapter, we are now more likely to recall events in the snapshots into which television framed them than we are from the words accompanying those snapshots.

The centrality of the visual image to televised news has been the subject of much scholarly speculation. Some hold that a story unaccompanied by film or videotape is less likely to receive any air time than one of comparable news value that lends itself to visual amplification. These scholars also contend that the length of time devoted to a story is in part a function of the sorts of visual material in it.[59] Ordinary language also reflects the dominance of television's visual messages. We do not speak of hearing television but of watching it.

Humans are about to set foot on the moon for the first time. The synoptic visual-verbal message would have been diminished by speechmaking in any traditional sense. As the world watched that first step, Neil Armstrong's words "That's one small step for man, one giant leap for mankind" were all that needed to be said.

The ability to create such moments within a speech is now more important to a politician's survival than the capacity to forge an artful speech that sustains an important argument. The application of the standards set by this definition explains why Congresswoman Barbara

Jordan's otherwise ordinary convention speech of 1976 was widely regarded as eloquent. For the first time in history a black woman keynoted a national major party convention. In the moment made eloquent by its fusion of speaker, speech, and occasion, she noted that "My presence here is one additional bit of evidence that the American Dream need not forever be deferred." Similarly, the address in which Lyndon Johnson urged passage of his civil rights package is remembered not for the lines of argument that impelled his claims but rather for the image of a Southerner standing before the Congress he had once led invoking the phrase that stood for the civil rights movement, "We Shall Overcome." Likewise, what we recall of Kennedy's most eloquent presidential address is the image of a U. S. president saying "'Ich bin ein Berliner'—Let them come to Berlin" before a huge West German audience pressing against the Berlin Wall.

Such moments often replace speeches. Pope John Paul II communicates reconciliation between Christians and Jews and our collective repentence for the horrors of the Holocaust by kneeling before a death wall at Auschwitz, with two former prisoners in their Auschwitz uniforms at his side. Two black athletes protest racism and assert their identification with the black power movement by clenched fists at an Olympic Awards ceremony. Speech in such settings would dilute the power of the nonverbal message being telegraphed to audiences, regardless of their native language, throughout the world.

Where in the past the eloquent person who chose the best from among the available means of persuasion had recourse to only verbal means, now eloquent speakers must bring a command of the stage and the dramas that can be played out on that stage. They must understand when the synoptic visual-verbal statement should be encased and when it should constitute the entire message.

What these visuals transmitted by the media reveal is the extent to which traditional argument—with its complement of data, warrant, and claims—has been replaced in American political discourse by staged dramatization of images that identify the politicians with us and associate them with images we approve or disapprove of.

In those moments in which comparable phrases and pictures merge, facets of the old and new mesh. So, for example, when, in September 1987, Pope John Paul II embraced an AIDS-stricken child and held the hand of an adult victim as he comforted him, the gestures established what words could only assert: that he would and that we should act compassionately toward even those suffering a dread disease. In a climate in which the quarantining of AIDS sufferers was being debated, victims were being denied access to jobs and health care, and school-age hemophiliacs were being shunned in the classroom, this was a dramatic display of caring.

By using both words and actions, Pope John Paul II increased the memorability of the message digested in the statement "God loves you all, without distinction, without limit." The same occurred when John Kennedy proclaimed "Let them come to Berlin."

The scope of the dramatic picture is narrow, however. If limited to the visual, how would Webster have repudiated the position of Hayne? How could the modern presidents subtly have shown that they and we had learned the lesson of Wilson's failed war? A visual symbol can associate one person, John Kennedy, for example, with a place, as it did when he spoke at Berlin, but the exact nature of the message he wished to convey is clear only in the synoptic phrase "Ich bin ein Berliner." And only words can ally his pride in Berlin's freedom with the pride of the Romans who said "Civis Romanus Sum."

In general, visual dramatization can increase the immediacy and resonance of a synoptic phrase but rarely can stand as an effective argument in its own right. Sacrificed in the move to show without telling is the capacity to redeem, redefine, contravene, and extend basic premises. Most often the visual moment is an assertion.

Because we lack a grammar to test whether a visual assertion can function as argument, we are particularly vulnerable to its use as a substitute for the reasoned invitation to judgment. The next chapter will explore the nature and prevalence of such pictures in the Reagan presidency.

Not only can the visual symbol function fraudulently as evidence but, by rendering suspect claims unsusceptible to rebuttal, it can pose a second hazard to the body politic. Unless the viewer is a sophisticated critic of the visual, an incumbent president can wield the dramatic moment so dexterously that its claims are difficult to undercut or rebut.

The moment repeated most often in the Nixon campaign of 1972 is drawn from the peroration of his speech to the Russian people delivered in Russia in May of that year. Nixon recalls placing a wreath at the memorial to the Russian war dead. There Nixon sees a monument to a young girl who died in the siege of Leningrad. Her name is Tanya. Aware that showing the cemetary, the wreath-laying, and a picture of Tanya will impress the image on the audience more forcefully than a shot of Nixon speaking, the advertisers use Nixon's words as an oral caption for the snapshots created by the event itself. The visual associations identify Nixon as a compassionate humanitarian who has opened a dialogue with Russia in the interests of peace for all the world's children. We experience Nixon experiencing the event. The synoptic image created by the fusion of words and pictures stands as a rebuttal to the widely held public belief that Nixon is a cold person. A person who would feel what we are told by Nixon that he is feeling is not the sort of person who would sustain the war in Vietnam for personal ends, as McGovern claims. McGovern is pitting words against our personal experience of Nixon experiencing the moment of identification with the children of the world through Tanya. In that contest, words cannot win.

When speakers used words to paint pictures in the past they did so knowing that such pictures can be profoundly moving. The pictures that politicians and the news media show us confirm that theory by being more moving than words alone could be. These digestive fusions of sight and sound are mere shards of political eloquence. Where in the past eloquence brought together "natural genius, greatness or importance of idea and circumstance, power of mind or intellectual quality of thought, and special activity of imagination and emotion incarnated in fine and appropriate language,"[60] in the last decades of the twentieth century its offspring is satisfied with synopsizing an important sentiment in memorable visual and verbal form on an appropriate stage so that it can be telegraphed to the national audience by the news media. The moving synoptic moment has replaced the eloquent speech.

6

Dramatizing and Storytelling

Ronald Reagan's adversaries, allies, and admirers agree that he is an effective communicator. Yet few consider him eloquent. Nowhere in the Reagan corpus is there a speech to rival FDR's first inaugural, Kennedy's speech in Berlin, or Johnson's speech to the Congress on civil rights. Nor are there passages that have come to speak his presidency as "nothing to fear but fear" and "Ask not what your country can do for you . . ." defined the presidencies of Roosevelt and Kennedy.

From Reagan's first inaugural, we remember his evocation of the national monuments as the cameras focused on the Washington, Jefferson, and Lincoln memorials. The words that formed the subscript have not lodged in memory. Likewise, we recall that by reading her words, Reagan captured a young woman's sentiments both about her father and about Normandy and at the same time paid tribute to the Normandy veterans, some present, and some, like the woman's father, absent. Words spoken in Reagan's State of the Union addresses do not linger; in place of them we remember Reagan's parade of heroes. Reagan's rhetoric invited us to honor a young man who dove into the freezing Potomac to save an airline crash victim, a soldier who risked his life to save others in the Grenadian incursion, a Vietnamese refugee who as a West Point cadet had earned academic honors, an elderly black woman who had devoted her life to caring for the children of drug addicts, a young girl who saved another child, and a young man whose science project was incinerated with the space shuttle Challenger but who, nonetheless, will pursue his love of science. More readily than the words Reagan spoke of them, we remember each person standing to applause in the House gallery.

Reagan's success as a communicator is attributable to his understanding of the medium that more than any other dominates our lives. The notion that Reagan is to television what FDR was to radio is a commonplace but one that camouflages an identifiable amalgam of skills that, in contemporary politics, gave Reagan his rhetorical edge. To a visual digestive medium, Reagan brings a talent for creating both verbal and nonverbal synoptic vignettes that capture his central claims. Better than any modern president, Reagan translated words into memorable televisual pictures. Where the next chapter describes Reagan's skillful use of what is heard, this centers on what is seen on television. Reagan's visual sense complements the conversational, intimate style through which he conveys a consistent public sense of himself and speaks through television in its own natural language.

Reagan's talent for synopsizing ideas in memorable pictures shows itself in four ways: (1) in his selection of props to illustrate his speeches; (2) in his ability to personify his central themes in the lives of ordinary citizens; (3) in his creativity in commandeering visual experiences we share; and (4) in his knack for narrative. By dramatizing and digesting, Reagan shows and tells in the visual bites television cameras crave. By evoking common visual experiences and reducing complex issues to dramatic narratives, Reagan uses an oral medium, speech, particularly speech on radio, to simulate our experience of an audiovisual medium, television. These four moves have an additional advantage: each, in and of itself, increases memorability.

Use of Televisual Props and Sets

Reagan is to television what corned beef is to rye. In his first rhetorical act as president Reagan demonstrated his fluency in the grammar and syntax of television. "This is the first time in our history that this ceremony has been held, as you've been told, on this West front of the Capitol," he said. That location enables Reagan to use television to underscore the central claim of his address, that heroism is both part of America's past and of her future. As he speaks of the national monuments, the cameras will lovingly transmit them to the living rooms of America. "Standing here, one faces a magnificent vista, opening up on this city's special beauty and history. At the end of this open mall are those shrines to the giants on whose shoulders we stand."

Presidential inaugurals commonly allude to or quote Washington,

Jefferson, Lincoln, or the Declaration of Independence. But Reagan is
the first to realize that he can render such allusions memorable by em-
bodying them in the nation's most famous landmarks. Where other
presidents used words to assert a connection with the venerated past,
Reagan invites the cameras visually to meld his presidency into those
of his great predecessors. He will show as well as tell. He will visually
associate as well as assert. "Directly in front of me, the monument to a
monumental man, George Washington, father of our country. A man
of humility who came to greatness reluctantly." (To add "is" to the first
phrase is to invest it with a patronizing tone. We know the Washington
monument is there; we don't need Reagan to tell us that. The absence
of the verb signals that this is a meditation, not a civics lesson.) Reagan
continues, "He led America out of revolutionary victory into infant nationhood. Off to one side, the stately memorial to Thomas Jefferson.
The Declaration of Independence flames with his eloquence. And then,
beyond the Reflecting Pool, the dignified columns of the Lincoln Memorial."

Continuing with the associative argument, Reagan weaves the theme
of the inaugural into the pictures the camera is capturing. "Beyond
those monuments to heroism is the Potomac River, and on the far shore
the sloping hills of Arlington National Cemetery, with its row upon row
of simple white markers bearing crosses or Stars of David." These images too illustrate his claim. "They add up to only a tiny fraction of the
price that has been paid for freedom. Each one of those markers is a
monument to the kind of hero I spoke of earlier."

Now comes the roll call with which the country identifies the victories
of its past. "Their lives ended in places called Belleau Wood, The Ar-
gonne, Omaha Beach, Salerno, and halfway around the world on
Guadalcanal, Tarawa, Pork Chop Hill, the Chosin Reservoir, and in a
hundred rice paddies and jungles of a place called Vietnam." Having
roused our disposition to assent by visually and verbally invoking one
noncontroversial symbol after another (e.g., Washington, Jefferson,
Lincoln, the Declaration of Independence, the cemetery, and a litany
of battles), Reagan rehabilitates the Vietnam war by including it. Relying on television's irresistible impulse to show and capitalizing on its
disposition to argue by visual association, Reagan has transformed a
body of revered national symbols into an extended visual aid. The panorama invites our respect for the founders, freedom, heroism, and the
Vietnam war. At the same time, these visual symbols visually bracket
his speech, functioning as the set on which he introduces his presidency.

A command of television is revealed as well in the language Reagan

speaks. Since the first student put quill to parchment, academic custodians of the language both have favored pupils who wrote in complete
sentences and feared for the future of those who captured their world
in elliptical phrases. By suppressing verbs not needed to make oral sense
of his ideas, Reagan risked a ruler to the wrist from those who think in
the language of the printed page. Those whose verbal reflexes were
shaped by television will neither mind nor notice. Reagan uses a style
we have learned from television. This is the abbreviated style in which
reporters and news anchors show and tell. He substitutes visual majesty
for the elevated language most inaugurals use to capture the momen-
tousness of the occasion.

Personifying Themes

Reagan is aware that he employs personification. "Mr. Rodriguez lives,"
Reagan told an audience in Texas, "a personification of courage and
inspiration to us all, and the holder of the highest award that we can
give, the Congressional Medal of Honor" (May 5, 1983). In Reagan's
rhetoric, personification abounds.

In his State of the Union messages, Reagan repeatedly created a support cast that included the members of the Court and of Congress as
well as "heroes" of his own choosing. By eulogizing flesh and blood
heroes, Reagan personifies his inaugural's claim that our nation is
teeming with heroism. "Some days when life seems hard," Reagan observed in one such annual message, "and we reach for values to sustain
us, or a friend to help us, we find a person who reminds us what it
means to be an American."

In the 1982 address to Congress that reminder took the form of
Lenny Skutnik, the young man who dove into the Potomac to save the
life of a survivor of an air crash, and Senator Jeremiah Denton, a former prisoner of war in Vietnam. Elsewhere it assumed the form of
"Sgt. Stephen Trujillo, a medic in the 2nd Ranger Battalion, 75th in-
fantry" who "was in the first helicopter to land at the compound held
by Cuban forces on Grenada. He saw three other helicopters crash."

The actions for which we honor Trujillo are noncontroversial. Rather
than killing the supposed enemy, he rescued his friends. "Despite the
imminent explosion of the burning aircraft, he never hesitated. He ran
across 25 yards of open terrain through enemy fire to rescue wounded
soldiers. He directed two other medics, administered first aid and returned again and again to the crash site to carry his wounded friends
to safety." Only an uncaring brute would fail to applaud such heroism.

Sergeant Trujillo embodies the theme of Reagan's first inaugural. As Congress and the American people applaud the soldier's heroism, Reagan transforms that approval into an endorsement of his intervention in Grenada. By so doing, the president demonstrates that, better than any other politician on the national stage, he understands the power of television to argue visually in ways that defy traditional evidence. (Courtesy Pete Souza, The White House)

Aware that their constituents are watching, Democrats and Republicans alike applaud.

The Democrats are about to learn that Reagan can quote such heroism for his purpose. In his next breath, he adds "Sgt. Trujillo, you and your fellow servicemen and women not only saved innocent lives, you set a nation free. You inspire us as a force for freedom, not for despotism, and yes, for peace, not conquest. God bless you." Just as those who were savoring the symbolism, the monuments, the national cemetery, and the famous battles found that the Vietnam war had slipped into the sanctuary, so too the Democrats discover that their applause for Trujillo's bravery has been transformed by Reagan into approval of the Grenadan "mission." Those who indicted the Grenadan "peace mission" as an "invasion" have been trapped on a set of Reagan's staging. In the digestive terms discussed in the last chapter, Reagan has reduced the "incursion" to the person of Trujillo and set that person as a character worthy of bipartisan, national applause. No imaginable words could have elicited a comparable Democratic response.

In his 1986 State of the Union address, Reagan enticed the Congress into approving his implication that it, not he, bore the blame for the unbalanced budget. "Now, Mr. Speaker," he said to House Speaker Tip O'Neill who would be retiring at the end of the year, "you know, I know, and the American people know—the federal budget system is broken; it doesn't work. Before we leave this city, let's you and I work together to fix it." Congress applauded. Reagan added: "And then we can finally give the American people a balanced budget." "I'm for that," said House Speaker Tip O'Neill softly from his seat behind Reagan.[1] Of course, O'Neill's words, which carried the implication that "we've been willing all along," were unheard by television's audience. Reagan's move "was classic" observed O'Neill's administrative assistant Christopher Matthews. "Reagan suggests that the government is the Congress and he is a citizen politician. He is thé people's ombudsman, their spokesman. The responsibility for the deficits belongs in the Congress. When he called upon the Speaker to do something about the deficit he wasn't saying that his own policies had quadrupled the deficit in five years. He was simply putting responsibility on the shoulders of the Speaker as he does when he holds rallies against the deficits which he has done twice on the Capitol grounds."

The Democrats in Congress lost as well in their choreographed response to a Reagan claim in his 1983 State of the Union address. In reply to Reagan's statement that "We who are in government must take the lead in restoring the economy," the Democrats in unison stood to applaud. They were trying, says Matthews, to make the point that it was his responsibility too.

But Reagan turned the tables. "He did a Jack Benny pause," Matthews recalls, and said, "And here all that time, I thought you were reading the paper." The members of Congress, their copies of his advance text in their hands, laughed. "All the members thought he meant reading the script along with him which is a reasonable thing to be doing," Matthews recalls. "At home everybody thought they were a bunch of Claghorns with their feet up on the desks reading the newspaper. He was able to portray the Congress as politicians and incumbents and himself as the American voice."

In his 1985 State of the Union address, Reagan added to his pantheon of heroes West Point cadet and Vietnamese refugee Jean Nguyen

In his 1986 State of the Union message, Ronald Reagan transformed his request for cooperation from Speaker O'Neill and the Congress into an implied claim that the Congress, not the president, bore primary responsibility for the large budget deficit. (Courtesy Pete Souza, The White House)

and founder of a home for the infants of drug-addicted mothers, Clara Hale. By applauding Nguyen, the Congress tacitly acknowledges the value of U.S. participation in the Vietnam war; she did after all escape from Vietnam with her family. At the same time, her success at West

Point hints that our failure to win in Vietnam may have deprived others there of the opportunity to make the kind of contribution that Nguyen is making.

By applauding Hale, the Congress approves Reagan's belief that without federal intervention, individuals can improve society. As the applause rises, Reagan smiles at Hale; returning his smile, Hale mouths a "Thank you" to Reagan. In that juxtaposition of images, Reagan has challenged the widespread belief that his programs disadvantage blacks. Reagan is using the grammar of television to assert what words could not credibly say and to secure visual signs of bipartisan approval of those questionable claims.

Magnifying the effectiveness of the appearance of Skutnik, Hale, and Nguyen is our ability to elaborate the story Reagan tells about each. The nation had watched mesmerized as, through the wonders of videotape replay, Skutnik dove again and again into the freezing Potomac. Subsequently, in newspaper, radio, and TV interviews, he recounted his experience. As Reagan remembers Skutnik's heroism we recall the images of it that television has impressed in our memory. We recall too the horror and helplessness we experienced as one rescue attempt after another proved futile or failed. On a day filled with tragedy. Skutnik's success provided a rallying point. Remembering the relief we felt on learning that the stewardess and Skutnik had both survived, we join in Congress' applause. Reagan has created a communal moment of thanksgiving that we otherwise would not have been able to experience. Regardless of party or political persuasion, we are grateful to Reagan, for he has vivified a conviction we dearly desire to hold as a truth. For Reagan, Skutnik demonstrates that heroes survive in America; at the same time, Skutnik justified Faulkner's conviction that "man will not merely endure; he will prevail."

Although neither Hale nor Nguyen had received the amount of national coverage earlier given Skutnik, both had previously told their stories in the national media. Nguyen appeared on the January 24 segment of CBS' "An American Portrait," in a sixty-second vignette. Hale was the subject of an article in a national weekly. These contexts enrich our experience of the honor Reagan pays them.

The power of Reagan's appeal was reflected in a comment made by David Johnson, executive director of the Democratic Senatorial Campaign Committee.[2] "Of course he was using them to demonstrate a point, and the point was the one he wanted to make and he's the president and a member of the opposition party and all that. I also felt all that, but the fact of the matter is the reaction I had was the one he wanted. I was proud of them."

Nor does it seem to matter that Reagan does not always have his stories straight. Martin Treptow, the hero enshrined in the national consciousness by Reagan's first inaugural, had not died under the circumstances described by Reagan. Neither was he buried beneath one of the televisual white crosses in National Cemetery. Instead, reporters located his grave in Indiana. But by then Treptow had become a legend, the specifics of his real life and death overshadowed by the meaning they had been assigned.

By arriving in Washington in a fur coat, Clara Hale frayed the image Reagan had hoped she would project. Riding to the State of the Union address in a limousine didn't help either. "We wished it would all go away," said a White House aide.[3] He needn't have worried. Such facts are the fetish of print reporters who, in the main, are unread by the masses who saw the symbolism Reagan wanted in the speech.

Evoking Common Visual Experience

So dextrous is Reagan's use of the grammar of television that it seems reasonable to conclude that it is deliberate. Evidence for this conclusion comes from his address to the nation announcing the formation of a new multinational force in Lebanon (September 20, 1982). There he argues in effect that his actions are justified not by what we have read or heard but by what we have seen. The visual evidence conveyed by television eliminates the need for additional words. "The scenes that the whole world witnessed this past weekend were among the most heartrending in the long nightmare of Lebanon's agony. Millions of us have seen pictures of the Palestinian victims of this tragedy. There is little that words can add, but there are actions we can and must take to bring that nightmare to an end. It's not enough for us to view this as some remote event in which we, ourselves, are not involved."

Those sentences could serve as the epitaph of traditional eloquence. When visual images can communicate meaning instantaneously to individuals of different languages and faiths around the world, the function of words changes. In such a world, words contextualize pictures and specify desirable or practical courses of ensuing action.

Interestingly, the act of interpreting these pictures calls forth a passage as formal and powerful as any in Reagan's speeches. "For the criminals who did this deed, no punishment is enough to remove the blot of their crime. But for the rest of us, there are things that we can learn and things that we must do. The people of Lebanon must have learned that the cycle of massacre upon massacre must end. Children are not avenged by the murder of other children. Israel must have learned that there is no way it can impose its own solutions on hatreds as deep and bitter as those that produced this tragedy."

Reagan's fear that we will view this as a "remote event in which we, ourselves, are not involved" hints at the liability in arguing televisually. Although neither side can yet make a compelling case, some scholars fear that much of the nonvoting electorate satisfies its need for political involvement by participating in politics vicariously.

Since the democratic ideal dictates that the president not act without justifying his action publicly, in a televisual world presidential words will link pictures to proposed action. This is the move Reagan makes in this speech.

Whenever possible, Reagan builds his arguments from a visual scene that he and the nation recently have experienced. So, for example, the president opened his November 22, 1982, address to the nation on strategic arms reduction by saying, "The week before last was an especially moving one here in Washington. The Vietnam veterans finally came home once and for all to America's heart. They were welcomed with tears, with pride, and with a monument to their great sacrifice. Many of their names, like those of our Republic's greatest citizens, are now engraved in stone in this city that belongs to all of us. On behalf of the Nation, let me again thank the Vietnam veterans from the bottom of my heart for their courageous service to America.

"Seeing those moving scenes, I know mothers of a new generation must have worried about their children and about peace. And that's what I'd like to talk to you about tonight—the future of our children in a world where peace is made uneasy by the presence of nuclear weapons" *(emphasis added).*

To refresh our memory of them and refashion their meaning, Reagan often evokes televised images on radio. In his address of April 23, 1983, he adds to these functions a third. Sixteen Americans have been killed in a terrorist attack on the U.S. Embassy in Beirut. Some critics question whether the presence of U.S. forces there is necessary. Others indict the Reagan administration for inadequately safeguarding the compound.

Reagan must displace these indictments that have been distilled in the pictures of an embassy reduced to rubble. He acknowledges the existence of such pictures but refuses to refreshen them. "The scenes of senseless tragedy in Beirut this week will remain etched in our memories forever." In place of the rubble, Reagan would position acts of heroism. "But along with the tragedy, there were inspiring moments of heroism." The bombing then has produced evidence to support a key claim of Reagan's inaugural! "We will not forget the pictures of Ambassador Dillon and his staff, Lebanese as well as Americans, many of them swathed in bandages, bravely searching the devastated embassy for their colleagues and for other innocent victims."

"We will not forget the image of young marines gently draping our nation's flag over the broken body of one of their fallen comrades." The language in which we habitually describe death in battle (i.e., fallen comrades) now contextualizes the pictures. "We will not forget their courage and compassion, and we will not forget their willingness to sacrifice even their lives for the service of their country and the cause of peace." Someone who knew nothing of the cause of their death would assume that they had died valiantly fighting for their country. Instead, of course, they died while sleeping in their bunks. A set of images damaging to Reagan is being displaced by another: heroic soldiers willingly sacrificing their lives in place of vulnerable, inadequately protected soldiers dying in their sleep.

When confronted by national tragedy the country turns to the only person who can speak on its behalf. In such circumstances a rhetorically skillful president can assume the role of head of the national family. The explosion of the space shuttle Challenger on January 28, 1986, bonded the country in a common experience. In such moments, we are aware that we are a community, a people, a nation, that to be an American is to share a common grief over deaths incurred in an act undertaken on behalf of the country as a whole. In stores, in schools, as they passed on the sidewalk, strangers stopped to ask others if they had heard.

Words were inadequate to convince those who had not seen the launch. When they turned to their television sets they saw that seventy-four seconds after lift-off, the shuttle carrying six astronauts and school teacher Christa McAuliffe had exploded in a ball of flame.

The trauma of the accident was magnified by the fact that it had a special audience. Because the flight was to have carried a school teacher into space, it was the focus of intensive educational efforts in the schools. A CBS/*New York Times* survey found that forty percent of the school children surveyed had watched the launch on television in their classrooms. This was a generation that had no recollection of the sense of danger that pervaded the earliest flights, one that until recently had invested its allowance in video space games. For this generation space was without menace. Nearly seventy percent identified McAuliffe, whose goal was to "humanize" the space age for children, as being like one of their own teachers.[4] Eighty-four percent of the older children reported that they were upset by the event. "Teenagers were most likely to describe their reaction as 'shock,' younger ones said they felt very sad."[5]

More than eighty percent of the nine to seventeen year olds said that they had spent a lot of time watching the television reports.

What they saw on television were replays of a scene that began familiarly: the shuttle on the launch pad, the shuttle propelling itself from the pad. Expecting to watch until its white trail disappeared into the heavens, viewers saw instead an explosion, the single column of white transformed into a large birdlike shape. Then parts of the Challenger began raining in white streaks from the sky. Throughout, the symbology was wrong. White is a symbol of life and rebirth, not death. Ascent into heaven is supposed to signal redemptive triumph, not tragedy.

As the videotape played and replayed, as one slow-motion remembrance of the tragedy gave way to another, as stop-action photography paused at the moment of explosion, Americans came to understand and accept that the crew was dead, the craft destroyed. The hope that somehow in the next replay the end would change gave way to agonized shock.

A state of national grief set in. Parents and children grieved not simply for the astronauts but for the parts of themselves that had been enraptured, uplifted, and invigorated by the conquest of space. In an era in which the nation had lost its first war and experienced its first presidential resignation, the space program's successful launches had served symbolically to assure us that the United States was still adventurous, resourceful, and a world leader.

The moments in which words fail are precisely the moments in which words are most needed. This complex situation required presidential words of assurance. In a moving nationally televised speech, written by Peggy Noonan, Reagan eulogized the astronauts and glorified the accomplishments of the space program. As head of the national family he consoled the children: "I want to say something to the schoolchildren of America who were watching the live coverage of the shuttle's takeoff. I know it's hard to understand, but sometimes painful things like this happen. It's all part of the process of exploration and discovery. It's all part of taking a chance and expanding man's horizons. The future doesn't belong to the fainthearted. It belongs to the brave. The Challenger crew was pulling us into the future, and we'll continue to follow them."

Challenging Reagan's ability to comfort the nation is the image of the explosion seared by repeated replaying into consciousness. If we recall the day in terms of the exploding shuttle, then it will remain for us a tragedy. If the day is instead to serve as one of rededication, Reagan must instate a more positive image. He does this in the closing words of the speech. "The crew of the space shuttle Challenger hon-

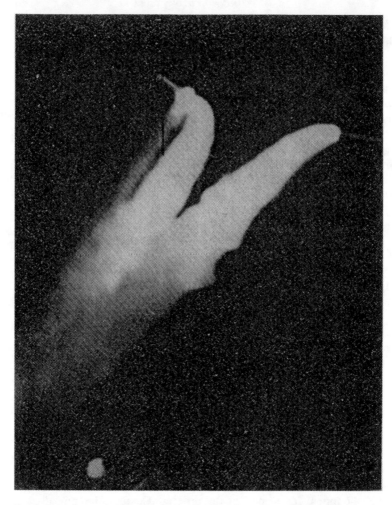

For hours, the nation watched transfixed as in replays the shuttle moved from launch to explosion. The trauma elicited by the nationally televised deaths of the astronauts was great. If the day was condensed in the national mind into the image of the explosion, then it would be memorialized as an unredemptive tragedy. The explosion raised doubts about our technological expertise and our confidence in the future, a future symbolized

in part by our successful space flights. In his speech to the nation on the
catastrophe, Reagan displaced the traumatic image of the incineration of
the craft with that of the astronauts waving goodbye. If this picture could
displace the explosion, then the day could be one of hope and heroism,
not of failure. (Courtesy NASA)

Speaking effectively on television requires an ability both to create the illusion of eye contact with an unseen audience and to converse with a camera. Delivering from a ghosted text requires a skill at speaking someone else's words as if they were your own and investing a script with the illusion of spontaneity. Most televised political speechmaking is built on these minor but not insignificant forms of deception. (Courtesy Mary Anne Fackelman-Miner, The White House)

ored us by the manner in which they lived their lives. We will never forget them nor the last time we saw them—this morning—as they prepared for their journey and waved goodbye, and slipped the surly bonds of Earth to touch the face of God." When NBC replayed Reagan's speech in prime time that evening, the picture of the waving astronauts was shown throughout this final paragraph. By evoking this image, Reagan invites us to displace the one of tragedy that has played and replayed throughout the day. Reagan's final words immortalize the astronauts in the words from a poem "High Flight" by John Gillespie Magee, Jr., an American flier killed while serving in the Royal Canadian Air Force in 1941.

Reagan has an easier task in his radio address to the flood victims in Monroe, Louisiana (January 2, 1983). There he transforms volunteers into personifications of an important civic virtue. They are to this radio address what Skutnik was to the televised State of the Union address. Reagan says, "The entire nation has watched the volunteers who have been filling and stacking sand bags. You exemplify the concept of neighbor helping neighbor, which is the very basis of our way of life."

The picture evoked in his radio address on domestic issues serves a more sophisticated and subtle function. Reagan eulogizes a man made famous by a photograph (January 22, 1983): "A week ago, Graham Washington Jackson, an ex-Navy musician, died in Atlanta at the age of seventy-nine. You probably don't recognize his name, but his face became familiar to millions of Americans when President Roosevelt died in Warm Springs, Georgia, in 1945. There's a very famous, very moving photo of Chief Petty Officer Jackson, tears streaming down his face while he played 'Going Home' on his accordian as FDR's body was borne away by train to Washington."

The picture Reagan calls to mind reinforces the assertion offered in the televised nonverbal exchange between Reagan and Clara Hale: Reagan understands and is responsive to the concerns of blacks. The eulogy for Jackson also places Reagan above petty politics or partisanship. After all, Jackson is immortalized for sorrowing over the death of a revered Democratic president. Jackson's other association with the presidency occurred in 1976 when he played the accordian at the Warm Springs ceremonies launching the general election campaign of Jimmy Carter. Without offering a scintilla of evidence, Reagan subtly identifies with blacks. By tapping a memorable moment and speaking a few kind words, Reagan reminds us of our common humanity, a humanity even dog-driven Democrats share for this brief moment with Ronald Reagan.

Reagan's tendency to synopsize issues in snapshots is evident as well in his favorite first-term rejoinder to criticism about his reluctance to negotiate arms limitation. "I've said before," he noted at a press conference on March 29, 1983, "I think it was summed up in a cartoon about the late Leonid Brezhnev when he was cartooned in one of your publications. The cartoonist had him speaking to a Russian general, and he said, 'I liked the arms race better when we were the only ones in it.' I think that you have to if you're going to negotiate you have to have some strength on your side."

In a meeting with news photographers, Reagan revealed the importance he attaches to the synoptic snapshot. "On a newspaper or a magazine page," he said, "I always look àt your work first, and so does everyone else. It's that still photo that captures the essence of the moment and sticks in our memory" (May 18, 1983). Reagan's use of words to create and evoke pictures suggests that one of his goals as a speaker is to capture the essence of the moment and make it stick in memory.

On a number of occasions, Reagan seems to be saying that this is his goal. "You know in Washington there's a very famous statue of our soldiers raising the flag at Iwo Jima," he told the flood victims in his radio address. "Well, maybe the sight of volunteers keeping back the force of river wafers by lifting sandbags would make another dramatic statue symbolizing America's character." Commenting on the importance of the photo of Jackson, Reagan notes that "Mr. Jackson symbolized the grief of the Nation back in 1945." For Reagan, Jackson will symbolize the fact that we are part of a common family.

Reagan's grasp of the grammar of television may well explain the frequency with which he draws evidence from novels and films. Popular novels, TV programs, and movies provide the national audience with communal experience. Reagan may be summoning the classic heroic moments in films or novels for the same reason that he summons our memory of news coverage of the tragedy in Lebanon or the dedication of the Vietnam Veterans Memorial: they created a strong retrievable emotional experience that large numbers share.

Such experiences are the raw stuff of which persuasion can be fashioned. So, for example, in his autobiography, he describes his youth as "one of those rare Huck Finn-Tom Sawyer idylls. There were woods and mysteries, life and death among the small creatures, hunting and fishing; those were days when I learned the real riches of rags."[6] Speaking to the sailors aboard the U.S.S. Constellation (August 20, 1981), Reagan recalled the final scene of a novel by Michener in which an "admiral, standing on the darkened bridge of his carrier, waiting for the pilots who had flown off the carrier's deck. . . . The admiral wondered at their selflessness, standing there alone in the darkness, and then in the book he asked aloud [sic], "Where do we get such men?" Mining a more recent film, Reagan responded to threats to overturn one of his proposals with a line made famous by actor Clint Eastwood in a Dirty Harry film: "Make my day."

As the Eastwood line suggests, appropriating the dialogue of film enables Reagan to say things he could not otherwise utter. Because it is said with a laugh, the Eastwood line telegraphs a tough, defiant posture without simultaneously undercutting Reagan's genial image. Reagan quoted a line by actress Clara Bow to accomplish a similar purpose, setting an otherwise strong statement in a comic frame: "You know, the actress Clara Bow once said of that famous Montana movie star, Gary Cooper—she said, 'When he puts his arms around me I feel like a horse' *(laughter)*. Well, for a conservative President like me to have to put his arms around a multibillion dollar deficit, it's like holding your nose and embracing a pig *(laughter)*. And believe me that budget deficit is as slippery as a greased pig" (August 11, 1982).

Reagan also quotes lines from films and novels that are either too profusely patriotic to be expressed directly by him or too purple for his otherwise plain style. So, for example, at the inaugural ball honoring Congressional Medal of Honor winners, he summarizes a scene from a novel by James Warner Bella. A commanding officer had fallen "mortally wounded." He called "the next in command over, who was to take over. And the lines I've never forgotten. He said to him as he was dying, 'There may be only one time, one moment in your life when you will be called upon to do the nasty thing that has to be done, when you are the only one that can serve your country in that moment.' He said, 'Do it or the taste will be forever ashes in your mouth.' The men you honor tonight have no taste of ashes in their mouths" (January 20, 1981).

Two of Reagan's recollections reveal his appreciation of the power of visual images. When *Birth of a Nation* came to his hometown, his "father simply announced that no member of our family would see that picture, because it was based on the Ku Klux Klan" (February 7, 1983, Question and Answer with local television anchors). In Reagan's next sentence we learn just how much power he ascribes to the visual image. "And to this day," he adds, "I have never seen that great motion picture classic." When asked whether he thinks that the television serial "The Winds of War" will help prevent the defense budget from being cut, Reagan observes that it is a possibility he has considered: "You know, I asked somebody the other day—having looked at a couple of installments of that myself—I said, 'Do you suppose that this could be a help to us' *(laughter)*—'because it reminds us of how blind so much of the world was to the threat that many years ago?'" (February 9, 1983).

On another occasion, film established incontrovertible fact for Reagan. In a speech commemorating the Days of Remembrance of Victims of the Holocaust (April 30, 1981), Reagan stated that he was "horrified" by claims that the Holocaust was invented:

Well, the old cliché that a picture's worth a thousand words—in World War II, not only do we have the survivors to tell us at first hand, but in World War II, I was in the military and assigned to a post where every week, we obtained from every branch of the service all over the world the combat film that was taken by every branch. . . . And I remember April '45. I remember seeing the first film that came in when the war was still on, but our troops had come upon the first camps and had entered those camps. And you saw, unretouched—no way that it could have ever been rehearsed—what they saw, the horror they saw. I felt the pride when, in one of those camps, there was a nearby town, and the people were ordered to come and look at what had been going on, and to see them. And the reaction of horror on their faces was the greatest proof that they had not been conscious of what was happening so near to them.

And that film still, I know, must exist in the military, and there it is, living motion pictures, for anyone to see, and I won't go into the horrible scenes that we saw. But it remains with me as confirmation of our right to rekindle these memories, because we always need to guard against that kind of tyranny and inhumanity.

On March 7, 1983, Reagan issued Proclamation 5024, a statement that designated March 13–19 "National Children and Television Week." The proclamation explains why even as an adult Reagan has avoided *Birth of a Nation* and why he suspects that his political cause will be aided by "Winds of War." It unpacks, as well, the premises that justify the care Reagan takes to speak television's language. Finally, it articulates what Reagan hopes to accomplish in his own use of television. Educing any of these conclusions would be risky if the proclamation simply reported well-established facts about television's influence. What makes it such an intriguing document is its eagerness to credit television with powers far beyond those confirmed by research. The proclamation stated:

Television has the power to shape thoughts, stir emotions, and inspire actions. It teaches, it sells, it entertains, it informs, and it has the capacity to influence powerfully the lives and values of our children. They learn much from television about the world, our society, and their place in it.

Television can communicate values that are consistent with our heritage and traditions and can portray those actions and attitudes that make for better citizens. It also can depict themes that are destructive of those values.

Knack for Narrative

Although his ideas are unoriginal, his language often pedestrian, the structure of his speeches at times haphazard, Reagan uses one form of discourse, the synoptic, dramatic narrative masterfully. He is a skilled storyteller. Better than any modern president, Reagan understands the power of dramatic narrative to create an identity for an audience, to involve the audience, and to bond that audience to him. Like all good storytellers, Reagan understands the importance of invoking sentiments in the audience through use of vivid detail and delivered conviction.

On at least one occasion, each of Reagan's unsuccessful predecessors employed narrative so effectively that the use raises the question: Why could they not duplicate Reagan's performance? The answer comes in the realization that in each instance the evocative narrative grows from their own lives or experience. None was able to step beyond personal experience to make memorable the moments felt by others.

In the conclusion of his 1968 convention address, Nixon translates his biography into an implied assertion that he will try to make America better for those less fortunate than he:

> Tonight, I see the face of a child. He lives in a great city. He is black, or he is white. He is Mexican, Italian, Polish. None of that matters. What matters, he's an American child. That child in that great city is more important than any politician's promise. He is America. He is a poet. He is a scientist, he is a great teacher, he is a proud craftsman. He is everything we ever hoped to be and everything we dare to dream to be. He sleeps the sleep of a child and he dreams the dreams of a child. And yet when he awakens, he awakens to a living nightmare of poverty, neglect, and despair. He fails in school. He ends up on welfare. For him the American system is one that feeds his stomach and starves his soul. It breaks his heart. And in the end it may take his life on some distant battlefield. To millions of children in this rich land, this is their prospect of the future. But this is only part of what I see in America. I see another child tonight. He hears a train go by at night and he dreams of faraway places where he'd like to go. It seems like an impossible dream. But he is helped on his journey through life. A father who had to go to work before he finished the sixth grade, sacrificed everything he had so that his sons could go to college. A gentle, Quaker mother, with a passionate concern for peace, quietly wept when he went to war but she understood why he had to go. A great teacher, a remarkable football coach, an inspirational minister encouraged him on his way. A courageous wife and loyal children stood by him in victory and also defeat. And in his chosen profession of politics, first there were scores, then hundreds, then thousands, and finally millions who worked for his success. And tonight he stands before you—nominated for President of the United States.[7]

For Lyndon Johnson, an effective moment of dramatic narrative occurred in New Orleans during the 1964 campaign. A white South-

erner, Johnson had fought for and signed the Civil Rights Act. In New
Orleans, he broke from his prepared text to take a personal stand on
that volatile issue. "Whatever your views are," he told the crowd, "we
have a Constitution and we have a Bill of Rights, and we have the law
of the land, and two-thirds of the Democrats in the Senate voted for it
and three-fourths of the Republicans. I signed it, I am going to enforce
it, and I am going to observe it, and I think that any man that is worthy
of the high office of President is going to do the same thing."

By Johnson's account, the applause was less than overwhelming. He
concluded with a story about Senator Joe Bailey, reared in Mississippi
but sent to the House and Senate from Texas. Bailey had been telling
Sam Rayburn that the South had a great future if it could develop its
resources. "I wish I felt a little better, Sammy," Bailey told Rayburn. "I
would like to go back to old Mississippi and make them one more Democratic speech. I feel like I have at least one more left in me."

"I looked over the members of the audience," Johnson recalled, "then
gave them the old Senator's final words to Mr. Rayburn on that occasion: 'Poor old Mississippi, they haven't heard a Democratic speech in
thirty years. All they ever hear at election time is "Nigger, Nigger,
Nigger." ' "8

Throughout his national career, Jimmy Carter rose to eloquence most
readily when speaking of his experiences as a Southerner. So, for example, his speech on the civil rights movement delivered at the Martin
Luther King Hospital in Los Angeles during the 1976 campaign is his
finest speech of the campaign. Carter opened his 1980 general election
campaign with another such speech (September 1, 1980). Addressing a
crowd in Tuscumbia, Alabama, Carter said:

> There are still a few in the South, indeed around the country—some I
> heard from today—who practice cowardice and who counsel fear and hatred.
> They marched around the State capitol in Atlanta when I was Governor.
> They said we ought to be afraid of each other, that whites ought to hate
> and be afraid of blacks, and that blacks ought to hate and be afraid of
> whites. And they would persecute those who worship in a different way
> from most of us. As a Southerner, it makes me feel angry when I see them
> with a Confederate battle flag, because I remember Judah P. Benjamin,
> who was Secretary of State of the Confederacy; he was a Jew. And I re-
> member General Pat Cleburne of Arkansas, who died in battle not very
> far from this very spot, and General Beauregard of Louisiana—brave men.
> Both were Catholics, and so were many others who served under that flag.
> And sometimes I see the raising of a cross, and I remember that the One
> who was crucified taught us to have faith, to hope, and not to hate but to
> love one another.
> As the first man from the Deep South in almost 140 years to be Presi-

dent of this nation, I say that these people in white sheets do not understand our region and what it's been through, they do not understand what
our country stands for, they do not understand that the South and all of
America must move forward.[9]

Such moments of powerful collective recollection occurred rarely in
the rhetoric of Carter, Johnson, and Nixon. When they appear, most
are highly personal and have been drawn directly from experience. In
such moments, they seem, in a phrase whose meaning has been lost in
overuse, to be speaking from the heart.

What differentiates Reagan's rhetoric from theirs is the ease with which
he forges such moments from the experiences of others and the consistency with which they recur. For Reagan, dramatic narrative is a rhetorical staple; for his predecessors, it was an exotic dish.

At the annual meeting of the National Alliance of Business (October
5, 1981), Reagan delivered the kind of speech that has become his
trademark. At the core was one of Reagan's central philosophical
premises: "There are hardheaded, no-nonsense measures by which the
private sector can meet those needs of society that the government has
not, can not, or will never be able to fill." Reagan translated that principle into a promise. "With the same energy that Franklin Roosevelt
sought government solutions to problems, we will seek private solutions."

In an age in which television has accustomed us to see as well as hear
political argument, the speech not only created pictures with words, but
also appropriated our recollection of televised or filmed actions. So, for
example, in a move I will discuss later, Reagan recalls Gary Cooper's
description of voluntarism from the movie *Mr. Deeds Goes to Town*. By
so doing, Reagan identifies himself with one of cinema's two most
memorable, plain-spoken, reform-minded, citizen-politicians. Deeds says,
"there will always be leaders and always be followers. It's like the road
out in front of my house. It's on a steep hill. And every day I watch
the cars climbing up. Some go lickety-split up that hill on high; some
have to shift into second; and some sputter and shake and slip back to
the bottom again. Same cars, same gasoline, yet some make it and some
don't. And I say the fellas who can make the hill on high should stop
once in a while and help those who can't."

To argue that rewards come to those who help, Reagan recalls a television interview with a young man sandbagging beachfront homes that
would otherwise be flooded. When asked why he and his friends were
doing it, he responded, "Well, I guess it's the first time we ever felt like
we were needed." That answer, says Reagan, "tells us something so true
about ourselves that it should be printed on a billboard."

Throughout, Reagan links our successful efforts in the past to present ones. "Now, I know there are cynics who dismiss the notion of Americans helping other Americans. They say that I speak of an America that never was and never can be. . . . Have they forgotten the great national efforts before there ever was a thing called 'foreign aid'? The American people organized to help Japan in the great earthquake, famine in India, 'Bundles for Britain.' The spirit is not dead.

"I wish the cynics would visit David and Flaka Fattah in Philadelphia. . . . This one couple did something that all the social welfare and law enforcement agencies had been unable to accomplish. They replaced the gang structure with a family structure. They actually took a gang of sixteen into their home . . . they're establishing what might be called an urban Boys Town."

Each of Reagan's stories argues implicitly for private action, not government intervention. Jose Salcido's wife had died of cancer "leaving him both father and mother of thirteen children. In an accident only the Lord can explain, one day the brakes on his truck didn't hold and he was crushed against a brick wall as he walked in front of the vehicle. The children who had lost their mother now had lost their father. But they were not orphaned." Neighbors, members of their parish, even strangers formed a citizens' committee to raise money to care for the children. Letting the words of others express his thoughts, Reagan reads a letter from one contributor: "This is for the children of Jose Salcido. It is for them to know there are always others who care; that despite personal tragedy, the world is not always the dark place it seems to be; that their father would have wanted for them to go on with courage and strength and still open hearts."

Lest his account of the success of his welfare reforms in California seem self-serving, he summons an event with both a happy and a humorous ending. When he was governor, a woman wrote saying that she had become so dependent on welfare that to retain her welfare status she had even turned down proposals of marriage. When Reagan's reforms went through, she left welfare and moved to Alaska where she had relatives. From Alaska she wrote to say that she had a "good job and that working now had given her a great deal of self-respect, for which she thanked me, and one line that I'll never forget. She said, 'It sure beats daytime television.' "

From this complex of elements, Reagan spins an affirmation of America's past and future greatness. "Americans are needed. They're needed to keep this country true to the tradition of voluntarism that's served us so well. And they're needed to keep America true to her values. In the days following World War II when a war-ravaged world could have slipped back into the Dark Ages, Pope Pius XII said: 'The American people have a genius for great and unselfish deeds; into the hands of America, God has placed an afflicted mankind.' Let those words be true of us today."

Where another president would have constructed this speech on a combination of statistical evidence and exhortation, Reagan built it instead on one story after another of individual initiative. Where another president would have searched for a way to embody his cause in a memorable phrase, Reagan sought instead to place it in memorable pictures. By identifying him with the cause of the needy, a number of the stories established Reagan's compassion and humanity; by illustrating the success of his welfare reforms in California, another underscored his competence and prophesied the success of his initiative at the federal level; by pairing the doubts of his unnamed critics with success stories, the speech insulated his proposal from their attacks. The dramatic accounts demonstrated as well a central theme of Reagan's presidency: the heroism of ordinary people. At the same time, they implied that our future could be as bright as our past. In an electronic age, this type of speech thrives. A synoptic moment can be lifted from practically any paragraph for replay on broadcast news; in an age of television, the speech invites the audience to see as well as hear its central claim.

Reagan's mastery of this form of speech is significant for a second reason. These speeches, which are the staples of his presidency, provide powerful and much needed reassurance that the country and its institutions are resilient, that our country's future is rich, and that we can unashamedly feel patriotism and pride.

Presidents from Johnson through Carter had recognized the country's need for reassuring rhetoric. Their failure to provide it is instructive, for where they faltered Reagan finally would succeed. His success is attributable to his grasp of the ways in which that reassurance can be translated into the concise, dramatic, evocative stories and scenes that in an electronic age substitute for traditional argument.

His predecessors did not fail for want of trying. Johnson pleaded with the public to quiet the criticism of his opponents. "I hope in the days to come that you will just stop, look, and listen as you hear these voices talking about what is wrong with your country, what is wrong with your Government, what is wrong with our men, what mistakes we have made. And ask them if they won't give a little equal time" to point out what is good (July 23, 1966).

LBJ's humor and hyperbolic praise feebly hid his hostility toward his critics in Congress. "Now I have made no secret of the fact that in my opinion there has never been a better Congress. There have been a few times in American history when a President of the United States would ever make a statement like that, though. I am not sure that all of you would want to make a statement like that if you would pick up a paper and see what the Congress says about me sometimes. George Washington, our first President, once warned that his Congress was about 'to form the worst government on earth.'

"Another great President, Theodore Roosevelt, said that he would like to turn sixteen lions loose on his Congress. When someone pointed out that the lions might make a mistake, he replied, 'Not if they stay there long enough' " (July 23, 1966).

Johnson's sermonizing also failed to satisfy, for it told people how he thought they should feel without uttering sentiments capable of summoning those feelings. "Your country is just like your family. If you spend all of your time talking about your wife and your boy and your girl and what they have done wrong and the mistakes that they have made (and you can find plenty that we have all made—none of us are perfect)—why, if you spend all of your time talking about your family that way, it will add to your problems; it won't solve them.

"So rather than be a martyr and start feeling too sorry for yourself, just think about how wonderful it is to be an American; how far we have come; how much we have done; how much better off we are than most of the people of the world."[10]

Where Johnson asserted that we have done much, Reagan would vividly and compellingly recall what we had done; where Johnson asserted that we were better off than others around the world, Reagan would demonstrate our blessings and invite us to join him in gratitude for them; where Johnson commanded audiences to believe, Reagan would beckon them.

From Johnson, Nixon inherited a country divided. "The country I had been elected to lead," he wrote, "had been on the ropes from domestic discord. The cities had been burning and beseiged; the college campuses had become battlegrounds; crime was increasing at an alarming rate; drug abuse and drug addiction were increasing; the military draft cast a disruptive shadow over the lives of young Americans."[11] By the end of his tenure, these problems seemed less incendiary; in their place was a problem Nixon had not anticipated: trauma over presidential betrayal of the public trust.

Nixon too suffered from an inclination to assert rather than evoke confidence in the future. But for him more so than Johnson, appeals for unity were based in the questions: If we are not the best, what will others around the world think of us and how will history judge us?

"Once a people decide that it doesn't matter whether they excel, once they resign themselves to be second best, then they find that they lose in every other way," he observed. "That is the beginning of the end of great civilizations.

"I say to you today: We cannot let that happen to America. Let us see to it that we recognize that this country has become great because people have dedicated themselves to making it the country it is" (July 31, 1971).

Better than Johnson, Nixon understood that the rhetoric of renewal and restoration must build on a high level of audience participation. Where Johnson lectured, Nixon invited positive responses to questions he framed: "The question for America is far more serious than the challenge that we confronted even in the dark days of Pearl Harbor. The question is our spirit. Do we have the spirit? Do we still have the drive? Do we still have the competitive urge to try to make this the best country in the world, to keep it the best country in the world?

"I think we have, and I think you are going out and tell the world that" (August 19, 1971).

Ultimately, however, no amount of discursive dexterity could enable Nixon to stitch together a country whose seams had been shredded by his complicity in Watergate. The unifying appeals themselves soured in his mouth when repeatedly they were used to divert public attention from Watergate. His rhetorical options exhausted, Nixon finally rationalized his resignation by arguing that by leaving the presidency he would help heal the country.

There were moments in Ford's brief term that suggested that he was correct in his assessment that the long national nightmare was over. Ford's credibility was damaged, however, when his pardon of Nixon raised the suspicion that it may have been the price of his presidency. Still, on the country's bicentennial in July 1976, a televised pictorial panorama, including the majestic tall ships and such national symbols as the Liberty Bell, evoked a common sense of national pride that could not be erased even by Ford's halting delivery of the accompanying patriotic words.

Without the benefit of the pictorial backdrop, Ford's later rhetoric could not relight the national fireworks. His campaign advertising conceded his limitations when, as images of that day paraded forth, it substituted a chorus singing "I'm Feeling Good about America" for Ford's Fourth of July speech. Still, Ford tried to revive our memories of that splendid day and to wrap his candidacy up in them. "On the Fourth of July we had a wonderful celebration of America's 200th birthday," he told an audience (September 25, 1976). "We have had a tough two years. We were divided. We have healed those divisions, and America today has a new spirit, a new spirit that has given us the capability to move out of our troubles into brighter skies." This is the rhetorical equivalent of a John Philip Sousa march without instruments. "We've had a wonderful Bicentennial anniversary," he told an audience in Mobile, Alabama (September 26, 1976). The day served as a tonic for Ford. "How many of you felt better on July 4 when we celebrated our 200th birthday? I know I did. I went to Valley Forge; I went to Philadelphia; I went to New York. I had the opportunity to see people of all walks of life in many states just get a new faith in America—a rebuilding, a rekindling of this great, great spirit that made America from 13 poor, struggling colonies 200 years ago to a nation of 215 million builders, people who today—whether they live on the East Coast, the North or the South or the East or the West—we're builders, and we've got that spirit." The spirit proved as evanescent as that last sentence. The pride that had been evoked by the patriotic symbols could not be recalled by Ford. Not even a thousand of his words could call forth one patriotic picture. Where Ford gladdened his scheduler's heart by recounting his itinerary on the Fourth, that report did little to recall our specific memories of the day.

Were Reagan given a comparable opportunity, he would instead have painted vivid word pictures evoking the image and meaning of the ships, the Liberty Bell, and the assembled thousands. During this collective recollection he would have rededicated us to basic principles and prophesied a future worthy of this reconstructed past.

Although malaise was not mentioned in the speech that reporters retrospectively dubbed the "malaise speech," Carter is now widely credited or blamed for adding "national malaise" (a phrase coined by Carter's pollster) to the presidential diagnoses of the country's maladies. He had promised to bring inflation down; it doubled. He had promised to balance the budget; it ballooned. He vowed to restore international faith in our country; on election day 1980, one year after they had been taken captive, American hostages remained imprisoned in Iran. Under his leadership, unemployment refused to ebb.

In the "malaise speech," the author of an autobiography titled *Why Not the Best?* publicly confessed that he had failed us and we him. Ostensibly about energy, the July 15, 1979, speech included an extended self-indictment of and by Carter. "But over those years the subjects of the speeches, the talks, and the press conferences have become increasingly narrow, focused more on what the isolated world of Washington thinks is important. Gradually you have heard more and more about what government thinks or what the government should be doing, and less and less about our nation's hopes, our dreams, and our vision of the future." Surprisingly, the speech does not go on to offer hopes, dreams, or visions.

The words Carter speaks instead are those spoken to him by advisers he assembled to help him evaluate his presidency.

"This from a Southern governor: 'Mr. President, you are not leading this nation—you're just managing the government. . . .' 'Don't talk to us about politics or the mechanics of government, but about an understanding of our common good.' 'If you lead, Mr. President, we will follow.' "

Having cleansed his soul, Carter turned to scrutinize the stained souls of the congregation. "In a nation that was once proud of hard work, strong families, close knit communities, and our faith in God, too many of us now tend to worship self-indulgence and consumption. Human identity is no longer defined by what one does, but by what one owns. But we've discovered that owning things and consuming things does not satisfy our longing for meaning. We've learned that piling up goods cannot fill the emptiness of lives which have no confidence of purpose."

The president from Plains accounts for the disenchantment of the public by noting: "We were sure that ours was a nation of the ballot, not the bullet, until the murders of John Kennedy and Robert Kennedy and Martin Luther King, Jr. We were taught that our armies were always invincible and our causes were always just, only to suffer the agony of Vietnam. We respected the Presidency as a place of honor until the shock of Watergate."

Where a man of the cloth might have shouted "Repent!" and set forth a regimen of corporal and spiritual works of mercy, Carter instead catalogues the "symptoms of this crisis of the American spirit," symptoms that include public belief that the next five years will be worse than the last, a decline in the productivity of American workers, a drop in personal savings and massive unwillingness to vote.

The speech glossed gloom with doom. "As you know, there is a growing disrespect for government and for churches and for schools, the news media, and other institutions," he said. Although the invited conclusion was too obvious to require words, Carter could not resist pronouncing it. "This is not a message of happiness or reassurance, but it is the truth and it is a warning." Just below the surface of Carter's populist "a government as good as its people" rhetoric lurked an aggravating impulse to preach.

After rehearsing our collective failings, Carter's path of restoration is singularly unsatisfying. The sides of the scale do not balance. His solutions are reminiscent of Lyndon Johnson's. Carter asks us to renew our faith "in each other, in our ability to govern ourselves." What is his role in this renewal? The strength "we need will not come from the White House but from every house in America." He also asks that we say nice things. "Whenever you have a chance, say something good about our country. With God's help and for the sake of our nation, it is time for us to join hands in America. Let us commit ourselves together to a rebirth of the American spirit. Working together with our common faith, we cannot fail." Almost a million Americans heard the speech that Carter considered one of his best.[12] Ronald Reagan's successful 1980 candidacy was constructed as a rebuttal to its claims about the American people. Judiciously, Reagan denied the speech's descriptions of the American people while reinforcing the indictments Carter had levied against himself.

By the end of the Carter presidency, "A sense of despair, of impotence, of frustration, permeated the political process," recalls *Washington Post* columnist Haynes Johnson.[13] "After a succession of failed presidencies, a feeling of instability had begun to surround the office. The range and complexity of problems appeared beyond the capacity of any person who became president."

By January 1986, things had changed. "Almost by sheer will of personality, by the effortless exuding of confidence, Reagan has reversed much of that feeling. The presidency is a stronger office today because of him." Indeed, Reagan overwhelmingly had won reelection in 1984 campaigning on the theme America's back and standing tall. So, the columnist tells Reagan, "some of us may passionately believe certain of your doses to be dangerous. Certainly we don't think you have a cure for all that ails us. But that doesn't stop us from admiring the way you administer your medicine. And when it comes to personal leadership qualities, whatever brand it is you bear ought to be patented as a national treasure." I will argue that the gold in this national treasure is, in part, a talent for using television to tell stories.

From Johnson through Carter, Reagan's predecessors recognized that the country required reassurances but lacked the temperament or talent to fashion them. The delivery of Ford and Carter was so poor, the conviction with which they conveyed scripted messages so minimal, that had their messages matched the country's need, they still might have foundered.

Classical rhetorical theorists recognized the role of public discourse in sustaining the state. This discourse, called epideictic by Aristotle, rehearsed the values of the citizenry, recalled the principles from which the government operated, and rededicated the people to the values and principles of the state. Pericles' funeral oration is a classic piece of epideictic as is the Gettysburg Address. Some occasions still inspire such ceremonial speech. From Reagan's predecessors, we heard it on the Fourth of July, Veterans' Day and in inaugural addresses. For Reagan, however, it is stock in trade.

By conserving and revitalizing, epideictic rhetoric sustains the communal sense of identity. In ages past oral epic poetry served this epideictic function; by transmitting from generation to generation the heroic tales of the past it ensured "a victory of memory over oblivion."[14] So, for example, the putative speaker in "The Song of Roland," a poem of the Middle Ages, says that the song is an "example." An "example" "revitalizes a moment in time and space—the instance of performance —with a therapeutic truth,. a meaning," that "re-presents itself each time anew through the phonic substance of speech."[15] An observer noted the effect of oral epic discourse on an audience in the Middle Ages:

> We call a *chanson de geste* that in which the deeds of heroes and of our ancient fathers are recited, such as the lives and martyrdoms of saints and the adversities that beset men of old for the Faith and for truth. . . . Moreover, this song must be ministered to the old people, to the laboring folk and to those of humble condition, so that by hearing miseries and calamities of others they may bear more easily their own and so that their own travails may become lighter. And thus this song brings about the conservation *(conservatio)* of the whole community.[16]

What the country required of its recent presidents was epideictic capable of vivifying the deeds of our ancient fathers and heroes and rendering them relevant to a contemporary audience. Such rhetoric would enable the American people once and for all to put behind them Vietnam, Watergate, Iran, the oil embargo, and a series of failed presidencies. Before attempting such discourse, a president might have been inclined to ask: "Are there commonly held values that have survived these divisive, depressing events? How can rhetoric be used to transcend our past differences, blunt the lingering bitterness, and propose a credible vision of the country's future and our future as a people?"

History provides a useful answer. Following the Civil War, the country was sundered as it had not been before and has not been since. Brother had fought brother. The South had been beaten into submission. Could rhetoric facilitate reconciliation in an atmosphere in which some were eagerly waving the bloody shirt? By recalling dramatic instances in which a common humanity had joined warring individuals in a higher purpose, a number of eloquent speakers began the task of reconciling North and South. After reliving the accounts and applauding the virtues embodied in them, audiences found themselves more disposed than they had before been to see good in their former enemies.

A classic speech of this sort was John Brown Gordon's "Last Days of the Confederacy."[17] During the war, a Confederate general, and, after, a U.S. Senator from Georgia, Gordon described himself simply as "a Southern man, a Southern soldier." His speech was "delivered with marked effect before large audiences in various parts of the country."[18] The text that survives was delivered in Brooklyn, New York, on February 7, 1901.

As do all effective narratives, Gordon's transports us out of ourselves into another time and place. The speaker and the audience are united in the common experience of the story. In that collective experience, they may find a commonality not otherwise apparent in the real world they inhabit. An involving recreation of the past can invite us to see ourselves, our world, and those with whom we have shared the tale in a new light. These are purposes that Gordon and Reagan share.

Gordon's speech is characterized by good-natured humor and reconciling dramatic narratives. Gordon notes, for example, that "we rapidly and cheerfully crossed the Potomac and then—a few days later—more rapidly and less cheerfully recrossed it. I think it is due to historical accuracy and to a proper respect for social regulations, to explain that no discourtesy whatever was intended by our unceremonious departure. Our visit was cut short by circumstances over which we did not have entire control, and for which we cannot be held exclusively responsible."

Having set the audience at ease, Gordon launches into his first lengthy narrative. He recounts seeing a Northern Major-General dying on the battlefield. "[A]s I rode by, intensely looking into his pale face, which was turned to the broiling rays of that scorching July sun, I discovered that he was not dead. Dismounting from my horse, I lifted his head with one hand, gave him water from my canteen, inquired his name and if he was badly hurt. He was General Francis C. Barlow, of New York . . . neither he nor I supposed he could live for one hour. I desired to remove him before death from that terrible sun. I had him lifted on a litter and borne to the shade in the rear." As Barlow said goodbye he begged Gordon to carry a message to his wife for him. "Tell her for me, that my last thought on earth was of her; tell her for me that you saw me fall in this battle, and that her husband fell, not in the rear, but at the head of his column; tell her for me, General, that I freely give my life to my country, but that my unutterable grief is that

I must now go without the privilege of seeing her once more, and bidding her a long and loving farewell."

Learning that Mrs. Barlow was just behind the Union line of battle, Gordon dispatched the message to her. Later that night word reached him that a "lady" was "on the line." Under guidance of Union officers, Mrs. Barlow was trying to reach her husband. Gordon ordered his staff to accompany her to her husband's side. Gordon assumed Barlow to be among the dead. The assumption was mistaken. Barlow recovered.

One year later, the Union general learned that Confederate General J. B. Gordon had died. Unaware that this was his ally's cousin, Barlow assembled his staff to express his sorrow at the death of the man who had safeguarded his wife through Confederate lines to his side.

Fifteen years passed. During that time each thought the other dead. Oblivious to the confusion, a mutual friend invited both to dinner. "Think of it!" says Gordon. "What could be stranger? There we met, both dead, each of us presenting to the other the most absolute proof of the resurrection of the dead.

"But stranger still, perhaps, is the friendship true and lasting begun under such auspices. What could be further removed from the realm of probabilities than a confiding friendship between combatants, which is born on the field of blood, amidst the thunders of battle, and while the hostile legions rush upon each other with deadly fury and pour into each other's breasts their volleys of fire and of leaden hail. Such were the circumstances under which was born the friendship between Barlow and myself, and which I believe is more sincere because of its remarkable birth, and which has strengthened and deepened with the passing years. For the sake of our reunited and glorious Republic may we not hope that similar ties will bind together all the soldiers of the two armies—indeed all Americans in perpetual unity until the last bugle call shall have summoned us to the eternal camping grounds beyond the stars?"

Throughout, Gordon forges appeals that transcend partisanship. He wishes, for example, that it were possible to lodge in the brain of every American youth the thought that "it is absolutely immaterial whether on this battlefield or that the blue or the gray won a great victory, for, thanks be to God, every victory won in that war by either side was a monument to American valor."

In vivid detail he invites the audience to reexperience the Confederate surrender, not as a moment of Union victory but as an affirmation of the common humanity of North and South. "The briny tears that ran down the haggard and tanned faces of the starving Confederates; the veneration and devotion which they displayed for the tattered flags which had so long waved above them in the white smoke of the battle; the efforts secretly to tear those bullet-rent banners from their supports and conceal them in their bosoms; the mutually courteous and kindly greetings and comradeship between the soldiers of the hitherto hostile armies; their anxiety to mingle with each other in friendly intercourse; the touching and beautiful generosity displayed by the Union soldiers in opening their well-filled haversacks and dividing their rations with the starving Confederates—these and a thousand other incidents can neither be described in words nor pictured on the most sensitive scrolls of the imagination."

Gordon concludes with a proclamation that "we unite in solemn compact that this American people shall know intestine war no more." From reconciling narratives, Gordon has forged common ground. By eliciting applause for values that transcend the differences over which the war was fought, he promotes reconciliation between North and South.

Like Gordon, Reagan builds epideictic from reconciling narrative. Like Gordon, Reagan argues from the evidence embodied in dramatic narrative. Such use of drama has been instrumental in accomplishing what Reagan defined as his mission as president: "What I'd really like to do," he said, "is go down in history as the President who made Americans believe in themselves again." [19]

Reagan's rhetoric is based on remembrance, restoration, and renewal. The theme was struck in Reagan's first speech as president, his inaugural address. "So," he said, "with all the creative energy at our command, let us begin an era of national renewal. Let us renew our determination, our courage, and our strength. And let us renew our faith and our hope" (January 20, 1981). "We have a decision to make," he told the Conservative Political Action Conference (March 20, 1986). "Will we continue with yesterday's agenda and yesterday's failures, or will we reassert our ideals and our standards, will we reaffirm our faith, and renew our purpose?"

Evidence abounds of Reagan's talent for and disposition toward storytelling. Indeed, he realizes that he must leash his storytelling impulse. "I could go on with these stories—I love them—" (July 27, 1982). "I've just got to tell one little story . . ." (December 8, 1982). Early in his presidency his command of the office was questioned by a prominent senator who complained that in a meeting all Reagan had done was relate anecdotes. So comfortable is Reagan with storytelling that he has delivered whole speeches that contain little else. Over half of his speech at the 84th annual dinner of the Irish American Historical Society (November 6, 1981) consisted of Irish jokes and anecdotes.

The anecdotes on which Reagan relies synopsize his claims and stow his argumentative burden; in the jargon of an earlier chapter, he understands the synecdochic nature of both dramatic visuals and dramatized verbal narrative. Responding to the criticism that he is long on stories but short on substance, Reagan said, "I think now and then to use an anecdote saves a lot of words sometimes to be able to tell something that illustrates what it is we're trying to do. If you have some example, for example, of bureaucratic dilly-dallying or repetitive things that aren't needed and you can tell that example, it saves several paragraphs of just trying to reason with someone in explaining what it is that you're trying to correct" (July 16, 1982).

Unlike his predecessor who seemed never to have met a statistic he didn't like, Reagan tends to misremember or misstate statistics, particularly in press conferences, and eagerly supplements or supplants them with stories. His remarks on January 26, 1983, provide an extreme but illustrative case.

> And there is a tendency to forget that in the long run it is out of that growing gross national product that every individual and every worker in this country is going to benefit.
>
> I know I have some figures, not with me here, about several years ago, what had happened when the taxes and the marginal rates were increased, but particularly the capital gains tax, and how the open market, the money markets, Wall Street, the billions of dollars that had been traded and sold in, well, to capitalize industries like your own, particularly smaller industries that were getting started, the entrepeneurs and so forth. Within a very few years, just a couple of years at the new higher rates, that had dwindled down to just a few million dollars, $15 million, I think. And only a couple of those entrepreneur-type companies that had gone to the marketplace for funding.

The questionable coherence of that statement is inadvertently set in a comic frame by Reagan's next sentence: "I think one of the challenges facing all of us on all of this is, there is a great lack of understanding among otherwise well-educated and intelligent people on things of this kind and the marketplace, how it functions and what is required to make it work."

Reagan then veers into a discussion of the increasing cost of higher education. His coherence improves slightly. Ultimately, he frames the question: "Have we become—it's so easy—be dependent on government that business practices that would be absolute imperatives in your own businesses are no longer applying, for example, in that field, to education."

Foundering, Reagan retreats to firm ground: from the conceptual to

the concrete, from analysis to anecdote: "I'm accused of telling anecdotes and so forth, but let me just give one example." As Reagan moves
into the narrative, sense returns to sentences; a grasp of grammar is
regained. "When I was Governor of California, I visited a State-supported
institution, higher education." Not yet into the story, Reagan's hold on
his sentences is still a bit shaky: "It was up in the north of our State in
what you would expect that a school of forestry and engineering and
so forth would be the principal functions there." Finally solidly within
the story, Reagan becomes surefooted. "But having been in the business I'd been in before I was Governor, I was proudly shown through
their theatre arts department. And I was shown their TV studios. They
even had a revolving stage so that they could have movable sets and so
forth and a shop for building them and a complete theatre. And I
couldn't resist. I finally said to the man in charge who was so proud of
this, I said, 'May I tell you that if any of your graduates ever make it
big in show business, Broadway, Hollywood, television, they will never
again perform in facilities equal to those that you've given them to learn
in.'" The audience laughs. Only then does Reagan do what the previous speaker initially had asked him to do, open the floor to questions.

Reagan's implied model of persuasion is that of Pascal, not Descartes.
Descartes held that facts coupled with logic should persuade; Pascal
unintentionally prophesied the power of the mode of communication
that is best suited for television when he noted that the heart has reasons that reason does not know. Reagan assigns evidentiary value to
rhetoric that cannot be vented in a Venn diagram.

The specific dramatic tale does not a generalization justify. Reagan
comfortably leaps from anecdote to generalized assertion. The dramatic tale has more power to involve and to propel that leap than do
the statistics that would better warrant the claim. If the speaker is credible, we are inclined to make the leap without rigorous testing. If a
trusted speaker tells the story with conviction, we suspend disbelief.

Reagan has a talent for recreation. "He is a person of warm sympa-
thies," notes speechwriter Peggy Noonan, "and this is apparent to people instinctively. When he talks about young boys involved in heroic
action he appears to be telling you a truth that he understands and
that (as a result) lives on its own as a truth." Reagan is able through
simple, direct, dramatic word pictures to evoke in audiences what he
himself seems to be feeling. In the process he violates the cultural axiom that boys neither cry nor admit to crying, an axiom given political
weight when what may or may not have been tears on the face of presidential aspirant Ed Muskie helped undercut his candidacy in 1972. In
response to the story of a British shopkeeper Reagan reports that "my

eyes were a little filled also." Reagan was making a film in Britain just after World War II. He stopped at a pub. Its owner, a "motherly looking lady" told him that GIs had frequented the pub during the war. " 'They called me Mom and the old man Pop.' And as she went on her voice was softening and she wasn't looking at me anymore; she was looking kind of beyond and into her memories. Her eyes were beginning to fill. And then she said, 'It was Christmas Eve. The old man and me were here all alone. And all of a sudden the door burst open, and in they came with presents for the both of us.' And the tears now had overflowed and were on her cheeks. And she said, 'Big strappin' lads they was from a place called Ioway.' "

Reagan artfully retells the experiences of others. Speaking of the travels of the Olympic Torch, Reagan vividly recreates scene after scene. In the process, he conveys his own pride in the actions of the citizens who carried the torch. His descriptions invite our pride as well. "In Richardson, Texas, it was carried by a fourteen-year-old boy in a special wheelchair. In West Virginia the runner came across a line of deaf children and let each one pass the torch for a few feet, and at the end these youngsters' hands talked excitedly in their sign language. Crowds spontaneously began singing, 'America the Beautiful' or 'The Battle Hymn of the Republic.'

"Then in San Francisco a Vietnamese immigrant, his little son held on his shoulders, dodged photographers and policemen to cheer a nineteen-year-old black man pushing an eighty-eight-year-old white woman in a wheelchair as she carried the torch."[20] As the crowd thundered its approval of this message of reconciliation, this dramatic insinuation that as the campaign theme had it, "America was back and standing tall," Reagan added, "My friends, that's America." The statement is about us, not about him.

By carrying it to us he comes to represent us in a way that his immediate predecessors never could. Lyndon Johnson's failed attempts are illustrative.

In his Christmas message of 1967 (December 24, 1967) Johnson talked about patriotism, but failed to evoke patriotic feelings. Speaking of his recent experience at the airstrip at Cam Ranh Bay, he noted: "In the hospital, I spoke with those who bore the wounds of war. You cannot be in such a place, among such men, without feeling grief well up in your throat, without feeling grateful that there is such courage among your countrymen. That was Christmas time in Vietnam—a time of war, of suffering, of endurance, of bravery and devotion to country."

Although he has failed to paint a memorable picture of the experience of the men in Vietnam, LBJ asks the country to remember them.

"I hope that all of you may remember, this Christmas, the brave young men who celebrate the Holy Season far from their homes, serving their country—serving their loved ones—serving each of us." He asks his audience to remember because he lacks the rhetorical wherewithal to evoke remembrance, to transfer what he says he feels into feelings they too can share. Instead, the audience is left with an account by Johnson of his own feelings. Where biography—a compelling account of the soldiers—is required, Johnson can muster only autobiography. Johnson seems unable to narrate without locating himself centrally in the scene and writing it ultimately about himself. Narrative reduces to narcissism.

Johnson seems aware that he lacks the verbal skill necessary to recapture either the experience of Vietnam or the sentiments of those waiting at home. "Now on the airstrip at Cam Ranh Bay, your sons and I exchanged 'Merry Christmas' and 'Happy New Year.' *I told them that I wished I could bring them something more*—some part of the pride you feel in them, some tangible symbol of your love and concern for them" *(emphasis added)*.

We hear the same problem in a speech delivered to the patients at the Bethesda Naval Hospital. "I just can't sum up in any words of mine how proud I am of the Marines, the Navy, the Army, the Air Force, and the Coast Guard, and the fellows that never look back. And when I feel pretty blue at night, and I issue the orders that you carry out, I do it with a heavy heart. But I never see one of your performances that I am not proud of you, and I wanted to come and tell you that before I checked out.

"Good luck to you. Tell all your families—your wives, your children, your mothers, and your fathers—that the President of your country is mighty proud of you" (October 21, 1965). The statement is about LBJ, not about the patients.

As we will see in a later chapter, most of us find it difficult to voice someone else's sentiments. Reagan's comfort in delivering the words of others and his ability to translate other persons' feelings through himself to a larger audience mean that he can take the words of a single citizen, raise them to the level of universal truth, and as spokesperson for the nation express them. The story of Martin Treptow, told in the first inaugural, is indicative of this skill:

"Under one such marker lies a young man, Martin Treptow, who left his job in a small-town barbershop in 1917 to go to France with the famed Rainbow Division. There, on the western front, he was killed trying to carry a message between battalions under heavy artillery fire.

"We're told that on his body was found a diary. On the flyleaf under the heading, My Pledge, he had written these words: 'America must win this war. Therefore I will work, I will save, I will sacrifice, I will endure, I will fight cheerfully and do my utmost, as if the issue of the whole struggle depended on me alone.' "

As he habitually does with such statements, Reagan then universalizes it, gives it status as an expression of our sentiments as a people. "The crisis we are facing today does not require of us the kind of sacrifice that Martin Treptow and so many thousands of others were called upon to make. It does require, however, our best effort and our willingness to believe in ourselves and to believe in our capacity to perform great deeds, to believe that together ·with God's help we can and will resolve the problems which now confront us." By embracing the beliefs expressed by Treptow through Reagan, we confirm our identity as Americans. "And, after all, why shouldn't we believe that? We are Americans."*

Reagan hoped to restore the country's pride in its military. In the process, he wanted to instill pride for what the country tried to accomplish in Vietnam. Both agendas are present in his speech honoring a Vietnam veteran.

Like all such acts, Reagan's reconstruction of the past is selective. In the choices he makes we see a speaker unburdening audiences of the trauma of Vietnam. As it was in his radio address on the bombing of the Beirut embassy, Reagan's unstated goal here is displacement of one set of images with another.

For many, the My Lai Massacre is a festering memory indicting the U.S. involvement in Vietnam. Without mentioning the traumas associated with My Lai, Reagan tries to replace our memories of the rapes, murders, and executions with the heroism of caring, compassionate soldiers. One speech supplants Lieutenant Calley with Sergeant Roy Benavidez.

In his remarks on presenting the medal of honor to the master sergeant (February 24, 1981), Reagan begins by recalling the homecoming the returning veterans received. "They were greeted by no parades, no bands, no waving of the flag they had so nobly served. There's been no 'thank you' for their sacrifice. There's been no effort to honor and, thus give pride to the families of more than 57,000 young men who gave their lives in that faraway war. . . . Pride, of course, cannot wipe

*Reagan can recreate Treptow for us in part because he is comfortable delivering other person's lines, a characteristic explored in the next chapter. But he can do it as well because his style so closely approximates ordinary speech. By contrast, John Kennedy's public speech style was so carefully crafted and formal that use of such material would have accentuated the differences between him and the person being quoted. It is not surprising that Kennedy was disposed to quoting Thucydides, Jefferson, and Shakespeare. Stylistically, he and they matched.

out the burden of grief borne by their families, but it can make that grief easier to bear. The pain will not be quite as sharp if they know their fellow citizens share the pain."

The speech invites us to experience that pride and in the process lessen the pain of the surviving families. "Back in 1970 Kenneth Y. Tomlinson wrote of what he had seen our young men do beyond and above the call of military duty in Vietnam—a marine from Texas on his way in at dawn from an all-night patrol stopping to treat huge sores on the back of an old Vietnamese man, an artilleryman from New Jersey spending his free time stacking sandbags at an orphanage to protect the children from mortar attacks, an Army engineer from California distributing toys he's bought in Hong Kong to the orphans his unit had adopted." There is no mention of the possibility that the old man was the victim of U.S. napalm or that the children had been orphaned by GIs. Where those who condemn the war will select such scenes, Reagan will spend his words capturing acts the country can be proud of.

The speech then catalogues the number of schools, hospitals, dispensaries, classrooms, churches, temples, and pagodas built by U.S. soldiers. To give faces to the statistics, Reagan turns to the rhetorical mode at which he excels—the dramatic narrative. At a facility funded by the contributions of marines there was an eleven-year-old boy, burned over three-quarters of his body. "He interrupted the game he was playing with visiting marines to say, 'All my life, I will never forget this place and these healing people. Some way I will repay them.'"

Just as those who condemned Vietnam as an immoral war drew their evidence heavily from those presumed by society to most merit protection, children and mothers, Reagan recounts the troop's generosity and humanitarianism toward these groups. "A Green Beret learned that a mother in a remote mountain village was having trouble in childbirth. He made his way to her home, carried her to a truck, and raced to Cam Ranh, where a Navy doctor delivered the baby. On Christmas he gave 1,500 orphans toothpaste, soap, candy, and nuts he'd collected from fellow servicemen."

Reagan concurs with Bob Hope's explanation of such humanitarianism. "I guess you know what kind of guys your sons and brothers and the kids next door are," noted Hope. Reagan adds, "Well, yes, we do know. I think we just let it slip our minds for a time. It's time to show our pride in them and to thank them." We are thanking them not for the death and destruction they occasioned but for their humanitarianism.

The valor and honor of the brothers, sons, and boys next door who fought in Vietnam are then personified in the heroism of Sergeant

Benavidez. The president recounts his deeds. After reading the citation, Reagan expresses the nation's gratitude to Benavidez and his comrades, living and dead. The expository nature of the account and its unemotional tone denature the speech of partisan overtones. Reagan is conscious of the style that both he and the citation are employing. "Let me read the plain, factual military language of the citation," he notes (February 24, 1981). This is not a polemic but a quiet act of commemoration, a communal act of honoring those values that we all cherish.

In the process of honoring the veterans, Reagan rehabilitates the Vietnam war. Insinuated into the speech is a premise that in any other context would shriek divisiveness. "They came home without a victory not because they'd been defeated, but because they'd been denied permission to win."

Because Reagan sounds sincere and seems to be expressing deeply held beliefs, he is able to say things that would sound mushy or manipulative coming from another speaker. "We can make America stronger not just economically and militarily," he stated in his acceptance address at the convention in 1984, "but also morally and spiritually. We can make our beloved country the source of all the dreams and opportunities she was placed on this good Earth to provide. We need only to believe in each other and in the God who has so blessed our land." It is difficult to imagine any modern president but Reagan delivering such lines with conviction. As *Washington Post* columnist Meg Greenfield has observed, he does not "exude anxiety or defensiveness or duplicity or aggression while he is speaking the most simple pieties."[21]

Reagan is able to do this in part because he wears the presidency lightly. He is not asking us to believe in him, as Carter, Johnson, and Nixon often did, but to believe in ourselves and in the country. Where Carter, Johnson, and Nixon occupied a central place in their own discourse, Reagan does not. Unlike Johnson whose rhetoric trumpeted his personal identification with the presidency, Reagan's bespoke the sentiments of a man not remade by the office. When asked by a reporter what voters saw in him, Reagan responded "I think, maybe, they see themselves and that I'm one of them."[22] Reagan's rhetoric is self-effacing; the rhetoric of Carter, Nixon, and Johnson often bordered on self-promotion or self-indulgence.

At times Johnson's statements about himself were simply formulaic. At others, they were self-indulgent. "I am not going to stay all night. I am just about through. I do want to present, though, my long-time beloved friend, the most distinguished Governor from the State of Texas, John Connally.

"And now I am going to take a little drive out here to Pryor and see some of my friends out there, have a light dinner, and go on home before it gets too dark. Good night."[23]

The presidency transfused Lyndon Johnson. Where Nixon spoke as The President and Johnson as Your President, Reagan speaks as a neighbor who stepped out of a shower one evening to find that he had been asked to lead the country for a while. The formal public speeches of Johnson and Nixon display the transformation effected by the presidency.

When on March 3, 1981, Walter Cronkite asked Reagan, "What's the greatest surprise that you've experienced in the Presidency?," Reagan noted, "it isn't as if suddenly something happens to you. I don't feel any different than I did before." The confinement of living in the White House didn't surprise him, he says because "I lived above the store when I was a kid, and it's much like that." Indeed, there was no dramatic moment in which he felt presidential. "You'd think that that'd be a very dramatic moment, and I was worrying that it was going to be a moment that would last all night, waiting for the returns to come in. I was in the shower and was called out of the shower, just getting ready to go out, late afternoon, when the President was on the other end of the phone. I was wrapped in a towel and dripping wet, and he told me that he was conceding. And that wasn't the way I'd pictured it."

Reagan jokes about the tendency of presidents to take credit for the work of others. "I'm going to make a statement here, but before I do, I just want to thank all of you. You're from the Office of Management and Budget, and you're the ones that have been working and slaving very hard, and all of us here are deeply grateful to you. And at which time I shall now read a statement in which I'll take all the credit" (March 9, 1981).

Presidents customarily claim that they draw inspiration from the people. The ways in which the various presidents have made that claim reveal much about their perceptions of the presidency and of themselves as presidents. Each statement was delivered at a time in which the president was in trouble: Johnson's while under attack over Vietnam, Nixon's while beset by critics over Watergate, Reagan's during the recession of 1982.

Speaking at the Fairfield County Fairgrounds in Lancaster, Ohio (September 5, 1966), Lyndon Johnson conceives of himself as powerful but burdened, his role as president as the protector of foreign and domestic tranquility, and his relationship with his audience as paternal. He says, "To the people who put these signs up, to the folks who had the posters, to all the folks who showed us a happy smile and gave us a warm hand today, I want to say to you that I shall return to your Capital tonight stronger and I hope wiser for having come your way.

"I am going to do everything that I can in the days ahead to keep prosperity at home and to bring peace to the world. I am going to try to be fair to my fellow man. I am going to try not to be bitterly partisan." Apparently being fair to his fellow man and avoiding bitter partisanship are worthy of less exertion than maintaining prosperity and bringing peace to the world. But in each instance, Lyndon Johnson and he alone is the agent.

To his audience he assigns less exalted functions. Speaking as their preacher and perhaps silently counseling himself as well, Johnson enjoins them to talk to each other, avoid feeling sorry for themselves, think about the sacrifices of the distant dead and count their blessings:

> All I am going to say to you is: You go home tonight and talk to your wife and to your children [women and children have no specific charge either to initiate conversation or respond] and to your family and don't feel sorry for yourself. Don't become a martyr. Don't complain about everyone around you. Think about how much better a world we are living in than our fathers lived in. Think about the sacrifices that our pioneer grandfathers and grandmothers made. Count your blessings and then say to yourselves: "I am going to do what is best for my country."

Johnson concludes with an exhortation that places him in the center of their universe. "I leave that judgment [presumably about what to do for your country] up to you. And when you do what is best for your country, you will do what is best for me."

Speaking at a dinner in Bel Air, California, on July 21, 1974, Nixon seemed a rhetorical disciple of his Democratic predecessor.

> You wonder sometimes, and I am often asked, you know, how do you really take the burden of the Presidency, particularly when at times it seems to be under very, very grievous assault. Let me say, it isn't new for it to be under assault, because since the time we came into office for five years, we have had problems. There have been people marching around the White House when we were trying to bring the war to an end, and we have withstood that, and we will withstand the problems of the future.
>
> People wonder, how does any individual, in these days when we have very high pressured campaigns, usually, in the media and the rest, taking on public figures, how does an individual take it, how does he survive it, how do you keep your composure, your strength, and the rest?
>
> Well, there are a number of factors. First, you have got to have a strong family, and I am proud of my family. But the second thing is, you have got to have also a lot of good friends, people that you have known through

the years, people who write you, who call you, or who see you and say 'We are sticking by you.' And I can assure you that no man in public life—and I have studied American history rather thoroughly—has ever had a more loyal group of friends, has never been blessed with, certainly, a more loyal group of friends who have stood by him through good days as well as tough days than I have.

A similar amalgam of ego-centrism, hyperbole, and didacticism occurred in Carter's rhetoric (October 7, 1978):

> If I can tap the strength and the courage, the dedication, the patriotism of the people of West Virginia and others like you in our country, we'll have an even greater nation than we have already. And as you well know, we still live in the greatest nation on Earth.

Where Carter, Nixon, and Johnson reside in the center of their discourse, Reagan is more self-effacing. He casts himself as narrator or raconteur, not high priest, king, or emperor. As they strain to adapt to their audiences, Nixon, Johnson, and Carter protest too much; by contrast, Reagan's rhetoric seems effortless. In the statements of his three predecessors we hear persons consciously speaking as president; their tone is decisive and categorical. Reagan is speaking as temporary custodian. In Reagan's house, says his rhetoric, the people rule; in the houses of his three predecessors, the president rules.

It is not *Reagan* who will renew and regenerate America. Instead, he says, "Through this long night of economic hardship, you the people, the heroes of America, American democracy, have measured up to Dr. Warren's admonition. With your continued help, through the magnificent reach of your determination, by the mighty force of your personal prayers, I know that this great, new season of hope will bring that day of renewal and national regeneration and will bring a better world for our children."

By giving the people power over their own destiny while affirming his confidence in them, Reagan minimizes his own accountability. By assuming the burden of the presidency, by magnifying the president as a responsible agent, and by taking a paternal posture, Carter, Nixon, and Johnson increase their accountability. When things go wrong, the president they have made themselves into will be blamed.

Because Reagan does not reside at the center of his discourse, he is better able than his predecessors to serve as national narrator, recounting the heroism, sacrifice, and patriotism of others in descriptive detail. His training as an actor is undoubtedly helpful. If we remain conscious that a specific actor is playing a specific part in a film and fail as a result to lose ourselves in the story, then the actor has failed. Reagan is able to set others center stage and to speak their sentiments. Like an effective actor he is able to transmit some of his own conviction to his audience. These abilities make it possible for him to help his audience experience pride in their country and fellow citizens. In short, these talents facilitate his effective use of epideictic rhetoric.

On a number of occasions, Reagan revealed an awareness of the power of the dramatic story to unify an audience. Scholars have made much of Reagan's accounts of the filming of Knute Rockne—All American. What they have missed is the lesson about the power of storytelling that Reagan drew from "Win one for the Gipper." Rockne reserved George Gipp's dying words until a game that occurred eight years after his death. He then used the story to inspire a team sundered by personal animosities. The Gipper's last words produced a unity that had otherwise eluded the team, enabling it to do the impossible. After noting "let's look at the significance of that story," Reagan recalls: "He told the story at halftime to a team that was losing, and one of the only teams he ever coached that was torn by dissension and jealousy and factionalism. The seniors on that team were about to close out their football careers without learning or experiencing any of the real values that a game has to impart. None of them had known George Gipp. They were children when he played for Notre Dame. It was to this team that Rockne told the story and so inspired them that they rose above their personal animosities. For someone they had never known, they joined together in a common cause and attained the unattainable" (May 17, 1981). As president, the man who played the Gipper has assumed the role of Rockne. In that capacity he relates one inspiring story after another in an attempt to unite the country in a common cause. As president, he reassures the country, as he did in his 1986 State of the Union address, that "In this land of dreams fulfilled where greater dreams may be imagined, nothing is impossible, no victory is beyond our reach, no glory will ever be too great. So now, it's up to us, all of us, to prepare America for that day when our work will pale before the greatness of America's champions in the 21st century."

As the presence of Skutnik, Trujillo, Hale, and Nguyen would suggest, Reagan also realizes the unifying power of the nonverbal statement. Reagan explicitly draws that conclusion in his recollection of the victory (March 2, 1983) of boxer George Forman in the Mexico City Olympics. "[B]ut when victory was announced and he stood in the middle of that ring and suddenly unfurled a small American flag and stood with that flag raised, it was a thrill, I think, for everyone in our country, I say it was in the turbulent sixties. He showed us that whatever divides us, it's not as strong as what keeps us together."

Throughout his first term, Reagan created vivid pictures of patriotism, heroism, and individual initiative. In his final broadcast speech of the campaign (November 5, 1984), he claimed: "I'm not sure anyone really knows when this new patriotism began or how it grew so quickly." He then synopsizes dramatic instances he has used in the past to instill the very patriotism whose origin he questions. "Was its seed first planted that day our POWs who had braved a horrendous captivity in North Vietnam, came home and said, 'God bless America?' " Or was it planted in the State of the Union address in which Reagan paid tribute to Senator Jeremiah Denton, the former POW, who uttered those words? Perhaps the seed was from any of Reagan's many retellings of his experience greeting the POWs in his California home.

By recalling an event of his own making, Reagan tacitly admits his hand in the creation of the "new" patriotism. "I treasure a memory of a visit to Normandy, where I met the boys of Pointe du Huc. And later at Omaha Beach, I read from the letter of a loving daughter who had promised her father, a Normandy veteran, that someday she would go back there for him. She would see the beaches and visit the monuments and place flowers at the graves of his fallen comrades. 'I'll never forget,' she wrote, and 'Dad, I'll always be proud.' "

Reagan's account of his experience at Omaha Beach illustrates the skills described in this chapter. The site of the Normandy invasion, the stage on which Reagan set the speech, beckoned memories of the young men who carried their country's cause onto the beaches on that earlier day. Also on the stage were the veterans and their families who had returned to commemorate the landing and the cause for which many of their friends had died. Television enabled Reagan to transport the national audience to the stage he had set in Normandy. Peggy Noonan, who wrote the speech, recalls: "I was thinking cinematically. After the President said 'These are the boys of Pointe du Hoc,' that's when the cameras would start to turn and then the President would say, 'These are the men who took the cliffs.' And suddenly you were going to look at these faces—I'm getting choked up—of these seventy-year old guys and you'd be very moved." Noonan's intuitions were accurate.[24]

The campaign film intercuts the speech at Pointe du Hoc with a second speech delivered at Normandy. In a segment from the second speech included both on the network newscasts and in the film, Reagan read from the letter of a woman whose father, a Normandy veteran, had recently died. She sat with the others in the audience before him. Tears appeared in her eyes as Reagan, his voice breaking with emotion, read of her desire to fulfill her father's wish to return to Normandy for the anniversary.

If eloquence survives in an electronic age, it is in such dramatic visualizations as Reagan's at Pointe de Hoc and Omaha Beach in 1984. These epideictic speeches commemorated the Allies' assault on Normandy in World War II. (Courtesy Bill Fitzpatrick, The White House)

That brief visual moment underscored the words of her letter to place in powerful, memorable form the key themes of Reagan's presidency. To the viewing public, it telegraphed the reconciliation of generations around the refurbished values of family, faith, and country. As Reagan shared her thoughts with the world, the woman was added to the album of snapshots of ordinary heros whose actions Reagan had elevated for public blessing.

At the core of the image was Reagan, displaying his compassion, pride, and patriotism by reading her words more movingly than she herself could have. In the process the president held up her sentiments as a mirror in which we could see our own. Reagan the reconciler. Reagan the patriot. Reagan the voice of the nation's feelings. Reagan the restorer of traditional American values. The dramatization was compelling, the staging unsurpassable, the visual argument politically potent.

As even wary Democrats find themselves assenting to this moment of national commemoration, Reagan massages the message into an affirmation of his political agenda. Just as legitimation of the war in Vietnam was insinuated into the epideictic of the first inaugural and into applause for Jean Nguyen, just as approval of the Grenadan invasion was intercut into the celebration of Trujillo's heroism, just as a benediction for nongovernment solutions to the nation's social problems was woven into the praise for Clara Hale, just as Congress was implicated in creation of the budget deficit when Reagan asked for the Speaker's cooperation in eliminating it, so too Reagan here has suborned epideictic to defend his policies. In the part of the speech included in the campaign film, the lesson Reagan draws from Pointe du Hoc is that we must always remember so that we will always be prepared to remain free. The statement prefigured "Prepared for Peace," the campaign slogan that would in 1984 synopsize Reagan's justification for increased military spending and for the controversial Star Wars system.

His message captured in this televisual moment, Reagan ensures that it will be impressed on the public consciousness. First the networks share it with their viewers. Then the Republicans replay it in their nationally aired convention film. It is broadcast again in the half-hour documentary aired on all three networks to launch the Reagan advertising campaign in the fall. By simply describing his experience of the occasion, Reagan can now summon that visual moment and the rich testimony it carries. This he does in his nationally televised speech on election eve 1984. His ability to do so testifies to his talent for employing the grammar of television to evoke feelings of pride and patriotism in the public.

7

Conversation and Self-Revelation

Ironic though it may seem, the first inaugural address of the modern presidency's most conservative politician was a revolutionary act. Accused by his opponents of wanting to lead the country headlong into the eighteenth century, Reagan nonetheless defied the patterns of discourse deified in the age of print; in their place, he innovatively inaugurated both his presidency and a new era in presidential communication by delivering a televisual speech. More than four decades after the first televised presidential address, the oldest man ever to be elected to the office demonstrated the power of a prime-time presidency.

While the inaugurals of most modern presidents read well, Reagan's oral prose signals that his speech was scripted to be seen and heard. Where most of his predecessors constructed speeches suitable for the print media of the nineteenth century, Reagan's was written to be spoken and seen through the electronic media of the twentieth.

Even the most formal of Reagan's speeches are written in a conversational style and delivered in a conversational voice. Where his predecessors brought a formal style and oratorical delivery to their inaugurals and State of the Union messages and a more casual style and delivery to press conferences and extemporaneous speeches, Reagan is consistently conversational in both environments. This consistency couples with his intimate conversational style to enable him to engage in an unprecedented level of self-disclosure on television. His moments of self-revelation invite us to conclude that we know and like him. At the same time, they provide a powerful warrant for claims that defy traditional forms of evidence and logic. By skillfully using the broadcast media to project his personality, he is able to deflect his critics' contentions that he is uncaring and disposed to use his role as Commander-in-Chief for military conquest. By engaging in judicious self-revelation, he is able to sidetrack charges of incipient senility, underscore his support for traditional values, and smooth the ideological edge from his sharper views.

Because we feel that we know him, because we have shared moments of intimacy with him, because we trust that he expresses convictions he holds dear, Reagan is able, when confronted with the tragic incineration of the space shuttle, to deliver the modern equivalent of Pericles' Funeral Oration. The ethos that he had cultivated in over five years of personal rhetoric enabled him to speak both for us and to us as he consoled the families, schoolchildren, and nation whose anticipation had turned to anguish.

Reagan's plain, conversational speech subtly strengthens his assertion that his is a presidency based in common sense and in trust in the people. In its use of contractions, informal transitions, and incomplete sentences, even Reagan's first inaugural mimicked ordinary speech. "[I]t's not my intention to do away with government," he said. "We're not, as some would have us believe, doomed to an inevitable decline." "I'm told that tens of thousands of prayer meetings are being held on this day, and for that I'm deeply grateful." "And after all, why shouldn't we believe?"

When he sensed that an idea was being lost, he doubled back to pick up a clarifying referent: "Those who say that we're in a time when there are not heroes, they just don't know where to look." As we do in conversation, Reagan bridged his ideas with informal transitions such as "Now," "well," "and," "but," and "so."

> We hear much of special interest groups. Well, our concern must be for a special interest group that has been too long neglected.
>
> Well, this administration's objective will be a healthy, vigorous, growing economy that provides equal opportunity for all Americans, with no barriers born of bigotry or discrimination.
>
> So, as we begin, let us take inventory.
>
> Now, so there will be no misunderstanding, it's not my intention to do away with government.
>
> Now, I have used the words "they" and "their" in speaking of these heroes.[1]

Reagan's inaugural address proclaimed that his would be a unique presidency. On an occasion on which even FDR and Harry Truman sought and spoke formal polished prose, Reagan's speech was pointedly conversational. What it sacrificed in elegance, it gained in identification with the audience. "He's a great communicator," says his former speechwriter Peggy Noonan, "because he's a very straightforward, plain-spoken communicator."[2]

Although Reagan long ago abandoned the Democratic party, his comfort with a casual public style is reminiscent of FDR's fireside chats. "To all of you who are so generously helping the cause of crippled children everywhere," FDR told a radio audience, "I also send my thanks and my best wishes. I like this kind of a birthday" (January 30, 1935).

Like the other presidents, Roosevelt spoke extemporaneously in a conversational style; otherwise he reserved this style to personalize his radio speeches to the people. By contrast, Reagan's speech, whether private or public, at the Waldorf or the Great Wall of China, is unselfconsciously conversational. In his State of the Union addresses, Reagan converses with Congress; FDR did not. "Yesterday, December 7, 1941— a date which will live in infamy—the United States of America was suddenly and deliberately attacked by naval and air forces of the Empire of Japan," FDR declared in his War Message to Congress (December 8, 1941). In a fireside chat with the nation the next evening, Roosevelt noted, "We are now in this war. We are all in it—all the way. Every single man, woman, and child is a partner in the most tremendous undertaking of our American history. We must share together the bad news and the good news, the defeats and the victories—the changing fortunes of war. So far, the news has been all bad. . . . The casualty lists of these first days will undoubtedly be large. I deeply feel the anxiety of all of the families of the men in our armed forces and the relatives of people in cities which have been bombed. I can only give them my solemn promise that they will get news just as quickly as possible."

Reagan uses a more casual vocabulary than his predecessors, often being colloquial where others would be formal. His labelling Quaddafi "flakey" was no fluke. He also is comfortable with the proverbs and truisms that lard our private vocabulary but are purged from public speech out of fear of appearing trite. Reagan condemns "blind alleys," advocates federal "belt tightening," and worries about being "out of time." Times are "fraught with danger"; nonetheless, we must "chart a new course," work "side by side" or "hand in hand," and make "hard choices." We are "swamped in a sea of red ink"; we want to "play on a level playing field." His realism is "rock-hard, clear-eyed, steady and sure." For him, achievements are "heroic," our longings "deep." For Reagan, the relationship between "deep" and "abiding," "plight" and "the poor," and "unfettered and free" is coital, if not conjugal. Of course, all of us, presidents and pedants alike, disinter our share of dead metaphors. In one fireside chat (December 29, 1940), FDR warns first that we cannot escape danger "by crawling into bed and pulling the covers over our heads" and later condemns those who believe that "we can save our own skins by shutting our eyes to the fate of other nations." Yet that same speech avers that "No man can tame a tiger into a kitten by stroking it," asks "Is it a negotiated peace if a gang of outlaws surrounds your community and on threat of extermination makes you pay tribute to save your own skins?," and announces "We must be the great arsenal of democracy."

The current president seems to shun the striking phrases sought by his predecessors. Reagan couches his premises and conclusions in conventionally expressed folk wisdom. "I have always believed," he told the representatives of the Sister Cities International Program (March 27, 1981), "that a lot of the problems in the world would disappear if people would start talking *to* each other instead of about each other." "Closing our eyes will not make reality disappear," he told Congress in his 1986 State of the Union message. Neither the ideas nor their expression is arresting. By contrast, FDR's phrasing of an old truth is striking. "When you see a rattlesnake poised to strike, you do not wait until he has struck before you crush him," he noted in a fireside chat delivered nearly three months before the "date which will live in infamy" (September 11, 1941). For FDR "a full pocketbook often groans more loudly than an empty stomach" (November 1, 1940), "the hand that held the dagger has stuck it into the back of its neighbor" (June 10, 1940), and selfish men "would clip the wings of the American eagle in order to feather their own nests" (January 6 1941).

When Reagan reaches for the felicitous phrase, more often than not it eludes him. In his 1986 State of the Union address, he inadvertently contrasts a compelling image of FDR's with a confusing one of his own. "As Franklin Roosevelt warned 51 years ago standing before his chamber, he said, welfare is '. . . a narcotic, a subtle destroyer of the human spirit.' And we must now escape the spider's web of dependency."

Still, Reagan's plain conversational style underscores the principles that he says guide his policies: common sense, confidence in the people, and a conviction that there are simple, though not easy answers. "All it takes is a little common sense and recognition of our own ability," he told the American people in 1981 (February 5,). "The American people brought us back—with quiet courage and common sense," he informed Congress in 1986 (February 4).

Reagan's syntax is as plain as his style. Seldom does he embed subordinate clauses in a single sentence; simple sentence structure reigns. "I mentioned that we will meet our commitment to national defense," he told Congress in 1986 (February 4). "We must meet it. Defense is not just another budget expense. Keeping America strong, free and at peace is solely the responsibility of the federal government. It is government's prime responsibility."

Nor are Reagan's sentences highly embellished. "His remarks carry punch because his nouns and verbs stand alone, making his style almost aphoristic," concludes rhetoric scholar Roderick Hart.[3] "This makes Ronald Reagan the sort of American whom Tocqueville wrote about, a person whose faith in certain simple values was so strong that his words needed no adornment."

The natural extension of Reagan's plain, conversational style is dialogue. He routinely closes his meetings with groups by inviting interchange. "I'd like to hear from you myself. So right now I think that's the end of the monologue. We can have a dialog, and the floor is open to hear your comments," he tells state legislators and county executives as he told other groups meeting with him at the White House (February 9, 1981).

Like FDR, Reagan understands that the broadcast media speak to individuals gathered most often in their homes. So, for example, in his first fireside chat after the bombing of Pearl Harbor, Roosevelt, in effect, invited the public to help him ensure that newspapers and radio stations did not report rumors about the war. He did that by speaking directly to "newspapers and radio stations" as the national audience eavesdropped. "To all newspapers and radio stations—all those who reach the eyes and ears of the American people—I say this: You have a most grave responsibility to the Nation now and for the duration of this war.

"If you feel that your government is not disclosing enough of the truth, you have every right to say so. But—in the absence of all the facts, as revealed by official sources—you have no right in the ethics of patriotism to deal out unconfirmed reports in such a way as to make people believe that they are gospel truth.

"Every citizen, in every walk of life, shares this same responsibility. The lives of our soldiers and sailors—the whole future of this Nation—depend upon the manner in which each and every one of us fulfills his obligation to our country."

The notion that Ronald Reagan is to television what FDR was to radio is a commonplace containing much truth. Each pioneered political uses of a medium; each used that medium to insulate his presidency from partisan attack. (Courtesy National Archives)

Suppressing the tendency to address the mass audience as a faceless mass, Reagan, like FDR, comfortably singles out special groups and people for direct address. This process simulates dialogue. In his tribute to the astronauts who had died in the explosion of the space shuttle, Reagan speaks directly to their families. "To the families of the seven, we cannot bear as you do the full impact of this tragedy, but we feel the loss and we're thinking about you so very much. Your loved ones were daring and brave and they had that special grace, that special spirit that says, 'Give me a challenge and I'll meet it with joy.'" (January 28, 1986).

The broadcast media gave both FDR and Reagan the ability to speak directly to individuals in their audiences. By contrast, when Lincoln wanted to make the same move he had to wait for the press to carry his words through the country. In a desperate attempt to head off civil war, Lincoln's first inaugural spoke directly to his "dissatisfied fellow-countrymen."

> In *your* hands, my dissatisfied fellow-countrymen, and not in *mine*, is the momentous issue of civil war. The Government will not assail *you*. You can

have no conflict without being yourselves the aggressors. *You* have no oath registered in heaven to destroy the Government, while *I* shall have the most solemn one to "Preserve, protect, and defend it."[4]

Realizing that reading and shooting are incongruous companions and recognizing the need to maintain dialogue with the South, Lincoln adds, "I am loath to close. We are not enemies, but friends. We must not be enemies. Though passion may have strained, it must not break our bonds of affection. The mystic chords of memory, stretching from every battlefield and patriot grave to every living heart and hearthstone all over this broad land, will yet swell the chorus of the Union, when again touched, as surely they will be, by the better angels of our nature" (March 4, 1861).

Other presidents occasionally have spoken directly to a part of their audience, but seldom as personally or as artfully as Lincoln, FDR, or Reagan. So, for example, in his November 3, 1969, speech on Vietnam, Nixon spoke to the young: "And now I would like to address a word, if I may, to the young people of this nation who are particularly concerned, and I understand why they are concerned, about this war.

> I respect your idealism.
> I share your concern for peace.
> I want peace as much as you do.

He then tries to show that his desire is in fact as strong if not stronger than theirs. The appeal to them has as its end enhancing his ethos. "There are powerful personal reasons I want to end this war. This week I will have to sign 83 letters to mothers, fathers, wives, and loved ones of men who have given their lives for America in Vietnam. It is very little satisfaction to me that this is only one-third as many letters as I signed the first week in office."

Similarly self-serving is Jimmy Carter's direct appeal at the 1980 Democratic convention to his defeated opponent, Teddy Kennedy. Carter is attempting to use the national audience to pressure Kennedy to embrace him and his campaign at the convention's close, an embrace Kennedy eludes. Here too the direct appeal seems self-interested, of use not to the country but to the "I" on whose behalf it was made. By contrast, Reagan's self-interest is submerged in his direct address. In such appeals, he speaks as spokesperson for the country, not as a partisan politician.

At the convention Carter noted, "I'd like to say a personal word to Senator Kennedy. Ted, you're a tough competitor and a superb campaigner, and I can attest to that. Your speech before this convention was a magnificent statement of what the Democratic Party is and what it means to the people of this country and why a Democratic victory is so important this year. I reach out to you tonight, and I reach out to all those who supported you in your valiant and passionate campaign. Ted, your party needs and I need you" (August 14, 1980).

The pedestrian quality of Reagan's conversational style reduces the likelihood that the audience will ask whether he is speaking his own or someone else's words. By talking about the speaking process, Reagan exorcises the ghostwriters whose presence is more palpable in the careful, often self-consciously crafted speeches of his predecessors.

By peppering prepared speeches with informal conversational cues, Reagan also minimizes the problem presidents face when speeches are written by different speechwriters. These homogenizing cues give the speeches an overall consistency that camouflages minor stylistic differences among his writers. Additionally, by delivering them with a level of conviction, apparent spontaneity, and sincerity that suggest they are his own, Reagan lessens our consciousness that he is reading the words of others. In these ways, Reagan sustains the credibility a speaker inadvertently can sacrifice if he or she appears to be reading someone else's words.

To read or not to read is a question that has vexed even those we remember as eloquent. "Gentlemen, reading from speeches is a very tedious business," Abraham Lincoln told an audience (July 10, 1858), "particularly for an old man who has to put on spectacles, and more so if the man be so tall that he has to bend over to the light."

Fortunately, the tedium is not always the message. Where viewers and listeners were painfully aware that Ford and Carter were reading rather than speaking to them and were conscious as well that neither relished the televised address, Reagan is able to speak the words on the text or TelePrompTer as if he were thinking them aloud for the first time. "He could make the phone book sound good," noted David Gergen, Reagan's assistant for communication in 1982, "providing you give him a page with Irish names."[5]

Truman's presidency provides a dramatic demonstration of the disabling consequences of asking an unskilled reader of other's scripts to deliver them with sincerity and conviction. Truman confessed that he had "poor ability to read a speech and put feeling into it."[6] His switch from script to the extemporaneous remarks that created "Give 'em hell, Harry", occurred when a difficult audience proved disdainful of his scripted address but was disarmed by his spontaneous afterthoughts.

"Give 'em hell, Harry" was the offspring of a speech to the American Society of Newspaper Editors (April 17, 1948). FDR's heir opened by reading from his scripted remarks. Then, unexpectedly, he moved to an extemporaneous statement. He spoke, wrote Jonathan Daniels, "in his own vocabulary, out of his own humor and his own heart."[7] Truman talked "in earnestness and almost intimacy with each man in the hall. He was suddenly a very interesting man of great candor who discussed the problems of American leadership with men as neighbors. He spoke the language of them all out of traditions common to them all." The editors' ennui was transformed into enthusiasm. What differentiates Reagan from Truman is Reagan's ability to convey a sense of intimacy, earnestness, candor, and conviction *while delivering a scripted statement.*

Reagan's delivery is a greater political asset than it would have been had he been preceded by effective speakers. So ineffective were Carter and Ford that occasionally their meanings disappeared in the awkward pauses that pocked their deliveries. Carter suffered an additional problem. By elevating his voice at the ends of sentences and failing to pause at periods, he sometimes managed to elide two sentences. "It isn't what he says that's the problem," one aide told James Wooten. "The problem is in the way he says it."[8] Poet and former senator and presidential candidate Eugene McCarthy characterized Carter as "an oratorical mortician. . . . He inters his words and ideas beneath piles of syntactical mush."

By mispronouncing words (e.g., technicological) and placing stresses in surprising places (e.g., mis'management), Carter subtly suggested that he and his audience belonged to warring linguistic communities. Even the presence of a script does not provide absolute protection from embarrassing errors, of course. Carter's mind was apparently on automatic pilot when in his acceptance address at the 1980 convention, he eulogized Hubert Humphrey. The name that tripped from Carter's tongue was the snide substitute used in the Carter camp to indict Humphrey's long-windedness. Humphrey supporters gasped audibly as Carter praised "Hubert Horatio Hornblower . . . Humphrey."

When delivering scripts, Reagan sounds and seems natural. "If he really wanted to help these people," commented Democratic media consultant Bob Squier after Reagan gave the U.S. senators advice on use of TV, "he would show them how to do his eye-crinkling, aw-shucks shoulder shrug."[9] Where Carter, Ford, and Johnson were distractingly self-conscious speechmakers, Reagan is at ease. As if to summon the next idea, he occasionally hesitates. Those with predistributed texts know something that the audience cannot tell, which is that the next thought has existed for hours in cold advance copies. So accomplished is Reagan in the seemingly spontaneous and sincere delivery of scripted words that with apparent conviction he delivered an indictment of his own administration when he merged two sentences of text in his convention address of 1984. Although the presence of speechwriters crimped the effectiveness of Ford and Carter, it poses no comparable problem for Reagan. Education as a lawyer or an engineer is poor preparation for comfortably delivering someone else's words in a conversational tone to an unseen audience. The profession that presupposes that ability is acting.

Reagan's ability to deliver his scripted speeches with sincerity and conviction gives him an edge over those tongue-tied and traumatized by the need to read a text. Without the safety net provided by a script, politicians can blunder as Carter did when, speaking extemporaneously at funeral services for Hubert Humphrey, he alluded to the memorial where Gandhi was "created." What Carter meant to say was "cremated."

A scriptless speaker is more likely than his text-bound counterpart to speak a senseless statement. Employees at the U.S. Embassy in India were puzzled when Carter confessed: "We are homesick for Amy. She happens to be in Colorado now, skiing for the first time. We don't have any snow in Georgia and this is her first experience; but our own country is so great and strong and, I hope, in its attributes, is enlightened, progressive and also beneficial." [10]

Relying on scripts has its price, however. The in-camera Tele-PrompTer enables politicians to create the illusion that they are looking at us when in fact they are staring into a camera; when it malfunctions the person who is looking so intently past millions of coffee tables into our hearts can sound foolish indeed. On one such occasion, Lyndon Johnson managed to deliver the same passage in one speech twice, prompting AP's Frank Cormier to note, "I actually wondered for a horrified moment if the President's mind had snapped under the strain." [11]

Extemporaneous remarks also can fuel the attacks of the opposition. Trying to argue that he was the victim of false accusations by the press, Truman in the 1948 campaign seemed instead to be confessing that he was guilty of wrongdoing. He said, "I have been in politics a long time, and it makes no difference what they say about you, if it isn't so. If they can prove it on you, you are in a bad fix indeed. They have never been able to prove it on me." [12]

If there was a single moment in the Truman presidency in which all concerned wished he had spoken with benefit of script, it occurred the morning of June 8, 1948. A last-minute decision placed Truman at the dedication of an airport. Truman was told only that the airport would honor "Wilmer Coates." On his arrival, a microphone was thrust at

Truman. Seeing veterans lining the street, Truman concluded that Coates had been a war hero. Truman aide, Ken Hechler recalls:

> The President started by expressing his pride in the honor he was able to pay to a native son. There was immediate consternation in the crowd; someone pulled on the President's coattails and whispered in his ear that the airport was being dedicated to a young woman.

But the embarrassment did not end there. Clearing his throat, the President started again. He referred to the fact that the young woman, whom he now assumed as a WAC, WAVE, or WAF, had bravely sacrificed her life for her country. Else why were the veterans all lined up? There was another interruption as more whispering and coattail tugging ensued. Wilma Coates was a teenager untouched by military service who had been killed hedgehopping with her boyfriend. "The President extended his profuse apologies to the father and mother of the young lady in whose honor the airport was being named."[13]

Because he can comfortably deliver from a text, Reagan is spared such moments. This talent reduces the number of occasions on which he is likely to misstate evidence or overstate his claims. Only in press conferences and debates does necessity dictate extemporaneous delivery with its attendant risks.

Reagan not only converses easily but engages television's audience in intimate conversation with a comfort that induces trust in him. The form of Reagan's sentences identifies him with his audience. He can speak for us, in part, because he speaks as we do. So, when in the first inaugural, he asserts that "Your dreams, your hopes, your goals are going to be the dreams, the hopes, and the goals of this administration, so help me God," his language patterns, and the sincerity with which he delivers such lines, dispose us to believe him.

Reagan's Stylistic Consistency

Often reporters' questions have exposed one presidential persona who mysteriously assumed another communicative guise when delivering public speeches on television. As butlers, barbers, former speechwriters, lovers, and even staffers traded confidences for copyrights and disclosed presidential conversations held behind closed doors, these often resembled neither the presidential responses to reporters' questions nor formal presidential speeches. Such revelations raised the possibility that the president was a trinity of persons. As the first person, the public candidate, Nixon in 1960 pontificated his disapproval of Truman's public swearing. The private third person later added the phrase "expletive deleted" to the public vocabulary. As a public speaker, Nixon was rated PG; his private conversations would have earned an R. The public Nixon's speech was clearly structured and demonstrated a lawyer's disposition toward carefully partitioned points; the transcripts revealed a very different private speaker, his thoughts meandering, his structure muddled.

The disparities extended beyond content. There are, of course, things we will reveal to intimates but conceal from a mass audience. Still, we expect a fundamental consistency in rhetorical style. It would come as a shock to learn that a president sounded like Churchill in public but Casey Stengal in private.

John Kennedy was another who displayed a marked contrast between private style and public speech. On April 11, 1962, in an opening statement at a news conference Kennedy spoke as public president. Although less stately than his inaugural, State of the Union addresses, or televised speeches to the American people, this statement, nonetheless, was more formal than Reagan's inaugural.

> The facts of the matter are that there is no justification for an increase in steel prices. The recent settlement between the industry and the union . . . was widely acknowledged to be noninflationary. . . . Steel output per man is rising so fast that labor costs per ton of steel can actually be expected to decline in the next 12 months. . . .
>
> In short, at a time when they could be exploring how more efficiency and better prices could be obtained . . . a few gigantic corporations have decided to increase prices in ruthless disregard to their public responsibilities.

In answers to reporters' questions, the conversational Kennedy emerged.

> . . . the suddenness by which every company in the last few hours, one by one as the morning went by, came in with their almost, if not identical, almost identical price increases . . . isn't really the way we expect the competitive private enterprise system to always work.

The contrast between the scripted Kennedy and the Kennedy of the answered question is marked. More pronounced is the contrast between either of these and the private Kennedy. In *The New York Times*, reporter Wallace Carroll revealed that Kennedy had privately told his staff, "My father always told me that all businessmen were sons of bitches, but I never believed it till now."[14] Years after Kennedy's death, Benjamin Bradlee recounted Kennedy's privately expressed views on the steel crisis. In the process, Bradlee confirmed that the comment about "sons of bitches" was not an aberration. A person familiar only with Kennedy's public speech would be hard pressed to guess that the following remarks were made by the president who asked "not what your country can do for you." "It's the way it was done," Kennedy said. "It looks like such a double cross. I think steel made a deal with Nixon not to raise prices until after the election. Then came the recession, and they didn't want to raise prices. Then when we pulled out of the recession they said 'Let Kennedy squeeze the unions first, before we raise prices.' So I squeezed McDonald [Dave McDonald, president of the steelworkers union], and gave him a good statesmanship leg to stand on with his workers. And they kicked us right in the balls. And we kicked back. The question really is: are we supposed to sit there and take a cold, deliberate fucking?"[15]

Such stylistic disparities raise intriguing questions. Which was the natural Kennedy style? Henry Fairlie concludes that it wasn't the style of the scripted speeches.

> He both forced it upon himself, and allowed it to be forced upon him. Not an inkling of it is to be found in his spontaneous replies at his press conferences; and although press conferences are different from speeches, there is usually a discernible connection between their styles. We must believe, for the evidence is ample, that in private John Kennedy was laconic and contained, cool and dry in his utterance. But what then happened when he rose to his feet? Whence came the magniloqence? His speeches are not spattered with the popular idiom that, even after the loftiest passages, brought Winston Churchill down to earth. John Kennedy spoke in public as Byzantine emperors appeared on state occasions: sheathed in gold, suspended between earth and heaven.[16]

If someone had slipped his conversation with Bradlee onto the front pages of the nation's newspapers as Kennedy was steeling himself against the possible personal indignities his conversation posited, I doubt that public concern would have centered on whether he expressed his real sentiments in public or in private. Rather, I would predict: some claiming to be aghast at the realization that the national sanctuary had been profaned; others gleefully noting that wealthy Catholics are still essentially wart-prone commoners; still others lecturing their children about naughty words while quietly cheering the calculating vigor and unvarnished manliness of Kennedy's convictions; finally, a small group finding in Kennedy's conversation a rationale for teaching sex education in the schools.

Indeed, Fairlie is not concerned with the impact of the inconsistent Kennedy personas on the public but rather with the origins of the mag-

The John Kennedy who spoke at press conferences was transformed into a loftier, more literary rhetor when delivering a scripted text. In private, a third Kennedy persona emerged. Such differences became important to the electorate when the White House transcripts revealed that the private and public Richard Nixons differed markedly not only in what they said but in how they said it. (Courtesy National Park Service. Photo by Abbie Rowe)

niloquent public style of "Let us never negotiate out of fear and let us never fear to negotiate."

Not until the political demise of President Richard Nixon did the public and press focus on the differences between public and private presidential speech. Not until the advent of President Ronald Reagan have scholars been required to explain the effectiveness of public use of what is ordinarily regarded as private conversational style.

In contrast to Kennedy, Ronald Reagan seems stylistically and tonally consistent whether functioning as public speaker, interviewee, question answerer, or inhabitant of the house at 16th and Pennsylvania. Where our sense of the others must reconcile the disparities in style, inviting the question, "Will the real president please stand up," our sense of Reagan jells easily with what else we know of who he is. He sounds like the same person regardless of setting. "Nobody is entirely him or herself in front of a microphone," notes Noonan. "You can't be. It's an inhibitor. The president's conversation in private is more relaxed and imaginative and colorful but his public and private self are very close." "What you see is what you get," concludes *Washington Post* White House reporter and veteran Reagan watcher Lou Cannon.[17] This, I would suggest, is one secret of his popularity and of his ability to insulate that popularity from the double-edged razors in some of his policies.

Not until the revelations of the Pentagon Papers and the Nixon White House transcripts would the differences between the public self of the president and the private self become a preoccupation of press and public. These private papers documented that presidents had dissembled in public statements. But the White House transcripts demonstrated, in addition, that what we saw stylistically in public did not correspond closely to Richard Nixon's patterns of private speech. In both cases truth was contained in the private conversation conducted behind closed doors; deceit wrapped itself in formal public rhetoric. Accordingly, the revelations subtly suggested that a private conversational style was the more trustworthy form.

The public belief that casual, conversational remarks reveal where formal public address conceals was evident before Johnson and Nixon. Dewey damaged his candidacy among blue-collar workers in general and railroad employees in particular when he lashed out at his train engineer for unexpectedly causing the train to lurch at a whistlestop. "That's the first lunatic I've had for an engineer. He probably ought to be shot at sunrise but I guess we can let him off because no one was hurt." The suggestion that Dewey's train had pulled out with a "jerk" was irresistible to comics and Democrats alike.[18]

The arrogant, callous tone of Dewey's remark and its failed attempt at humor seemed to corroborate Alice Roosevelt Longworth's characterization of him as the man atop the wedding cake. Indeed, if not harnessed, the man atop the wedding cake might hurl hands full of icing at the blue-collar help. More recently, Jesse Jackson's 1984 run for the Democratic nomination was hampered when a reporter revealed that, in what Jackson had taken to be an off-the-record conversation, he had referred to Jews as Hymies, a comment in sharp contrast to the rhetoric of reconciliation implied in the phrase the "rainbow coalition."

Although I suspect that it is true, I am not prepared to argue that differences between a public and private speech style will necessarily damage a public figure. Instead, I believe that consistency between public and private styles is uniquely advantageous when the style is a competent but personable one. Were a president's public and private style off-putting, this obviously would not be the case. However, when one's popularity is constructed on a consistency between private and public speech and an artful self-revelation, the impact of disclosures that this president said one thing and did another is particularly damaging. As I will argue later, the revelations of Irangate threatened two of Reagan's most powerful means of personal identification with the American people.

Reagan's inaugural previewed the style that would characterize his presidency. Structurally and stylistically there was little difference between the inaugural address and the new president's remarks that afternoon as he signed the Federal Employee Hiring Freeze Memorandum. At the signing, he said, "This—for the benefit of the oral press—this is an order that I am signing, an immediate freeze on the hiring of civilian employees in the executive branch. I pledged last July that this would be a first step toward controlling the growth and size of government and reducing the drain on the economy for the public sector. And beyond the symbolic value of this, which is my first official act, the freeze will eventually lead to a significant reduction in the size of the federal work force. Only rare exceptions will be permitted in order to maintain vital services. Now I am happy to be taking this action in this historic room, a sign of what I hope will be full cooperation between Congress and the executive branch" (January 20, 1981).

Reagan's consistent conversational bent contrasts even to the practice of the president eulogized for his plain "Give 'em hell" style. Unlike Reagan, Truman employed one style when delivering a scripted speech on a formal occasion and quite another on less formal occasions. In his inaugural, he said, for example (January 20, 1949):

> Democracy alone can supply the vitalizing force to stir the peoples of the world into triumphant action, not only against their human oppressors, but also against their ancient enemies—hunger, misery, and despair.
> On the basis of these four major courses of action we hope to help create

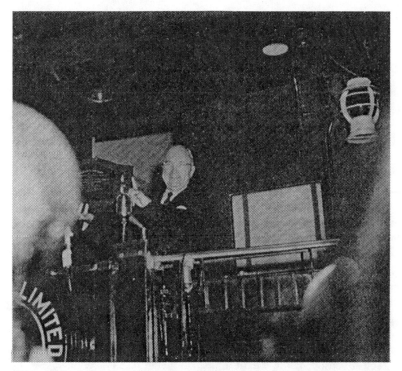

Although he "gave 'em hell" while whistlestopping, in his inaugural address
Harry Truman adopted the formal style scripted for him by his writers. (Courtesy Political History Division, Smithsonian)

the conditions that will lead eventually to personal freedom and happiness
for all mankind.

If we are to be successful in carrying out these policies, it is clear that
we must have continued prosperity in this country and we must keep ourselves strong.

Slowly but surely we are weaving a world fabric of international security
and growing prosperity.

The next day a very different sounding Harry Truman thanked the
Women's Division of the Democratic National Committee for giving
him a bronze of himself (January 21, 1949).

I do appreciate most highly . . . what the Women's Division . . . has done
in organizing this meeting, and in presenting me with myself.

Nobody, of course, can understand what he looks like to other people. He can only see one side of himself, and if he looks in the mirror, he is not right sure whether that is true or not, because he thinks he's better looking than that. . . .

I went down to the Capitol this morning to have breakfast with the Missouri delegation. In spite of the fact that I got to bed at 3 o'clock and got up at 5:30, I made it down there in time. . . .

I do want to thank you most sincerely for this cordial expression of your kindness and admiration for your President. I hope that it will not be necessary, at some future date, to have it destroyed, as I have seen done with public men who have been awarded things of this kind, while they were yet alive. I hope that you will always feel that I should have had this in the beginning, and shall continue to have it in the future.

Although Truman had won the 1948 election with hard-hitting, plain-spoken extemporaneous speeches, his inaugural address was encased in cadenced, crafted prose.

Reagan's Use of Self-Disclosure

Because he comfortably employs a consistent conversational style, Reagan is able publicly to disclose facets of himself and facts from his past that protect him politically. Although his style did not meet the traditional criteria of eloquence, it was often effective and endearing.

Self-disclosure is not meant to be trumpeted to an assembled throng but spoken softly to intimates. By self-disclosure I do not mean the routine mining of one's own past for the nuggets of accomplishment that can be alchemized into political gold. Phrased in pedestrian form, they proclaim "what I did as congressman, senator, governor, general or astronaut I will do as president." Of these, Reagan has his share. But, additionally, Reagan's conversational delivery and consistent sense of public self enable him to use his *personal* past in uncommonly effective ways to underscore central themes and undermine attacks.

Scholars of interpersonal communication tell us that openness invites openness; disclosure, disclosure. Self-disclosure can accelerate our sense of intimacy in a relationship. Reagan's judicious use of personal revelation accounts, in part, I suspect, for the fact that even his opponents profess to like him as a person. Reagan wears this affection as political armor, insulating him from the slings of outraged opponents and from the sting of unpopular policies.

We lack the vocabulary to speak of *public* intimacy. For us, intimacy and privacy are intertangled. Decorum dictates that we speak personal words quietly and in ways that do not attract public notice. The keepers of public etiquette condone words of love whispered to an intimate other in a crowded room. But shout the same words to the same person in the same place, and what was once condoned as endearing will be condemned as exhibitionistic. The same is true about other personal facts and feelings; we do not shout secrets, we confide them. Reagan understands that television speaks not to crowds but to individuals; accordingly, it is suited to self-disclosure. While speaking quietly and conversationally, he confides in us.

Along the same lines, we expect intimacy to occur between individuals, not between an individual and a mass audience. Consequently, some in his audiences squirmed when in 1976 Jimmy Carter closed his campaign speeches by proclaiming to the anonymous masses, "I love you."

The broadcast media enable a president to speak to us as individuals in the privacy of our homes. Roosevelt transformed this realization into an intimate radio style; Reagan, whose professional life started in radio, expanded his range to include television. Where FDR and occasionally JFK were proficient in use of the broadcast media, most other modern presidents were deficient. "President Johnson never really felt at home in front of a television camera," notes his former aide Jack Valenti.[19] "Like many a politician bred to fight and speak in local union halls, clubhouses, and spacious arenas before large groups of people, LBJ never felt comfortable staring at a red light atop some contraption with a single lens that was staring back at him. It was too drained of human juices, too lacking in the stir and stomp of a public responding to his exhortations."

By disclosing the private details of the lives of public figures, the press has eased the way for Reagan's public intimacy. Contrasting Washington D.C. in 1960 and 1986, columnist David Broder observes that "the intrusiveness of the media has grown."[20] Frank Cormier of the Associated Press told Broder, "There was a much greater tendency then to be protective of sources in general and politicians in particular. They don't get that kind of coddling now. Reporters saw John Kennedy in the back seat of a limousine with a woman who wasn't his wife, and nothing was said or written. Today, there would be tremendous competitive pressures to report that."

Some conclude that such revelations by the press have damaged the presidency. "The collapse of restraints over what is and is not printed in the press and displayed on video is a spike in the heart of the presidency," notes Valenti. While unremitting vigilance by the press has damaged some presidents, it has benefitted others in an unexpected way. By basting the public's belief that it is entitled to such information, such revelations have disposed us to not only accept but welcome comparable revelations by presidents themselves. Reagan's disclosures are at one with the culture that consumes televised docufiction about the lives of its celebrities, carries home *People* magazine, and at checkout counters casts more than an inconspicuous glance at *The National Enquirer.*

In one sense, Reagan's personal public style simply magnifies a trend already present in the modern presidency. A computer-based analysis of the speeches of the presidents from Truman through Carter revealed a steady increase in rhetorical familiarity and self-reference.[21] Reagan's personalized discourse is a natural extension of that trend. What differentiates him from most of his predecessors is the artfulness of his use of familiar speech.

Reagan's low-key style lends itself to personal statements about his past and his feelings. To seem credible, such statements cannot sound either crafted or scripted; their delivery must seem spontaneous and sound sincere. The formality of John Kennedy's public speech style lent itself to wit, but not intimacy. There is virtually no personal discussion by Kennedy about himself in his televised political speeches. When such material emerged, it was either on the campaign trail or out of camera range. And even then the level of disclosure did not approach Reagan's. So, for example, in his toast to President de Gaulle of France at the dinner at the Elysee Palace (May 31, 1961), Kennedy noted, "it is not difficult for this President of the United States to come to France. I sleep in a French bed. In the morning my breakfast is served by a French chef. I go to my office, and the bad news of the day is brought to me by my Press Secretary, Pierre Salinger, not in his native language, and I am married to a daughter of France." When speaking publicly about this daughter of France, the president of the New Frontier antiseptically titled her "Mrs. Kennedy."

Alternatively, speech that casts the public in the role of voyeur invites squirming. Nixon's nationally televised farewell to the White House staff was self-disclosive in ways that raised apprehensions quieted only by the fact that his signed letter of resignation was being transmitted as he spoke.

The revelation itself must make sense in the context of the relationship in which the candidate or president engages us. As the previous chapter's illustrations from the rhetoric of Johnson and Nixon suggested, self-disclosure for its own sake seems exhibitionistic or narcissistic.

In the 1976 campaign, Jimmy Carter revealed facts of his past artfully. From a repertoire of stories about federal inefficiency and his own proficiency as Georgia's governor, Carter projected a government as good as its people.

Once president, he could not find a comparable resource to explain himself and his presidency. When he mined his past in the 1980 campaign, Carter unearthed arguments not for his own reelection but for the election of Truman or Roosevelt. Repeatedly in his campaign addresses, Carter noted, "I grew up as a small boy during the Great Depression. I was born in 1924. I saw the Democrats, under Franklin Roosevelt, change my life. Our family didn't have electricity on the farm. Franklin Roosevelt was for the REA; the Republicans were against it. I saw old people in so-called poor folks homes. Franklin Roosevelt and the Democrats thought we ought to have Social Security; Republicans were against it. . . . I remember when I got a little bit older, we thought that elderly citizens ought to have some health care. I believe Harry Truman put forward Medicare. My opponent, Governor Reagan, got started in politics traveling around the country almost professionally speaking out against Medicare" (October 21, 1980). When it came to building the case for his own four years as president, the peanut farmer, who in 1976 had reminded voters that he knew what it was like to manage a small business and to work with his hands, was transformed into a sermonizer and a statistician.

What presidents have revealed and concealed about their illnesses points up the disclosive difference between Reagan and his predecessors. After leaving the hospital in November 1955, Eisenhower told those who had gathered to say goodbye at Lowry Air Force Base:

> Again it is time for Mrs. Eisenhower and me to say good-bye to Denver after a summer's stay. This time we leave under somewhat unusual circumstances. As you know, I have spent some time in the hospital. Such a time is not wholly a loss.
>
> Misfortune, and particularly the misfortune of illness, brings to all of us an understanding of how good people are.
>
> To General Griffin, the staff at Fitzsimons, the medical staff, the nurses, the clinical technicians, the enlisted men—all of the people that even clean out the hospital: my very grateful thanks, because they have done so much, not only to take care of me, but to make my stay as pleasant as possible. . . .
>
> Then, Mrs. Eisenhower and I have both been touched by the volume of messages that have come in—telegrams and letters and flowers and gifts. And finally we have been especially grateful for the knowledge that over this country and over the world friends have sent up their prayers for a sick person. . . .
>
> And I hope that those people who have sent in messages—and Mrs.

Eisenhower has not been able to reach them all; she did her best—that they will know, through this little talk, that we are eternally thankful to them.

So uncomfortable was Johnson with discussing his surgery that he spoke of its intended beneficiary in first personal plural, a habit carried over from his discussion of his legislative accomplishments. But here "we" created the impression that "Mrs. Johnson" planned to undergo the operation with him (November 13, 1966 News Conference):

> We will leave San Antonio tomorrow morning, 9 or 10 o'clock. Mrs. Johnson has an engagement in Washington at 3 o'clock. We will be there ahead of that time.
> We plan to go into Bethesda Naval Hospital Tuesday afternoon, will spend the afternoon and evening there and will undergo surgery early Wednesday morning.
> It is anticipated that we will have an anesthetic and the operations will take perhaps less than an hour. Within an hour we will be out from under the influence of the anesthetic.
> I have talked to the Vice President. . . .
> We expect that we will be in the hospital for a very few days and then we will be returning to Texas. I am hopeful that I can spend a good portion of my time on the Budget between now and the first of the year; and the State of the Union Message.

Nixon's response to his first hospitalization in thirteen years (July 20, 1973) revealed both his facility and his inabilities as a communicator. His thanks to the staff of the hospital and to his own staff are gracious. Unlike Johnson, Nixon speaks of himself in first person. He jokes that he's heard from everyone in the country who has ever had pneumonia. In a move that Reagan will raise to a minor art form, Nixon reads a charming letter from a child. "Dear President Nixon," the boy writes. "I heard you were sick with pneumonia. I just got out of the hospital yesterday with pneumonia and I hope you did not catch it from me. Now you be a good boy and eat your vegetables like I had to. . . . If you take your medicine and your shots, you will be out in 8 days like I was. Love, John W. James III, 8 years old."

Like Reagan, Nixon has an impulse to speak directly to the letter writer. It is a form of address he cannot sustain. "Well, John W. James III, I got out in 7 days, so I did a little bit better than he did. But perhaps my case of pneumonia was not as difficult as his. I will take his advice. I will eat my vegetables. . . ."

Had Nixon simply added that he was now ready to get back to work, the speech would have used self-revelation in a manner suitable to a president—graciously, self-effacingly, even charmingly. Instead, he veered into the sort of inadvertent confession that fed the fears of both friendly and hostile Nixon watchers. The person who emerges from behind the words is self-aggrandizing; he postures; his ploys are worrisomely transparent. His attempts to seem heroic are mock-heroic. "[O]ur friends in the press . . . the whole Nation . . . and . . . thousands who have written me" will want to know, says Nixon, that his doctors have advised him to "slow down a little now and take some time off and relax a little more." The words he attributes to them sound as contrived as those in which Carter in the 1980 debate conveyed his daughter's concerns about nuclear war. According to Nixon, they said: "Mr. President, now look, you have excellent health, you have been very fortunate that you have established a modern record of 4½ years in the White House without having missed a day because of illness, but you have got to realize you are human."

Having awarded himself a place in the *Guinness Book of Records* for his record-breaking attendance in office, Nixon relays his melodramatic reply. "No one in this great office at this time in the world's history can slow down. This office requires a President who will work right up to the hilt all the time. That is what I have been doing. That is what I am going to continue to do. And I want all of you [his staff] to do likewise."

Nixon then implies that he is willing, perhaps eager, to sacrifice his health in the service of his country. "Oh, I know many say, 'But then you will risk your health.' Well, the health of a man is not nearly as important as the health of the Nation and the health of the world." Having suggested his indispensability to the nation and the world, he adds, "I don't say this heroically," although one might reasonably infer that that is his intent.

Next, without directly saying so, Nixon hints that his critics have caused · his illness. At the same time, he reiterates his resolve not to resign. "Another bit of advice, too, that I am not going to take—oh, it really isn't advice. I was rather amused by some very well-intentioned people who thought that perhaps the burdens of the office, you know, some of the rather rough assaults that any man in this office gets from time to time, brings on an illness and that after going through such an illness, that I might get so tired that I would consider either slowing down or even, some suggested, resigning." Such suggestions, he says, are "plain poppycock."

After rehearsing the accomplishments of his administration and forecasting the tasks ahead, he reveals the purpose to be served by all this pathos. "There are these and other great causes that we were elected overwhelmingly to carry forward in November of 1972. And what we were elected to do, we are going to do, and let others wallow in Watergate, we are going to do our job."

As Nixon and Johnson's comments suggest, one risk of public self-revelation is that more will be revealed than intended. Nixon and Johnson's self-referential statements provided more fodder for students of psychology than either would have wished. Their statements have become confessions unprotected by priestly seal, inviting not confidence but concern.

Where they fail, Reagan succeeds. In a radio address following his surgery for rectal colon cancer, Reagan was, in the words of *The New York Times*, "unusually personal."[22] First, Reagan thanks "some very special people" including the doctors and nurses and those who wrote, called, and included him in their prayers. One of the nicest cards, he notes, "was the one from the nurses down the hall who sent me a card from the new babies in pediatrics. It was signed with their little patients' tiny footprints."

He then moves to a gentle self-indictment for ignoring the warning signs: "We all tend to ignore the signs that something may be wrong with us." Reagan understands that he can speak directly to specific groups in his audience and does that here. "So if you're listening to this right now and it reminds you of something that you've been putting out of your mind, well, pick up the phone, call your doctor or local hospital. Just tell them Dr. Reagan sent you." As America's Dutch uncle, Reagan is asking that we learn from his mistake. In the process, he reinforces the belief that he and we are much alike.

Eisenhower, Kennedy, and Johnson spoke of their wives as "Mrs."; Reagan's nationally aired radio speech is a lace-trimmed valentine for "Nancy." "First Ladies aren't elected and they don't receive a salary. They've mostly been private persons forced to live public lives. Abigail Adams helped invent America. Dolly Madison helped protect it. Eleanor Roosevelt was FDR's eyes and ears. Nancy Reagan is my everything."

Delivered without postage, the spoken love letter continues. Through national radio, Reagan is now talking to a woman who is seated with him in the same hospital room. "When I have thought on these days, Nancy, I remember your radiance and your strength, your support, and for taking part in the business of this nation." The fact that the sentence won't parse increases its credibility. Emotions after all do not dance to grammar's dictates. "Thank you, partner," he adds. "By the way, are you doing anything this evening?" The press recounts that "At that point Mrs. Reagan, who was seated near her husband, began to weep."[23]

Reagan is the first president to share moments of intimacy with a national audience in a way that does not seem self-serving or vulgar. There was intimacy in LBJ's display of his gall bladder scar but intimacy of the sort that violated decorum. In a sense, that act symbolized a problem for LBJ—he could not readily find words to translate his own sentiments into those of others. He showed what he should have kept shirted because he could not say what needed to be said.

As I have indicated, Reagan's personal statements are politically dexterous because they invite an affection that protects him from attack. By pre-empting or rebutting charges to which he otherwise is vulnerable, the statements serve a second political purpose as well. Like the visual assertions of the previous chapter, these statements act as evidence, but evidence that by traditional standards would not constitute proof. So, for example, Reagan summons a night before Christmas long past to certify three claims important to his 1980 candidacy: (1) that his age is an asset, not a liability, for only a candidate his age could have lived through the '30s Depression; (2) that he is unwilling to bring down inflation by increasing unemployment; (3) that he is a compassionate person who will not repeat the country's past mistakes.

In his nationally telecast speech announcing his candidacy in 1980 Reagan told the story in these words:

> I've lived·through one depression. I carry with me the memory of a Christmas eve when my brother and I and our parents exchanged our modest gifts. There was no lighted tree as there had been on Christmases past. I remember watching my father open what he thought was a greeting from his employer. We all watched. And yes we were hoping it was a bonus check. It was notice that he no longer had a job. And in those days the government ran radio announcements·telling workers not to leave home looking for jobs. There were no jobs. I'll carry with me always the memory of my father sitting there holding that envelope, unable to look at the rest of us. I cannot and will not stand by while inflation and joblessness destroy the dignity of our people.

In the middle of the 1982 recession, Reagan returned to that story to certify his personal commitment to solving the problem of joblessness. In his October 13, 1982, televised speech to the nation, some of the inferences invited in the first telling became explicit premises.

> I have a special reason for wanting to solve this problem in a lasting way. I was 21 and looking for work in 1932, one of the worst years of the Great Depression. And I can remember one bleak night in the thirties when my father learned on Christmas Eve that he'd lost his job. To be young in my generation was to feel that your future had been mortgaged out from under you, and that's a tragic mistake we must never allow our leaders to make again. Today's young people must never be held hostage to the mis-

takes of the past. The only way to avoid making those mistakes again is to learn from them.

Reagan's personal revelation has served other important purposes. Like the fact of his survival, Reagan's freshening of the assassination attempt skillfully sabotaged those who sought to read senility into every press conference stumble. The account was included in the film shown at the Republican convention of 1984 and replayed in the campaign's nationally aired documentary film. These films revive our own memories of our experience of the hours after the assassination attempt as news footage of the shooting played and replayed in our living rooms. In the Reagan documentary, we see that footage once again, this time with its sound muted. The surviving president narrates. In a calm, controlled voice he tells what he experienced and what he learned from it.

Reagan's recovery is reassuring. The memories of the assassinations of Robert and John Kennedy and Martin Luther King, Jr., remain painful for many in the audience. Three much younger men have been killed. His close brush with death, his good-natured response to it, and his calm recollection of it counter concerns about his age. He is not only physically strong and psychologically resilient but a testament to his own themes. By surviving, he joined his own pantheon of ordinary heroes who were able, when their country required it, to do the impossible. The campaign's recreation of these traumatic days helps insulate Reagan from his fumblings in the first debate with Mondale. Unaware that the slowness of his actual recovery was covered up, viewers can say of his performance in the debate, "He just had a bad night."

But the personal recollections accomplish even more than this. Although our society is premised on the separation of church and state, it nonetheless requires that the president function as the secular head of the country's national religion. Presidents find it difficult to telegraph their religious convictions to a public that includes atheists, agnostics, and Seventh Day Adventists. When they try, most fail. Their remarks about God seem formulaic. Playing on our expectation that a close brush with death will change one's life, Reagan explains that he, in effect, has committed the rest of his life and presidency to God. In the context of his personal statement about the assassination, we do not find the statement unusual or offensive.

If transferred to a public speech, the same claim would raise questions. So, in subsequent addresses, Reagan refers to the experience elliptically. "We are a nation of idealists," he said in his 1986 State of the Union message, "yet today there is a wound in our national conscience. America will never be whole as long as the right to life granted by our

Creator is denied to the unborn. *For the rest of my time,* I shall do what I can to see that this wound is one day healed" *(emphasis added).* Those for whom religion is salient are more likely than the rest to read into that statement: "For the rest of [the borrowed time God has given me]." Others who are less likely to remember the story about his conversation with Cardinal Cooke can hear the claim to mean "For the rest of my term as president."[24]

The form of self-disclosure and the context that occasioned it permit Reagan to utter what a president would otherwise say at some political risk.

I didn't know I was shot. In fact I was still asking, 'What was that noise?' I thought it was firecrackers. And the next thing I knew, Jerry, the secret service had simply grabbed me here and threw me into the car and then he dived in on top of me. And it was only then that I felt a paralyzing pain and I learned that the bullet had hit me up here. When I walked in they were just concluding a meeting in the hospital of all the doctors associated with the hospital. When I saw all those doctors around me I said I hoped they were all Republicans. I've been asked about a visitor that I had while I was recuperating back in March of 1981, Cardinal Cooke. He was a wonderful man, a most dedicated man, and just one of the most kindly men that I have ever met. And we were talking about some of the—call them coincidences that had happened at the time of the shooting and that I had heard after I'd started to recover. And he said that in view of them God must have been sitting on my shoulder. Well, he must have been. I told him that whatever time I've got left, it now belongs to someone else.

Reagan also uses personal revelation to take the hard ideological edge off of some of his controversial claims. After noting that there were 45½ pages of want ads in the *LA Times* on the Sunday he was last there and after arguing that companies were begging people to take their jobs, Reagan backs away from the implication that the unemployed don't want jobs with a humorous piece of self-disclosure:

I look back and I feel sorry for some of the young people today, because one of the better jobs I ever had in my life was the job I had working my way through college. I washed dishes in the girls' dormitory (January 26, 1983).

Like Roosevelt and Kennedy, Reagan uses humor to deflect serious questions. Playing such humor through requires a lightness of tone, a seeming spontaneity, an off-handedness that Nixon, Johnson, Ford, and Carter seemed to lack. If humor is to succeed, the speaker must appear good natured but not enraptured with his or her own cleverness. A subtle sense of surprise that the humor is appreciated helps. Humor is particularly important in a president because it establishes that the person doesn't take himself too seriously. Intuitively, we suspect that mirth and megalomania don't mix.

Kennedy seemed to enjoy language play. He called himself a textual deviant, for example, and recast the language of a cigarette ad to say that he was reading more [newspapers] now but enjoying it less.

FDR, Kennedy, and Reagan used humor to parry and pre-empt attacks. In the most decisive moment of his 1984 campaign, Reagan sealed his reelection by parrying concerns about his age with humor in the second presidential debate. He also pokes fun at his former professions. "I know once when I was out on the mashed potato circuit before I—well, that was when I was unemployed—" (March 17, 1981). Alternatively, he notes, "in all my years in Hollywood, I was never a song and dance man; that's how I wound up an after-dinner speaker" (September 9, 1982). Recalling that his final movie was *Hellcats of the Navy*, Reagan told cadets at the Naval Academy that if he were given another script "it would probably be for *The Old Man and the Sea.*"

Because he earned his living as an actor, the notion that he is the pawn of his staff, a front man for the ideas of others, a script reader, is one he must cope with. He does this in part by revealing an instance in which he used his skills as a communicator to engage in friendly fabrication. The story, says reporter and Reagan expert Lou Cannon, is "Reagan's own favorite . . . from the more than six hundred games he recreated" as a radio announcer. As with many of Reagan stories, discrepancies emerge in the retelling. Sometimes, in his autobiography, the batter is reported to have been Augie Galan; in other tellings it is Billy Jurges.[25]

Reagan's account goes like this: When he was announcing a ball game over radio, the wire carrying the needed information went dead. Improvising, Reagan claimed that the batter hit one foul, then, stalling for time, claimed that he'd hit another and finally a third. "And he kept on fouling them until I was beginning to set a world record for a batter hitting successive fouls" *(laughter).*

When the information from the actual game began to flow again, Reagan learned that "Billy popped out on the first ball pitched." One scholar concludes that this story, "shows us just how comfortable he can be with illusion. Having taken himself and his listeners into an imaginative stadium, the future President instantly turned to outright fiction to avoid losing his audience. Unwilling to break the spell by which he held them, Reagan simply lied, albeit harmlessly and for a motive which no one could hold against him."[26] Yet in later retellings, Reagan seems aware that that is a possible conclusion and, with an aside, moves to blunt the inference that the story might predict presidential behavior. "I don't suppose being in the business I'm in now I should ever tell you that I faked something out that way," Reagan noted after relating the baseball story to the Mathews-Dickey Boys Club (July 22, 1982). After repeating the story to a group of high school students in Chicago, he adds (January 19, 1983), "But maybe I shouldn't tell that. You—people are suspicious enough of those of us in politics."

Reagan is comfortable recalling stories about his own past mistakes, recollection that invites audience identification. He tells of giving a speech in Mexico while he was governor. At the end, he sat down to so little applause that he was "a little embarrassed. So, when the next fellow got up and started speaking to the audience in Spanish, and they were applauding—well, I beat them to it after every time. I was so embarrassed I applauded longer and louder than anybody, until our Ambassador leaned over and said to me, 'I wouldn't do that if I were you, he's interpreting your speech' " (September 17, 1982). Reagan demonstrates his skill as a communicator by revealing that he does not take the label "Great Communicator" too seriously. "I used to find," he told an audience, "when I was Governor myself, sometimes, that I'd go home and make very eloquent speeches in the shower" (September 7, 1981).

Reagan's instinctive move to deflect a tough issue with humor is evident in his repeated efforts to set aside a reporter's question about a Justice Department report alleging the existence of discriminatory federal statutes. Initially, Reagan says that it hasn't reached him yet. The reporter claims that it has. Reagan jests, "Don't tell me I'm losing my memory" (laughter) and proceeds to defend his appointment of women to positions in government. Undeterred, the reporter reiterates that he has the report and adds that it reveals the occurrence of sexual harassment. Reagan parries: "Harassment?" (laughter) "Now, Sarah, just a minute here with the discussion, or we'll be getting an R rating" (laughter). The banter continues with the reporter insisting that Reagan does indeed have the report. Finally, the president concludes, "I'll look into that and see what it is, but I don't recall anything that really had an X rating that ever was handed to me" (laughter) (July 29, 1982).

Reagan's spontaneous humor went a long way toward countering the charge that he is a creature of the scripts of others. When asked after his cancer surgery how he felt "on the inside," Reagan volleyed, "The same as I do on the outside" (December 30, 1985). Reagan's most facile use of humor occurred in a moment of national crisis. With an assassin's bullet lodged within an inch of his heart, Reagan's one-liners reassured the nation that he would survive. "Honey," he told his wife, "I forgot to duck." To his surgeons he said, "Please tell me you're Repub-

licans." "Reagan's critics had sometimes deplored his one-liners as un-
convincing inventions of his speechwriters," noted an article in the
Washington Post.[27] "But in this moment of crisis, Reagan's wit was revealed as genuine—and as a graceful and courageous response to pain
and adversity."

Where Reagan is the master of the one-liner, John Kennedy's ban-
tering humor took a more sophisticated form. He deflected the claim
that his father's money was buying the 1960 election for him by reporting that his father wanted to buy no more votes than necessary to
win. Pressed about the possible influence of the Vatican on his presidency, Kennedy responded that he now understood why Henry the
Eighth set up his own Church. Challenged over the appointment of his
brother as Attorney General, he responded, "I don't see anything wrong
with my trying to give him some legal experience before he goes out to
the private practice of law."

With a smile, Kennedy thwarted a challenge by Lyndon Johnson at
the Democratic convention of 1960. In a strongly worded speech before the Massachusetts and Texas delegates, Johnson touted his record
in the Senate and criticized that of an unnamed opponent. Because
Kennedy's response is humorous it makes its point without blatantly
alienating Johnson or his supporters. More important, Kennedy managed to avoid responding to Johnson's claims about the demonstrable
weaknesses in his record as a senator from Massachusetts.

Kennedy noted that Johnson "made some general references to perhaps the shortcomings of other Presidential candidates, but as he was
not specific, I assume he was talking about some of the other candidates and not about me. I have found it extremely beneficial serving in
the Senate with Senator Johnson as leader. . . . it is true that Senator
Johnson made a wonderful record in answering those quorum calls,
and I want to commend him for it. I was not present on all those occasions. No, and I was not the majority leader. As Lyndon knows, I
never criticized. In fact, on every occasion, I said that I thought Senator Johnson should not enter the primaries, that his proper responsibility was as majority leader, and that if he would let Hubert, Wayne,
and me settle this matter, we could come to a clear-cut decision."[28]

FDR also used humor to avoid serious political charges. Fala entered
the history books as the dog whose Scotch soul was tormented by the
thought that someone was lying about how he was transported home.
"These Republican leaders have not been content with attacks on me,
or my wife, or on my sons. No, not content with that, they now include
my little dog, Fala. Well, of course, I don't resent attacks . . . but Fala
does resent them. . . . I think I have a right to resent, to object to

libelous statements about my dog" (September 23, 1944). For FDR, humor was also a weapon of attack. The Landon sunflower, he told reporters, was " 'yellow but had a black heart and was fit only for parrot food.' [T]o which someone added that it was dead in November."[29]

Humor also made indictments of his opponents more palatable. On September 29, 1936, in a speech in New York, Roosevelt launched his political campaign by recounting:

> In the summer of 1933, a nice old gentleman wearing a silk hat fell off the end of a pier. He was unable to swim. A friend ran down the pier, dived overboard and pulled him out; but the silk hat floated off with the tide. After the old gentleman had been revived he was effusive in his thanks. He praised his friend for saving his life. Today, three years later, the old gentleman is berating his friend because the silk hat was lost.[30]

To mute the possibility that he is revelling in his own greatness, Reagan's descriptions of his accomplishments are often either couched in humor, as is the confession to have enjoyed washing dishes in a girls' dorm, or include a statement that pulls his experience into line with our own. The latter move is evident in Reagan's recollection of a particularly clever comeback to the challenge of a young dissident. " 'Your generation cannot understand its own sons and daughters,' the young man argued. 'You didn't grow up in an era of space travel, of jet travel, of cybernetics, computers figuring in seconds what it used to take men years to figure out.' And he went on like that. And usually you only think of the answer after you're gone, but the Lord was good to me. And he talked long enough that I finally interrupted him, and I said. 'Wait a minute. It's true what you said. We didn't grow up, my generation, with those things. We invented them' " (February 7, 1983).

Reagan does not credit his rejoinder to his native superiority. Instead, he implies that, like the rest of us, it would have been more usual for him to find the perfect response hours after it was too late. But with the help of the Lord and the verbosity of the adversary, he managed to come back with the perfect response. Because he's handled the story with a light touch, we appreciate both the story and the storyteller.

Where Reagan is self-deprecating, Nixon was self-aggrandizing. One charms, the other chafes. "If anyone listened as I did to what was said at that mass . . . ," Nixon noted on one occasion (September 7, 1970). "Rather than saying 'Democrats for Nixon,' " he observed during the 1972 campaign, "why not 'Democrats for America.' That is what it is really all about" (September 23, 1972). "When I was your age," he told an audience, "or perhaps a little younger—let's see 1932 to 1939—in those years, I was in high school, later went on to college, then to law

school, finished law school, and incidentally, worked all the way through."
(September 25, 1972). "I remember, since I was somewhat of a student
of history, that when I went to Duke University in 1934, after a very
good college education at Whittier in California, I was utterly convinced that Ulysses S. Grant was the best general produced on either
side" (October 12, 1972). In his final speech as president, Nixon said,
(August 9, 1974), "I had a little quote in the speech last night from
T.R. As you know, I kind of like to read books. I am not educated, but
I do read books."

Reagan's disclosures about his relationship with his wife both underscore his commitment to family values and rebut critics who, early in
his administration, had characterized her as extravagant and uncaring.
The warmth and affection they convey about each other silently underscore Reagan's claims. His effectiveness as a champion of family values
is a tribute to his skills as a communicator. As the country's first divorced president, a person reportedly not close to his own children,
Reagan exhibits his commitment to family by publicly showing his devotion to his wife.

The fact that the Reagans are comfortable on camera is evident when
comparing a scene from a Ford commercial in 1976 with one from a
Reagan commercial in 1984. In the Ford ad, the president and Mrs.
Ford walk stiffly toward the White House. They appear to have placed
their arms around each other under duress. The moment is awkward.
In the Reagan half-hour documentary, the president and Mrs. Reagan
walk easily together. While watching the Fords, the audience feels like
Heisenberg aware that the process of observing alters the objects being
observed. By contrast, the Reagans are natural. We seem to be walking
with them. Gone is our sense that we are intruders. The Ford ad seems
voyeuristic; the Reagan believable. They are relaxed about being private in public; we are comfortable with their comfort. Reagan's tribute
to his wife from his hospital room simply extends into words what we
have seen to be true elsewhere.

By making it difficult to focus effectively on his personal or program-
matic consistency, Reagan's judicious use of self-revelation, humor, and
public conversation complicates the press's pursuit of two of its stock
lines of inquiry. The day-to-day, forum-to-forum sameness of Reagan's
style subtly underscores the notion that he is politically and philosoph-
ically self-consistent.

In a way that makes little logical but much emotional sense, we are
not disposed to see inconsistency in his actions toward the Russians, for
example, even when it does exist. How after all is it that he is negoti-
ating with Gorbachev when the Evil Empire according to rhetoric past

has broken every promise it ever made and is bent on destruction of our way of life? When changes in position are apparent, the trust inspired by Reagan's consistent revelatory communication style disposes us to believe that he is acting in what he perceives to be the best interest of the country.

This coupled with the self-disclosure also gives the Reagan presidency an opacity. We expect candor of someone employing such a style. We also observe how he has altered the political landscape with this style. What was an "arena," an image conjuring up gladiators, is for Reagan a living room. Yet, while smiling and shrugging, Reagan managed to both parry and brazen the Caesars who tried to engage him there. When his undoing came, it was at his own hand.

Reagan's self-disclosive response to Irangate posited consistency between the public president who had denied that he had authorized a trade of arms for hostages and the private individual who had in fact approved the deal. In his apologia of March 4, 1987, Ronald Reagan simultaneously invited the affection built on public/private consistency and minimized his legal culpability. The cost was high. Accomplishing these ends required that Reagan sacrifice his ability to lead the nation. To the extent that the self-defense succeeded, Reagan became a titular head of government. Resounding silence met his plea after the June summit that the country rally behind his efforts to reduce the deficit. Reagan had become a British monarch without bloodline, capable of ceremonial leadership but having no claim to formulate policy.

The first term of Reagan's presidency disassociated a command of fact from a capacity to govern. The person who stumbled over details in press conferences and in his first debate of the 1984 campaign was reelected in a wash of public confidence that he had nonetheless managed to bring "America back" economically and militarily. His ability to delegate was prized as well. Carter's ads of 1980 bragged that he worked late; Reagan took pride in spending evenings at "home." Reagan's narratives worked in service of convictions that he conveyed with a sincerity carrying a cogence of its own.

To absolve himself in a self-consistent way, Reagan must basically argue that in an important foreign policy matter others were in charge. If he is capable of re-exerting control now, why didn't he then? He either gives up that right and sacrifices the ability to lead, or asserts the capacity of exerting control nonplausibly.

Reagan accounts for the inconsistency between his earlier claim that he did not trade arms for hostages and the Tower Commission's Report that such a deal was made by saying, "A few months ago I told the American people I did not trade arms for hostages. My heart and my best intentions still tell me that is true, but the facts and the evidence tell me it is not." He told the American people what he believed and still believes. The facts, which he says he accepts, speak otherwise. Here is a person overcome by his own convictions, convictions so powerful that they occlude his vision of what is. By contrast, we have no doubt as Watergate unravels that Richard Nixon knew exactly what had happened, knew it was illegal, pursued it anyway, and then conspired to cover it up.

Are Reagan's convictions now under control or will they continue to both distract him from questions that should be asked and overshadow facts he should command? The speech moves to confirm that Reagan is still overwhelmed by his convictions. In a revealing juxtaposition of ideas, Reagan first explains that he mistakenly let his concern for the hostages spill over into geopolitical strategy, failing to ask enough specifics about the Iran affair. Then, rather than detailing the specifics he should have commanded, Reagan spends a paragraph addressing the hostage families, a move that argues that he remains preoccupied with the hostages and hence remains incapable of asking the right questions.

> I undertook the original Iran initiative in order to develop relations with those who might assume leadership in a post-Khomeini Government. It's clear from the Board's report [not clear to him but clear from the board's report], however, that I let my personal concern for the hostages spill over into the geopolitical strategy of reaching out to Iran. I asked so many questions about the hostages' welfare that I didn't ask enough about the specifics of the total Iran plan.

After positing a limited capacity to ask questions, as if he may ask only a certain amount without exhausting his quota, Reagan veers into an emotional statement about the very hostages who supposedly distracted his attention at a previous critical time. "Let me say to the hostage families, we have not given up. We never will, and I promise you we'll use every legitimate means to free your loved ones from captivity."

Since Reagan's public persona never was dependent on a command of factual detail and since his conveyed sense of genuine conviction was consistently a characteristic of who he was perceived to be, the defense arguing that he was motivated by ideological conviction but lost track of the details was one capable of reconciling the public Reagan and the one revealed in the Tower Commission Report. If, alternatively, he was integrally involved in the decision-making process, his public disclaimer of the arms deal must have been a lie. As an involved decision maker and lier, Reagan could plausibly be painted as a probable co-conspirator in the efforts to cover up the illegalities revealed in the Congressional investigation.

The March 4, 1987, speech of self-defense presupposes that Reagan is an amiable ideologue victimized by his past success as a delegator. His low-key, conversational manner and his narratives about honor, hard work, and individualism make it difficult to view him as a crazed ideologue—a Rasputin. Rather, he is to be watched with a wariness born of affection.

Three times in the speech Reagan concedes that he is not the repository of either fact or truth. First, he could not speak to the American people until the Tower Commission had determined what happened. Nor can he speak to the issues left unresolved by the Report. Like the people, he must await "the continuing investigations of the court-appointed independent counsel and the two Congressional investigating committees." Finally, because record-keeping was inadequate, he couldn't remember when he approved the arms deal. Facts inhere in records, not in Reagan. Irangate has established the need for the president to command the facts. The speech has established that ideology can blind Reagan to fact. Throughout he tells us that he has become a character in a story that must be told by someone else. The paternal role assumed by the tribal storyteller can no longer be his.

Such a president requires competent advisors who scrupulously will act within the law and who resolutely will confront the ideologue in Reagan with the facts. In the past, Reagan has delegated poorly. His solution to this problem is once again to delegate. This time to a new chief of staff, a new national security adviser, and a new director of the CIA. But having magnified their credibility and credentials, Reagan undercuts their role by reducing them to furniture to be moved—"I am considering other changes in personnel, and I will move further furniture as I see fit in the weeks and months ahead." Furniture cannot be trusted to guide an ideologically driven president.

Finally, Reagan assures the country that he's learned his lesson and will move on. It's the "healthiest way to deal with a problem." But the speech shows a president who has not learned. He is still preoccupied with hostages, still not in command of either the facts or the truth, and still confident that in delegation is salvation.

Reagan's style had enabled him to speak for us; to the extent that we must now be wary of his ideologically driven actions and alert to the possibility that under their influence he will tell us what by any other name would be a lie, we distance ourselves from him. If his patriotism has led to actions we disapprove of, then his rehearsal of our patriotism can only be an end in itself, not a means of securing assent to policy.

Entrusted with ceremony but not policy, Reagan can follow the public will, as he did in the Soviet arms agreement; he can't lead it.

But as a figurehead, Reagan cannot readily be made out to be a crook. Because he did not command the facts, he cannot be accused of direct involvement in illegalities; because he was ideologically blinded he can rationalize any involvement that is uncovered; because he retains·our affection, we are ill disposed to seek the vengeance whispered in the shadows of past attempts to impeach.

Where Nixon's detailed, articulate, strategic apologiae confirmed one after the other that he was both capable and disposed to wield detail and truth for his purposes, Reagan's poor performance at the June 1987 economic summit increased the credibility of his claim that he was not involved in the intricacies of the Iran/Contra affair. How could one suppose that Reagan was a conspiring accomplice in such detailed doings when at the post-summit Vienna press conference he could neither recall the name of the UN Security Council nor remember his own strategy to stabilize the dollar? Such misstatements subtly underscore his claim that it is not true that "behind the scenes" he "violated the law" and did "all sorts of shady things to try and violate the Congress' restriction on aid to the freedom fighters" (May 27, 1987).

Moreover, if not forgivable, his failing is at least understandable. Long before Oliver North became a household name, Reagan had proclaimed publicly that the Contras were the moral equivalent of the founding fathers. His actions then were consistent with his public discourse. What actions would we have denied France had they benefitted George Washington during the Revolution? "I made it plain," Reagan reminded reporters in his May 27, 1987, news conference, "[I] went to the public trying to arouse public opinion in this country, in support of our position so that they would influence their representatives in Congress to continue providing the aid." Throughout, Reagan was able to contend as he did in his January 27, 1987, State of the Union address that "The goals were worthy. I do not believe it was wrong to try to establish contacts with a country of strategic importance or to try to save lives. And certainly, it was not wrong to try to secure freedom for our citizens held in barbaric captivity."

Unlike Nixon's, these actions were neither venal nor self-interested. Reagan's impulses are noble and cause-driven. His failing is that he proved a True Believer in a cause that could not be fully championed without congressional consent. And Reagan's cause is less menacing: "freedom fighters," not an anti-war activist, military support abroad, not a break-ins at home. Understandable. Perhaps even forgivable. But as a flaw, fatal in one we expect to lead.

8

The Divorce Between
Speech and Thought

"The evening of February 27, 1933, at Hyde Park was cloudy and cold.
. . . Inside the warm living room a big, thick-shouldered man sat writing by the fire. From the ends of the room two of his ancestors looked down from their portraits. . . . Franklin D. Roosevelt's pencil glided across the pages of yellow cap paper. 'I am certain that my fellow Americans expect that on my induction into the Presidency I will address them with a candor and a decision which the present situation of our Nation impels.' The fire hissed and crackled; the large hand with its thick fingers moved rapidly across the paper. . . . Phrase after phrase followed in the President-elect's bold, pointed, slanting hand. Slowly the yellow sheets piled up. By 1:30 in the morning the inauguration speech was done."[1] James MacGregor Burns' description of the composition of this important speech was consistent with that reported four years earlier by Roosevelt intimate and speechwriter Samuel Rosenman, who wrote: "The speech was one of those very few of which the President wrote the first draft in his own hand. He wrote it on yellow legal paper, sitting by the fire at Hyde Park on the night of February 27. The original manuscript is now in the Roosevelt Library at Hyde Park."[2]

Indeed, in the Roosevelt Library is a draft of the inaugural written in Roosevelt's hand. Appended to it is a memo typed by the president-elect and dated March 25, 1933. "This is the original manuscript of the Inaugural Address as written at Hyde Park on Monday, February 27,

THE WHITE HOUSE
WASHINGTON

March 25, 1933.

This is the original of the Inaugural
Address - March 4th, 1933 - and was used by me
at the Capitol. Practically the only change,
except for an occasional word, was the sentence
at the opening, which I added longhand in the
Senate Committee Room before the ceremonies
began.

Franklin D Roosevelt

****

So eager was FDR to take credit for writing his first inaugural that he tran
scribed in longhand the draft written by a speechwriter and fabricated a story
about his authorship of the speech. (Courtesy Franklin D. Roosevelt Library,
Hyde Park, New York)

1933. I started it about 9:00 P.M. and ended it at 1:30 A.M. A number
of minor changes were made in subsequent drafts but the final draft is
substantially the same as this original."
    One problem mars these compelling accounts. FDR did not draft his

The draft of the inaugural that FDR copied onto a yellow legal pad survives in the Franklin D. Roosevelt library as a testament to the fact that in one sense he did *write* his own speech.

famous first inaugural. As Roosevelt speechwriter Raymond Moley has documented, it was he who wrote the draft. To corroborate his claim, Moley dug out the notes FDR dictated, his own elaborations, and his outline of the speech. Moley's evidence suggests that on February 27, at Hyde Park, FDR examined his ghost's draft of the inaugural address. "He read over my draft carefully," Moley recalled, "and then said that he had better write out the text himself because if Louis Howe . . . failed to see a draft in his [Roosevelt's] handwriting, he would 'have a fit.' "[3]

The president and his ghost then edited the longhand copy of the draft. In the morning, Louis Howe added the inaugural's most famous line, "the only thing we have to fear is fear itself." Not until 1964 did Moley learn of Roosevelt's claim to authorship. In the meantime, FDR's ruse had outfoxed the author of *Roosevelt: The Lion and the Fox* as well as jurist, FDR speechwriter, and confidante Samuel Rosenman. Both learned the hard way that politicians are all too ready to take credit for someone else's words.

Since much of what we know about our leaders is learned from what they say to us, their speechwriters help shape our perceptions of them. Such scribes may shape public policy as well. "I learned early in the Administration," wrote Carter aide Hamilton Jordan, "that the persons who control the President's rhetoric exert an enormous influence over his actions and policies. For when a President says something, it moves pending issues, policies, and thinking in one direction or another and often defines the terms on which the battle, in Congress or among the voters, will be fought. . . . The battles over a President's words are really struggles over the heart and soul of his Presidency."[4]

The increasing presence of such struggles signals a change from the time of Demosthenes, Cicero, and even Lincoln and Churchill. In the past, responsibility for discovering *(inventio)*, structuring *(dispositio)*, and expressing argument in apt language *(elocutio)* resided more centrally with the speaker than it now does. Although I've spoken throughout these chapters of the thoughts, understandings, insights, and convictions mirrored in presidential speeches, all that you or I can know with surety is that the people involved spoke the words that embodied those thoughts, understandings, insights, and convictions. This chapter explores the implications of the division of labor that in modern times has sundered speaking from thinking, the act of delivering a message from the process of conceiving it.

The Ghosts of Speeches Past

For almost as long as there have been speakers, speechwriters have created their words. The first may have been Moses who was, by his own admission, "slow of speech and slow of tongue." God instructs Moses to "put words" in Aaron's mouth.[5]

Since Athenians were required to represent themselves in court, the F. Lee Baileys of ancient Greece were speechwriters, not speakers. Litigants lacked the time or the talent to become rhetoricians, notes classicist R. C. Jebb. Accordingly, they found it "worthwhile to buy their rhetoric ready made."[6] Antiphon was the first known logographer to compose speeches for pay. Fifteen ghosted speeches by Antiphon survive from the fifth century B.C.[7]

In place of the ghosts of courtrooms past who wrote the words of defendants and plaintiffs, we now have lawyers who speak for their clients. But where the leaders of the body politic were then expected to forge their own thoughts into words and to weather the verbal challenges of their adversaries and the members of the audience, today most political leaders rely on the language of others.

Since the birth of their profession, speechwriters have been condemned for corrupting public discourse. In Plato's *Phaedrus,* an Athenian politician reportedly berated Lysias for being a speechwriter.[8] In 1950, the Supreme Court described the ghosting process as "the custom of putting up decoy authors to impress the guileless."[9]

Formerly cast as whores, speechwriters are more often being seen as handmaidens. "Not too long ago," observed historian Ernest May in 1953, "topical indexes contained the reference: 'Ghost Writing—see Forgery'; now the searcher is referred instead to—Authorship; Collaboration."[10]

Then, as now, some have placed their eloquence in service of inept, inarticulate, and occasionally even evil leaders. Seneca, for example, helped Nero write his maiden speech as Roman emperor and assisted as well in composing Nero's eulogy of the emperor resurrected in the series *I, Claudius.*

The leader whose dying words reportedly were "Et tu, Brute" may have had help composing "Veni, vidi, vici." He was in good company. Both Alexander the Great and Pope Julius II employed ghostwriters. Hidden hands moved across the texts of the father of our country as well. Alexander Hamilton, James Madison, and John Jay gave the prose of George Washington a touch of rhetorical class.[11]

Had Hamilton written the country's first presidential farewell in Washington's own style, he would have violated the first president's request to make it honest, unaffected, and simple. Washington told Hamilton: "Even if you should think it best to throw the whole into a different form, let me request, notwithstanding, that my draught may be returned to me (along with yours) with such amendments and corrections, as to render it as perfect as the formation is susceptible of; curtailed, if too verbose; and relieved of all tautology, not necessary to enforce the ideas in the original or quoted part. My wish is, that the whole may appear in a plain stile; and be handed to the public in an honest; unaffected; simple garb."[12]

Ghostwriters helped Andrew Jackson convert "his vigorous but illiterate thoughts into respectable prose."[13] Indeed, Jackson's Nullification proclamation, written by Secretary of State Edward Livingston, bears the signatures of both Livingston and Jackson.

A bit more than a century later, speechwriting became a profession that dared speak its name. In 1952, American University aroused controversy when it announced a new course in speechwriting, the first in the country. Not everyone welcomed the new profession with flowers and champagne. "We admit there are a lot of ghost writers in Washington," responded commentator and reporter Eric Sevareid. "And we claim that is one reason government has become less articulate, its leaders less able to move and excite the American people. We don't understand government leaders who are too busy to write their own speeches, for a man's own words are the man's own self. He wouldn't dare use a false face or a false name: it is equally fraudulent to use false words."[14]

The battle lines had been drawn a decade earlier when Walter Lippman equated failure to write one's own speeches with failure to say one's own prayers and write one's own love letters. "The truth," argued Lippman, "is that anyone who knows what he is doing can say what he is doing, and anyone who knows what he thinks can say what he thinks. Those who cannot speak for themselves are, with very rare exceptions, not very sure of what they are doing and of what they mean. The sooner they are found out the better."[15]

Even as American University was enrolling its first aspiring wordsmiths, presidential candidates were denying that they kept company with such creatures. Those who swore that Ike and Adlai wrote their own prose lived to retract it. When Democratic candidate Adlai Stevenson was asked whether he composed his own speeches, he replied, "I am blushing—appropriately, I hope."[16] The blush was indeed appropriate but not for the reason he implied; Stevenson's Elks Club was filled not with hunters but with writers. Republicans as well as Democrats dissemble about the origins of their speeches. In the same campaign, General Eisenhower claimed, "All my prepared talks are thrown out the window."[17] If so, someone outside not only caught them but pitched them back in, for Ike too relied on scripted texts.

The appetite of the broadcast and print media for fresh material dictates that few of those able to write their own speeches have the time to do so. Prior to their incarnations as presidential candidates, both Ike and Stevenson had crafted speeches for others. Given the time, both presumably could have drafted their own pronouncements.

At least some of the time, Ike and Stevenson had a second excuse for relying on scripted texts. In 1952, a televised speech had to be written out before it could be delivered because the script had to be pre-timed to fit half-hour or hour-long live broadcasts. That justification for speechwriting has eroded. Presidents no longer time their statements to end as the second hand is signalling a break to the next half hour's programming. When the speech is aired as a public service by the networks, commentators either fill in the unexpired time or the station returns to normal programming. If the speech is aired in purchased time, it can be edited by the president's media advisers if too long or supplemented with other material if it is too short to fit the units in which air time is sold.

Repeated delivery of the same unaltered speech is also less likely in the broadcast age. In times past, a politician could recycle the same speech to one local gathering after another without risk that reporters would convey its substance to the nation. So, for example, through repeated delivery, William Jennings Bryan perfected the lines of argument immortalized in his "Cross of Gold" speech. Had he wanted to make the same move in 1988, he would either have had to add newsworthy items to the speech each day or sacrifice access to the national news audience. More important, by the convention at which the supposedly fresh speech was supposedly spontaneously delivered, the speech would have been yesterday's news to those interested in politics. Its punch would have been spent in preconvention news clips.

When television was live, politicians deviated from their pretimed scripts at some political peril. Because he was out of time, Nixon was cut from the air near the end of his famous "Checkers Speech" before he could tell his audience the address to which he wanted their supportive letters and telegrams sent. Adlai Stevenson routinely disappeared from the screen, his time up, before he had completed his speeches. Consequently, the eloquent peroration to his election eve speech in 1952 was unheard by the country until aides were able to purchase additional time for it later in the evening. Because he habitually was revising the text even as he approached the podium and because he delivered speeches at varying rates, Stevenson failed to deliver even pretimed speeches within the allotted minutes.

Accusing one's opponents of being the creatures of the scripts of others did not originate with Democratic attacks on the actor turned president, Ronald Reagan. In 1962 Nixon implied that his victorious rival, JFK, was a "puppet who echoed his speechmaker." "A public figure when he's running for President shouldn't be just a puppet who echoes his speechmaker. The ideas should be *his*, the opinions *his*, the words *his*. . . . I think it's important that the guy at the top communicates directly what he believes—even if it's pedestrian and dull. It's easier for Kennedy to get up and read Sorensen's speeches. But I don't think it's responsible unless he believes it deeply himself."[18] Yet, once in the presidency, Nixon assembled a speechwriting staff so sizeable that it overshadowed all but FDR's. Until Richard Nixon's presidency, speechwriters were camouflaged on the payroll as administrative aides. Nixon changed that title to writing and research staff.[19]

"It is a form of hypocrisy for politicians to imply that they write all their own speeches," notes Bill Moyers, former Johnson aide and speechwriter.[20]

It is more usual than not to find the speaker playing some role, however minor, in the writing of a major political address. On occasion speakers show more sense about the process than their ghosts do. When FDR found excessive alliteration in the draft of a speech, he pared it out. So, for example, a draft of the four freedoms speech (January 6, 1941) contained the claim "In the future days which we seek to make secure, we look forward to a world founded fundamentally upon four essential human freedoms."[21] By the next draft, "fundamentally" had vanished.

Others should have welcomed help when it was offered. Daniel Webster, one of the finer orators of the nineteenth century, volunteered to draft William Henry Harrison's inaugural address. Although Harrison insisted on penning his own speech, he did let his newly appointed Secretary of State take a look at it. Later, Webster revealed that his contribution to the address was killing "seventeen Roman proconsuls as dead as smelts."[22] Although smeltless, Harrison's speech is undistinguished.

Some of our most eloquent presidents, including Lincoln and Wilson, occasionally had a helping hand; several including FDR and Kennedy made extensive use of the writing talents of others. Wilson's "neutrality of thought" proclamation (August 10, 1914), long thought to have been of his own making, turned up in original draft in the hand-writing of counselor to the State Department Robert Lansing.[23]

Lincoln's first inaugural benefitted from help by William Seward who was responsible for suggesting part of the speech's most famous paragraph.[24] In Lincoln's revision, we see eloquence at work. Seward had written, "I close. We are not, we must not be, aliens or enemies, but fellow-country(men) and brethren. Although passion has strained our bond of affection too hardly, they must not, I am sure they will not, be broken." Lincoln substituted: "I am loathe to close. We are not enemies, but friends. We must not be enemies. Though passion may have strained, it must not break our bonds of affection."[25]

Many of the memorable sentences spoken by our leaders have been borrowed. A newsman travelling with "Black Jack" John J. Pershing is credited with inspiring "Lafayette, we are here." Although Henry Clay said it, "I'd rather be right than President" was originally phrased by Senator William C. Preston.[26] Louis Howe is credited with "nothing to fear but fear itself," Samuel Rosenman with "I pledge you, I pledge myself, to a New Deal for the American people," Thomas Corcoran with "This generation of Americans has a rendezvous with destiny." "I shall go to Korea," was written by Emmet John Hughes. Ike's farewell warning about the military industrial complex was penned by Malcolm Moos. John Kenneth Galbraith supposedly wrote "Let us never negotiate out of fear, but let us never fear to negotiate."[27] Peggy Noonan contributed Reagan's claim that "the freedom fighters of Nicaragua . . . are the moral equivalent of our Founding Fathers."

Some speechwriters have more authority than others. In the 1956 presidential campaign, the Republican National Committee gave a ghost the task of churning out daily attacks on the Democrats. Assorted Republicans had agreed to sponsor the resulting billingsgate, sight unseen. "Many times the fellow to whom the statements were attributed was campaigning far out in the hinterlands when his statement was released in Washington. He learned what a colorful talker he was only by reading himself in the newspapers."[28]

The tactic had ample precedent. In the final two years of the Hoover administration, Democratic publicist Charles Michelson issued attacks in the names of prominent Democrats with their permission. "[W]henever Hoover made some public statement, Michelson immediately pounded out an answer on his typewriter, selected the most effective name from his list of 'ghostees,' and within an hour had the Democratic comment laid down in mimeographed form on the desk of every Washington correspondent."[29]

Something comparable occurs when a passage passes from ghost to newsprint without pausing even momentarily in the purported speaker's mind or mouth. In 1960, speechwriter William Ewald recalled that candidate Nixon sometimes would deliver his stock canned stump speech from the platform "while a variety of handouts, labeled 'excerpts,' on a variety of subjects sailed off from his train or plane from coast to coast." On the premise that it would increase grocery prices twenty-five percent and cost two million jobs, one such undelivered excerpt excoriated Kennedy's farm plan. The next morning Ewald heard two reporters complain that "That excerpt on Kennedy's farm plan was uncalled for."[30] As a practical matter, since Nixon had never delivered it, the claim, quite literally, was *uncalled for*. By contrast, when Carter tired of delivering texts, he endorsed the sentiments expressed in the undelivered speeches.[31]

As FDR's memo about writing his inaugural attests, speakers are reluctant to confess that the words they speak are not their own. The exceptions have been noteworthy. After reading a passage from one of his speeches, Warren G. Harding commented, "I never saw this before. I didn't write this speech and I don't believe what I just read."[32] While running for a Senate seat in Oregon in 1956, Douglas McKay concluded a long speech with the announcement: "And now I'd like to say a few words of my own."[33] In a letter published in *Life Magazine*, Eisenhower thanked a writer for the fine result produced by one of his presidential speeches. "On every side I have had compliments concerning the content of the talk," noted the president. "I am sorry you could not take over also its delivery."[34]

Often, the speaker's delivery betrays the existence of ghosts behind the speech. New York Mayor John F. Hyland occasionally met his text for the first time in delivery. A story that may be apocryphal recounts His Honor delivering a joke he had not before seen. Unexpectedly convulsed in laughter by his own newfound wit, the mayor broke his glasses. The words that moments before had provided him with such pleasure were a blur. Faced with a script now as undecipherable to him as the Rune Stone, he was incapable of improvising the remainder. An aide, although not the one who'd written the speech, stepped forward to deliver the rest of the speech.[35]

Relying on speechwriters carries risks. As a member of FDR's Cabinet, Harold Ickes used the services of writers in the Department of the Interior. By doing so, "Ickes inadvertently did himself an injustice as far as his later life was concerned, for he built up, with the help of ghosts, a reputation for cleverness in repartee and pungency in writing that he failed notably to maintain upon leaving office."[36]

Some embarrassments were more immediate. Invited to speak at an important gathering in New York, two high government officials separately called the State Department for a speech. The U.S. Advisor to the UN, Dr. Isadore Lubin, was noticeably distressed as he listened to the speech being delivered by the Secretary of Labor, Lewis B. Schwellenbach. Schwellenbach was giving word for word the speech Lubin had in his pocket. When his turn came, Lubin confessed.[37]

The Need for Ghosts

The pressures that prompt politicians to hire squads of speechwriters rather than extemporize their way through political life include: the need to place advanced copies of the speech text in the hands of reporters to increase the likelihood of coverage and ensure accurate reporting and the necessity of putting the text on the TelePrompTer to enable politicians to sustain eye contact with the audience.

Additionally, careful phrasing is often required to ensure that a presidential speech will not be misinterpreted by those here and abroad listening for nuances. "The major speech that will be reported throughout the state or nation, or, perhaps, throughout the world, needs careful preparation," notes rhetoric scholar Ernest Bormann. "Each word must be weighed and the viewpoints pooled when a speech is prepared. The organization is full of experts who expect to be and usually are consulted when important statements are being drafted."[38] This was a lesson Jimmy Carter learned the hard way in spring 1977 when he talked about Israel's need for "defensible borders." The Arab states were alarmed. Israel rejoiced. Carter inadvertently had employed an Israeli code word which the diplomatic community took to mean the right to retain the territory gained during the 1967 war.

So, speechwriting is not to democracy what syphilis was to monarchy. Speechwriters have insinuated themselves into the great chain of being by providing leaders with a valued service. By shielding audiences from attack by toxic prose, wordsmiths occasionally engage in corporal works of mercy. H. L. Mencken said that the natural style of Warren Harding seemed like "a string of wet sponges; it reminds me of tattered washing on the line; it reminds me of stale bean-soup, of college yells, of dogs barking idiotically through endless nights. It is so bad that a sort of grandeur creeps into it."[39] "He invariably utters the expected," noted Mencken, "which is but another name for the not worth hearing. One half looks for him to abandon connected speech at any moment, and to start a mere chaotic babbling of stereotyped phrases: 'Please remit,'

'Errors and omissions excepted,' 'For review only,' 'Apartment to let.'
'Oh, say, can you see,' "[40] When Harding died, e. e. cummings memorialized his ability to write a "simple declarative sentence with seven
grammatical errors." The poem concludes:

> somebody might hardly never not
> have been unsorry, perhaps.[41]

Of course, a speechwriter may simply replace one set of rhetorical
problems with another. On May 14, 1920, Warren G. Harding proclaimed: "America's present need is not heroics but healing, not nos-
trums but normalcy, not revolution but restoration, not agitation but
adjustment, not surgery but serenity, not the dramatic but the dispassionate, not experiment but equipoise, not submergence in internation-
ality but sustainment in triumphant nationality." Economist and professor Jacob Hollander claimed to have written "normality" not "normalcy."
Years later he told a student "Poor Warren Harding . . . What he did
with that word showed a lot that was wrong with the man.[42] One might
ask, as well, what such anguished, awkward, aberrational alliteration
announces about its author?

In recent times too speechwriters have increased the effectiveness of
the speaker's message. McGovern's writers replaced his long, complex
sentences with shorter ones. Humphrey's writers not only shortened his
sentences but cut his speeches as well. Nixon's writers controlled his
tendency to ramble. Reagan's dignify anecdotes with argument.

The dilemma for public figures who wish to speak their own thoughts
in their own words is that they feel compelled to give more speeches
than they can conceive and capture in language. The number of speeches
by a president has risen dramatically in modern times. In the nineteenth century, presidents and presidential candidates rarely delivered
public addresses. The belief that the office should seek the person not
the person the office meant that, with few exceptions, those desiring
the presidency did not deliver campaign addresses. Once president, the
leaders of the nation dispatched most of their messages in writing by
messenger. From Jefferson's time until Wilson's, even the State of the
Union address, then called the annual message, was a written document. Veto messages and farewells were also scripted, not spoken. The
inaugural address was among the very few orally delivered pieces of
presidential discourse.

Spurred by the advent of the broadcast media and by changed conventions in campaigning, political speechmaking has increased. "Comparing 1945 to 1975, public speeches by America's chief executives increased almost 500%. . . . Jimmy Carter averaged one speech a day

during *each* of his 4 years in the White House."[43] In 1972, the *National Journal* calculated that more "than a half-million words annually flow out of the White House in a torrent of paper and ink."[44]

Still, if politicians are speaking more now, they seem to be enjoying it less. "I know you wish you could get out of writing so many speeches," Kennedy told his speechwriter Ted Sorensen in 1959. "I wish I could get out of giving so many, but that's the situation we're both in for the present."[45] "Of the many things demanded of him" in spring 1978, "Carter was tired most of all of giving speeches," noted his speechwriter James Fallows.[46] Both Kennedy and Carter might have taken a lesson from Abraham Lincoln. When a crowd gathered outside his hotel to cheer him, Lincoln came to the balcony and said (June 17, 1864):

> Fellow-citizens: I attended the Fair at Philadelphia today in the hope that possibly it might aid something in swelling the contributions for the benefit of the soldiers in the field, who are bearing the harder part of this great national struggle in which we are engaged. . . . . having said at the Fair what I thought was proper for me to say there in reference to that subject, and being more of a politician than anything else, and having exhausted that branch of the subject at the Fair, and not being prepared to speak on the other, I am without anything to say. I have really appeared before you now more for the purpose of seeing you . . . and allowing you to see me a little while (laughter) and, to show to you that I am not wanting in due consideration and respect for you, when you make this kind demonstration in my honor. At the same time I must beg of you to excuse me from saying anything further.[47]

More bothersome than the increased number of presidential and congressional speeches is the number of them delivered on matters of little consequence. Wouldn't the Republic be better served if the president invested the time he now spends congratulating Miss Teenage America, thanking farmers who delivered the national Thanksgiving turkey, and recycling the same set of anecdotes before another fraternal or civic organization in reading history, studying the writings of the world's great thinkers, pondering the meaning of the war photos exhibited at the Corcoran Gallery, reflecting on the nature of the office, and thinking out major speeches? Eliminating inconsequential speeches, labelled "Rose Garden Rubbish" by the press, would free the president for more important thoughts and activities and at the same time save the forests cut to print such speeches and the library space required to house them.[48]

By multiplying the occasions on which a president speaks, we invite premature articulation. Nixon speechwriter Aram Bakshian explains: "The word will come down that the President wants to talk about a particular policy area. But the policy may not be ready yet and the apparatus may not be ready to move yet, with the result that you very often are reduced to saying, 'Well, let's give them at least five things we're doing about this. So you end up with this itemized list of new initiatives which will sometimes take on a life of their own that they wouldn't have had otherwise. They are things that wouldn't have happened if it weren't for the speech."[49]

Magnifying the need for speechwriters is the increased complexity of the political world. Not only does Congress pass more legislation now than it did a century ago but the proposed legislation speaks to a greater variety of issues. To secure media coverage, members of Congress must say or do something that is concise, memorable, and relevant to the day's news agenda. In a media age, speechlessness is next to recklessness. Silence sacrifices name recognition and mandates using other means to tell the voters back home "I'm working." Congresspersons who do not sponsor and speak on legislation are vulnerable to their opponents' charge that they are "do nothings."

No single individual has the time or talent to search and seize the details, proposals, and language of the contemporary debates on subjects as dissimilar as the Sandanistas, sugar supports, and the snail darter. "A Senator or Congressman has to be so many things to so many people now," notes veteran congressional observer Roger Mudd, "that they don't have an hour in the day anymore to sit down and collect their thoughts."[50]

Members of Congress and presidents find that the solution is not in themselves but in their staffs. "The truth is that a senator is a syndicate," wrote the pseudonymous Rufus Dart II in *Scribner's Magazine* in 1932.[51] "No man who talks as much as the average senator can possibly wring from his own brain the enormous volume of words he spouts, or even be sure of their source. . . . There is probably no spot in the government where the literary ghost is so truly ghostly as in the Senate, and the shortest route to the number of senators who never have quoted one, consciously or not, is to take a census of the few who, for excellent reason, never speak at all."

The same is true today. "In Congress, it's a continuum," says *New York Times* congressional reporter Steve Roberts. "Some people are handed a script and pushed out there and read it; some, probably rare, do write a draft themselves; most are somewhere in between; they might get a draft, they might make changes in it; some days they have the time to do it; sometimes they don't. A high percentage of the speeches have sizeable input from someone other than the lawmaker. Every senator has a speechwriter on the payroll. There's no secret there."[52]

Changes in the Nature and Function of Political Speech

With the increased complexity of the legislative world, with the prolif-
eration of staff to keep the congressperson abreast of the issues, with
the advent of a national eavesdropping audience has come a changed
role for the congressional speech. "The role floor speeches play in the
legislative process is almost infinitesimal," observes Roberts. "People do
not make up their minds on the basis of floor speeches. The speeches
there are designed to summarize arguments, to gain press coverage
and with the advent of television to inform the general public. But does
any Senator or Congressman sit in front of his TV or sit on the floor
and say 'My God, that guy has really made the point. I'm going to
change my vote?' I'd be surprised if that happens half a dozen times in
a year." "With the pressure on members of Congress to declare themselves, take an early position, to be distinctive, minds are made up so
early that it's a rare day on Capitol Hill when a speech actually changes
a vote," notes Mudd.[53] "It can come on floor amendments and on spur
of the moment changes in the bill but most of this stuff is canned and
is delivered à la Mack Mattingly."

The media, argues Roberts, have changed the nature of the legislative process. The audience for the congressional speech is now not so
much the other members of Congress but the public that can be influ-
enced and mobilized by persuasive speech carried whole to a small part
of the audience by C-SPAN and digested for a larger audience by print
and broadcast news. "Members use the media to reach out to the public, to generate support which then rebounds on Congress." Senator
Philip Gramm's speeches on the deficit reduction proposal, Gramm-
Rudman, had such an impact, in Robert's judgment.

What is lost in the changed character of congressional speechmaking
is the refinement of argument borne of a direct and spontaneous clash
of ideas. When the substance of congressional hearings is the scripted
speech and question and the substance of floor debates is the pre-
fashioned text, both leadership and legislation are torn from the moor-
ings provided by the search for arguments, evidence, and language to
cogently sustain a case. When the building of an argument is separated
from its presentation, the case can neither be strengthened nor tested
in public debate. Chained to the phrases and proof in the text, the
presenter is ill prepared to do anything but repeat what has already
been said. Where the great legislation of the nineteenth century was
forged on the floor of Congress through give and take, the testing and
defense made possible when the presenter commands the case, the legislation of the last twenty years has more often been the by-product of

political trades and the loyalties of voting blocks than of public discussion.

Where it once occurred in the public forum, the testing of political ideas now occurs in back rooms, in public between the press and a politician or between adjacent snippets of speeches juxtaposed for public consumption by the media.

When a politician enters a forum clutching a text, public discussion is likely to be replaced by declamation. In the process, the existential risk that once accompanied public argument is lost and with it the susceptibility to persuasion that comes of mind confronting mind rather than script confronting script.

By divorcing the speaking of ideas from conception of them, ghostwriting also has clouded our ability to know the person who would lead. Insinuating speechwriters between the speaker and the message means that in most instances on the national public stage the speech will not reveal the actual speaker the way speeches of the past did or literature routinely does. Few politicians today can say with Henry Miller: "Every line and word is vitally connected with my life, my life only, be it in the form of deed, event, fact, thought, emotion, desire, evasion, frustration, dream, revery, vagary, even the unfinished nothings which float listlessly in the brain like the snapped filaments of a spider's web. There is nothing really vague or tenuous—even the nothingnesses are sharp, tough, conscious that the web I am spinning is made of my own substance."[54] Where Walt Whitman could say of his work, "Who touches this touches a man," most politicians would be required to confess, "Who touches this speech touches a speechwriter."

So, while it was possible for such scholars as Adrienne Koch to "rebuild and portray [Jefferson's] pattern of thinking" from his writings and speeches, to do the same for a contemporary politician is difficult, if not impossible. "If, on the basis of letters and speeches, a scholar should try to analyze Franklin Roosevelt's mind," notes Ernest May,[55] "he would emerge with a figure made up of Roosevelt and the fragments of Roosevelt's ghosts—Rosenman, Sherwood, Michelson, Grace Tully, Missey Le Hand, even the sprightly apparition of Harold Ickes."

The change is an important one for, as Bormann argues, an audience can only know a speaker by what he says if the speaker honestly presents himself as he really is. "When he reads a speech that reveals to his audience a quiet humor, an urbane worldliness, subtle and incisive intellectual equipment, then he should be that kind of man. If his collaborators . . . are responsible for the 'image' revealed in the speech, and if the speaker has different qualities and intellectual fiber, the speech is a deceit and it can be labeled as ghostwritten and condemned as unethical."[56]

As a practical matter, as I noted earlier, those who study a modern president's speech are analyzing not a single person but a syndicate. In an age in which voters increasingly vote for a person, not a party, the amalgam of advisers, writers, and an elected official that is the public president should be one that the voter can come to know and know well. How else can a citizen intelligently chose one candidate over another?

In the past, when candidates' party affiliations predicted their positions, fathoming their personal temperaments and talents was not a prerequisite of intelligent voting. In this age of personal politics, voters require more information about the mind and dispositions of the candidates than routine ghosting will permit.

As the Romans noted in the expression *stylus virum arguit*, our style betrays us. When crafted by others, style is sundered from the consciousness and the viscera of the speaker. Stylistic preferences that betray the person's weaknesses can be purged; strengths such as decisiveness, clarity, and self-effacement can be superimposed in their stead. When this occurs, language becomes a mask, the politician an actor.

Exposing the consciousness and the reflexes of those who would lead is important for a second reason. If the syndicate governed, a president speaking its words would provide a sense of the future leader's sensibilities. But, in some sensitive areas, it is the president alone who represents us, making decisions on our behalf.

International summitry is a political fact of life. At a summit, the president cannot consult with a gaggle of ghosts. The syndicate steps back. The single person of the communicating president steps forward. The matters at issue are consequential. What Roosevelt said to Stalin and Churchill at Yalta reconfigured Europe, what Kennedy said to Khrushchev at their first meeting may have precipitated the Cuban Missile Crisis, what Carter said to Begin and Sadat led to the Camp David Accords. None of these encounters was scripted.

Face-to-face contact between world leaders enables one to size up the other. "When I reflected on my encounters with him just after they ended, a picture of Khrushchev, the man, formed in my mind," recalled Richard Nixon. "Always on the offensive, he combined an instinctive feeling for his adversary's weaknesses with an almost compulsive tendency to press an advantage—to take a mile when his opponent gave an inch and to run over anyone who showed even the slightest sign of timidity. . . . He was a man who did his homework and prided himself on knowing as much about his opponent's position as he did about his own. . . . Despite his appearance of being highly emotional, he demonstrated to me that when anything of importance was being discussed, he was sober, cold, unemotional, and analytical."[57] Such assessments influence subsequent decisions on both sides. The electorate deserves the chance to try to ascertain the mental agility and disposition of those who will represent the United States in such close encounters.

The fact that the president can launch nuclear weapons provides another compelling rationale for giving the electorate the opportunity to see the minds of candidates at work. When they occur, debates provide one such chance. Others would be desirable.

Ghosting not only enables leaders to conceal what we need revealed but also, by providing words on demand, transfers policy-shaping powers to individuals more skilled in the nuances of language than legislation. In a White House haunted by ghosts, those elected to lead are inclined to cede constitutionally specified powers to those selected to write.

Increased presidential involvement in important speeches would benefit both the president and the country. When integrally involved in the speech's construction, the president is more likely to consider the circumstances that form the context of the message, as well as the speech's character and consequences. So, for example, Reagan insiders reveal that one means of getting him involved in an issue of importance to them is to make sure that he collaborates in the writing of a speech on that topic.

Such involvement clearly does not always occur, even on major speeches. "So great was Eisenhower's confidence in Hughes," noted another of Ike's writers, "that Hughes could begin the drafting of a talk scheduled, say, for Seattle as Ike's plane went wheels up, Seattle-bound, from Washington's National Airport; or finish drafting a speech for seven o'clock on nationwide TV at 6:50 P.M., pushing the page across the desk to the relaxed and waiting speaker."[58]

One would hope that presidential aide David Stockman is accurate when he notes that it is unusual for a presidential speech to be fashioned by the combination of fiction and frenzy that characterized the creation of Reagan's September 24, 1981, speech on his economic plan.

> The TV speech was scheduled for Thursday evening. . . . Six different drafts of the speech were now circulating inside the White House. But as of Tuesday evening, no one knew what the contents or thrust of the message would be. . . . By late afternoon [of the day of delivery] the President's speech was still being chopped, scissored, and pasted together in the Roosevelt Room. This was unusual to say the least. Ordinarily, nationwide

presidential addresses are wrapped up days ahead of time. Gergen, Deaver, the speech writers, and I were all shouting and throwing papers around, trying to make it come together. . . . [Reagan's speech contained] strong words, but they were a caricature of the truth, and they marked a profound turning point. On September 24, 1981, the Reagan Administration went into hiding from the massive fiscal disorder it had unleashed only months before.[59]

Nowhere in Stockman's account is Reagan credited with being part of the process of creating either the speech or the positions it expressed.

The extent of Reagan's conceptual involvement was called dramatically into question when in his press conference of June 12, 1986, he showed no sign of remembering words he had spoken credibly and with conviction three days earlier. In a speech at Georgetown University on June 9 Reagan had noted that "Just as the men and women of the resistance [the Contras in Nicaragua] have decided what they must do, so too, have [Soviet leader Mikhail] Gorbachev, [Cuban President Fidel] Castro, [Palestine Liberation Organization Chair Yasser] Arafat and [Libyan leader Moammar] Gadhafi."[60] When asked in his press conference what effect likening Gorbachev to these leaders would have on a possible summit, Reagan responded, "I didn't think I lumped him in with them." "It was in the speech," insisted the questioner. Reagan replied: "I—I certainly—then, it was a bad choice of words, because I didn't mean to do that. . . . I must have goofed someplace, because, believe me, I don't put him in the same category."

Mel Grayson, a speechwriter for Vice President Spiro Agnew, tells an equally troubling tale.

> "Vice President Agnew told the Supermarket Institute in Houston today," said the newscaster, "that unless the food industry does a better job of holding down prices, the government will step in and clamp a ceiling on them." That shift in administrative policy came as a surprise to just about everybody in America, including the administration. For the President and his key advisers had nothing to do with it. Nor for that matter did Vice President Agnew. The idea of tossing the price control bombshell at the food industry had been mine, all mine, and mine alone. . . . [I]t occurred to me that night . . . that in many important respects the world is being run by us public relations ghost writers.[61]

Ghosting's Effects on Speakers

Whether their presence is cause for rejoicing or lament, speechwriters are a fact of life. The pluses for the speaker already have been noted. But there are minuses as well.

When the ghosted text contains words the speaker can say truthfully and comfortably, speechwriting's divorce of speaking from thinking simply obscures our view of the thought processes and mind of the speaker, denies the speaker the advantages that come from writing one's thoughts, and deprives the public and the political process of public rhetorical exchange of ideas that can refine proposals and educate the audience. When the ghosted text sunders the speech act from the speaking self additional problems emerge.

Ghosts who try to capture the feelings that a leader should or does have cast speakers as John Alden. Gerald Ford's response to a passage in a ghosted text seems strange. "As I read his draft, tears came to my eyes. 'I am indebted to no man,' he had written, 'and only to one woman, my dear wife.' Hartman understood my feelings perfectly."[62] Why, we justifiably might ask, couldn't you write that for yourself, Mr. President? What is the effect of having another select the language in which to speak one's intimate self? Have elected officials arrived at a point at which ghosts are required either to feel for them or to translate their intimate feelings into language?

Perhaps ghosted speeches have done to politicians what Hallmark cards have done to the relationships between lovers and live-ins, mothers and children. With a ready-made expression available for $1.00, we are no longer disposed to express our own feelings with pen on paper. Signing our name to ratify someone else's expression of our feelings of friendship, love, or sorrow fractures the relationship between our personal self and personal expression. Induced by the convenience of it all to conclude that we either shouldn't or can't convey our own feelings, card carrying noncommunicators take comfort in the ads' assurances that they have cared enough to send the very best.

As alarming are the possibilities that purchasing and signing a card replace feeling the sentiments it expresses; reliance on such formulaic expressions endangers our capacity to feel friendship, love, or sorrow; by obviating the need for self-expression, such cards suppress the creativity that in times past memorialized deeply felt emotion in the world's great love sonnets and elegies.

If both feeling and expression are governed by the law "use it or lose it," the impact of ghosts on a leader's capacity to lead could be ghastly. Those who live by scripts alone may find that their own ability to think, speak, and write have gone the way of our sixth toe. One might speculate, for example, that President Reagan's reliance on speechwriters and before them scriptwriters played a role in his disposition to accept information about the Iran/Contra dealings uncritically and to trust his aides to act in his best interest. Casually and routinely delegating the responsibility for searching out the data to support claims, testing the relationship between fact and assertion, and locating the precise, expressing word may dull both a leader's disposition and ability to perform those tasks for himself. Why would we expect someone who embraces the words of others to suddenly become an active, inquiring, scrutinizing manager of information when offered a plan for aiding the Contras?

But where critic Roderick Hart would have presidents spend more time thinking about thinking,[63] I would add that they should spend more time in the active process of determining what questions are worth answering, gathering and testing data, studying historical precedents, weighing alternative proposals, considering the criticisms levied by their toughest adversaries and most thoughtful friends, and then thinking through the language in which to invite the country to their answers.

By separating self from the speech act, the ghosting process also invites a sundering of persona from person. In the process those who live by the script may lie by the script. If a speaker is the composite of the thoughts and words of others, why not use those words to create a persona dissimilar from the person delivering the text? The question gained currency when, in September 1987, news accounts revealed that presidential hopeful Senator Joseph Biden (D. Delaware) had appropriated not simply the words of the British Labor Party leader Neil Kinnock but his family history as well.* Both in a presidential debate at the Iowa State Fair on August 23, 1987, and in an interview taped by the National Educational Association three days later Biden spoke Kinnock's word and past as if they were his own.

In May 1987 Kinnock's Labor Party had aired a statement by Kinnock in his race against British Prime Minister Margaret Thatcher's Tories. Although the Labor Party lost the election, the spot was credited with boosting Kinnock's standing by twenty percent in the polls. In it Kinnock had asked: "Why am I the first Kinnock in a thousand gen-

*Such larceny is precedented in American politics. In March 1845 speaker of the House John White of Kentucky bade his colleagues farewell in words stolen from another farewell—the one delivered by Vice-President Aaron Burr as he left the Senate in March 1805. When the theft was detected, White was pilloried by those his words had originally impressed. A half year later he committed suicide. Included among the appropriated lines was a condemnation of efforts "by misrepresentation and traduction, to weaken the public respect and confidence in the immediate Representatives of the people." Plagiarism is not necessarily deadly, however. In his eulogy of the Duke of Wellington, the nineteenth-century orator and statesman Benjamin Disraeli pirated a section of Adolphe Theirs' eulogy of Marshal Gouvion-Saint-Cyr. The theft was noted and widely condemned. Disraeli went on to become British Prime Minister.

erations to be able to get to university? Why is Glenys [his wife] the first woman in her family in a thousand generations to be able to get to university? Was it because all our predecessors were thick?"

The speech went on to ask why his ancestors who worked in the Welsh coal mines had failed to prosper:

> Did they lack talent? These people who could sing and play and recite and write poetry? These people who could make wonderful, beautiful things with their hands? Those people who could dream dreams, see visions? Why didn't they get it? Was it because they were weak? Those people who could work eight hours underground and then come up and play football? Weak?
>
> Does anybody really think that they didn't get what we had because they didn't have the talent or the strength or the endurance or the commitment? Of course not. It was because there was no platform upon which they could stand.

Although his ancestor who worked in the mines was an engineer and despite the fact that some of his predecessors had been college educated, Biden concluded his appearance at the Iowa State Fair by saying:

> I started thinking as I was coming over here, why is it that Joe Biden is the first in his family ever to go to a university? Why is it that my wife, who is sitting out there in the audience, is the first in her family to ever go to college? Is it because our fathers and mothers were not bright? Is it because I'm the first Biden in a thousand generations to get a college and a graduate degree that I was smarter than the rest?"

Where Kinnock had exhumed his Welch progenitors, Biden beckoned his Irish ones:

> Those same people who read poetry and wrote poetry and taught me how to sing verse? Is it because they didn't work hard? My ancestors, who worked in the coal mines of northeast Pennsylvania and would come up after twelve hours and play football for four hours? No, it's not because they weren't as smart. It's not because they didn't work as hard. It's because they didn't have a platform upon which to stand.

As they dug deeper than any engineering miner, the press found that Biden had borrowed from the speeches of Robert Kennedy and Hubert Humphrey as well. There is remarkable ideological fidelity in these choices. Of the public personae of three liberals, Biden was fashioning a fourth. No one would fault his choice of ancestors were he not proclaiming that he was self-created. This act of rhetorical parthenogenesis invites us to ask, Is there a person who is Joseph Biden or is he simply a persona constructed of the feelings and history of others? And were he elected, how would we know who it was who was leading? Or whether the person who today is Kinnock and yesterday was RFK might not tomorrow submit to the allure of a new master text?

A speaker's problems are compounded when the sentences are the product of a covey of writers. When more than one ghost is writing for an individual, that person is more disposed to speak in somewhat dissimilar voices. The problem is not a new one. During the Revolutionary War, George Washington concealed his own "awkward style and unready pen"[64] behind the rhetoric of three secretaries who served as ghostwriters. David Humphreys wrote Washington's victory statement on the surrender of Cornwallis as well as Washington's responses to the audiences that gathered to celebrate the British evacuation of New York. The speeches are artful. By contrast, Washington's Farewell Order to the Armies of the United States "had a heavy introduction, superfluous statements within, and a feeble exhortation." The reason? Humphreys was too ill to write it; the substitute writer was not up to the task.[65]

Although professional wordsmiths claim to adopt the style and substance of the putative author, the speakers on occasion find that they are speaking someone else's soul. Reliance on writers can carry ideological implications. In the 1964 presidential race, Barry Goldwater may have been the victim of the ideological and rhetorical extremism of his writers.[66] "Barry Goldwater has been held to account for the strident language and the impolitic opinions of another man named Barry Goldwater," argues Richard Rovere.[67] "Almost everything that has ever appeared under his name has been cast in a rhetoric alien to his mode of thinking and speaking." Since Goldwater approved the books and articles that Rovere mined, he was, of course, ultimately responsible for their content. But if Rovere is correct, the Arizona senator's reliance on the thoughts and words of others counterfeited his own convictions and damaged his presidential prospects.

Sometimes the shadow cast by the speech reflects the substance of the speaker but the style of the writer. Although Ted Sorensen wrote in a manner that he believed paralleled Jack Kennedy's, it was a style fundamentally dissimilar from that of either Lyndon Johnson or Bobby Kennedy. Yet, for brief periods, Sorensen wrote for both.

Because JFK's ghost wrote Lyndon Johnson's first presidential speech to Congress, its style is eerily reminiscent of the late president's. The speech is not simply Johnson's eulogy of Kennedy but Sorensen's as well. What was unnoticed in the moving moment as the country continued to grapple with the meaning of Kennedy's life and death was that the speech was not written from the soul of the new president but from that of Kennedy's aide, friend, and speechwriter. Indeed, as what we had come to know as Kennedy's style pours through the text, it seems to hint that Kennedy might somehow have written his own eulogy.

But while the Kennedy/Sorensen style lives on in Johnson's speech, some of Sorensen's sentiments do not. Sorensen would have had Johnson say "the greatest leader of our time has been struck down by the foulest deed of our time—and I who cannot fill his shoes must occupy his desk." Between the time Sorensen dispatched his final draft and Johnson's delivery, the reference to Johnson's inadequacy was deleted.[68]

By delivering an announcement of candidacy written by Sorensen, Bobby Kennedy projected a persona different from that voters would come to know in the 1968 primaries. Such claims as "At stake is not simply the leadership of our party or even our country; it is the right to the moral leadership of the planet" echoed the deceased president, an echo underscored by the fact that Bobby Kennedy announced his candidacy in the same Senate room used by his older brother. But RFK's natural style was more direct and urgent, his rhetoric less lofty and more anguished than his brother's. In 1967 he had asked "Do we have a right here in the United States to say that we are going to kill tens of thousands, make millions of people . . . refugees, kill women and children? . . . I very seriously question whether we have that right. . . . Those of us who stay here in the United States must feel it when we use napalm, when a village is destroyed and civilians are killed."[69] Additionally, Robert Kennedy's speeches were less carefully crafted than his older brother's. Rhetorically there were two Robert Kennedys: one spoke the words of Ted Sorensen in his announcement of candidacy, the other adopted a discernibly different style in carrying his case to the American people.

If the scripted speech is not to raise suspicions about the character of the speaker, its style and substance must correspond to the style and substance of the public person the voters know or will come to know. In subtle ways, use of multiple speechwriters can undercut that sense. For example, two very different Nixons emerged in the closing weeks of the 1968 campaign. One attacked his opponent sharply: "Mr. Humphrey's political philosophy has failed him—and it has failed America." Humphrey is a candidate "who turns his back on the present and lives in the past. His team has had its chance. We now ask for the chance to succeed where it has failed." The other Nixon was gracious and gentle in his treatment of the Minnesotan. "Vice President Humphrey is a man I respect. He is a man of honor and a man of his convictions. And he honestly believes in the old ways. I believe in a new way." The first Nixon stripped Humphrey of his office by referring to him as "Mr.," not "Vice President." The first Nixon spoke of Humphrey's failure. The second Nixon mentioned instead Vice President Humphrey's old ways. The difference between the two Nixons was the difference in speechwriters. The first speech was written by Patrick Buchanan; the second by Raymond Price.[70]

When a speaker's words are scripted by a conglomerate of speechwriters, subtle but detectably different personae begin to speak through the mouth of the same person, a fact hardly reassuring to those seeking to find the person behind the public candidate. So, for example, Nixon speechwriter William Safire notes that "When Nixon wanted to take a shot at somebody, he turned to Buchanan, who could do so with relish, and who could also provide concise, hard-hitting suggested answers in a press conference briefing book. When Nixon wanted a vision of the nation's future, or wanted to express his compassion for the dependent, or to deal with urban affairs, he turned to Price, and later to the staff Ray headed. When he wanted to deal with the work ethic or economic matters, political philosophy or a touch of humor, he worked with me."[71] The Nixon who spoke through the words of Buchanan differed from the Nixon who spoke though the words of Price who differed from the Nixon who spoke through the words of Safire.

Still, behind each of these personae was Richard Nixon whose hand is evident in most of his major speeches. By contrast, under Gerald Ford, presidential speechwriters occasionally framed policy in the words they chose, words Ford delivered as written. This caused John Casserly, one of Ford's speechwriters, to ask, "How and why are we speechwriters given so much latitude? What makes any of us presume that we can attempt to put such words in the President's mouth?"[72]

The question "Does he or doesn't he?" resulted. Only his speechwriters knew for sure. "I have written in Mr. Ford's Concord, Massachusetts, speech for tomorrow that 'now is the time for reconciliation—not recrimination,' " wrote Casserly in his diary. "But I am also aware that in a Monday night television interview with CBS News, he will probably blame Congress again 'for not voting immediately the requested aid to Vietnam.' (As a matter of fact, that is precisely what happened.) This is contradictory. The country could not have 'reconciliation' at the 200th anniversary of the battle of Concord on Saturday and 'recrimination' on Monday. It seems to me that we are a split personality. I favor reconciliation if we are to get anywhere with Congress, but obviously my boss does not entirely agree with that."[73]

When a speech is jointly authored by two ghosts it can engage itself in battle. Bryce Harlow, a writer for Ike, produced detailed, headline inviting, hard-hitting argumentative speeches. One of Ike's aides observed that at its extreme this style could include "blood flowing in the gutters, virgins raped on every street corner, rockets fired off, purple in every sentence."[74] By contrast, ghost Kevin McCann wrote a more studied, lyrical prose. When they collaborated on a eulogy to Al Smith, the result was liverwurst on a croissant. From McCann: "Since the beginning of time men have deluded themselves—or have been deluded by other men—with fantasies of life free from labor or pain or sacrifice, of limitless reward that requires no risk, of pleasure untainted by suffering." From Harlow: "Newly passed legislation provides more generous tax treatment of some one-half million individuals and families with heavy medical, dental, or hospital bills."[75]

The speechwriters do not always merit the blame for speeches at war with themselves, however. The speech by Carter that the *Washington Post* titled "Two Different Speeches" was the by-product of Carter's inability to reconcile Vance and Brzezinski's views on the Soviet Union. Carter stapled Vance's memo to Brzezinski's, reworded the documents, and delivered the resulting speech to the U.S. Naval Academy in June 1978. "It had an obvious break in the middle," notes former Carter speechwriter James Fallows, "like the splice in a film; as one newsman who had read the advance text said, after hearing Carter come to the end of the conciliatory material and move into the Brzezinski section, 'And now—War!' "[76]

As the same ghost moves from employer to employer, the identifiable persona of that speechwriter may stalk the national stage. The speeches of Lindsay, Muskie, McGovern, and Edward Kennedy share stylistic and substantive similarities not simply because these public figures are ideological or temperamental kin but because at different times, they employed the same speechwriter—Bob Shrum. Shrum writes from a Catholic past, a past evident in the litany with which the Methodist McGovern's 1972 convention address closes. His is also a rhetoric of repentance and redemption. McGovern calls on the nation to repent over Vietnam; Edward Kennedy invites the convention to repudiate the false principles that have masqueraded as Democratic philosophy and return to true Democratic values. "The idea of redemption is at the heart of the whole liberal experiment," says Shrum. "I remember as a kid when liberalism was in fashion and the Church was trying to explain why it had always been for it. We read papal encyclicals like *Rerum Novarum*. There is a political and religious mix in my experience."[77] "There is a certain historical context, a set of feelings and beliefs I have about recent American history that I write out of," he adds. "The heroes are Franklin Roosevelt, John and Robert Kennedy. No matter who I'm writing for, one will probably find more references to them than to anyone else." Shrum's prose also reveals a preference for analogical argument, comparing present to past.

Sometimes the persona of the speechwriter steps through the speech to address the audience in powerful language not native to the speaker. The finest speech of the Eisenhower presidency embodies the sensibilities and style of its author, Emmet John Hughes, more clearly than those of the president speaking them. The poignant appeal for peace and an end to the arms buildup was delivered by Ike to the American Society of Newspaper Editors April 16, 1953. In it he said, "Every gun that is made, every warship launched, every rocket fired signifies, in the final sense, a theft from those who hunger and are not fed, those who are cold and are not clothed. This world in arms is not spending money alone. It is spending the sweat of its laborers, the genius of its scientists, the hopes of its children. The cost of one modern heavy bomber is this: a modern brick school in more than thirty cities. . . . This is not a way of life at all, in any true sense. Under the cloud of threatening war, it is humanity hanging from a cross of iron." Eisenhower's aide William Bragg Ewald characterized that final metaphor as "too religious, too literary, too emotional for Eisenhower's invention."[78] Like the speech, it was the expression of Ike's Catholic amanuensis, Hughes.

Most of us cannot comfortably and convincingly deliver words written by someone else. So significant was this problem that in the late 1930s the notion of ghost*readers* was proposed. "[T]rained voices corresponding to those of prominent men can be groomed for the job of impersonation," noted *The Literary Digest*.[79] "So far as is known, radio ghost-speaking has not yet been tried, but is in the offing."

A number of years later, it was tried but for different reasons. Winston Churchill did tell the House of Commons: "We shall fight on the beaches . . . we shall fight in the hills . . . we shall never surrender." But because he was too preoccupied with the Dunkirk invasion to spare the time to record the address, British actor Norman Shelley impersonated Churchill's delivery in the broadcast of the speech heard overseas. The ruse, which was approved by Churchill, was uncovered in 1979.[80]

More usually, the presence of a ghosted text is betrayed by the speaker's stilted delivery. When Harry Truman read from a text, noted Herbert Corey writing in *Nation's Business*, "he sounded like a grown up small boy unwillingly reading an address to Dear Teacher."[81] George McGovern "is uneasy when delivering speeches written by others," noted the *National Journal* in 1972.[82]

Occasionally, the speaker of someone else's words is their victim. Intending to indict Watergate as "this bizarre incident" one corporate head condemned it as "this brassiere incident."

An inability to deliver scripted words with sincerity and conviction can undercut their substance. By reading his speech about Chappaquiddick, Edward Kennedy drew attention to its careful phrasing and underscored the revelation in the press that following the accident former Kennedy speechwriters had been summoned to the Kennedy enclave.

Likewise, prose that is too precise can betray the presence of speechwriters. Writing about one of Nixon's confessions of non-complicity in Watergate, John Osborne noted, "The weakness of his account leaped from a betraying phrase in a reference to his 1972 campaign. 'It is clear,' he said, 'that unethical as well as illegal activities took place in the course of that campaign. None of these took place with my specific knowledge or approval.'" This phrasing prompted Osborne to conclude, "A president who was as innocent of knowledge and involvement as Mr. Nixon claimed to be would not have had to have his lawyers and drafters write that none of it took place with his *specific* knowledge and approval."[83]

When questioned by those troubled by this realization, speechwriters respond as did Emmet Hughes. Ike's aide noted that writers may "give important inflections" to what the president says. "But the only decision of political moment belongs, wholly and unqualifiedly, to the President. Whatever he publicly declares is profoundly his."[84]

We are not alarmed to learn that a speechwriter has penned the dry detail of presidential recitations on the budget. Such words neither speak nor pretend to bespeak the soul of their speaker. But a moment of quiet unease attends the realization that the intimate, disclosive words that Reagan spoke from his Bethesda hospital room after cancer surgery were penned, in part at least, by someone else, as was his moving tribute to the "boys at Pointe du Hoc." ("These are the boys of Pointe du Hoc. These are the men who took the cliffs.") In both instances, the sentences Reagan spoke were those of speechwriter Peggy Noonan. Consistent with the unwritten code of the speechwriter, Noonan states that speechwriters collaborate with Reagan.[85] Given enough time, she contends, Reagan himself could have written the speech at Pointe du Hoc. The speechwriter's role in constructing the public articulate Reagan was demonstrated dramatically in summer 1986 when Noonan and fellow writer Ben Elliott resigned from the White House; after that, the quality of Reagan's speeches plummeted. "[T]he president needs some new speech writers," observed Lou Cannon. "His long-winded ramblings in Dixie were so devoid of quotable rhetoric or substance that they failed to qualify as stories for the evening network news."[86]

In a sense, reliance on speechwriters devalues speechmaking. When audiences are unaware of the presence of ghosts, the process of communicating their words subtly deceives. When audiences are aware, argues Bormann, "the fact that the highest leaders of the nation use ghostwriters serves as a powerful indirect suggestion that speechmaking is an unimportant part of leadership and one that the personage in high leadership position delegates to hired flunkies."[87]

Because speechwriters are expected to write and not tell, it's difficult to know how much political discourse is ghosted. But even if the practice is as pervasive as reporters allege and scholars suspect, it probably poses less imminent danger than dragonflies or dandruff if writers simply are writing what, time permitting, the speakers could and would write themselves.

Yet, if presidents are speaking their own convictions and selves in the words of another, as the defenders of ghosting aver, then on a number of important occasions their convictions lacked consistency. In 1968, did Richard Nixon view "Vice President" Hubert Humphrey as a person worthy of respect whose flaw was a reliance on old ideas or did he see "Mr. Humphrey" as a failure whose policies had failed America? Did Gerald Ford stand for reconciliation or retribution? And, in the most momentous instance, was John Kennedy the president of detente as his speech at American University made him out to be or the president of defiant democracy projected two weeks later in the "Ich Bin Ein Berliner" speech at the Berlin Wall? There is after all a chasm between the contention that we aspire to make the world safe for diversity to enable each nation to develop "according to its own traditions and its own genius . . . and all bound together by a respect for the rights of others" and the claim "There are some who say we can work with the communists. Let them come to Berlin."

Since the contentious passage in the Berlin speech was spoken extemporaneously and the conciliatory speech at American University scripted, the possibility exists that Kennedy was a cold warrior in Camelot whose strident rhetorical tendencies were softened by Sorensen. Sorensen offers an alternative but not incompatible explanation: "His famous 'Ich bin ein Berliner' speech illustrated both the spontaneous eloquence an aroused audience could arouse in him and the dangers of stump speeches on foreign policy. He sounded as though he were rallying opposition to the very kind of collaboration with the Soviets he was then seeking on the Test Ban Treaty and other matters. . . . [T]he incident illustrated JFK's dilemma: he was at his most forceful best when discussing extemporaneously as an individual those world issues about which he cared the most; but those were the very issues which required him to speak as President from a carefully prepared and distributed text."[88]

Regardless of the scope of the speechwriter's role, and the evidence suggests that that scope is larger with some presidents than with others, one of the major changes in communication in the twentieth century is the extent to which not only the public political words spoken but the ideas they express originated in someone else's mind. The resulting double standard is stark. When students fail to acknowledge the sources from which their essays are drawn or, worse, when they expropriate the language of another, we righteously cry plagiarism and penalize them; once the student attains the status of senator, congressperson, or president, the rules change. Feigning authorship of another's thoughts and words is then not only expected but publicly funded.

Although the practice of placing one person's words in another person's mouth dates at least to Moses, only recently has it become sufficiently pervasive to invite the questions: Are some public officials simply mouthpieces? Does this process dull the politician's ability to think clearly, refine that ability, or leave it untouched? What are the implications for governance if leaders are reduced to messengers voicing the messages of others? Does the uncritical acceptance of the words of another dull one's disposition to ask tough questions of subordinates, such as Oliver North and William Casey, about how policy is being executed?

The omnipresence of speechwriters has changed the rhetorical requirements for those who would be president. The candidate able to speak the words of others with sincerity and conviction will have the advantage over those whose tone and inflections betray the act of deception. Candidates for public office also must be prepared to deny, either directly or indirectly, that they often are speaking someone else's sentences.

Rhetoric scholar Ernest Bormann would define the very act of ghostwriting as deception: for him ghostwriting is "the practice of using collaborators to deceive the audience and make the speaker appear better than he is."[89] To distinguish between known speechwriters and those kept hidden, former Nixon writer William Safire defined the former as speechwriters and the latter as ghostwriters. In *The New Language of Politics*, Safire argues that "Only a president, who the public has come to recognize is too busy to prepare his own messages, can afford to permit it to become known who writes his speeches." Ghostwriters "surreptitiously" prepare messages "for public figures below the highest levels."[90]

Whether to Exorcize or Enshrine the Ghosts

Of a leader we should expect thoughtful, well-conceived ideas, a capacity to translate them into major speeches, essays, or books, and an ability to deliver such messages cogently and convincingly to a national audience.

Of course, as Voltaire observed, speech can also be an effective means of concealing thought. In speeches conceived in their own minds and written by their own pens, speakers are unlikely to deliberately reveal anything that would disappoint their mothers. Yet their concealing is revealing. In examining speakers' choices from among the available means of persuasion, we can divine a sense of the claims they either cherish or think they should cherish, the sorts of evidence toward which they gravitate or think they should gravitate, and the seriousness with which they take themselves and the world. By contrast, the advent of the speechwriter raises the question: has the speaker any self or thoughts to reveal?

The advantages of reuniting thinking and speaking are many. If elected officials and those who aspire to that status were expected to participate in the creation of their major speeches, changes or subtle shifts in policy might increasingly be the product of careful counsel and informed presidential consent, not of last minute shadings by unelected ghosts.

The quality of policy making and public leadership might increase, as well. Throughout history, theorists of communication have noted the educative value of forging thought into language. Most have agreed with Francis Bacon that "Reading maketh a full man; conference a ready man and writing an exact man." What is less noted is the value of sustained contact with a set of ideas. As he considered their meaning in speech after speech, on occasion upon occasion, Daniel Webster's concept of both the Constitution and the law matured. So too did Lincoln's grasp of the meaning of war, union, liberty, and country. The Gettysburg Address expresses an intricate universe in memorable language because Lincoln had absorbed the legacy of the founders, understood the principles on which government must rest, and had fathomed the importance of fraternity to the body politic. Had his earlier speeches been ghosted, his address at Gettysburg might have been neither little noted nor long remembered. Likewise, Jefferson's précis of American principles in the Declaration of Independence is the by-product of years of thought, reading, and writing on these same issues. In Woodrow Wilson's writings as a college professor, we see the Fourteen Points foreshadowed. Had he not considered such matters repeatedly, again and again faced a blank page, pen in hand, and learned from critics, opponents, and audiences who responded to the early incarnations, I suspect that the reasons and language for which that war was fought would have been not only different but less memorable.

A contemporary search for a Wilson, a Lincoln, or a Jefferson yields a very small number of public figures willing and able to undertake the difficult process of crystallizing thought in language. One such was Martin Luther King, Jr., whose "I Have a Dream" speech embodied lived ideas forecast in earlier speeches, letters, and essays. In jail, at the pulpit, in rallies, King had reached for the language that would invite audiences to understand the common humanity of blacks and whites and the meaning of making real the promises of democracy. The eloquence of that speech flows from King's command of a rich rhetorical tradition, from his ability to voice his own and his people's convictions, and from his unremitting struggle to enable his audiences to witness the world as he had come to experience it.

The moments in which ideas and language meet are simultaneously times of conception and birth. As they listen to responses from audiences, columnists, and critics, speakers have additional opportunities to evaluate their thoughts and expressions, to reform or refine. From such encounters should come more disciplined public thought, more thoughtful public policy, conceptions of the political world carved in marble, not written in water. None of this is likely from politicians when their words are ghosted.

Out of repeated attempts to give language to shared principles can come a definitive speech. I would argue that the speech Edward Kennedy delivered at the Democratic convention of 1980 defined and defended liberalism so well because it was forged out of the experiences of a ghost who had grappled with questions about the relevance of liberalism for four different candidates of like disposition and in that soulsearching had found an answer that satisfied him, Kennedy, and the convention. Edward Kennedy's speech is as much a *cri de coeur* of Shrum's as of Kennedy's.

Similarly, the finest speech of the Eisenhower presidency, his address on disarmament to the newspaper editors, is an expression of the conscience and sensibilities of Emmet John Hughes. Reagan's most deliberative address, his speech to the British Parliament, speaks the education and language of Tony Dolan. The speech delivered by JFK in

THE DIVORCE BETWEEN SPEECH AND THOUGHT

the finest rhetorical hour of his presidency, his speech at American University, is a summative speech by Sorensen. I do not doubt that these speeches expressed the convictions of those who delivered them. I do doubt that Ike, JFK, Edward Kennedy, or Reagan could have written those speeches. As White House writer Peggy Noonan notes, "the fractionation" of the time of members of Congress and the president means that they cannot readily fuse creativity, conviction, concentration, and art to create eloquence. The Websters, Lincolns, Jeffersons, and Wilsons of today are the Shrums, Sorensens, Hughes, Noonans, and Dolans.

One irony comes in the fact that the presence of some writers on the national stage is more long-lived than that of any of their employers. Shrum's language gained national attention when spoken by Lindsay; then Lindsay's public role narrowed. Shrum's vision and language survived in the speeches of Muskie during the period that the senator from Maine was considered the Democratic front-runner for the 1972 election; when Muskie's star faded, Shrum reemerged as a wordsmith for 1972 Democratic nominee McGovern and in that role commanded a national audience no longer available to Lindsay or Muskie. Although McGovern lost the presidency and then his Senate seat, Shrum's political presence was reincarnated in Edward Kennedy who would seriously challenge his party's incumbent president. The opportunity to write for four like-minded individuals of different background and temperament in different settings against different challengers should provide the perfect crucible for intellectual and rhetorical growth. In a talented writer such an accumulation of experiences coalesces to produce an occasional masterpiece.

Speechwriters such as Shrum become repositories not only of the lines of argument and appeals of political days past but also of the lessons learned by candidates no longer part of the national scene. Shrum is, in a sense, an archive of the lessons and language of the Lindsay, Muskie, McGovern, and Kennedy candidacies. As Shrum signs on to a new campaign so too does that archive. Reflection on the meaning of these failed candidacies is likely to culminate in the sort of speech Kennedy delivered at the 1980 Democratic convention.

Another irony is that those demonstrably capable of writing eloquent speeches may be incapable on their own of securing the stage to showcase them. Even if fate smiled a Pepsodent smile full of uncapped teeth, Dolan, Noonan, Shrum, or Sorensen probably could not win the presidency. Occasionally, a speechwriter who has placed important ideas and eloquent words in the mouth of a prominent leader will conclude that he too is qualified for a post of high leadership. Emmet John Hughes resigned as Ike's chief speechwriter after his request to become U.S. Ambassador to the UN was overruled by John Foster Dulles. When Sorensen sought elective office, he lost. As interesting is the likelihood that some of the eloquent leaders of our past would today be denied high public office. Because he was all but disabled by his apprehension about speaking in public, were he alive today Thomas Jefferson probably would be ghosting someone else's speeches.

The tacit duplicity entailed in speaking someone else's words and, by worrisome implication, in speaking someone else's thoughts has prompted scholars of speech to recommend ways of acknowledging the presence of the person behind the presidential text. These include a credit, similar to those run at the end of regular television programming, that would disclose the identity of the speechwriter. "Why could not a presidential address be followed by a short paragraph flashed on the screen which read 'The first three drafts of this speech were prepared by Sam Rosenman, the fourth and fifth drafts by Ted Sorensen; and the finishing touches were added by the President himself' "?, asks rhetoric scholar Franklyn Haiman.[91] "If such a practice were to have a chilling effect on the extent to which presidential speeches were written by ghosts, then so much the better." Among the advantages Haiman attributes to this proposal is its ability to debunk the myth "that those in positions of authority—as well as many in their audiences—wish to create and perpetuate . . . a myth that authority figures are all-seeing, all-knowing and all-doing—a cult of leadership which endows the father or mother figure with superhuman capacities and turns away from the reality that in any group, organization or society the functions of leadership are, to one degree or another, inevitably shared."[92] Haiman's proposal is based on an Edenic view of human nature. What would stop FDR and those of like disposition from savoring the apple even as the credits disavowed the assistance of serpents of any sort?

Those interested in fleshing out ghosts also invite reporters to include the identity of the speechwriter in accounts of the speech. As a practical matter, notes *Newsweek* reporter Howard Fineman, such identification is given only when the speech is particularly memorable or controversial. So, for example, Peggy Noonan was identified as the author of Reagan's shuttle speech because the speech was eloquent; Tony Dolan was identified as the author of the phrase "evil empire" because that characterization of the Soviet Union was controversial. The writers were identified in reports of Reagan's speech at Strasbourg, notes *Washington Post* reporter Lou Cannon, because the conflict between Patrick Buchanan, Reagan's communication chief, and Bud McFarlane, diplomatic adviser, made authorship a newsworthy matter.

In general, reporters assume that the informed public is aware that presidential speeches routinely are ghosted. Bernard Weinraub of *The New York Times* adds that since most presidential speeches are ultimately written by committee, identification of authors would not only be cumbersome but would reveal little that is newsworthy.

Were the networks to resurrect postspeech analyses, the identification of the pens producing presidential prose would be commonplace. Whether *in pacem* or not, that oral art form seems to be permanently interred.

"The problem now," notes Roger Mudd, "is that there aren't networks anymore that do decent post presidential speech analysis. Back in the '6os until the Agnew Des Moines speech, to be chosen to do a post presidential speech or press conference analysis was an assignment of honor. You got the day off to get ready. They gave you fifteen minutes, sometimes thirty minutes, to discuss in detail the metamorphosis of the speech, what he left in, what he left out. An audience got a real sense of the meaning and thrust of a speech. The Agnew [attack] scared a lot of the networks into dropping analysis. Now I don't think it will ever come back because of the intense commercial competition among the networks. They want to go right back to 'Spencer for Hire' and 'Hill Street Blues.'"

More important than changing the scowls of speech scholars to smiles (an advantage of great moment to their parents, friends, lovers, fellow carpoolers, editors, students, and children), reportorial focus on the birthing and chromosomal characteristics of speeches could help the electorate come to know the person who is president. What view of the public, for instance, propelled Jimmy Carter to patronize audiences in prepared texts, texts he carefully edited, but to use "words from the engineering books and Brzezinski's fanciest theories" when speaking extemporaneously?[93] What of the contradictions between the extemporaneous Ford and the scripted Ford, the extemporaneous Kennedy and the scripted Kennedy? What disposition enables a person to either read or say something he does not believe? Alternatively, what feat of attitudinal agility permitted Ford and JFK to embrace antagonistic positions on the same issue? What does Nixon's ability to assume antithetical postures toward his opponent reveal about him?

A different recommendation inhered in poet Robert Frost's view of the world. During lunch with some of Ike's aides in 1954, Frost asked why anyone should have his writing done for him. The staff responded that the world had become so large that no individual could manage his own writing. "When the world becomes that large," Frost replied, "perhaps it's time to break up into smaller worlds."[94]

If politicians could leash their speaking schedules, they might find their legislative load lightened as well. Political scientists have questioned the tendencies of recent Congresses to see legislation as an all-purpose solution, a sign that the system has responded, prima facie evidence that a pressing problem has yielded to the ingenuity of elected officials. In an ideal world, politicians, including those penultimate politicians who become presidents, would propose policy only when needed and only after thinking it through carefully.

If politicians spoke less, they also would have more time to invest in important speeches. "Presidential campaign ritual requires that the candidate be shuttled from coast to coast as many times as possible, assuring maximum physical exhaustion, and minimum opportunity to prepare his statements," noted two-time presidential nominee Adlai Stevenson in 1960. "The result is the ever greater use of the ghost writer and the ever greater difficulty of knowing the candidate himself."[95]

Had the country liked Stevenson better than Ike, the Illinoisan would have found that some of these problems plague presidents, as well. "Presidents are called upon to speak too often," notes a former Johnson speechwriter, "manufacturing words of no lasting significance for gatherings of little consequence to them."[96] Presumably, the nation would survive if the president sacrificed his annual statement about the national turkey.

When in an unrealistic mood, one might hope for a means that would entice candidates for office to offer the electorate and an assembled panel of questioners at least one thirty-minute statement, of their own composing, answering such questions as why they were seeking the office, what issues would preoccupy them, what they approved and disapproved of in the conduct of their predecessors, where they would like to take the country, God and the Congress willing.

We have had flickering glimpses of candidates who should have been able to answer such questions and couldn't. Teddy Kennedy's responses to the questions of Roger Mudd in 1980 are notable for that reason as are the explanations delivered by John Glenn in his ads in the early primaries of 1984. Ronald Reagan's poor performance in press conferences, in the first debate of 1984, and in his closing statement of the last debate of that year are also worrisome. Nothing in the scripted performances of these candidates betrayed the conceptual inadequacies found in these extemporaneous presentations. The frightening thought is that some of our leaders may have succeeded because they either shunned such occasions or contrived to use them as a forum in which scripted answers could be disgorged from memory.

The picture that emerges from these dabs of information is bleak, a Munch, not a Degas. Since we have few public occasions in which the mind of the candidate or leader can be seen unshielded by speechwriters, it is now possible to elect someone whose primary qualifications are a knack for creating news McNuggets, a willingness to speak the thoughts of others, a talent for doing so with sincerity and conviction, and a tolerance for feigning enthusiasm when delivering the same stock stump speech for the seventh time in a single day.

In the eighteenth-century treatise *Discours sur l'Eloquence*, theorist Jean François Marmontel argued, "L'éloquence est dans l'âme, et non dans la parole." Emerson concurred. There can be no eloquence, he contended, unless there is a "man *(sic)* behind the speech." If these cultural analysts are correct, then the explanation for the absence of eloquence is plain. What is required is a leader able to bring to politics what Edmund Burke brought. "Burke is so great because, almost alone in England, he brings thought to bear upon politics," noted Matthew Arnold.[97] "He saturates politics with thought."

9

Mating the Best of the Old and the New

"Were it left to me to decide whether we should have a government without newspapers, or newspapers without a government," wrote Thomas Jefferson two centuries ago, "I should not hesitate a moment to prefer the latter. But I should mean that every man should receive those papers and be capable of reading them."[1] What Jefferson did not envision was a literate reader dispatching the newspaper to the bottom of the birdcage, its political news unread even by the bird. Nor could he suppose that his great-grandchildren's great-grandchildren would search some major newspapers in vain for an instance of extended political argument, a transcribed speech, for example, or a published debate.

The last century had its share of abbreviated messages but the newspaper was not their home. Bites of information and slogans inhabited street and parade banners, processional torches, and broadsides. Newspapers were made of longer stuff. Although partisan, the papers of Jefferson's day were substantive.

Nor could Jefferson foresee the reader who today devours the sports page, comics, advice columns, and the horoscope and then turns away sated without having digested any information about the state of the nation or the world. More astonishing to him would be the fact that nearly everyone does receive television, a medium not confined to the literate, yet few elect to watch what political substance is found there.

I do not mean to idealize Jefferson's America. Jefferson was as concerned about public apathy then as we are now. The fact that the public wasn't reading political materials spawned his concern. And Jefferson's world included slaves, women, and landless men who were disenfranchised regardless of how well-read they were. Moreover, as the *Federalist Papers'* fears of demagoguery remind us, some of the public discourse that did reach the citizenry fell short of the ideal.

Still, those who sought substance could find it. They located it not simply on the printed page but in themselves. In the House of Burgesses and in the Constitutional convention, the founders spoke their own thoughts in their own words, engaged the ideas of others, and were engaged. Of such engagements our government was forged.

Today the search for substance is more readily thwarted. Abbreviated forms of communication abound. Our cultural literacy has eroded. The allusive has become elusive. So too has our ability to conceive speeches that invite a reconsideration of who we are as individuals and as a people. Without understanding who we have been and what it has meant, it is difficult to reconceive where we are going or ought to go. Our ability to create reasoned, informed public assent has waned. The great modern exercises of the old eloquence—George Marshall framing the Marshall Plan, Winston Churchill warning about the descent of an Iron Curtain, Eisenhower and JFK arguing for arms limitation, and John Kerry repudiating the war in Vietnam—stand out because the rhetorical terrain surrounding them is so flat.

None of this means that it is either possible or desirable to scorn the new. Joseph Welch at the Army-McCarthy Hearings, JFK at Berlin, Barbara Jordan at the Democratic convention, and Ronald Reagan at Normandy were eloquent in ways uniquely televisual. And their eloquence served the country well.

If this is television at its rhetorical best, its worst can be found in a 1968 Republican ad that wordlessly allied Democratic presidential nominee Hubert Humphrey with war, social unrest, and poverty. By juxtaposing unrelated images, the ad made an argument that if expressed verbally would have elicited disbelief or ridicule. As "Hot Time in The Old Town Tonight" played jauntily in the background, a smiling Humphrey was intercut with soldiers crouched behind sand bags in Vietnam. Another intercut. This time between Humphrey and the chaos in the streets of Chicago at the 1968 Democratic convention. Another intercut. Humphrey and Appalachian poverty. And in the background the unremitting sound of "Hot Time." Discordant music tied the scenes of battles, riots, and poverty. "Hot Time" coupled one frame of the smiling Humphrey to another. Humphrey lived in a world untouched by poverty, war, or rioting the ad implied. The juxtaposed images wordlessly whispered that Humphrey had either caused these conditions or was indifferent to them.[2] As disconcerting as the existence of this message is the realization that those unable to spot verbal sophistry are even less likely to unmask its visual cousins.

In this ad we see realized the fears that prompted Kant to condemn rhetoric as "'the art of deluding by means of fair semblance . . . which borrows from poetry only so much as is necessary to win over men's minds to the side of the speaker before they have weighed the matter, and to rob their verdict of its freedom.'"[3] Such uses of the available means of persuasion confirm Plato's concern that rhetoric can artfully make the untrue appear true.

By contrast, the great eloquence of the past had as its end judgment (krinate), the end Aristotle saw for all rhetoric. In the society envisioned by Aristotle, the audience listened to all sides of a case and then judged it justly. Deliberation conjoined practical wisdom (phronesis) and judgment. The "most characteristic function of a man of practical wisdom is to deliberate well. . . . In an unqualified sense, that man is good at deliberating who, by reasoning, can aim at and reach the best thing attainable to man by action."[4]

The notion that the end of rhetoric is judgment presupposes that rhetoric consists of argument—statement and proof. Morselized ads and news bites consist instead of statement alone, a move that invites us to judge the merit of the claim on the ethos of the speaker or the emotional appeals (pathos) enwrapping the claim. In the process, appeal to reason (logos)—one of Aristotle's prime artistic means of persuasion—is lost.

In some settings the ethos of a speaker is sufficient to sustain a case. Greek speakers enhanced their ethos by establishing their practical wisdom (phronesis), good will (eunoia), and worthy moral character (arete). Creating the illusion that a speaker possessed practical wisdom, good will, and worthy character was difficult in a city-state in which the audience and the speaker were neighbors. With the advent of an electorate of millions and a country spanning oceans, direct experience of the character of a speaker is unattainable for most of those called on to judge public discourse. When we see a potential leader through the filter provided by pseudo-events, news bites, or nuggetized ads and then can know for certain only that most politicians do not speak their own words, ethos is a less reliable anchor for belief.

So we are left with the mode of proof that, taken alone, was suspect for Aristotle and Plato alike. "It is not right to pervert the judge by moving to anger or envy or pity," noted the father of Greco-Roman rhetoric, "one might as well warp a carpenter's rule before using it." The audience cannot judge if the ruler is bent. Much snippetry bends the measure. If the electorate is to deliberate fully and judge justly, public discourse must be enriched by *logos* as well as *ethos* and *pathos*, statement as well as proof. The absence of these basic ingredients of classical rhetoric may help explain the much lamented volatility of the electorate. Discourse based in warranted *ethos* and compelling *logos*, statement and proof, provides a sense of surety about what we know and believe that cannot be attained by *pathos* alone.

No longer are we educating speakers or citizens capable of Aristotelian deliberation. In classical times the model orator was one who had "interiorized all that [was] best in the culture, and who [could] apply this wisdom in the public forum, influencing his fellow citizens to think and act on particular issues in accord with their common heritage. In a very real sense, the classical orator served as the voice of cultural continuity."[5]

But should a speaker speak as a voice of cultural continuity, few would now recognize it. Unmoored from our own great literature and from the lessons of history, we are unable to form the sorts of powerful enthymemes that bond citizens sharing a rich common culture and tradition. Those immersed in the study of history, their minds sharpened by philosophy, their values polished by great literature and poetry, their critical acuity fine-edged by careful study of the masterpieces, know the look and sound of leadership and the forms and shapes of demagoguery. One reason for studying Hitler, for example, is, as Kenneth Burke noted, "to discover what kind of 'medicine' this medicine-man has concocted, that we may know, with greater accuracy, exactly what to guard against, if we are to forestall the concocting of similar medicine in America."[6]

Those unschooled in the past readily confuse elegance with eloquence, conviction with cogency. Unable to recognize leadership when we see it, we careen from election to election searching for a candidate who compensates for the weaknesses of the president who has most recently failed us. After Nixon, an honest blue-jeans-wearing populist whose lack of Washington experience was considered a blessing; after Carter, competence and a confidence in the country; after Reagan, a command of detail and a strong management style.

From history we learn that what you see isn't always what you get. The past reveals that leadership often requires telling the citizenry truths it does not want to hear, that one test of the maturity of a people is a willingness to act on facts requiring sacrifice. A lived knowledge of the sounds of great words makes it easier to spot counterfeit ones and makes us less susceptible to policy claims warranted not by reasoned proof but by *pathetic* appeals.

Ronald Reagan practices much that is powerful of the new eloquence but little of the old. Some moments in Reagan's presidency illustrate the advantages television provides the electorate; others synopsize the changed nature of eloquence in an electronic age; and some reveal what we're missing. To illustrate, I would like to return to his speeches at Normandy. Earlier we concentrated on the speeches themselves. Here we see them transformed by inclusion in a televised campaign documentary. The film not only shows Reagan making the speeches but visually illustrates his words with filmed footage of the landing. The fact that speechwriter Peggy Noonan wrote the words Reagan is speaking is camouflaged by Reagan's conversational, intimate style and by the obvious emotion he is feeling as he chokes back tears during the address. In quiet words spoken over his delivery of the speech Reagan discloses his private thoughts as the ceremony was progressing. Throughout the segment he is retelling the story of a daughter's devotion to her veteran father's memory. He acts as her spokesperson and ours. By reading her letter with feeling, he invites us to share his patriotic emotions. The speech vivifies family values, heroism, and the value of the individual and makes compelling the nation's obligation to remember Normandy. It also reconciles generations.

As the segment opens, Reagan is speaking at Normandy.

> We stand on a lonely windswept point on the northern shore of France. But forty years ago at this moment the air was dense with smoke and the cries of men and the air was filled with the crack of rifle fire and the roar of cannon. Here in Normandy the rescue began. At dawn on the morning of the sixth of June 1944 . . .

As the sound of his speech fades, the presence of Reagan as narrator emerges. Since the audience is seeing pictures of the veterans, Reagan can and does move into the abbreviated speech of the television anchor: "sixty-two of the rangers who scaled the cliffs there at Pointe du Hoc now back forty years later at the scene of their heroic action." The speech continues, "These are the boys of Pointe du Hoc. These are the men who took the cliffs." Then, as narrator, Reagan reveals what he was feeling as he delivered the Normandy speech.

> It was a very moving experience. They were what General Marshall called our secret weapon, the best damned kids in the world. Where do we find them? Where do we find such men? And the answer came almost as quickly as I'd asked the question. Where we've always found them in this country,

on the farms, the shops, the stores and the offices. They just are the product of the freest society the world has ever known.

We return to the speech.

Someday, Lis, I'll go back, said Private First Class Peter Robert Zanatta of the 37th engineer combat battalion and first assault wave to hit Omaha Beach. Lisa Zanatta Henn began her story by quoting her father who promised that he would return to Normandy. She ended with a promise to her father who died eight years ago of cancer. "I'm going there, Dad. And I'll see the beaches and the barricades and the monuments. I'll see the graves and I'll put flowers there just like you wanted to do. I'll feel all the things you made me feel through your stories and your eyes. I'll never forget what you went through, Dad. Nor will I let anyone else forget. And Dad I'll always be proud." Through the words of his loving daughter who is here with us today, a D-Day veteran has shown us the meaning of this day far better than any president can. It is enough for us to say about Private Zanatta and all the men of honor and courage who fought beside him four decades ago. We will always remember. We will always be proud. We will always be prepared so we may be always free.

As this discourse demonstrates, Reagan's style is to conversational, intimate, electronic communication what the speeches of Cicero were to fiery oratory idealized in his time: each defined the state of the art.

The mesh between Reagan's natural style and the appetites of both television and the citizenry is serendipitous. Unlike Bryan, Reagan benefits from the habits engendered by his rhetorical past, not because it gave him a wide-ranging flexible rhetorical repertoire but because the limited one it refined met the needs of the country and the dispositions of the electronic media in the early 1980s. By repeating his habitual moves, Bryan failed. By transplanting his past successes, Reagan triumphs. He is by background a radio announcer turned actor on a medium that requires a conversational, intimate style, a comfort with self-disclosure, and the ability to convincingly deliver the words of another; that training has tuned his sense of visual communication to the point that he can assert with pictures more effectively than with words, a talent suited to the synecdochic medium of television. By disposition and practice, he was a storyteller at a time when storytelling met a powerfully felt societal need.

In short, the influence of Reagan's past as a speaker works to his advantage in most instances. As a speaker for General Electric and as a political speaker on the chicken and cherry-pie circuit, Reagan polished crowd-pleasing speech, long on illustrations, short on statistical detail. His natural tendency is to see the world through dramatic vignettes.

Ironically, the "Great Communicator's" effectiveness resided in his use of a style once condemned as rhetorically effeminate. Few today would seriously argue a correlation between eloquence and one's testosterone level. Still, as Chapter 4 noted, for centuries, august theorists of communication damned or at least demeaned the "effeminate" style of communication and discounted those ostensibly created to conceive children but not ideas. Females could not hold their own at the rostrum, said these gendarmes of public discourse, because they supplanted thinking with feeling, data with drama, reasoning with emoting, arguing with empathizing. Where scientifically structured data were required, women told stories. Women were indicted for an inability to conceal; Reagan unselfconsciously revealed. Women were condemned for feeling, expressing, and acting on emotion. As he recalled the death of American soldiers in the bombing in Lebanon, repeated a veteran's words about Normandy, or retold the story of how his father received a pink slip one Christmas Eve, Reagan unashamedly evinced emotion—his voice caught, his eyes teared, he looked down and pursed his lips as if to control strong feelings. The outward signs of inward conviction streamed forth as he rehearsed tales of national pride, patriotism, and honor as well. And rather than situating his claims in statistics, Reagan preferred to lodge them in stories.

The ironies extend beyond Reagan's rehabilitation of an "effeminate" style. The president who seemed for more than a term to confirm that a command of fact was irrelevant to competence may well be instrumental in redeeming discourse based in a command of detail. More so than any modern leader Reagan seemed sworn to the advice reportedly given to Mark Twain by his editor, "Don't let the facts get in the way of a good story." So routine were factual and statistical errors in his responses to press questions that his stumbles stopped securing headlines. Here too the times conspired to minimize the political damage. As Chapter 1 noted, audiences are no longer trained in history, literature, or the classics. Reagan's mass audience was unlikely to detect errors of historical fact. Although the press could locate no trace of the welfare queen Reagan claimed lived in luxury, he clung to the story, with no noteworthy political fallout.

As important was the possibility that commanding the facts did not necessarily yield effective governance. With a vengeance, Jimmy Carter documented his answers in press conferences. By the tangible indicator—the misery index—with which he had skewered Ford in 1976, his own presidency failed. Although economists would argue that a high price was exacted for it in the form of an unprecedented national debt, the misery index was reduced by the president who stumbled over figures and avowed a simple faith in "supply-side economics."

Reagan benefitted as well from our sense that we are drowning in a flood of information. As practically every congressional debate on an economic or military matter attests, statistics and scholars can be marshalled on both sides of any issue. Reagan's stories and simple principles drew order out of this chaos.

So important was the ordering of ideas to the traditional theorist that Aristotle made *dispositio* one of his five canons of rhetoric. When Descartes stripped rhetoric of style and delivery, discovering and ordering ideas remained. Once outside a narrative structure, Reagan's ability in this regard falters. His speech on Lebanon and Grenada abuts two very different situations with barely a transition for glue. His penchant for endings produced a speech to Congress with not one peroration but three! Thinking the first signalled the end of the address, Congress applauded vigorously, prompting Reagan to observe, correctly, that he should have ended there.

Until the Tower Commission and the Irangate hearings revealed the need for a president to command and intelligibly structure the facts, the public found in Reagan a kindred spirit. If the speech at Normandy marks the rhetorical pinnacle of the Reagan presidency, its low point occurred on November 13, 1986. That evening, Reagan told the American people "Now you are going to hear the facts from a White House source. And you know my name." The speech then went on to both misstate fact and to deceive. "We did not—repeat, did not, trade weapons or anything else for hostages," said Reagan, "nor will we." As the public was to learn and Reagan later was to admit, we had traded weapons for hostages.

Although it embodies what passes in an electronic age for eloquence, Reagan's rhetoric leaves much to be desired. A command of history enables a leader to learn from the past; a command of fact enables him to test the legitimacy of his inferences. Reagan's leaps from the single anecdote or personal experience to the general claim are sound only if his anecdote is accurate, typical, and representative of a larger universe of experiences. His subordination of fact to conviction and truth to ideological convenience ultimately cost him his credibility.

One might wonder as well whether his reliance on speechwriters and before them scriptwriters played a role in his disposition to accept information uncritically, to trust his aides to act in his best interest. When one relinquishes the responsibility for searching out the data to support claims, to test the relationship between fact and claim, to search for the precise, expressive word, one may also dull the disposition to test the language others use to persuade you, to challenge the facts as others present them to you, to assume an active rather than a passive role in the informational process.

What Reagan did well was revivify and reinforce; what he did poorly was advance our understanding of ourselves, our country, and its institutions. Such understandings cannot be conceived in the clichés that constitute Reagan's vocabulary. Jefferson, Lincoln, Wilson, and FDR saw and spoke their world in fresh language. The conceptual power behind Pericles' Funeral Oration, Burke's "On Conciliation with America," Lincoln's inaugurals, Wilson's Fourteen Points address, FDR's second and fourth inaugurals, and Marshall's articulation of the Marshall Plan is palpable. There are no comparable speeches in the Reagan corpus. At his best, Reagan reassured as he did at Normandy and in his speech in the wake of the shuttle explosion. At their best, his eloquent predecessors reconceptualized.

There is no reason to doubt that speeches that mesh the best of the old and the new can be fashioned in the ninth decade of the twentieth century. The key question is: If they were, would they be heard by an audience disposed to absorb their political information in the brief bits and bites of network news and political advertising? A canny, risk-taking politician might gamble and craft such a speech for delivery in a forum that naturally attracts a large audience. Keynote addresses and acceptance speeches at conventions fall into this category as do election eve speeches by the major party nominees. In each of these forums we expect a long speech—which by today's standards means a speech of over thirty minutes—enough time to assume the burdens of disclosing the historical context that produced the topic, defining terms, summarizing alternative postures and weighing their advantages and disadvantages, evidencing and dramatizing key positions, and synthesizing the issue in a memorable way. A canny politician might buy time simultaneously on all three networks, heavily advertise an important speech, and then deliver one. Were such a speech to succeed politically, others might follow.

Some of the politicians on the national stage show a disposition to combine the old and the new eloquence. In his keynote address at the Democratic convention of 1984, Mario Cuomo's style and delivery were conversational. But, unlike Reagan, who hews tightly to his scripted texts in formal settings, Cuomo reworked the script as he was delivering it, a process that enabled him to adapt to audience response.

Indicating an understanding of Reagan's strengths, the speech attempted to supplant one of Reagan's central images with two others.

While acknowledging that Reagan's shining city on a hill existed for some, the speech dramatized the existence of another city inhabited by elderly people who "tremble in the basements of the houses . . . people who sleep in the city's streets."

Cuomo also offered a fresh metaphor for the body politic: a wagon train. "The Republicans believe the wagon train will not make it to the frontier unless some of the old, some of the young and some of the weak are left behind by the side of the trail. . . . We Democrats believe in something else. We Democrats believe that we can make it all the way with the whole family intact." If either the image of the desperate city or the wagon train had pervaded the speech it would have been more effective. Nonetheless, Cuomo's impulse to displace Reagan's verbal dramatizations was an apt one, the alternative images promising.

Cuomo also made good use of personal disclosure to build a political case. Near the close of the speech, he said:

> That struggle to live with dignity is the real story of the shining city. It's a story I didn't read in a book, or learn in a classroom. I saw it, and lived it. Like many of you. I watched a small man with thick calluses on both his hands work fifteen and sixteen hours a day. I saw him once literally bleed from the bottoms of his feet, a man who came here uneducated, alone, unable to speak the language, who taught me all I needed to know about faith and hard work by the simple eloquence of his example. I learned about our kind of Democracy from my father and I learned about our obligation to each other from him and from my mother. They asked only for a chance to work and to make the world better for their children and to be protected in those moments when they would not be able to protect themselves. This nation and its government did that for them.
>
> And that they were able to build a family and live in dignity and see one of their children go from behind their little grocery store in South Jamaica on the other side of the tracks where he was born, to occupy the highest seat in the greatest state in the greatest nation in the only world we know, is an ineffably beautiful tribute to the Democratic process.

An editor might have improved the story by either cutting the reference to his father's bleeding feet or providing a context in which to understand it. Had the story reflected less on the speaker and more on the prospective nominees, it would have better served Mondale's purposes. As it was, however, it set in place a vivid persona for a candidate who might have been contemplating a presidential run in the future.

In short, at the convention Cuomo established that he could argue cogently but conversationally and both dramatize and visually assert as well. In subsequent statements on abortion, on the nature of governance, and on eliminating discrimination, Cuomo demonstrated a conceptual power not apparent in the keynote address. His Chubb Fellowship lecture at Yale is illustrative. It contained a quotable digestive statement begging to be lifted into headlines and news clips. "[W]e campaign in poetry. But when we're elected, we're forced to govern in prose." The phrasing was fresh. It labelled his philosophy "Progressive Pragmatism," called for a new party, the "Common Sense Party," and suggested a visual symbol for the party—a profile of Thomas Paine. At Yale, he could presuppose a familiarity with Thomas Paine. Were the speech spoken on television, clues about Paine's identity would be required lest the audience infer incorrectly that Thomas Paine is the guy who founded the much advertised firm of Paine-Weber.

Where the keynote address established and then abandoned two dramatic images, the speech at Yale is structured to preview its central claim in a dramatic image that reappears to recap the speech.

> Galileo, as you know, described the world as he saw it, a world that circled the sun in constant orbit. Many people had trouble accepting this. They were taught the earth was the center of the universe and never moved. It challenged their perception of the universe and, they believed, challenged the basis of their faith. So, with the help of the Inquisition, they forced Galileo to kneel before their tribunal and retract his assertion that the earth moved. They made him say the earth was stationary because God had created it that way. Galileo knelt and spoke the words they forced him to speak: he denied the earth orbited the sun. But as he arose, those around him heard him say in a quiet voice. 'E pur si mouve' (But still it moves).

Cuomo closes the speech by saying, "But I hope I will be strong enough to know all of this and still be able to say, 'E pur si mouve.' "

Cuomo understands the dilemmas entailed in communicating effectively in an electronic age. In the same speech he observed: "[S]ticking by your principles requires that you explain your principles, and in this age of electronic advocacy this process can often be tedious and frustrating. This is especially so when you must get your message across in twenty-eight-second celluloid morsels, when images prove often more convincing than ideas.

"Labels are no longer a tendency in our politics. In this electronic age, they are our politics." Whether Cuomo will surmount these difficulties remains to be seen. He shows promise of being able to do so.

The search for a substantive Democratic alternative to Reagan and the need to provide a cogent answer to the question "Where's the Beef?" propelled Colorado senator and 1984 presidential hopeful Gary Hart to deliver a nationally televised half-hour speech before the 1984 New York primary. Broadcast outside prime time, poorly advanced, delivered inadequately, the speech failed to either draw an audience or provide needed fuel for Hart's faltering candidacy. Still, the move suggested respect for the speech as a form of electoral communication. Prior to the pictorial exposé in spring 1987 Hart effectively had used speeches to stake down substance in the pre-primary jockeying of 1986. Dean of Washington columnists and reporters David Broder recognized the significance of Hart's move:

> Last week, Hart laid out the broad principles of a foreign policy of "enlightened engagements," and some of its specific applications, in three speeches at Georgetown University. A few weeks back 'he published a book on military strategy and Pentagon management called "America Can Win." Earlier this year and in 1985, he introduced legislation and gave major speeches on trade and monetary policy, education, job-training and economic development.
>
> His work has an intellectual coherence that goes well beyond the level of the average stump speech. The foreign-policy lectures hang on the assumption that "the diffusion of power" to Europe, Japan and the Third World countries necessitates a new look at the Soviet-American contest. That thesis can be debated by those who still see a bipolar world.
>
> Even more challenging are some of Hart's specific proposals. He argues that U.S. banks may be required to write down some of their loans to debt-ridden Third World countries. He advocates pressuring the South Korean government to permit open political opposition. He says it is time to raise the issue of redistributing the NATO defense responsibilities in Western Europe. . . .
>
> Whether Hart is right or wrong in all his views, he is genuinely trying to start a Democratic debate. He is not alone in this enterprise. New York Governor Mario Cuomo has given some notable speeches in the past 15 months and former Virginia governor Charles Robb is also trying to define a program and philosophy for his party.[7]

Broder's analysis is important for three very different reasons. First, when Broder talks, others listen. If candidates come to believe that the press does not live by news McNuggets alone but by the substantive speech as well or at least that such speeches will garner serious treatment, then an incentive for such discourse is added to the political mix.

Second, Broder's column on Hart like others on Cuomo's speeches suggests that two-step flow of a new sort is alive and well. That hoary paradigm suggested that ideas are transmitted through media to opinion leaders and from them to followers. In the case of Hart and Cuomo, ideas are conveyed through speeches, unheard by the public, but received by opinion leaders (columnists) and digested by them for consumption by the public. But unlike broadcast reports, these print reports are synopsizing not the effect of the speech or its strategic intent but its content.

Third, Broder's synopsis of Hart's stands is coupled with praise for the coherence of the view informing them, praise that tacitly invites those serious about politics to read and hear the speeches themselves. Broder's hope that a substantive debate is in the offing is one that could be realized if the candidates were to use the debates sprinkled throughout the primaries to engage the specifics of each other's proposals and then follow up the debates with thoughtful speeches that advance the issue agenda rather than simple repeating stock phrases. Especially promising is the Dartmouth College proposal that each candidate devote a full-length speech and question-and-answer session to the issues raised in one of a series of commissioned scholarly essays.

Conspire with me for a moment in creating a political world bent on increasing the thoughtful speechmaking in presidential campaigns and in the presidency itself. This world would be constructed from the classroom up. By studying speeches, students would learn both to listen critically and to argue their own claims cogently. In history and great literature, students would find a base from which enthymemes could build; by studying poetry and foreign languages as well as great rhetoric they would refine their abilities to choose well from among the available means of persuasion. These preparations behind them, students would be readied for civic participation by practice in the art of speaking.

Like the first groundhog, speechmaking would poke into the schoolyear, perhaps at commencement; then, finding an early spring, on other important academic occasions. Chancellors might revive the practice of defining the university's mission in inaugural addresses. If one delivered the contemporary equivalent of John Henry Newman's "Idea of a University," the Board of Regents probably wouldn't mind. The agenda for the year might be spelled out in a State of the University address. Speeches at civic ceremonies might follow.

While students were speaking more, heads of state would be speaking less. Keynesian principles would be applied to the presidency. Presidential speeches seem to be in oversupply; demand is down. Fewer speeches might merit more attention.

In our projected wonderland, the presidents who were speaking less would have more time to spend weighing evidence, challenging arguments, and only then selecting the words that would convey that process and its conclusions to the nation. The burdens on grandparents would increase as their children's children turned to them incredulously to ask "Did somebody really write a president's speeches for her when you were little?"

In this utopia, the political process would conspire as well to invite elaborated thought rather than stock phrases and slogans. As the primaries winnow the number of candidates to a handful, the length of time each is given for an opening statement would increase. In the California primary, we would be hearing ten-minute broadcast speeches from the final few. Candidates would debate in depth and at length.

As a gesture demonstrating that we have put the British burning of the White House behind us, we would adopt a political communication model from our mother country. Since this is utopia, the legal obstacles and profit-taking needs of the broadcasters would dissolve. In the closing days before each vote, the local stations in each primary state would make ten-minute slots available to each candidate at no charge. The only requirement would be that the candidate spend that time speaking directly to the voters on a common topic. Such a move would guarantee that no candidate would be denied access to the electorate for want of the money to produce ads and buy ad time. This practice would be repeated in the general election, where, in the closing month of the campaign, each major party candidate could be given some prime time each week in which to address an issue of central concern. On election eve, when the attention span of the electorate peaks, the candidates each would be given a half hour in which to differentiate themselves from their opponents and define their visions of the future.

Newspapers too would contribute by following the practice of *The New York Times* and printing a version of each candidate's stock stump speech. In addition, a partial page would be devoted each week to reproducing the two or three most noteworthy paragraphs spoken or written by each candidate. This unfiltered access to the electorate would reward those who step beyond the stock speech and the news bite to contribute thoughtfully to the discourse of the campaign. And it would serve the very different requirements of those active communication participants who from the first straw poll compulsively seek out political information and those whose interest in political information is not aroused until the closing weeks of the campaign. By focusing on what is new in the speech of a candidate, the media serve well the needs of the first group and speak past the second.

Candidates who believed that a speech well expressed their candidacies might reproduce major sections of the speech as a print ad in the most influential newspapers the morning after delivering it to the nation. Spot ads could increase readership and viewership by forecasting

the speech. The techniques of Madison Avenue could be placed in service of substantive discourse. Subsequent ads then could digest a longer
message rather than functioning as parts that are simultaneously the
whole.

Broadcast news would follow suit by broadcasting four- to five-minute
clips from each stock speech. To accommodate the varying informational levels of those whose political interest coincides with the first frost,
the first corn, and the first political handshake in New Hampshire, some
channel regularly might air the stock speeches of the candidates still in
the running. News reports could add to their focus on the effect of a
speech and its strategic intent a clip carrying the substance of the speech
itself. Instead of paraphrasing what the candidates said, they could show
them saying it. The thirty-one million homes that currently receive
C-SPAN's ongoing campaign coverage and the millions more tuned to
CNN are experiencing the advantages of this world already. Were it
not for the vigilance of C-SPAN, the nation would never have heard
Joe Biden recall as his own the words of a British candidate.

Television and radio stations should encourage rather than discour-
age the five-minute time buys that make it possible for a candidate to
develop ideas at greater length.

At the conventions, reporters and television and radio crews could
conduct their interviews off the floor, thereby making it possible for
interested delegates to listen to the speeches. CNN and C-SPAN would
continue to provide interested viewers with the ability to see and hear
gavel-to-gavel coverage of entire speeches.

When a candidate delivered a nationally broadcast speech, TV and
print digests could preview it. By treating it as they would treat a major
presidential address, news reporters could create the expectation that
the public watch, listen, and read.

Recognizing that speechmaking flourishes when rewarded by press
attention, all reporters great and small would repent their absence on
the campaign trails of the 1986 elections, an absence that enabled candidates in many campaigns to reduce their public dialogue to ads. Candidates for office would not necessarily be expected to speak often.
They would be expected to speak thoughtfully, knowledgeably, and well.
Audiences would be able to expect time to question positions. Those
candidates whose slogan might be "I came, I saw but I never spoke"
would find their silence noted in stories, questioned in columns, and
chided in editorials.

Reporters and candidates would return to the model of the 1950s
when "the highlight of a typical day was a formal speech to an impor-

tant audience. These speeches," recalls David Broder, "distributed to the press in advance, provided the copy for most of that day's news coverage, as well as raw material for second-day stories analyzing policy shifts or comparing one candidate's positions with his opponents's."[8]

The media would commemorate the twentieth anniversary of Spiro Agnew's dramatic condemnation of post-speech analysis by celebrating the first anniversary of the rebirth of this honorable form. Every newspaper that ever coveted Walter Kerr would now wish for its own Tom Shales or John J. O'Connor.

To the prosecutorial function the press has adopted since Watergate would be added the obligation to educate the electorate. Questions that require exposition of a policy position would receive smiles of approval from editors watching press conferences. Thoughtful, reasoned discourse would be as likely to be covered by reporters as leaks, scandals, hyperbolic accusations, and confessions.

Viewership for "The MacNeil-Lehrer News Hour" would rise dramatically as would public attention to documentaries and readership of the news in newspapers. A book calling for the opening of the American mind and another on cultural literacy would displace diet books and three-second management guides on the list of nonfiction best sellers.

Politicians could answer the question "Where's the Beef" by noting "In the Speech." Use of spots would be accepted as a useful part of the electoral process. They could preview, emphasize, recap, and create redundancy for longer messages. Relying on spots, however, would come to stand as an indictment.

Rather than condemning every morselized bit of information as demeaning to democracy, we would encourage a mix of long and short forms; the longer messages would afford context and substance, the shorter, synopses. Those spots that contribute to our understanding of candidates and their positions would be applauded as would the sixty-second point/counterpoints on issues recently pioneered by the creators of the McLaughlin Group.

To make possible both enthymemes and enlightened discourse, educators would thoughtfully consider the recommendations of those who see ways to increase both visual and verbal literacy. Our schools would teach students to recognize and reject faulty premises, data, and claims, whether visual or verbal. In this rush to traditional cultural sources we would not ignore the possibility that atraditional sources can conserve culture as well. Although the mere anticipation of it might have caused Churchill to choke on his cigar, Iron Maiden's "Aces High," which replays a portion of Churchill's most famous speech, is perpetuating a new generation's memories of the prime minister's eloquence and his country's cause.

Television's powerful recapturing of our past would also be put to good use. We would fund and then watch programming such as "Roots," "Eyes on the Prize," and Bill Moyers' PBS segments recounting what our forbearers were doing in Philadelphia two hundred years ago.

As we consider the future, we would have as one goal making the world safe for deliberation, for another, making deliberation possible, for a third, making it probable. If it becomes impossible, our horizon holds dystopia. We will reach a point at which the citizenry will damn as incomprehensible a modern incarnation of Burke's "On Conciliation" or Demosthenes' "On the Crown." In this nightmare of a future, a president would not only not be able to write a coherent speech but would be unable to conceive of what one would look or sound like. Some citizens would comfort and then ultimately confound the hovering social scientists by feigning comprehension of complex issues. More people, for example, would express an opinion on U.S. policies in Nicaragua than could identify the fighting factions, the position supported by the president, or the part of the world housing that small country.

Decades later, as historians struggled to find the snapshots and fifteen-second phrases that would explain to a listless public how public speech came to be displaced by slogans and how oratory gave way to aphorism, they might divine prophetic significance in a November evening in 1887 when a Chinese diplomat and a French author addressed the Gridiron Club in Washington D.C. Since the diplomat spoke only halting English, he opted to address his audience in Chinese. Not comprehending a word, his audience searched for nonverbal signals. At the end of a particularly intense passage, a daring few applauded. As the diplomat smiled his approval, others followed suit. Soon the crowd was punctuating the passionately delivered passages with rousing signs of approval. Noting the success of the diplomat, the French author too elected to use his native tongue. Having mastered the art of feigning comprehension and aided by a few in the audience who did understand French, the audience applauded at the pauses in his speech as well. Upon his return to France, the author, Paul Blouet, wrote an account of his visit to the United States that praised the American audience for being as fluent in Chinese and French as in its native English. The Americans were too embarrassed to let on what had really happened.

If the world parsed neatly into such opposed alternatives, the simple-minded two-sidedness of it all would find a comfortable home in our current concepts of news and ads. However, in a complex world, there are no ready answers to the questions: Can an eloquence that conjoins the best of the old and new survive in the electronic age? And, if so, can anyone other than David Broder and the speaker's immediate family be enticed to listen? If the answer to these questions ultimately is "no," the fault, Demosthenes, is not in our television sets but in ourselves.

Notes

Preface

1. Dionne, p. 83.
2. Works. 28, p. 757.
3. Cochrane, p. 494.
4. Morrow, pp. 76–77.

Chapter 1

1. Plutarch, pp. 354–56.
2. Lincoln, December 26, 1839, vol. 1, p. 178.
3. Churchill, p. 132.
4. British Orations (June 3, 1940), p. 358.
5. Ibid., p. 359.
6. Jebb, vol. 1, p. lxxi.
7. Ibid., p. lxxiv.
8. Whately, p. 10.
9. Jebb, p. lxxiv.
10. Modern Eloquence, vol. 6, pp. 898–99.
11. In British Orations from Ethelbert to Churchill, pp. 330–31.
12. Safire, On Language, pp. 52–53.
13. Quoted by Baskerville, p. 38.
14. Quoted by Thonssen and Baird, p. 47.
15. Miller, pp. 326–27.
16. Bennett, p. 16.
17. Ibid., p. 20.
18. Chronicle, p. 18.
19. Cheney, p. 12.
20. In Crocker and Carmack, p. 18.

21. *The Well-Tempered Critic*, p. 26.
22. *The Chronicle of Higher Education*, October 24, 1984, p. 36.
23. Lucian, p. 157.
24. *Ibid.*, p. 147.
25. Charles Kendall Adams, p. 85.
26. *Ibid.*, pp. 3–6.
27. *Ibid.*, p. 177.
28. Wiley, pp. 1–15.
29. Moran, p. 132.
30. *Ibid.*, p. 71.
31. In Crocker and Carmack, pp. 11–12.
32. Brougham, *Speeches*, Vol. IV, p. 387.
33. Macaulay, *Essays*, p. 51.
34. In Crocker and Carmack, p. 15.
35. I, v.
36. II, lxxxvi.
37. Pond, in *Modern Eloquence*, p. 898.
38. Macauley, p. 316.
39. *De Oratore* II, xxii ff.
40. Burke, Edmund, p. 228.
41. See footnote 174, *op. cit.*
42. *De Doctrina*, Book IV, Chap. 3.
43. Part 8 of the oration.
44. Milton, *Complete Poetry*, p. 671.
45. Miller, in "The Praise of Eloquence," p. 329.
46. X, ii, 11–29.
47. Ward, pp. 27 ff.
48. *Phaedrus*, pp. 275–76.
49. Kennedy, p. 111.
50. Introduction, *The World's Famous Orations*, vol. 1, pp. xiv–xv.
51. Goodrich, p. 25.
52. Webster, p. 240.
53. Transcript from tape.
54. Winans, p. 240.
55. "Elements of CIA Style," *Harper's*, vol. 270 (January 1985), p. 16.

Chapter 2

1. The rhetorical implications of the exchange between Bryan and Darrow in the Scopes Trial have received little sustained treatment. Robert T. Oliver comments simply: "The end of his [Bryan's] life reached an anticlimax in the Scopes trial, where he was ridiculed by the master satirist Clarence Darrow for his stubborn insistence upon his faith in the literal truthfulness of every word of the Bible" (*History of Public Speaking in America* [Boston: Allen and Bacon, 1966], p. 481). Writing in *A History and Criticism of American Public Address*, Myron G. Phillips notes only that "The details of the trial are unimportant. It is enough to say that Bryan pitted himself against a clever adversary, Clarence Darrow; that technically Bryan won his case and, with the eyes of the world centered upon him died at the close of the

trial, as eloquent in death as he had been in life" (ed. William Norwood
Brigance [New York: Russell and Russell, 1960). Essays discussing Bryan
as orator include: Margaret Wood, "William Jennings Bryan," in *American
Public Address: Studies in Honor of Albert Craig Baird* (Columbia: University
of Missouri Press, 1961), pp. 153–169; John H. Sloan, "Bryan Versus 'Bosses'
at Baltimore," in *SSSJ* (Summer 1967), pp. 260–72; John H. Sloan, " 'I
Have Kept the Faith': William Jennings Bryan and the Democratic Na-
tional Convention of 1904," *SSSJ* (Winter 1965), pp. 114–23; Jack Mills,
"The Speaking of William Jennings Bryan in Florida, 1915–1925," *SSSJ*
(January 1949), pp. 137–69.

2. *Time* (July 20, 1925), p. 17.
3. *Time* (July 20, 1925), p. 28.
4. *St. Louis Labor* (July 21, 1925), reprinted in L. Sprague de Camp, *The Great
Monkey Trial* (New York: Doubleday and Co., Inc., 1968), p. 413.
5. *Baltimore Sun* in Sprague, p. 436.
6. *The Nation* (August 5, 1925), p. 154.
7. Information contained in judge's charge to Jury. *The World's Most Famous
Court Trial: State of Tennessee v. John Thomas Scopes*. Hereafter cited as
Trial.
8. de Camp, p. 436.
9. de Camp, p. 413.
10. Scopes and Presley, p. 216.
11. Reprinted in Wrage and Baskerville.
12. *Ibid.*, p. 119.
13. *Ibid.*, p. 110.
14. *Ibid.*, p. 114.
15. Trial, p. 177.
16. Trial, p. 282.
17. Trial, p. 284.
18. Quoted by de Camp, p. 429.
19. Trial, p. 288.
20. Trial, p. 299.
21. Trial, p. 300.
22. Trial, p. 304.
23. Trial, p. 172.
24. Trial, p. 176.
25. Trial, pp. 286–87.
26. Trial, p. 290.
27. Trial, p. 291.
28. Bryan, *Letters to a Chinese Official*, pp. 88–89.
29. Trial, p. 292.
30. Trial, p. 293.
31. Trial, p. 294.
32. Trial, p. 294.
33. Trial, pp. 298–99.
34. de Camp, p. 403.
35. de Camp, p. 403.
36. de Camp, p. 430.
37. "Journal of Mary B. Bryan," quoted by Coletta, p. 269.

Chapter 3

1. Stallworthy, p. 11.
2. Tacitus, *Works*, 36, p. 764.
3. Stallworthy, p. 135.
4. Steiner, *After Babel*, p. 230.
5. *Inflammare animos audientium.*
6. *Brutus*, vi. 26.
7. *De Doctrina*, IV. Chap. 13.
8. Lowell, p. 449.
9. Katz, pp. 389–90.
10. *A New Dictionary of Quotations on Historical Principles*, p. 338.
11. Peterson, front page.
12. *The American Tradition in Literature*, ed. Bradley, II, p. 727.
13. *Rhetoric*, p. 1355a.
14. III *Rhetoric*, I, p. 1404a.
15. White, p. 35.
16. X, 18.
17. Cf. IX, III, 102.
18. Baldwin, pp. 93–94.
19. *The Philosophy of Rhetoric*, p. 7.
20. Baskerville, p. 58.
21. Burns, *Power to Lead*, p. 127.
22. *Ibid.*, p. 128.
23. *Philosophy of Rhetoric*, p. 24.
24. *Ibid.*, pp. 3, 23.
25. Burke, *Journal of General Education*, p. 203.
26. Rosenman, p. 271.
27. Kearns, p. 253.
28. *Crisis*, p. 335.
29. *Ibid.*, p. 61.
30. Wright, pp. ix–x.
31. Winans, p. 231.
32. *Ibid.*, p. 90.
33. P. 41.
34. Ruffin, p. 159.
35. Mathews, pp. 19–20.
36. *Public Speaking*, p. 205.
37. *Lectures on Rhetoric and Oratory*, p. 379.
38. Ruffin, p. 132.
39. Ong, *Fighting*, p. 141. In *The American Tradition in Literature*, ed. Bradley, p. 743.
40. In *The American Tradition in Literature*, ed. Bradley, II, p. 743.
41. *Webster's Ninth New Collegiate Dictionary*, New York: Merriam Webster, 1983, p. 830.
42. *Public Speaking*, p. 94.
43. Pascal, 26th *Pensée*.
44. Bacon, *De augmentis*, VI. 3.
45. Fenelon, pp. 92–93.

46. Sumner, IX, p. 409.
47. Garrow, p. 265.
48. *Ibid.*, p. 272.
49. Williams, p. 273.
50. Transcript. CBS News, October 4, 1984.
51. Interview with Stahl, October 1986.
52. Sennett, pp. 4, 25.
53. Transcript from audiotape.
54. Cohn, p. 197.

Chapter 4

1. Bierce, *Dictionary*, p. 142.
2. Brownmiller, p. 112.
3. *Ibid.*, p. 113.
4. Hunter College Women's Studies Collective, p. 406.
5. *Politics* VII, 12. 1335B, pp. 17–19.
6. *The Descent of Man*, Part 11, ch. VIII.
7. *Institutes*, XI. III, 19.
8. Fraser, p. 4.
9. Pomeroy, p. 175.
10. Tolchin, p. 87.
11. Hunter, p. 417.
12. Lerner, p. 63.
13. *New Dictionary of Thoughts*, p. 735.
14. *Politics* 1, 13. 1260a: 20–30; III. 4.1277b: 21–25.
15. 1 Tim. 2:9–15.
16. Linda Kerber, pp. 212–13.
17. O'Faolain, pp. 191–92.
18. Quoted by Kramarae, p. xvii.
19. Winthrop's Journals, Vol. II, p. 225; cited by Morgan, p. 44.
20. Bassuk, pp. 139–51.
21. Gilman, pp. 72 ff.
22. McPhee and Fitzgerald, p. 50.
23. Valenstein, pp. 3–11.
24. *Politics* 1, 13, 1260b 28–31.
25. HA IX, 1 608b, 16–17.
26. Wilson, no page.
27. EN VII, 7–8; Pol 1.13 1259b, pp. 35–38.
28. Rossi, p. 233.
29. *Ibid.*, p. 173.
30. *Ibid.*, p. 163.
31. Fraser, p. 246.
32. Wessley, pp. 289–303.
33. Szasz, p. 130.
34. Berg and Berry, p. 125.
35. Demos, p. 125.
36. *Op. cit.*, p. 95.
37. Demos, p. 93.

38. Campbell, p. 52.
39. Rossi, p. 166.
40. Speech to the Troops at Tilbury on the approach of the Armada in 1588. Peterson, pp. 89–90. Maria Theresa of Austria made a comparable claim upon ascent to the throne in 1741. "I am only a woman," she said, "but I have the heart of a King." See Macartney, p. 47.
41. Pomeroy, p. 172.
42. *Great Debates in American History*, vol. 4, p. 307.
43. Pomeroy, p. 175.
44. Putnam-Jacobi, p. 94.
45. *Institutes*, x, 11, 12.
46. Webster, vol. 1, p. 307.
47. See, for example, Raymond, p. vi.
48. Channing, p. 111.
49. Rossiter, p. xv.
50. *Ibid.*
51. Atkinson, pp. 112–13.
52. XI, III, 19.
53. Mason, p. 13.
54. Atkinson, p. 113.
55. Ramus, p. 34; 70 (Paris 1567). For Peacham (p. 61), the manly figures of sentences were "martial" while those of words were "effeminate, and musical." Words give "color and beauty" while the figures of sentences give "life." Similarly, for Hobbes (p. 524) sentences have a "certain manly majesty,.which far surpasseth the soft delicacy of dainties of the former figures."
56. Sprat II, p. 116.
57. *Ibid.*
58. Duberman, p. 27ff.
59. Borgatta and Stimson, pp. 89–100; Hall, p. 145.
60. Dosser, pp. 241–58.
61. Greene, p. 12.
62. Hall, p. 143.
63. Exline, pp. 201–9.
64. Feshbacker, pp. 315–38.
65. Vaux, pp. 85–110.
66. Barron, pp. 24–72.
67. Stewart, Cooper, and Friedley, p. 114. The same distinction wears different language in the literature on personality. There males are cast as agency oriented and females as tending toward communion. Some attribute the task orientation of men to their more aggressive personalities; by this logic, women's more nurturant personalities dispose toward maintenance of group well-being. Carlson, pp. 17–32.
68. Cf. Chodorow, pp. 6–7.
69. Arkin and Dobrofsky, pp. 151–68; Stein and Hoffman, pp. 136–50.
70. Lipman-Blumen, pp. 91–126.
71. Bernard, pp. 135–64.
72. Gilley and Summers, pp. 33–37.
73. Mitchell-Kernan, p. 328.

74. Burgoon, Dillard, and Doran, pp. 283–94.
75. Benze and Declercq, pp. 278–83.
76. Swacker, pp. 76–83.
77. Gardiner, p. 185.
78. Bogan, p. 13.
79. Ruthven, p. 93.
80. Bettleheim, p. 153.
81. Guazzo, I, p. 69.
82. *Ibid.*
83. *Spectator*, 3, p. 376.
84. Bromberg-Ross, pp. 9–11. Bogan; Harding; Kalcik, pp. 3–11.
85. Sadker and Sadker, pp. 54–57.
86. Infante, pp. 96–103.
87. Johnson and Stanwick, Chapters 1 and 2.
88. Hedlund et al., p. 518.
89. Werner and Bachtold, pp. 79–83.
90. Constantini and Craik, p. 226.
91. Interview. September, 1987. Blakely is the Director of Advertising for Smith and Harroff.
92. Shabad and Andersen, pp. 18–35.
93. Nie et al., p. 319.
94. Quoted by Campbell and Jerry, in press.
95. Gehlen, p. 39.
96. Smith, pp. 384–96.
97. Cf. Baxter and Lansing, p. 57.
98. Campbell et al., p. 490.
99. Baxter and Lansing, p. 50.
100. Benze and Declercq, pp. 278–83.

Chapter 5

1. Reprinted in Miller, *George Mason*, p. 39.
2. *Works of John Adams*, II, 512.
3. *The Writings of Thomas Jefferson* (ed. 1869), VII, pp. 304, 407, quoted by Becker in *The Declaration of Independence*, pp. 25, 26.
4. *The Writings and Speeches of Daniel Webster*, vol. 4, pp. 244.
5. Lincoln, *Works*, vol. 2, pp. 466–67.
6. See Lincoln (February 14, 1860), vol. 3, p. 520, vol. 2, p. 461.
7. *Vital Speeches*, p. 611.
8. (February 15, 1973), *Vital Speeches*, p. 267. A campaign commercial of Nixon's in 1968 foreshadows Nixon's synecdochic repudiation of Kennedy's theme. In the commercial, Nixon stated: "I am asking not that you give something to your country, but that you do something with your country; I am asking not for your gifts, but for your hands."
9. Heffner, p. 109.
10. (September 30, 1917), *The Works of Theodore Roosevelt*, Memorial ed. vol. XX, p. 520.
11. (September 6, 1918), National ed., XIX, 270. See also Memorial ed., vol. XXI, p. 284.

12. 52:127–28.
13. 1:144.
14. 9:201–2.
15. 17:301–3.
16. (January 22, 1917), Richardson, XVI, pp. 8199–204.
17. Lodge, p. 208.
18. (September 1917), *The Works of Theodore Roosevelt*, National ed., vol. XIX, p. 19.
19. *Congressional Record*, April 4, 1917, p. 253.
20. Taylor, *What Eisenhower Thinks*, p. 91.
21. Truman, Vol. II, p. 383.
22. September 25, 1961, in *Public Papers* (1961), p. 619.
23. Nixon, "Remarks at the Dedication of the Woodrow Wilson International Center for Scholars" (February 18, 1971), *Public Papers* (1971), p. 188.
24. September 27, 1934, *Speeches on Foreign Policy*, ed. H. H. E. Craster (New York: Books for Library Press, 1940; rpt: 1971), p. 6.
25. "Negroes Speak of War" (July 1934), Foner, pp. 788–89.
26. October 6, 1938, *In Search of Peace* (New York: G. P. Putnam and Sons, 1939), p. 215.
27. October 27, 1938, *Speeches on Foreign Policy*, p. 211.
28. "Speech-Written on the Eve of Death, to have been delivered at the Jefferson Day Dinner, 13 April 1945," in *Nothing to Fear*, p. 456.
29. September 20, 1963, in *Papers* (1963), p. 366.
30. Sorensen, *The Kennedy Legacy*, pp. 192–93.
31. Chamberlain, p. 200 (June 10, 1963), *Papers of the Presidents* (1963), p. 460.
32. *Ibid.*, p. 462.
33. *Ibid.* (October 26, 1963), p. 817.
34. February 18, 1971, *Papers* (1971), p. 188.
35. Jefferson, in Richardson, vol. 1, p. 311.
36. Seymour, I, p. 288.
37. *Papers* (1900–1902), ed. Link, vol. 12, p. 57.
38. In Richardson, vol. XVI, pp. 8199–204.
39. November 19, 1919, Borah, pp. 223–31.
40. October 2, 1935, in *The Public Papers*, p. 410. See also October 17, 1935, p. 423; October 23, 1935, p. 425.
41. Vandenberg, p. 10.
42. Quoted by Schlesinger, *The Crisis of the Old Order, 1919–1933*, p. 378.
43. Maxim Hudson, "Faith, Hope, Charity, and Prohibition," *Address to the Phillipsburg Kiwanis Club*, Lake Hopatcong, New Jersey, August 12, 1925, p. 27; Ernest H. Cherrington. "Address Before Congress on Behalf of the Committee of One Thousand," Washington D.C., December 1913, p. 7.
44. In the *Selected Works*, pp. 68–69.
45. *Ibid.*, p. 83.
46. Reprinted in Stanton, ed., *History of Woman Suffrage*, II, pp. 94–95.
47. *Ibid.*, p. 94.
48. Catt and Shuler, p. 46.
49. *Ibid.*, p. 47.
50. *History of Woman Suffrage*, II, p. 94.

51. p. 49.
52. Buhle, p. 231.
53. Catt and Shuler, p. 40.
54. Catt and Shuler, p. 50.
55. Catt and Shuler, p. 72.
56. *History of Woman Suffrage*, II, p. 94.
57. p. 127.
58. Election Debriefing, University of Maryland, November 1984.
59. Gunter, p. 171.
60. Bryant, *Rhetorical Dimensions of Criticism*, p. 122.

Chapter 6

1. *Washington Post*, February 5, 1986, A5.
2. *Washington Post*, February 8, 1985, C2.
3. *Wall Street Journal*, January 28, 1986, p. 1.
4. CBS/NYT Poll, p. 2.
5. *Ibid.*
6. Reagan, *Where's the Rest of Me?*, p. 13 ff.
7. Nixon, *RN*, p. 315.
8. Johnson, *The Vantage Point*, p. 110.
9. Carter, *Keeping Faith*, pp. 556–57.
10. Johnson's rhetorical dispositions are well analyzed by Kearns and Turner.
11. Nixon, *RN*, p. 979.
12. Carter, *Keeping Faith*, p. 121.
13. January 12, 1986, A3.
14. The phrase is Vance's, pp. 374–403.
15. *Ibid.*, p. 381.
16. Ibid., p. 382.
17. *Modern Eloquence*, ed. Reed, pp. 471–94.
18. *Ibid.*, p. 471.
19. Quoted by Cannon, p. 320.
20. Erickson, p. 107.
21. Quoted by Cannon, p. 371.
22. Cannon, p. 306.
23. Johnson, *Public Papers* (1966), p. 415.
24. Rosenbaum, p. 251.

Chapter 7

1. Unless otherwise indicated, the dates in parentheses that follow quotes from presidential speeches correspond to the dates listed in public papers for those texts.
2. Interview with Noonan, 1986.
3. Hart, *Verbal Style*, pp. 220–21.
4. Richardson, vol. 6, p. 11.
5. *New York Times*, October 6, 1982, A26.
6. Hechler, p. 67.
7. Daniels, pp. 347–48.

8. *New York Times*, January 26, 1978, A15.
9. Lloyd Grove, *Washington Post*, "Presidential Teleprompting," June 6, 1986, D1.
10. *New York Times*, January 26, 1978, A15.
11. Turner, p. 135.
12. Hechler, p. 74.
13. *Ibid.*, p. 76.
14. *New York Times*, April 23, 1962, p. 262.
15. Bradlee, p. 77.
16. Fairlie, *The Kennedy Promise*, pp. 72–73.
17. Interview with Cannon, 1986.
18. Hechler, p. 99.
19. .Valenti, pp. 119–20.
20. "The Politics of Change," in *The Washington Post Magazine*, February 2, 1986, p. 151.
21. Hart, *Verbal Style*, pp. 46–48.
22. *New York Times*, July 21, 1985, p. 22.
23. *Ibid.*
24. Transcript from tapes.
25. Lou Cannon, "Reaganisms of the Year," *Washington Post*, December 30, 1985, A2.
26. Erickson, p. 15.
27. February 6, 1986, C4.
28. Adler, p. 52.
29. Schlesinger, *The Politics of Upheaval*, p. 623.
30. *Ibid.*, p. 621.

Chapter 8

1. Burns, p. 161.
2. *Working with Roosevelt*, pp. 89–90.
3. Moley, pp. 96–119.
4. Jordan, p. 312.
5. Exodus 4.
6. Jebb, I, p. 3.
7. Brigance, p. 10.
8. *Phaedrus*, p. 258.
9. May, p. 463.
10. *Ibid.*, p. 459.
11. Einhorn, p. 42.
12. Washington, pp. 48–49.
13. Gunderson, p. 239.
14. Jeffrey and Peterson, p. 116.
15. Safire, *The New Language*, p. 414.
16. Bendiner, p. 15.
17. *Ibid.*
18. Levy, p. 105.
19. Einhorn, p. 429.
20. Interview with Moyers, 1984.

21. Crowell, p. 280.
22. Fuess, p. 46.
23. Fleming, p. 70.
24. Fuess, p. 47.
25. Tarver, p. 13.
26. Gunderson, p. 22.
27. Bonafede, p. 314.
28. Lewis, p. 39.
29. Clapper, p. 67.
30. Ewald, p. 303.
31. Fallows, p. 33.
32. Einhorn, p. 43.
33. Lewis, p. 42.
34. Gunderson, p. 24.
35. Bendiner, p. 15.
36. Farrar, p. 112.
37. *Ibid.*, p. 116.
38. Bormann, "Ghostwriting and the Rhetorical Critic," p. 284.
39. Mencken, p. 39.
40. *Ibid.*, p. 23.
41. Goldman, p. 14.
42. Ibid., p. 11.
43. Hart, *Verbal Style*, p. 2.
44. Bonafede, p. 311.
45. Sorensen, p. 60.
46. Fallows, p. 33.
47. Lincoln, vol. VII, p. 393.
48. See McDonald, p. 11.
49. Chapel, "Speechwriting," pp. 67–68.
50. Interview with Mudd, June 1986.
51. Dart, pp. 273–74.
52. Interview with Roberts, June 1986.
53. Interview, June 1986.
54. "Reflections on Writing," p. 28.
55. May, p. 460.
56. "Ethics," *Quarterly Journal of Speech*, p. 267.
57. *Leaders*, p. 175.
58. Ewald, p. 231.
59. Stockman, pp. 319–26.
60. *Washington Post* (June 12, 1986), p. A19.
61. Grayson, p. 65.
62. Ford, *A Time to Heal*, p. 26.
63. Hart, *Sound of Leadership*, pp. 190–214.
64. Brigance, p. 10.
65. *Ibid*, p. 11.
66. Rovere, p. 37.
67. *Ibid.*
68. The two texts survive in the Sorensen files, JFK Library.
69. William Chafe, p. 357.

70. Noonan, p. 20.
71. *Before the Fall*, p. 100.
72. Casserley, p. 58.
73. *Ibid*, p. 77.
74. Ewald, p. 150.
75. *Ibid.*, p. 157.
76. Fallows, p. 43.
77. Interview with Shrum, June 1986.
78. Ewald, p. 227.
79. July 10, 1937, p. 38.
80. *Washington Post* (October 4, 1979), DI.
81. Corey, p. 78.
82. (February 26, 1972), p. 356.
83. John Osborne, pp. 94–95.
84. *Ordeal*, p. 25.
85. Interview with Noonan, 1986.
86. *Washington Post*, (July 29, 1986), A2.
87. *Communication Education*, p. 305.
88. Sorensen, *The Kennedy Legacy*, pp. 125–26.
89. Bormann, "Ethics of Ghost Written Speeches," p. 420.
90. Safire, *The New Language*, 1968, p. 414.
91. *Communication Education*, p. 303.
92. *Communication Education*, p. 302.
93. Fallows, p. 43.
94. Ewald, p. 160.
95. *The Papers of Adlai E. Stevenson*, vol. 7 (May 16, 1960), p. 490.
96. McPherson, p. 43.
97. Arnold, p. 266.

Chapter 9

1. Jefferson, pp. 411–12.
2. Jamieson, p. 246.
3. "Of Aesthetic Judgment," Sect. 53.
4. Aristotle, *Nicomachean Ethics*, 1141b, 7–14.
5. Halloran, "Tradition and Theory," p. 235.
6. Burke, *Philosophy*, p. 191.
7. Broder, *The Washington Post*, June 15, 1986, p. F7.
8. Broder, *Behind the Front Page*, p. 240.

Bibliography

Abramowitz, Mildred W. "Eleanor Roosevelt and the National Youth Administration 1935–1943: An Extension of the Presidency." *Presidential Studies Quarterly* 14 (Fall 1984), pp. 569–80.

Adams, Charles Kendall, ed. *Representative British Orations.* New York and London: G. P. Putnam's Sons, 1900.

Adams, Henry. *The Education of Henry Adams.* New York: The Modern Library, 1918.

Adams, John G. *Without Precedent.* New York: W. W. Norton, 1983.

Adams, John. *Works of John Adams,* ed. Charles Frances Adams. Boston: Little Brown, 1850–1856.

———. *Lectures on Rhetoric and Oratory.* Intro. J. Jeffrey Auer, and Jerald L. Banninga. New York: Russell & Russell, 1962.

Addison, Joseph. *The Spectator,* ed. George A. Aitken. Vol. 8, London: John C. Nimmo, 1898.

Adler, Bill. *More Kennedy Wit.* New York: Bantam Books, 1965.

Anderson, Judith. *Outspoken Women: Speeches by American Women Reformers 1635–1935.* Dubuque, Iowa: Kendell Hunt, 1984.

———. "Sexual Politics: Chauvinism and Backlash?" *Communication Quarterly* 21 (1973), pp. 11–16.

Angle, Paul M. *By These Words.* New York: Rand McNally, 1954.

Arendt, Hannah. *The Human Condition.* Chicago: University of Chicago Press, 1958.

———. *Lectures on Kant's Political Philosophy,* ed. Ronald Beiner. Chicago: University of Chicago Press, 1982.

Aristotle. *Rhetoric.* Trans. John Henry Freese. Cambridge, Mass.: Harvard University Press, 1947.

Arkin, W., and L. R. Dobrofsky. "Military Socialization and Masculinity." *Journal of Social Issues* 34 (1978), pp. 151–68.

Arnauld, Antoine, and Claude Lancelot. *The Port-Royal Grammar.* The Hague: Mouton, 1975.

Arnold, Matthew. "The Function of Criticism at the Present Time." In *Lectures and Essays in Criticism.* Ann Arbor: The University of Michigan Press, 1962, pp. 258–85.

Atkinson, Max. *Our Master's Voices.* London: Metheun, 1984.

Auer, J. Jeffrey. "The Image of the Right Honourable Margaret Thatcher." *Central States Speech Journal* 30 (1979), pp. 289–310.

———. "Response." *Communication Education* 33 (1984), pp. 306–7.

Augustine. *On Christian Doctrine.* In *Great Books of the Western World.* Vol. 18. Chicago: Encyclopaedia Britannica, 1952.

Bacon, Francis. *Advancement of Learning.* In *Great Books of the Western World.* Vol. 30. Chicago: Encyclopaedia Britannica, 1952.

Baker, Ray Stannard, ed. *Woodrow Wilson, Life and Letters.* Garden City, N.Y.: Doubleday, 1927–1939.

Bakshian, Aram Jr. "The Ghosts of Forbidden City," *Washingtonian* 12 (October 1976), p. 132ff.

Baldwin, Charles Sears. *Medieval Rhetoric and Poetic.* Gloucester, Mass.: Peter Smith, 1959.

Barclay, Martha Thomson. "Distaff Campaigning in the 1964 and 1968 Presidential Elections." *Central States Speech Journal* 21 (1970), pp. 117–22.

Barron, Nancy. "Sex-Typed Language: The Production of Grammatical Cases." *Acta Sociologica* 14 (1971), pp. 24–72.

de Bary, William Theodore, ed. *Sources of Indian Tradition.* New York: Columbia University Press, 1958.

Barzun, Jacques. *The Selected Writings of John Jay Chapman.* New York: Farrar, Straus and Cudahy, 1957.

Baskerville, Barnet. *People's Voice: The Orator in American Society.* Lexington: University Press of Kentucky, 1979.

Bassuk, Ellen. "The Rest Cure: Repetition or Resolution of Victorian Women's Conflicts?" In *The Female Body,* ed. Susan Rubin Suleiman. Cambridge, Mass.: Harvard University Press, 1986.

Baxter, Sandra, and Marjorie Lansing. *Women and Politics.* Ann Arbor: University of Michigan Press, 1981.

Beasley, Maurine. "Lorena A. Hickok: Journalistic Influence on Eleanor Roosevelt." *Journalism Quarterly* 57 (Summer 1980), pp. 281–86.

———. "Eleanor Roosevelt's Press Conferences: Symbolic Importance of a Pseudo-Event." *Journalism Quarterly* 61 (Summer 1984), pp. 274–79, 338.

———. "Eleanor Roosevelt's Vision of Journalism: A Communications Medium for Women." *Presidential Studies Quarterly* 16 (Spring 1986), pp. 66–75.

Beck, Lois, and Nikki Keddie. *Women in the Muslim World.* Cambridge, Mass.: Harvard University Press, 1978.

Becker, Carl. *The Declaration of Independence.* New York: Vintage Books, 1958.

Beiner, Ronald. *Political Judgment.* Chicago: University of Chicago Press, 1983.

Bendiner, Robert. "Ghosts behind the Speechmakers." *The New York Times Magazine,* August 17, 1952, p. 15ff.

Bennett, W. Lance. "The Ritualistic and Pragmatic Bases of Political Campaign Discourse," *Quarterly Journal of Speech* 63 (October 1977), pp. 219–38.
Bennett, William J. "To Reclaim a Legacy." *Chronicle of Higher Education* 28 (November 1984), p. 16
Benson, Thomas W. "Conversation with a Ghost." *Today's Speech* 16 (1968), pp. 71–81.
———. "Inaugurating Peace: Franklin D. Roosevelt's Last Speech." *Speech Monographs* 36 (1969), pp. 138–47.
Benson, Thomas, and Michael H. Prosser, eds. *Readings in Classical Rhetoric.* Bloomington and London: Indiana University Press, 1972.
Benze, J. G., and E. R. Declercq. "Content of Televised Political Spot Ads for Female Candidates." *Journalism Quarterly* 62 (1985), pp. 278–83.
Berg, Christine, and Philippa Berry. "Spiritual Whoredom': An Essay on Female Prophets in the Seventeenth Century." In *Feminist Literary Theory*, ed. Mary Eagleton. Oxford: Basil Blackwell, 1986.
Bernard, Jessie. "Talk, Conversation, Listening, Silence." *The Sex Game.* New York: Atheneum, 1972, pp. 135–64.
Berryman, C. L. "Instructional Materials for Teaching a Course in 'Women in Communication.'" *Communication Education* 28 (July, 1979), pp. 217–21.
Bettleheim, Bruno. *The Uses of Enchantment.* New York: Alfred Knopf, 1977.
Bierce, Ambrose. *The Collected Works of Ambrose Bierce.* New York and Washington: The Neale Publishing Co., 1909.
———. *The Devil's Dictionary.* New York: Dover Publications, 1911; 1958.
Bischoff, Friedrich A. *Interpreting the Fu.* Wiesbaden: Franz Steiner Verlag, 1976.
Blair, Hugh. *Lectures on Rhetoric and Belles Lettres.* London: W. Strahan, 1783.
Blankenship, Jane, Marlene G. Fine, and Leslie K. Davis. "The 1980 Republican Primary Debates: The Transformation of Actor to Scene." *Quarterly Journal of Speech*, 69 (1983), pp. 35–36.
Bloch, Maurice, ed. *Political Language and Oratory in Traditional Society.* London: Academic Press, 1975.
Bloom, Allan. *The Closing of the American Mind.* New York: Simon and Schuster, 1987.
Bogan, Meg. *The Women Troubadours.* New York: W. W. Norton Co., 1976.
Boguet, Henry. *An Examen of Witches.* n.p., John Rodker, 1929.
Bonafede, Dom. "Report: Speechwriters Play Strategic Role in Conveying, Shaping Nixon's Policies." *National Journal* 19 (February 1972), pp. 311–20.
Boneparty, Ellen. "Women in Campaigns: From Lickin' and Stickin' to Strategy." *American Politics Quarterly* 5 (July 1977), pp. 298–300.
Borah, William E. "Speech on the League of Nations." In *Great Issues in American History*, ed. Richard and Beatrice K. Hofstadter. New York: Vintage Books, 1969.
Borgatta, Edgar F., and J. Stimson. "Sex Differences in Interaction Characteristics." *Journal of Social Psychology* 60 (1963), pp. 89–100.
Bormann, Ernest G. "Ethics of Ghostwritten Speeches." *Quarterly Journal of Speech* 47 (1961), pp. 262–67.
———. "Ghostwriting Agencies." *Today's Speech* (September 1956), pp. 20ff.
———. "Ghostwriting and the Rhetorical Critic." *Quarterly Journal of Speech* 46 (1960), pp. 284–88.

————. "Response." *Communication Education* 33 (1984), pp. 304–5.
Bosmajian, Haig A. "The Abrogation of the Suffragists' First Amendment Rights." *Western Journal of Speech Communication* 38 (Fall 1974), pp. 218–32.
Braden, Waldo. *The Oral Tradition in the South.* Baton Rouge: Louisiana State University Press, 1983.
Bradlee, Benjamin C. *Conversations with Kennedy.* New York: W. W. Norton, 1975.
Bradley, Scully, Beatty, Richmond and E. Hudson Long, eds. *The American Tradition in Literature.* New York: W. W. Norton, 1967.
Brake, Robert J. "Women Orators: More Research?" *Today's Speech* 15 (November 1967), pp. 20–22.
Brake, Robert J. and Robert D. Neuvey. "Woman Orators: An Opinion Survey." *Today's Speech* 21 (Fall 1973), pp. 33–37.
Brandenburg, Earnest. "The Preparation of Franklin D. Roosevelt's Speeches." *Quarterly Journal of Speech* (April 1959), pp. 214–21.
Brewer, David J. *The World's Best Orations.* 10 vol. St. Louis: Ferdinand P. Kaiser, 1899.
Brigance, W. Norwood. "Ghostwriting: Before Franklin D. Roosevelt and the Radio." *Today's Speech* (September 1956), pp. 10–12.
Brigance, W. Norwood, ed. *A History and Criticism of American Public Address.* New York: Russell and Russell, 1960.
British Orations from Ethelbert to Churchill. London: J. M. Dent and Sons Ltd., 1960.
Broder, David S. "Ghosts of Speeches Past." *Washington Post,* December 4, 1977, Sec C, p. 7.
Bromberg-Ross, JoAnn. "Storying and Changing: An Examination of The Consciousness-Raising Process." *Folklore Feminists Communication* 6 (1975), pp. 9–11.
Brougham, Henry Lord. *Speeches of Henry Lord Brougham.* Edinburgh: Adam and Charles Black, 1838.
————. *Sketches of Public Characters.* Philadelphia: E. L. Carey, and A. Hart, 1839.
Brown, Maud Morrow. "Sarah McGehee Isom." *Southern Speech Communication Journal* 25 (Fall 1959), pp. 27–33.
Brownmiller, Susan. *Femininity.* New York: Fawcett Columbine, 1984.
Bryan, William Jennings. *The First Battle.* Chicago: W. B. Conkey Co., 1896.
————. *Letters to a Chinese Official.* New York: McClure, Phillips and Co., 1906.
Bryan, William Jennings, ed. *The World's Famous Orations.* 10 vols. New York: Funk and Wagnalls Co., 1906.
Bryant, Donald. *Rhetorical Dimensions in Criticism.* Baton Rouge: Louisiana State University Press, 1973.
Bryant, Donald, ed. *The Rhetorical Idiom.* Ithaca, N.Y.: Cornell University Press, 1958.
Bryant, Donald C., and Carroll C. Arnold et al. *An Historical Anthology of Select British Speeches.* New York: The Ronald Press, 1967.
Bryant, Donald, and Karl R. Wallace. *Fundamentals of Public Speaking.* New York: Appleton-Century-Crofts, 1953.

Bryce, James. *The American Commonwealth.* New York: The Macmillan Co., 1911.
Buhle, Paul, and Marijo, eds. *The Concise History of Woman Suffrage.* Urbana: University of Illinois Press, 1978.
Bulwer, John. *Chirologia and Chironomia,* ed. James W. Cleary. Carbondale and Edwardsville: Southern Illinois University Press, 1974.
Burghley, William, Lord. *Precepts.* London: Thomas Jones, 1637.
Burgoon, Michael, J. P. Dillard, and N. E. Doran. "Friendly or Unfriendly Persuasion." *Human Communication Research* 10 (1983), pp. 283–94.
Burke, Edmund. *Reflections on the Revolution in France.* New York: Penguin, 1982.
Burke, Kenneth. *A Grammar of Motives.* Berkeley: University of California Press, 1962.
———. *Permanence and Change.* Los Altos, Calif.: Hermes Publications, 1954.
———. *The Philosophy of Literary Form.* Berkeley: University of California Press, 1973.
———. "Rhetoric—Old and New," *The Journal of General Education* V (April 1951), pp. 202–9.
———. *A Rhetoric of Motives.* Berkeley: University of California Press, 1969.
Burks, Don M., ed. *Rhetoric, Philosophy and Literature: An Exploration.* West Lafayette, Ind.: Purdue University Press, 1978.
Burns, James MacGregor. *The Power to Lead.* New York: Simon and Schuster, 1984.
———. *Roosevelt: The Lion and the Fox.* New York: Harcourt, Brace, 1956.
de Camp, L. Sprague. *The Great Monkey Trial.* New York: Doubleday and Co., 1968.
Campbell, Angus, Philip E. Converse, Warren E. Miller, and Donald E. Stokes. *The American Voter.* New York: John Wiley and Sons, 1960.
Campbell, George. *The Philosophy of Rhetoric,* ed. Lloyd Bitzer. Carbondale: Southern Illinois University Press, 1963,
Campbell, Karlyn Kohrs. "Femininity and Feminism: To Be Or Not To Be A Woman." *Communication Quarterly* 31 (Spring 1983), pp. 101–8.
———. "Stanton's 'The Solitude of Self': A Rationale for Feminism." *Quarterly Journal of Speech* 66 (October 1980), pp. 304–12.
———. "The Rhetoric of Women's Liberation: An Oxymoron." *Quarterly Journal of Speech* 59 (1973), pp. 74–86.
———. "Style and Content in Early Afro-American Feminists." *Quarterly Journal of Speech* 72 (November 1986), pp. 434–45.
Campbell, Karlyn Kohrs, and E. Claire Jerry. "Woman and Speaker: A Conflict in Roles." In Sharon Brehm, ed. *Social Roles and Personal Lives.* Westport, Conn.: Greenwood Press, 1987.
Cannon, Lou. *Reagan.* New York: G. P. Putnam and Sons, 1982.
Caplan, Harry. *Of Eloquence.* Ithaca, N.Y.: Cornell University Press, 1970.
Carlson, R. "Understanding Women: Implications for Personality Theory and Research." *Journal of Social Issues* 28 (1972), pp. 17–32.
Carnegie, Dale. *Public Speaking.* New York: Pocket Books, 1926.
Carter, James E. *Public Papers of the President.* Washington, D.C.: Government Printing Office, 1977–1980.

Carter, Jimmy. *Keeping Faith*. New York: Bantam Books, 1982.

Casserly, John J. *The Ford White House*. Boulder: Colorado Associated University Press, 1977.

Catt, Carrie, and Shuler. *Woman Suffrage and Politics*. New York: Charles Schribner's Sons, 1923.

Chafe, William H. *The Unfinished Journey*. New York: Oxford University Press, 1986.

Chamberlain, Neville. *In Search of Peace*. New York: G. P. Putnam and Sons, 1939.

Channing, Edward. *Lectures Read to Seniors in Harvard*, eds. Dorothy I. Anderson, and Waldo Braden. Carbondale: University of Southern Illinois Press, 1968.

Chapel, Gage W. "Christian Science and the Nineteenth Century Woman's Movement." *Central States Speech Journal* 26 (1975), pp. 142–49.

———. "Speechwriting in the Nixon Administration." *Journal of Communication* 26 (1976), pp. 65–72.

———. "Speechwriting in the Ford Administration: An Interview with Presidential Speech Writer Robert Orben." *Exetasis* 3 (July 15, 1976), pp. 16–17.

Cheney, Lynn. *American Memory: A Report on the Humanities in the Nation's Public Schools*. Washington, D.C.: National Endowment for the Humanities, 1987.

Chodorow, Nancy. *The Reproduction of Mothering*. Berkeley: University of California Press, 1978.

Cicero. *Brutus*, trans. G. L. Hendrickson; *Orator*. Trans. H. M. Hubbell. Cambridge, Mass.: Harvard University Press, 1971.

Clagett, Marshall. *Greek Science in Antiquity*. New York: Abelard-Schuman Inc., 1955.

Clapper, Raymond, and J. George Frederick "Is Ghostwriting Dishonest?" *Forum* (February 1939), pp. 67–71.

Cochrane, Robert, comp. *The Treasury of British Eloquence*. London: William P. Nimmo, 1877.

Cody, Sherwin, ed. *A Selection from the World's Great Orations*. Chicago: A. C. McClurg and Co., 1928.

Cohn, Roy. *McCarthy*. New York: Lancer Books, 1968.

Coletta, Paolo E. *William Jennings Bryan*. Lincoln: University of Nebraska Press, 1969.

Connors, Robert J., Lisa S. Ede, and Andrea A. Lunsford, eds. *Essays on Classical Rhetoric and Modern Discourse*. Carbondale: Southern Illinois University Press, 1984.

Conrad, Charles. "Agon and Rhetorical Form: The Essence of 'Old Feminist' Rhetoric." *Central States Speech Journal* 32 (Spring 1981), pp. 45–53.

Constantini, Edmond, and Kenneth Craik. "Women as Politicians." *Journal of Social Issues* 28 (1972), pp. 217–36.

Cook, Bruce. "Ghost Writing." *Commonweal* 102, May 9, 1975, pp. 105–8.

Copeland, Lewis, ed. *The World's Great Speeches*. Garden City, N.Y.: Garden City Publishing Co., 1942.

Corey, Herbert. "Ghosts that Haunt the Hustings." *Nation's Business* (August 1948), pp. 43–45, 78.

Cottin, Jonathan, and Andrew J. Glass. "Report: Democrats Depend on

Speechwriters for their Ideological Images." *National Journal* (February 26, 1972), pp. 350–59.

Coughlin, Elizabeth Myette and Charles Edward Coughlin. "Convention in Petticoats: The Seneca Falls Declaration of Woman's Rights." *Communication Quarterly* 21 (1973), pp. 17–23.

Coward, Harold G. *The Sphota Theory of Language*. Dehli: Motilas Banarsidass, 1980.

Cowley, Malcolm. "The Haunted House." *The New Republic* 108 (April 12, 1943), pp. 481–82.

Crocker, Lionel. *An Analysis of Lincoln and Douglas as Public Speakers and Debaters*. Springfield, Ill.: Charles C Thomas, 1968.

Crocker, Lionel, and Paul A. Carmack. *Readings in Rhetoric*. Springfield, Ill.: Charles C Thomas, 1965.

Croll, Morris W. *Style, Rhetoric and Rhythm*, ed. J. Max Patrick et al. Princeton, N.J.: Princeton University Press, 1966.

Crowell, Laura. "The Building of the 'Four Freedoms' Speech." *Speech Monographs* 22 (November 1955), pp. 266–83.

Crowned Masterpieces of Eloquence. London: International University Society, 1920.

Crowther, J. G. *The Social Relations of Science*. London: The Cresset Press, 1941.

Crump, J. I. Jr. *Intrigues: Studies of the Chan-Kuo Ts'e*. Ann Arbor: The University of Michigan Press, 1964.

Custard, Harry Lewis, and Edith May Custard, eds. *Wisdom of Emerson*. Tucson, Arizona: Unity of World Knowledge Publ., 1965.

Dalbiac, Lilian. *Dictionary of Quotations* (German). New York: Frederick Ungar Publ., n.d.

Daniels, Jonathon. *The Man of Independence*. Philadelphia: Lippincott, 1950.

Dart II, Rufus. "The Ventriloquists of Washington." *Scribner's Magazine* (November 1932), pp. 268–74.

De Britaine, William. *Humane Prudence*. 10th ed. London: Richard Sare, 1710.

Debs, Eugene. *Eugene Debs Speaks*, ed. Jean Y. Tussey. New York: Pathfinder Press, 1972.

Dees, Diane. "Bernadette Devlin's Maiden Speech: A Rhetoric of Sacrifice." *Southern Speech Communication Journal* 38 (Summer 1973), pp. 326–39.

Demos, John Putnam. *Entertaining Satan*. New York: Oxford University Press, 1982.

Devlin, L. Patrick. "The Influences of Ghostwriting on Rhetorical Criticism." *Today's Speech* (Summer 1974), pp. 7–12.

Dhanamjaya. *The Dasarupa*. Trans. George C. O. Haas. Dehli: Motilas Banarsidass, 1962.

Dionne, E. J. Jr. "The Elusive Front-Runner." *The New York Times Magazine*, May 3, 1987, pp. 28–40; 70.

Dionysius of Halicarnassus. *On Literary Composition*, ed. W. Rhys Roberts. London: Macmillan and Co., 1910.

Dixon, Peter. *Rhetoric*. London: Methuen and Co., 1971.

Donaldson, Alice. "Women Emerge as Political Speakers." *Communication Monographs* 18 (1951), pp. 54–61.

Donker, Marjorie, and George M. Muldrow. *Dictionary of Literary—Rhetorical Conventions of the English Renaissance*. Westport, Conn.: Greenwood Press, 1982.

Dosser, David A., Jack O. Balswick, and Charles F. Halverson, Jr. "Male Inex-
pressiveness and Relationships." *Journal of Social and Personal Relation-
ships* 3 (1986), pp. 241–58.
Douglass, Frederick. *The Frederick Douglass Papers*, ed. John W. Blassingame.
New Haven and London: Yale University Press, 1979.
———. *Frederick Douglass*, ed. Benjamin Quarles. Englewood Cliffs, N.J.: Prentice-
Hall Inc., 1968.
Duberman, Lucille. *Gender and Society*. New York: Praeger, 1975.
Ebeling, Harry. "Aimee Semple McPherson: Evangelist of the City." *Western
Journal of Speech Communication* 21 (Summer 1957), pp. 153–59.
Einhorn, Lois J. "The Gosts Unmasked: A Review of Literature on Speech-
writing." *Communication Quarterly* 30 (Winter 1981), pp. 41–47.
Eisenhower, Dwight D. *Public Papers of the President*. Washington, D.C.: Govern-
ment Printing Office, 1953–1960.
Ek, Richard A. "Victoria Woodhull and the Pharisees." *Journalism Quarterly* 49
(Fall 1972), pp. 453–59.
Ellmann, Mary. *Thinking about Women*. New York: Harcourt, Brace, 1968.
Emerson, Ralph Waldo. "Society and Solitude." In *The Complete Works of Ralph
Waldo Emerson*. Cambridge, Mass.: Riverside Press, 1904.
———. *Emerson: A Modern Anthology*, eds. Alfred Kazin, and Daniel Aaron.
Cambridge, Mass.: Riverside Press, 1958.
Enos, Richard Leo. "The Persuasive and Social Force of Logography in An-
cient Greece." *Central States Speech Journal* 25 (1974), pp. 4–10.
Erickson, Paul D. *Reagan Speaks: The Making of An American Myth*. New York:
New York University Press, 1985.
Erskin, H. "The Polls: Women's Role." *Public Opinion Quarterly* 35 (Summer
1971), pp. 275–90.
Ewald, William Bragg, Jr., *Eisenhower the President*. Englewood Cliffs, N.J.:
Prentice-Hall, 1981.
Exline, R., D. Gray, and D. Schutte. "Visual Behavior in a Dyad as Affected by
Interview Control and Sex of Respondent." *Journal of Personality and So-
cial Psychology* 1 (1965), pp. 201–9.
Fairlie, Henry. "The Decline of Oratory." *The New Republic* (May 28, 1984) pp.
15–19.
———. *The Kennedy Promise*. New York: Dell Publishing, 1972.
Fallows, James. "The Passionless Presidency." *Atlantic* 243 (May, 1979), pp. 33–
46.
Farrar, Larston D. "Live Ghosts in Washington." *The American Mercury* 83 (1956),
pp. 108–19.
Farrell, Kathleen, and Theodore Otto Windt, Jr. "Presidential Rhetoric and
Presidential Power: The Reagan Initiatives." In *Essays in Presidential Rhet-
oric*, eds. Theodore Otto Windt and Beth Ingold. Dubuque, Iowa: Ken-
dall/Hunt, 1983, pp. 310–22.
Farrington, Benjamin. *Science and Politics in the Ancient World*. New York: Barnes
and Noble, 1966.
Fenelon. *Dialogues on Eloquence*. Trans. W. S. Howell. Princeton, N.J.: Univer-
sity of Princeton Press, 1951.
Ferraro, Geraldine A. *Ferraro: My Story*. New York: Bantam Books, 1985.
Feshbacker, N. D. "Sex Differences in Empathy and Social Behavior in Chil-

dren." In *The Development of Prosocial Behavior*, ed. N. Eisenberg. New York: Academic Press, 1982. pp. 315–38.

Filler, Louis, ed. *Wendell Phillips on Civil Rights and Freedom*. New York: Hill and Wang, 1965.

Fischli, Ronald. "Anita Bryant's Stand Against 'Militant Homosexuality': Religious Fundamentalism and the Democratic Process." *Central States Speech Journal* 30 (Fall 1979), pp. 262–71.

Fisher, John. "A Footnote on Adlai E. Stevenson." *Harper's Magazine* 231 (November 1965), pp. 18–29.

Fisher, Walter. "Reaffirmation and Subversion of the American Dream." *Quarterly Journal of Speech* 59 (1973), pp. 160–67.

———. "Rhetorical Fiction and the Presidency." *Quarterly Journal of Speech* 66 (1982), pp. 1–8.

Fleming, Eugene D. "Ghosts in the Closet." *Cosmopolitan* 147 (August 1959), pp. 68–71.

Foner, Philip S., ed. *The Voices of Black American: Major Speeches by Negroes in the United States, 1797–1971*. New York: Simon and Schuster, 1972.

Ford, Gerald. *A Time to Heal*. New York: Harper & Row, 1979.

———. *Public Papers of the President*. Washington, D.C.: Government Printing Office, 1974–1977.

Foss, Sonja K. "Teaching Feminist Rhetoric: An Illustrative Syllabus." *Communication Education* 27 (September 1978), pp. 328–35.

———. "Equal Rights Amendment Controversy: Two Worlds in Conflict." *Quarterly Journal of Speech* 65 (1979), pp. 275–88.

Foss, Karen and Sonja Foss. "The Status of Research on Women and Communication." *Communication Quarterly* 31 (Summer 1983), pp. 195–204.

Fox-Davies, Arthur Charles. *The Book of Public Speaking*. London Caxton Publishing Co., n.d.

Franklin, Benjamin. *Autobiography*. New York: Holt, Rinehart and Winston, Inc., 1948.

Frye, Northrop. *The Well-Tempered Critic*. Bloomington: Indiana University Press, 1963.

Fuess, Claude M. "Ghosts in the White House." *American Heritage* 10 (December 1959), p. 45ff.

Fukuzawa Yukichi. *The Autobiography of Fukuzawa Yukichi*. Trans. Eiichi Kiyooka. Tokyo: The Hokuseido Press, 1940.

Gandhi, Mahatma. *The Message of Mahatma Gandhi*, ed. U.S. Mohan Rao. New Delhi: Publications Division of the Ministry of Information and Broadcasting, Government of India, 1968.

———. *The Selected Works of Mahatma Gandhi*. Ahmedabad: Navajivan Publishing House, 1968.

Gardiner, Judith Kegan. "On Female Identity and Writing by Women." In *Writing and Sexual Difference*, ed. Elizabeth Abel. Chicago: University of Chicago Press, 1982. pp. 177–91.

Garrow, David J. *Bearing the Cross: Martin Luther King, Jr., and the Southern Christian Leadership Conference*. New York: William Morrow and Co., 1986.

Gehlen, Frieda L. "Women in Congress." *Trans-action* 6 (October 1969), p. 39.

Giles, Herbert A., ed. *Gems of Chinese Literature*. New York: Paragon Book Reprint Co., 1965.

Gilley, H. M., and C. S. Summers. "Sex Differences in Use of Hostile Verbs." *Journal of Psychology* 76 (1970), pp. 33–37.

Gilman, Charlotte Perkins. *The Yellow Wallpaper*. Boston: Small, Maynard, 1899; rpt. New York: Feminist Press, 1973.

Gilroy, Harry, "Survey of the Ghost Writers." *The New York Times Magazine*, March 27, 1949, p. 20ff.

Gold, Ellen Reid. "The Grimke Sisters and the Emergence of the Women's Rights Movement." *Southern Speech Communication Journal* 46 (Summer 1981), pp. 341–60.

Goldman, Eric. "Party of One." *Holiday* 31 (1962), p. 11ff.

Gonda, Jan. *The Ritual Sutras*. Wiesbaden: Otto Harrassowitz, 1977.

———. *Vedic Literature*. Wiesbaden: Otto Harrassowitz, 1975.

Goodrich, Chauncey A,, ed. *Select British Eloquence*. New York: Bobbs-Merrill Co., 1963.

Goss, Judy Baker and David Ritchey. "Sarah Bernhardt's First 'Farewell' tour, 1905–1906: Little Rock, Arkansas Welcomes Camille." *Central States Speech Journal* 30 (Winter 1979), pp. 360–67.

Gould, Lewis L. "Modern First Ladies in Historical Perspective." *Presidential Studies Quarterly* 15 (Summer 1985), pp. 532–40.

Graham, Mary W. "Margaret Chase Smith." *Quarterly Journal of Speech* 50 (December 1964), pp. 390–93.

Grayson, Mel. "Ghosts at the Podium." *Advertising Age* 49 (October 9, 1978), pp. 65–66.

Great Debates in American History. New York: Current Literature Publishing Co., 1913.

Greene, Chris. "Women: The Emotional or the Expressive Sex?" *Psychology Today* (June 1986), p. 12.

Griffith, Allen Ayrault. *Elocution and Oratory*. St. Louis: Christian Publishing Co., 1879

Gronbeck, Bruce. "The Functions of Presidential Campaigning." *Communication Monographs* 45 (1978), pp. 268–80.

Guazzo, Steeven. *The Civile Conversation of M. Steeven Guazzo*. Trans. George Pettie (1581). London: Constable, 1925.

Gubar, Susan. "'The Blank Page' and Issues of Female Creativity." In *Writing and Sexual Difference*, ed. Elizabeth Abel. Chicago: University of Chicago Press, 1982. pp. 73–93.

Gunderson, Robert G. "Political Phrasemakers in Perspective." *Southern Speech Communication Journal* 26 (1960), pp. 22–26.

Gunter, Barrie. "Forgetting the News." *Mass Communication Review Yearbook* (1983), pp. 165–72.

Habermas, Jurgen. *Communication and the Evolution of Society*. Boston: Beacon Press, 1979.

———. *Knowledge and Human Interests*. Trans. J. J. Shapiro, Boston: Beacon Press, 1971.

———. *Legitimation Crisis*. London: Heinemann, 1976.

Haiman, Franklyn S. "Ghostwriting and the Cult of Leadership." *Communication Education* 33 (October 1984), pp. 301–4.

Hall, Judith A. *Nonverbal Sex Differences.* Baltimore: Johns Hopkins University Press, 1984.
Hallett, Judith P. *Fathers and Daughters in Roman Society.* Princeton, N.J.: Princeton University Press, 1984.
Halloran, S. M. "On the End of Rhetoric, Classical and Modern." *College English* 36 (February 1975), pp. 621–31.
————. "Tradition and Theory in Rhetoric." *Quarterly Journal of Speech* 62 (October 1976), pp. 234–42.
Hamill, S.S. *The Science of Elocution.* New York: Nelson & Phillips, 1876.
Hammerback, John C. "William F. Buckley, Fr., On Firing Line: A Case Study in Confrontational Dialogue." *Communication Quarterly* 22 (Summer 1974), pp. 23–30.
Hance, Kenneth G. et al. "The Later National Period: 1860–1930." In *A History and Criticism of American Public Address* ed. William Norwood Brigance. Vol. I. New York: McGraw-Hill, 1943, pp. 111–52.
Hancock, Brenda Robinson. "Affirmation by Negation in the Women's Liberation Movement." *Quarterly Journal of Speech* 50 (1972), pp. 264–71.
Han Fei Tzu. *Basic Writings.* Trans. Burton Watson. New York and London: Columbia University Press, 1964.
————. *The Complete Works of Han Fei Tzu.* Trans. W. K. Liao. London: Arthur Probsthain, 1939.
Harding, Susan. "Women and Words in a Spanish Village." In *Toward An Anthropology of Women,* ed. Rayne Reiter. New York: Monthly Review Press, 1975.
Hart, Roderick P. "The Language of the Modern Presidency." *Presidential Studies Quarterly* XIV, 2 (1984), pp. 265–88.
————. *The Political Pulpit.* West LaFayette, Ind.: Purdue University Press, 1977.
————. *Verbal Style and the Presidency.* Orlando: Academic Press, 1984.
————. *The Sound of Leadership.* Chicago: University of Chicago Press, 1987.
Hayward, John, ed. *Silver Tongues.* London: Michael Joseph Ltd., 1937.
Hechler, Ken. *Working with Truman.* New York: G.P. Putnam's Sons, 1982.
Hedlund, Ronald D., Patricia K. Freeman, Keith E. Hamm, and Robert M. Stein. "The Electability of Women Candidates: The Effects of Sex Role Stereotypes." *Journal of Politics* 41 (1979), pp. 513–24.
Heffner, Richard D. *A Documentary History of the United States.* New York: New American Library, 1965.
Heidegger, Martin. *Poetry, Language, Thought.* Trans. Albert Hofstadter. New York: Colophon Books, 1971.
Ad Herrennium. Trans. Harry Caplan. Cambridge Mass.: Harvard University Press, 1954.
Highet, Gilbert. *A Clerk of Oxenford.* New York: Oxford University Press, 1954.
Hillbruner, Anthony. "Frances Wright: Egalitarian Reformer." *Southern Speech Communication Journal* 23 (Summer 1958), pp. 193–203.
Hirsch, E. D., Jr. *Cultural Literacy.* Boston: Houghton-Mifflin Co., 1987.
Hitler, Adolph. *Mein Kampf.* New York: Reynal and Hitchcock, 1939.
————. *The Speeches of Adolph Hitler.* Trans. Norman H. Baynes. London: Oxford University Press, 1942.
Hobbes, Thomas. *The English Works of Thomas Hobbes.* London: John Bohn, 1840.

Honan, William H. "The Men Behind Nixon's Speeches." *The New York Times Magazine*, January 19, 1969, p. 20ff.

Hope, Diana Schaich. "Redefinition of Self: A Comparison of the Rhetoric of the Women's Liberation and Black Liberation Movements." *Communication Quarterly* 23 (Winter 1975), pp. 17–25.

Horner, Winifred Bryan, ed. *The Present State of Scholarship in Historical and Contemporary Rhetoric.* Columbia and London: University of Missouri Press, 1983.

Horowitz, Maryanne Cline. "Aristotle and Women." *Journal of the History of Biology* 9 (1976), pp. 183–213.

Howell, Wilbur Samuel. "John Locke and the New Rhetoric." In *Philosophers on Rhetoric*, ed. Donald G. Douglas. Skokie, Ill.: National Textbook Co., 1973.

Howes, Raymond F., ed. *Historical Studies of Rhetoric and Rhetoricians.* Ithaca, N.Y.: Cornell University Press, 1961.

Liu Hsieh. *The Literary Mind and the Carving of Dragons.* Trans. Vincent Yu-chung Shih. New York: Columbia University Press, 1959.

Hudson, Lee. "Belting the Bible: Madalyn Murray O'Hair vs. Fundamentalism." *Western Journal of Speech Communication* 36 (Fall 1972), pp. 233–40.

Hughes, Emmet John. *The Living Presidency.* New York: Coward, McCann & Geoghegan, 1972.

———. *The Ordeal of Power: A Political Memoir of the Eisenhower Years.* New York: Atheneum, 1963.

Hume, David. "Of Eloquence." In *Essays.* London, 1882, pp. 163–74.

Hunter College Women's Studies Collective. *Women's Realities Women's Choices.* New York: Oxford University Press, 1983.

Infante, Dominick A. "Motivation To Speak on a Controversial Topic." *Central States Speech Journal* 34 (1983), pp. 96–103.

Ingold, Beth, and Theodore Otto Windt, Jr., "Trying to 'Stay the Course': President Reagan's Rhetoric During the 1982 Election." *Presidential Studies Quarterly* 14 (1984), pp. 87–97.

Izutsu, Toshihiko. *Language and Magic.* Tokyo: Keio Institute of Philological Studies, 1956.

Jamieson, Kathleen Hall. *Packaging the Presidency: A History and Criticism of Presidential Campaign Advertising.* New York: Oxford University Press, 1984.

Japp, Phyllis M. "Esther or Isaiah?: The Abolitionist-Feminist Rhetoric of Angelina Grimke." *Quarterly Journal of Speech* 71 (1985), pp. 335–48.

Jarrard, Mary W. "Emerging ERA Patterns in Editorials in Southern Daily Newspapers." *Journalism Quarterly* 57 (Winter 1980), pp. 606–11.

Jebb, Richard C. *The Attic Orators.* London: Macmillan and Co., 1876.

———. *Essays and Addresses.* Cambridge: Cambridge University Press, 1907.

Jefferson, Thomas. *The Life and Selected Writings of Thomas Jefferson*, eds. A. Koch and W. Peden. New York: Random House, 1944.

Jeffrey, Robert, and Owen Peterson. *Speech.* New York: Harper & Row, 1975.

Johnson, Fern L. "Political and Pedagogical Implications of Attitudes Towards Women's Language." *Communication Quarterly* 31 (Spring 1983), pp. 133–38.

Johnson, Fern L., and Lynda Goldman. "Communication Education for Women:

A Case for Separatism." *Communication Education* 24 (November 1977), pp. 319–26.

Johnson, Lyndon B. *Public Papers of the President.* Washington, D.C.: Government Printing Office, 1964–1969.

———. *The Vantage Point.* New York: Holt, Rinehart and Winston, 1971.

Johnson, Marlyn, and Kathy Stanwick. *Profiles of Women Holding Office.* New Brunswick, N.J.: Rutgers University Press, 1976.

Johnson, Seneca. "In Defense of Ghost Writing." *Harper's Magazine* 179 (October 1939), pp. 536–43.

Jones, Edgar R. *Selected English Speeches.* London: Oxford University Press, 1913.

Jordan, Hamilton. *Crisis.* New York: Berkeley Books, 1982.

Kahler, Erich. *The Inward Turn of Narrative.* Trans. Richard and Clara Winston. Princeton, N.J.: Princeton University Press, 1973.

Kalcik, Susan. " '. . . Like Ann's Gynecologist or the Time I Was Almost Raped.': Personal Narratives in Women's Rap Groups." *Journal of American Folklore* 88 (1975), pp. 3–11.

Kant, Immanuel. *Critique of Judgment.* Trans. James Creed Meredith. Oxford: Clarendon Press, 1952.

Katz, William J. *Eyewitness: The Negro in American History.* New York: Pitman Publishing Co., 1968.

Kearns, Doris. *Lyndon Johnson and the American Dream.* New York: New American Library, 1976.

Kendall, Kathleen Edgerton, and Jeanne Y. Fisher. "Frances Wright on Women's Rights: Eloquence Versus Ethos." *Quarterly Journal of Speech* 60 (February 1974), pp. 58–68.

Kennedy, George A. *Classical Rhetoric and Its Christian and Secular Tradition.* Chapel Hill: University of North Carolina Press, 1980.

———. *Greek Rhetoric Under Roman Emperors.* Princeton, N.J.: Princeton University Press, 1983.

Kennedy, John F. "Acceptance Speech." *Vital Speeches* (August 1960), p. 611.

———. *Public Papers of the President.* Washington, D.C.: Government Printing Office, 1961–1964.

Kennedy, Patricia S. and Gloria H. O'Shields. *We Shall Be Heard: Women Speakers in America.* Dubuque, Iowa: Kendall Hunt, 1983.

Kerber, Linda. *Women of the Republic.* Chapel Hill: University of North Carolina Press, 1980.

Kessler, Lauren. "The Ideas of Women Suffragists and the Portland *Oregonian.*" *Journalism Quarterly* 57 (Winter 1980), pp. 597–605.

Kirkland, Mrs. C. M. *Patriotic Eloquence.* New York: Charles Scribner and Co., 1866.

Kondracke, Morton. "Speech, Speech! Author, Author!" *The New Republic* (July 5, 1982), pp. 21–25.

Kramer, Cheris. "Women's Speech: Separate But Unequal?" *Quarterly Journal of Speech* 60 (February 1974), pp. 14–24.

Kramarae, Cheris. *Men and Women Speaking.* Rowley, Mass.: Newbury House, 1980.

Kroll, Becky Swanson. "From Small Group to Public View: Mainstreaming the

Women's Movement." *Communication Quarterly* 31 (Spring 1983), pp. 139–47.

Kurzeja, Wayne Samuel. *Presidential Quotient.* Chicago: Chicago Review Press, 1984.

La France, Marianne and Clara Mayo. "A Review of Nonverbal Behavior of Women and Men." *Western Journal of Speech Communication* 43 (Spring 1979), pp. 96–107.

Lawson, John. *Lectures Concerning Oratory,* ed. E. Neal Claussen and Karl R. Wallace. Carbondale: Southern Illinois University Press, 1972.

Lechner, Sister Joan Marie. *Renaissance Concepts of the Commonplaces.* New York: Pageant Press, 1962.

Legge, James. *The Chinese Classics.* Shanghai, 1935.

Lerner, Gerda. *The Creation of Patriarchy.* New York: Oxford University Press, 1986.

Levenson, Joseph R. *Confucian China and Its Modern Fate.* Berkeley: University of California Press, 1968.

Levy, Alan. "Richard Nixon's Biggest Crisis." *Redbook* 119 (July 1962), p. 105.

Lewis, Peter. "Ghost Town." *The New York Times Magazine,* April 10, 1960, p. 39ff.

Lincoln, Abraham. *The Collected Works of Abraham Lincoln,* ed. Roy P. Basler. New Brunswick, N.J.: Rutgers University Press, 1953.

Lindstrom, Monty. "Speech and Kava on Tanna." In *Vanuatu,* ed. Michael Allen. New York: Academic Press, 1981.

Linkugel, Wil A. "The Speech Style of Anna Howard Shaw." *Central States Speech Journal* 13 (Spring 1962), pp. 171–78.

———. "The Women Suffrage Argument of Anna Howard Shaw." *Quarterly Journal of Speech* 49 (April 1963), pp. 165–74.

———. "The Rhetoric of American Feminism: A Social Movement Course." *Communication Education* 23 (March 1974), pp. 121–30.

Lipman-Blumen, Jean. "Achieving Styles: A Model, An Instrument, and Some Findings." In *Achievement and Achievement Motives,* ed. J. Spence. San Fransisco: W. H. Freeman, 1983, pp. 91–126.

Locke, John. *Locke Selections,* ed. Sterling P. Lamprecht. New York: Charles Scribner's Sons, 1928.

———. *The Works of John Locke.* Germany: Scientia Verlag Aalen, 1963.

Lodge, Henry Cabot. "Speech in U.S. Senate." *Congressional Record* (April 4, 1917), p. 208.

Lomax-Cooke, Carolyn. "The Speaker and the Ghost." *Vital Speeches* XLVIII (December 1, 1981), pp. 125–28.

Longinus. *On the Sublime,* ed. D. A. Russell. Oxford: Clarendon Press, 1964.

Lowell, James Russell. "Abraham Lincoln." In *Essays English and American,* ed. Charles W. Eliot, *The Harvard Classics.* New York: P.F.F. Collier and Son, 1938.

Lu Chi. *Wen Fu.* Trans. E. R. Hughes. New York: Pantheon Books, 1951.

Lucian. *Lucian.* Trans. A. M. Harmon. London: William Heinemann, 1925.

Macartney, C.A. *Maria Theresa and the House of Austria.* London, 1969.

Macaulay, Lord. *Essays, Critical and Miscellaneous.* Boston: Phillips, Sampson, and Co., 1855.

————. *Lays of Ancient Rome and Miscellaneous Essays and Poems*. London: Every-man's Library, New York: Dutton, 1910.

————. "On The Athenian Orators." In *Miscellaneous Works of Lord Macauley*. New York: Harper and Brothers, n.d., pp. 444–58.

Malleus Maleficarum. Trans. Rev. Montague Summers. New York: Benjamin Blom Inc., 1928.

Mansfield, Dorothy M. "Abigale S. Duniway: Suffragette with Not-so-Common-Sense." *Western Journal of Speech Communication* 35 (Winter, 1971), pp. 24–29.

Martin, Donald R., and Vicky Gordon Martin. "Barbara Jordan's Symbolic Use of Language in the Keynote Address to the National Women's Conference." *Southern Speech Communication Journal* 59 (Spring 1984), pp. 319–30.

Masaco, Kunihiro. "The Japanese Language and Intercultural Communication." *The Japan Interpreter* 10 (1976), pp. 267–83.

Mason, John. *An Essay on Elocution and Pronunciation* (1748). Menston, England: The Scholars Press, Ltd., 1986.

Mathews, William. *Oratory and Orators*. Chicago: S. C. Griggs and Co., 1887.

Maxa, Rudy. "James Fallows: Presidential Wordsmith Says Once Is Enough." *The Washington Post Magazine* (July 23, 1978), p. 4.

May, Ernest R. "Ghost Writing and History." *American Scholar* 22 (Autumn 1953), pp. 459–65.

McAdoo, Eleanor Wilson, ed. *The Priceless Gift: The Love Letters of Woodrow Wilson and Ellen Axson Wilson*. New York: McGraw-Hill Book Co., 1962.

McDavitt, Elaine E. "Susan B. Anthony, Reformer and Speaker." *Quarterly Journal of Speech* 30 (1944), pp. 173–80.

McDonald, John B. "Rose Garden Rubbish." *Wall Street Journal* (January 1, 1977), p. 11.

McFarlin, Annjennette. "Ahllie Quinn Brown: Black Woman Elocutionist." *Western Journal of Speech Communication* 46 (1980), pp. 72–82.

McGee, Michael Calvin. "The Origins of 'Liberty': A Feminization of Power." *Communication Monographs* 47 (1980), pp. 23–45.

McIlvainy, J. H. *Elocution*. New York: Charles Scribner and Co., 1870.

McPhee, Carol, and Ann Fitzgerald, comp. *Feminist Quotations*. New York: Thomas Y. Crowell, 1979.

McPherson, Harry. "Beyond Words." *The Atlantic* (1972) pp. 39–45.

McPherson, Louise. "Communication Techniques of the Women's Liberation Front." *Communication Quarterly* 21 (Spring 1973), pp. 33–38.

Mencken, H. L. *A Carnival of Buncombe*. Chicago: University of Chicago Press, 1984.

Miller, Henry. "The Wisdom of the Heart." In *Reflections on Writing*. Norfolk, Conn.: 1941.

Miller, Perry, ed. *The American Puritans*. New York: Doubleday, 1956.

Milton, John. *Complete Poetry and Selected Prose of Milton*. Intro. Cleanth Brooks. New York: Modern Library, 1950.

————. *Of Reformation in England*. In *The Complete Prose Works of John Milton*. Vol. 1. New Haven, Conn.: Yale University Press, 1953, pp. 519–617.

Mitchell-Kernan, Claudia. "Signifying." In *Mother Wit from the Laughing Barrell*, ed. Alan Dundes. Englewood Cliffs, N.J.: Prentice-Hall, 1973.

Mohrmann, G.P., Charles J. Stewart, and Donovan J. Ochs, eds. *Explorations in Rhetorical Criticism*. University Park: The Pennsylvania State University Press, 1973.

Moley, Raymond. *The First New Deal*. New York: Harcourt, Brace and World Inc., 1966.

Moore, Charles A., ed. *Philosophy and Culture East And West*. Honolulu: University of Hawaii Press, 1968.

Moran, Lord. *Churchill: From the Diaries of Lord Moran*. Boston: Houghton Mifflin Co., 1966.

Morgan, Edward S. *The Puritan Family: Religion and Domestic Relations in Seventeenth-Century New England*. New York: Harper & Row, 1966.

Morrow, Lance. "Decline and Fall of Oratory." 116 (August 18, 1980), pp. 76–77.

Motter, T. H. Vail, ed. *Leaders of Men*. Princeton, N.J.: Princeton University Press, 1952.

Muller, Adam. *Twelve Lectures on Rhetoric*. Ann Arbor, Mich.: University Microfilms International, 1978.

Murphy, James J., ed. *Renaissance Eloquence*. Berkeley, Calif.: University of California Press, 1983.

———. *A Synoptic History of Classical Rhetoric*. New York: Random House, 1972.

Murphy, Richard. "Problems in Speech Texts." In *Papers in Rhetoric and Poetic*. Iowa City: University of Iowa Press, 1964.

Nakamura, Hajime. *Ways of Thinking of Eastern Peoples*. Honolulu: University of Hawaii Press, 1964.

Natanson, Maurice, and Henry W. Johnstone, Jr., eds. *Philosophy Rhetoric and Argumentation*. University Park: The Pennsylvania State University Press, 1965.

Needham, Joseph. *The Grand Titration*. Toronto: University of Toronto Press, 1969.

———. *Science and Civilisation in China*. Cambridge: Cambridge University Press, 1983.

Nelson, Jeffrey. "The Defense of Billie Jean King." *Western Journal of Speech Communication* 48 (Winter 1984), pp. 92–102.

Neustadt, Richard E. *Presidential Power*. New York: The New American Library, 1960.

A New Dictionary of Quotations on Historical Principles, ed. H. L. Mencken. New York: Alfred A. Knopf, 1966.

The New Dictionary of Thoughts, ed. Tryon Edwards. New York: Standard Book Co., 1966.

Nichols, Marie Hochmuth. *Rhetoric and Criticism*. Baton Rouge: Louisiana State University Press, 1967.

Nie, Norman H., Sidney Verba, and John Petrocik. *The Changing American Voter*. Cambridge, Mass.: Harvard University Press, 1979.

Nisbet, Robert. "What to Do When You Don't Live in a Golden Age." *The American Scholar* (1982), pp. 229–41.

Nixon, Richard. *Leaders*. New York: Warner Books, 1982.

———. *RN: The Memoirs of Richard Nixon*. New York: Grosset and Dunlop, 1978.

————. *Papers of the President*. Washington, D.C.: Government Printing Office, 1969–1974.

North, Helen. *Sophrosyne*. Ithaca, N.Y.: Cornell University Press, 1966.

O'Barr, William M., and Jean F. O'Barr, eds. *Language and Politics*. Mouton: Mouton and Co., 1976.

O'Brien, Lawrence F. *No Final Victories*. New York: Ballantine Books, 1974.

O'Faolain, Julia, and Lauro Martines, eds. *Not in God's Image*. New York: Harper Torchbooks, 1973.

Oberdorfer, Don. "Vast Ghostland, of Washington." *The York Times Magazine* (April 26, 1964), p. 25ff.

Ohmann, Richard. "In Lieu of a New Rhetoric." *College English* 26 (October 1964), pp. 17–22.

Oliver, Robert T. *Communication and Culture in Ancient India and China*. Syracuse, N.Y.: Syracuse University Press, 1971.

————. *A History of Public Speaking in America*. Boston: Allen and Bacon, 1966.

Ong, Walter J. *Rhetoric, Romance and Technology*. Ithaca, N.Y.: Cornell University Press, 1971.

————. *Fighting for Life*. Ithaca and London: Cornell University Press, 1981.

Ortega y Gasset, Jose. *The Dehumanization of Art and Other Writings on Art and Culture*. Garden City, N.Y.: Doubleday, 1956.

Osborne, John. *The Fifth Year of the Nixon Watch*. New York: Liveright, 1974.

Parker, Edward G. *Reminiscences of Rufus Choate*. New York: Mason Brothers, 1860.

Partnow, Elaine, ed. *The Quotable Woman*. New York: Facts on File, 1977.

Pattison, Robert. *On Literacy*. New York: Oxford University Press, 1982.

Paul, Herbert. *Famous Speeches*. London: Sir Isaac Pitman and Sons Ltd., 1910.

Peacham, Henry. *The Garden of Eloquence* (1593). Intro. William G. Crane. Gainsville, Fla.: Scholars' Facsimiles and Reprints, 1954.

Pearce, W. Barnett and Bernard J. Brommel. "Vocalic Communication in Persuasion." *Quarterly Journal of Speech* 58 (October 1972), pp. 298–306.

Pearce, W. Barnett, and Sharon M. Rossi. "The Problematic Practices of Feminism: An Interpretive and Critical Analysis." *Communication Quarterly* 32 (Fall, 1984), pp. 277–86.

Pearson, Judy C. "Conflicting Demands in Correspondence: Abigale Adams on Women's Rights." *Communication Quarterly* 23 (Fall 1975), pp. 29–33.

Pearson, Lionel. "Cicero's Debt to Demosthenes." *Pacific Coast Philology* III (April 1968), pp. 49–54.

————. "The Development of Demosthenes as a Political Orator." *Phoenix* XVIII (1964), pp. 95–109.

Pederson, Lucille M. "Pedagogical Methods of Teaching 'Women in Public Speaking'." *Communication Education* 30 (July 1981), pp. 256–65.

Peterson, Houston, ed. *A Treasury of the World's Great Speeches*. New York: Simon and Schuster, 1954.

Phifer, Gregg. "Edith Bolling Wilson: Gatekeeper Extraordinary." *Communication Monographs* 38 (1971), pp. 277–89.

Phillips, J. A. *The History of An Idea: Eve*. New York: Harper & Row, 1984.

Pindar. *The Odes of Pindar*. Trans. Sir John Sandys. Cambridge, Mass.: Harvard University Press, 1978.

Pinola, Mary, and Nancy E. Briggs. "Martha Wright Griffiths: Champion of Women's Rights Legislation." *Central States Speech Journal* 30 (Fall 1979), pp. 228–40.

Platz, Mabel, ed. *Anthology of Public Speeches.* New York: The H. W. Wilson Co., 1940.

Pliny. *Letters.* Trans. William Melmouth. Cambridge, Mass.: Loeb Classical Library, 1915.

Plutrarch. *Lives of the Noble Greeks,* ed. Edmund Fuller. New York: Dell, 1959.

Polanyi, Michael. *Personal Knowledge.* London: Routledge & Kegan Paul, 1962.

———. *The Tacit Dimension.* Garden-City, N.Y.: Anchor Books, 1967.

Pomeroy, Sarah B. *Goddesses, Whores, Wives, and Slaves.* New York: Schocken Books, 1975.

Porter, Ebenezer. *Lectures on Eloquence and Style.* New York: Gould and Newman, 1836.

Postman, Neil. *Amusing Ourselves to Death.* New York: Viking, 1985.

Powell, Jody. *The Other Side of the Story.* New York: William Morrow and Co., 1984.

———. "A Presidential Ghost Story." *Newsweek* (January 11, 1971), pp. 21–22.

Priestley, Joseph. *A Course of Lectures on Oratory and Criticism,* ed. Vincent Bevilacqua and Richard Murphy. Carbondale: Southern Illinois University Press, 1965.

The Public Orations of Demosthenes. Trans. Arthur Wallace Pickard-Cambridge. Oxford: Clarendon Press, 1912.

Purnell, Sandra E. "Rhetoric/Rape: Communication as Inducement to Assault." *Bulletin of Speech Communication* 16 (1976), pp. 20–21.

Putnam-Jacobi, Mary. *Common Sense Applied to Woman Suffrage* New York: G. P. Putnam's Sons, 1894.

Quintilian. *Institutio Oratoria.* Trans. H. E. Butler. London: William Heinemann, 1921.

Ramus, Peter. *Rhetorica.* Paris, 1567.

Ray, Robert F. "Ghostwriting in Presidential Campaigns." *Central States Speech Journal* 8 (Fall 1956), pp. 8–11.

Raymond, Robert. *The Patriotic Speaker.* New York: A. S. Barnes and Burr, 1864.

Reagan, Ronald. *Public Papers of the President.* Washington, D.C.: Government Printing Office, 1981–1987.

———. *Where's the Rest of Me?* New York: Duell Sloan and Pierce, 1965.

Reed, Thomas B. *Modern Eloquence.* Philadelphia: John D. Morris and Co., 1923.

Reid, Ronald. "The Boyleston Professorship of Rhetoric and Oratory, 1806–1904: A Case Study in Changing Concepts of Rhetoric and Pedagogy." *Quarterly Journal of Speech* 45 (October 1959), pp. 241–57.

Richards, I. A. *Mencius on the Mind.* London: Kegan Paul, Trench, Trubner and Co., 1932.

———. *The Philosophy of Rhetoric.* New York: Oxford University Press, 1936.

Richardson, James D., ed. *A Compilation of the Messages and Papers from the Presidents.* 20 Vols. New York: Bureau of National Literature, Inc., 1927–1987.

Ritter, Ellen M. "Elizabeth Morgan: Pioneer Female Labor Agitator." *Central States Speech Journal* 22 (Winter 1971), pp. 242–51.

Roberts, Steven. "TV May Quicken the Senate's Pulse." *New York Times* (June 8, 1986), p. 5.
Roosevelt, Franklin D. *The Public Papers and Addresses of Franklin D. Roosevelt.* New York: Random House, 1938.
Roosevelt, Mrs. Franklin D. "Speech Training for the Youth." *Quarterly Journal of Speech* 27 (October 1941). pp. 369–71.
Roosevelt, Theodore. *The Works of Theodore Roosevelt.* Memorial Edition. New York: Charles Scribner's Sons, 1923–1926.
Rosenbaum, Ron. "Who Puts the Words in the President's Mouth?" *Esquire* (December 1985), pp. 242–51.
Rosenman, Samuel I. *Working with Roosevelt.* New York: Harper and Brothers, 1952.
Rosenthal, Paul I. "The Concept of the Paramessage in Persuasive Communication." *Quarterly Journal of Speech* 58 (February 1972), pp. 15–30.
Rosenwasser, Marie J. "Rhetoric and the Progress of the Women's Liberation Movement." *Communication Quarterly* 20 (Summer 1972), pp. 45–56.
Rossi, Alice S., ed. *The Feminist Papers: From Adams to de Beauvoir.* New York: Columbia University Press, 1973.
Rossiter, Margaret W. *Women Scientists in America.* Baltimore: Johns Hopkins University Press, 1982.
Rovere, Richard H. "The Minds of Barry Goldwater." *Harper's Magazine* (September 1964), pp. 37–42.
Ruffin, J. N. *Forms of Oratorical Expression and their Delivery.* London: Simpkin, Marshall, Hamilton, Kent and Co., 1920.
Ruthven, K. K. "Feminist Literary Studies." In *Feminist Literary Theory: A Reader,* ed. Mary Eagleton. London: Basil Blackwell, 1986.
Sadker, M. P., and D. M. Sadker. "Sexism in the Classroom of the 80s." *Psychology Today* (March 1985), pp. 54–57.
Safire, William. *Before the Fall.* New York: Belmont Tower Books, 1975.
———. *On Language.* New York: Times Books, 1980.
———. *The New Language of Politics.* New York: Random House, 1968.
———. "Ringing Rhetoric: The Return of Political Oratory." *The New York Times Magazine,* (August 19, 1984), p. 22ff.
Sandford, William Phillips. *English Theories of Public Address, 1530–1828.* Dissertation, Ohio State University, 1929.
Sandys, John Edwin. *A History of Classical Scholarship.* New York: Hafner Publishing, 1964.
Sargent, Epes. *The Standard Speaker Containing Exercises in Prose and Poetry for Declamation.* Philadelphia: Charles Desilver, 1857.
Saxton, Mrs. Scott. *The New Elocution Reader.* Denver, Col.: 1894.
Schlesinger, Arthur M., Jr. *The Coming of the New Deal.* Boston: Houghton Mifflin Co., 1959.
———. *The Crisis of the Old Order, 1919–1933.* Boston: Houghton Mifflin Co., 1957.
———. *The Politics of Upheaval.* Boston: Houghton Mifflin Co., 1960.
Schmidt, Ralph N. "The Message of Olympia Brown—Preacher." *Communication Quarterly* 12 (April 1964), pp. 2–5.
Schram, Martin. "Carter's Faults as Speechmaker Hinder Effort to Lead U.S." *The Washington Post* (December 30, 1977), p. A2.

―――. *The Great American Video Game*. New York: William Morrow and Co., 1987.
Schwartz, Howard. "Senator Smith Speaks on Speaking." *Today's Speech* 15 (1967), pp. 19–22.
Scopes, John T., and James Presley. *Center for the Storm: Memoirs of John T. Scopes*. New York: Holt, Rinehart and Winston, 1967.
Scott, Robert L. "A Synoptic View of Systems of Western Rhetoric." *Quarterly Journal of Speech* 61 (December 1975), pp. 439–47.
Sears, Lorenzo. *The History of Oratory*. Chicago: S. C. Griggs and Co., 1896.
―――. *Wendell Phillips*. New York: Benjamin Blom, 1909.
Sennett, Richard. *The Fall of Public Man*. New York: Alfred Knopf, 1977.
Seymour, Charles, ed. *The Intimate Papers of Colonel House*. Boston: Houghton Mifflin Co., 1926.
Shabad, Goldie, and Kristi Andersen. "Candidate Evaluations by Men and Women." *Public Opinion Quarterly* 43 (Spring 1979), pp. 18–35.
Shelby, A. "The Southern Lady Becomes an Advocate." In *Oratory in the New South*, ed. Waldon W. Braden, Baton Rouge: Louisiana State University Press, 1979.
Sheridan, Thomas. *A Course of Lectures on Elocution* (1762). Menston, England: The Scholar Press, Ltd., 1968.
Sherwood, Robert E. *Roosevelt and Hopkins*. New York: Bantom Books, 1950.
Shrum, Robert. "Engineering the Politics of Love." *New Times* (July 9, 1976), pp. 34–40.
―――. "No Private Smiles." *New Times* (July 11, 1976), p. 23ff.
Sidney, Sir Philip. "The Defense of Poesy." In *English Essays from Sir Philip Sidney to Macauley. Harvard Classics*. New York: P. F. Collier Son, 1937.
Silvestri, Vito N. "Emma Goldman, Enduring Voice of Anarchism." *Today's Speech* 27 (1969), pp. 202–25.
Simons, Herbert. "Requirements, Problems and Strategies: A Theory of Persuasion for Social Movement." *Quarterly Journal of Speech* 56 (February 1970), pp. 2–11.
Smith, Adam. *Lectures on Rhetoric and Belles Lettres*, ed. John M. Lothian. London: Thomas Nelson and Sons Ltd., 1963.
Smith, Craig R. "Contemporary Political Speech Writing," *Southern Speech Communication Journal* 42 (Fall 1976), pp. 52–67.
―――. "Addendum to 'Contemporary Political Speech Writing.'" *Southern Speech Communication Journal* 42 (Winter 1977), pp. 191–94.
Smith, T. W. "The Polls: Gender and Attitudes Toward Violence." *Public Opinion Quarterly* 48 (1984), pp. 384–96.
Smithey, William Royall, ed. *Virginia Oratory*. Charlottesville: Virginia Historical Publications, 1934.
Solomon, Martha. "The Rhetoric of STOP ERA: Fatalistic Reaffirmation." *Southern Speech Communication Journal* 44 (Fall 1978), pp. 42–59.
―――. "'The Total Woman': The Rhetoric of Completion." *Central States Speech Journal* 32 (Summer 1981), pp. 74–84.
―――. "Stopping ERA: A Pyrrhic Victory." *Communication Quarterly* 31 (Spring 1983), pp. 109–17.
Sorensen, Theodore C. *Kennedy*. New York: Harper & Row, 1965.
―――. *The Kennedy Legacy*. New York: New American Library, 1969.
Spacks, Patricia Meyer. *Gossip*. New York: Alfred A. Knopf, 1985.

BIBLIOGRAPHY 289

Sprat, Thomas. *History of the Royal Society.* London: Printed for the Royal Society, 1667.

Stanton, Elizabeth Cady, Susan B. Anthony, and Matilda Joslyn Gage, eds. *History of Woman Suffrage.* New York: Source Book, 1881; rpt. 1970.

Stallworthy, Jon, ed. *The Oxford Book of War Poetry.* New York: Oxford University Press, 1984.

Stein, P. J., and S. Hoffman. "Sports and Male Role Strains." *Journal of Social Issues* 34 (1978), pp. 136–50.

Stelkovis, Walter J. "Ghostwriting: Ancient and Honorable." *Today's Speech* (January 1954), pp. 17–19.

Stern, Edith M. "The Cash-and-no-Credit Business." *The Saturday Review* (October 26, 1940), pp. 11–12.

Stevenson, Adlai E. *The Papers of Adlai E. Stevenson,* ed. Walter Johnson. Boston: Little, Brown and Co., 1977.

"Stevenson's Ghost Writers." *U. S. News and World Report,* (September 26, 1952), pp. 57–59.

Stewart, Lea P., Pamela J. Cooper, and Sheryl A. Friedley. *Communication between the Sexes.* Scottsdale, Ariz.: Gorsuch Scarisbrick, 1986.

Stockman, David. *The Triumph of Politics.* New York: Harper & Row, 1986.

Strother, David B. *Modern British Eloquence.* New York: Funk and Wagnalls, 1969.

Sumner, Charles. *The Works of Charles Sumner.* Boston: Lee and Shepard, 1874.

Swacker, Marjorie. "The Sex of the Speaker as a Sociolinguistic Variable." In *Language and Sex,* eds. Barrie Thorne and Nancy Henley. Rowley, Mass.: Newbury House, 1975, pp. 76–83.

Szasz, Thomas. *The Manufacture of Madness.* New York: Harper & Row, 1970.

Tacitus. *Complete Works of Tacitus.* Trans. Alfred John Church, and William Jackson Brodribb. New York: The Modern Library, 1942.

———. *Dialogus De Oratoribus,* ed. Charles Edwin Bennett. Boston: Ginn and Co., 1894.

Tarver, Jerry. *Professional Speech Writing.* Richmond, Va.: Speech Writing Institute, 1982.

Taylor, Allen, ed. *What Eisenhower Thinks.* New York: Thomas Y. Crowell Co., 1953.

Taylor, Warren. *Tudor Figures of Rhetoric.* Whitewater, Wisc.: The Language Press, 1972.

Thompson, Wayne N. "Barbara Jordan's Keynote Address: Fulfilling Dual and Conflicting Purposes." *Central States Speech Journal* 30 (Fall 1979), pp. 272–77.

———. "Barbara Jordan's Keynote Address: The Juxtaposition of Contradictory Values." *Southern Speech Communication Journal* 44 (Spring 1979), pp. 223–32.

Thonssen, Lester, and A. Craig Baird. *Speech Criticism: The Development of Standards for Rhetorical Appraisal.* New York: Ronald Press, 1948.

Thorpe, Clarence DeWitt. *The Aesthetic Theory of Thomas Hobbes.* Ann Arbor: The University of Michigan Press, 1940.

Tolchin, Martin, and Susan. *Clout: Womanpower and Politics.* New York: Coward, McCann and Geoghepan, Inc., 1973.

"The Trouble with Ghosts." *Time* (December 5, 1949), p. 25.

Treichler, Paula A. and Cheris Kramarae. "Women's Talk in the Ivory Towers." *Communication Quarterly* 31 (Spring 1983), pp. 118–32.
Trent, Judith S. "Political Communication and Women: A Course Proposal." *Communication Education* 30 (1981), pp. 162–71.
Truman, Harry S. *Public Papers of the President.* Washington, D.C.: Government Printing Office, 1947–1953.
———. *Years of Trial and Hope.* Garden City, N.Y.: Doubleday, 1956.
Turner, Kathleen. *Lyndon Johnson's Dual War.* Chicago: University of Chicago Press, 1985.
Tuve, Rosemond. *Elizabethan and Metaphysical Imagery.* Chicago: University of Chicago Press, 1947.
Twitchell, D. Y. "Susan B. Anthony." In *A History and Criticism of American Public Address,* ed. Marie K. Hockmuth, Vol. 3, New York: Longmans, Green, 1955.
Valenstein, E. S. "The Practice of Psychosurgery: A Survey of the Literature (1971–1976)." In *Psychosurgery.* Washington, D.C.: Government Printing Office, 1977.
Valenti, Jack. *Speak Up with Confidence.* New York: William Morrow and Co., 1982.
Vance, Eugene. "Roland and the Poetics of Memory." In *Textual Strategies,* ed. Josue V. Harari. Ithaca, N.Y.: Cornell University Press, 1979, pp. 374–403.
Vandenberg, Authur. *The Private Papers of Senator Vandenberg.* Cambridge, Mass.: The Riverside Press, 1952.
Van Over, Raymond, ed. *Sun Songs: Creation Myths from Around the World.* New York: New America Library, 1980.
Vaux, A. "Variations in Social Support Associated with Gender, Ethnicity, and Age." *Journal of Social Issues* 41 (1985), pp. 89–110.
Vickers, Brian, ed. *Rhetoric Revalued.* Binghamton, N.Y.: Center for Medieval and Early Renaissance Studies, 1982.
Wagner, Gerard A. "Sojourner Truth: God's Appointed Apostle of Reform." *Southern Speech Communication Journal* 28 (Winter 1962), pp. 123–30.
Wallace, Karl R. "The Substance of Rhetoric: Good Reasons." *Quarterly Journal of Speech* XLIX (October 1963), pp. 239–49.
Wamboldt, Helen Jane. "Speech Teacher to the First Lady of the World." *Communication Quarterly* 12 (November 1964), pp. 5–6.
Ward, John. *Systems of Oratory.* London: J. P. Ward, 1759.
Ward, Samuel Ringgold. *Autobiography of a Fugitive Negro.* New York: Arno Press, 1968.
Warner, Marina. *Monuments and Maidens: The Allegory of the Female Form.* New York: Atheneum, 1985.
Washington, George. *The Writings of George Washington.* Washington, D.C.: Government Printing Office, n.d.
Watson, Burton. *Early Chinese Literature.* New York: Columbia University Press, 1962.
Weaver, Judith L. "Edith Bolling Wilson as First Lady: A Study in the Power of Personality, 1919–1920." *Presidential Studies Quarterly* 15 (Winter 1985), pp. 51–76.
Weaver, Richard M. *The Ethics of Rhetoric.* South Bend, Ind.: Regnery/Gateway Inc., 1953.

Weber, Max. *From Max Weber*, eds. H. H. Gerth and C. W. Mills. New York: Oxford University Press, 1958.

Webster, Daniel. *The Writings and Speeches of Daniel Webster*. Boston: Little, Brown and Co., 1903.

Wells, John, ed., *A Crossroads of Freedom*. New Haven, Conn.: Yale University Press, 1956.

Werner, Emmy E., and Louise M. Bachtold. "Personality Characteristics of Women in American Politics." In *Women in Politics*, ed. Jane Jacquette. New York: John Wiley and Sons, 1974, pp. 79–83.

Wessley, Stephen E. "The Guglielmites: Salvation Through Women." In *Medieval Women*, ed. Derek Baker. Oxford: Basil Blackwell, 1978.

Whalen, Ardyce. "The Presentation of Image in Ella T. Grasso's Campaign." *Central States Speech Journal* 27 (Fall 1976), pp. 207–11.

Whately, Richard. *Elements of Rhetoric*. New York: Harper and Brothers, 1893.

Widgery, Robin Noel. "Sex of Receiver and Physical Attractiveness of Source as Determinants of Initial Credibility Perception." *Western Journal of Speech Communication* 38 (Winter 1974), pp. 13–17.

White, James Boyd. *When Words Lose Their Meaning*. Chicago: University of Chicago Press, 1984.

Whitney, Henry C. *Life on the Circuit with Lincoln*. Boston: Estes and Lauriat, 1892.

"Who's Writing LBJ's Speeches?" *U. S. News and World Report* (June 28, 1965), p. 57.

Wiley, Earl W. "Lincoln the Speaker." *Quarterly Journal of Speech* 20 (February 1934), pp. 1–15.

Will, George F. *Statecraft as Soulcraft*. New York: Simon and Schuster, 1983.

Wills, Garry. *Reagan's America: Innocents At Home*. Garden City, N.Y.: Doubleday, 1987.

Wilson's Arte of Rhetorique (1560), ed. G. H. Mair. Oxford: Clarendon Press, 1909.

Wilson, Woodrow. *Constitutional Government in the United States*. New York: Columbia University Press, 1961 (c. 1908).

———. *A Crossroads of Freedom: The 1912 Campaign Speeches of Woodrow Wilson*, ed. John Wells. New Haven, Conn.: Yale University Press, 1956.

———. *Life and Letters*. Garden City, N.Y.: Doubleday, Doran and Co., 1927–1939.

———. *The New Freedom*. New York: Doubleday, Page and Co., 1918.

———. *The Priceless Gift: The Love Letters of Woodrow Wilson and Ellen Axson Wilson*, ed. Eleanor Wilson McAdoo. New York: McGraw-Hill Book Co., 1962.

———. *The Papers of Woodrow Wilson*, ed. Arthur Link. Princeton, N.J.: Princeton University Press, 1963.

———. *The Public Papers of Woodrow Wilson*. Authorized ed. New York and London: Harper and Brothers, 1925 (c. 1927).

———. *Selected Literary and Political Papers and Addresses of Woodrow Wilson*. New York: Grosset and Dunlap, 1921.

Winans, James Albert. *Public Speaking*. New York: The Century Co., 1917.

Windes, Russel, Jr. "Adlai E. Stevenson's Speech Staff in the 1956 Campaign." *Quarterly Journal of Speech* 46 (1960), pp. 32–43.

Winter, Irvah Lester. *Public Speaking*. New York: The Macmillan Co., 1916.

The World's Most Famous Court Trial: State of Tennessee v. John Thomas Scopes. Cincinnati, Ohio: National Book Co., 1925.

Wood, Julia T., and Charles Conrad. "Paradox in the Experiences of Professional Women." *Western Journal of Speech Communication* 47 (Fall 1983), pp. 305–22.

Woolbert, Charles Henry. *The Fundamentals of Speech.* New York: Harper and Brothers, 1920.

Wrage, Ernest J., and Barnet Baskerville, eds. *Contemporary Forum: American Speeches on Twentieth-Century Issues.* New York: Harper & Row, 1962.

Wright, Arnold, ed. *Great Orations.* London: Hutchinson and Co., 1903.

Yates, Frances. *The Art of Memory.* Chicago: The University of Chicago Press, 1966.

Yoakam, Doris G. "Pioneer Women Orators of America." *Quarterly Journal of Speech* 23 (April 1937), pp. 251–59.

———. "Women's Introduction to the American Platform." In *A History and Criticism of American Public Address,* ed. William Norwood Brigance, Vol. I, New York: McGraw-Hill, 1943, pp. 153–92.

Zacharis, John C. "Emmeline Pankhurst: An English Suffragette Influences America." *Communication Monographs* 38 (1971), pp. 198–206.

Zall, P. M., ed. *Abe Lincoln Laughing.* Berkeley: University of California Press, 1982.

Index

Aaron, 205
Abel, 29
Abzug, Bella, 88
Acceptance speech, 27
Ad Herrenium, 48
Adam, 71–73
Adams, Henry, 47
Adams, John Quincy, 54, 78, 92
Addison, Joseph, 83
Advertising, 7, 10, 13, 14, 22, 29, 48, 57, 62, 251
Aeneas, 45
Agnew, Spiro, 113, 219, 235, 252–53
Alden, John, 220
Alexander the Great, 205
Anderson, Paul Y., 32
Anecdote, 11, 150–54, 212, 213
Anthony, Susan B., 110–11
Antiphon, 205
Antitheses. See Figures of speech
Apostrophe. See Figures of speech
Arafat, Yasser, 219
Archai, 95, 99
Archias, Licinus A., 16, 25
Arete, 240
Aristotle, 18, 20, 21, 24, 48, 68, 71, 73, 240, 245
Arlington Cemetery, 44
Army-McCarthy hearings, 63, 239
Arnold, Matthew, 237

Arrangement. See Canons of rhetoric
Asquith, Herbert, 100
Atkinson, Max, 79
Attic orators, 20, 25, 55
Augustine, 25, 46
Austen, Jane, 18
Autobiographical, self-disclosive discourse, 63

Bacon, Francis, 56
Bailey, F. Lee, 205
Bailey, Joseph, 138
Baker, Howard, 7
Bakshian, Aram, 213
Barlow, Francis C., 148
Barlow, Mrs. Francis C., 149
Beauregard, General Pierre, 138
Beecher, Henry Ward, 111
Beecher, Lyman, 46
Begin, Menachim, 50, 59, 61, 67, 217
Begum Speech, 53
Bella, James Warner, 135
Benavidez, Roy, 155–56
Benjamin, Judah P., 138
Bible, 20, 24, 28, 29
Biden, Joseph, 221–22, 252
Bierce, Ambrose, 67
Birth of a Nation, 135–36
Blair, Hugh, 53, 55, 78

Blakely, Ed, 85
Blouet, Paul, 254
Bolingbroke, Henry St John, 20
Borah, William, 106–107
Bormann, Ernest, 211, 216, 229–30
Boston Massacre address, 15
Bow, Clara, 135
Bradlee, Benjamin, 176–77
Bradley, Tom, 7
Brezhnev, Leonid, 131, 133
Brzezinski, Zbignew, 235
Broder, David, 183, 249–50, 252, 254
Brougham, Henry, 20
Brutus, 29
Bryan, William Jennings, 28, 31–32, 52,
    53, 207, 243
Buchanan, Patrick, 225, 234
Buddha, 39–40
Bunker Hill oration, 24
Burke, Edmund, 20, 24, 29, 237, 246
Burke, Kenneth, xi, 50, 241
Burke, Yvonne Braithewaite, 85
Burns, James MacGregor, 201
Burr, Aaron, 221
Bush, George, 23
Bush/Ferraro debate, 112

Caesar, Julius, 28, 29
Cain, 29
Calhoun, John, ix, 20
Calley, Lieutenant John, 155
Camp David Accords, 61
Campaign discourse, 49
Campbell, George, 48
Campbell, Karlyn Kohrs, 76
Cannon, Lou, 179, 228, 234
Canons of rhetoric
    arrangement, 21
    delivery, 3, 21, 25–26, 30, 52–54,
        207, 210, 245
    dispositio, 204, 245
    elocutio, 204
    inventio, 204
    memory, 18, 21–25, 43–44, 60–67,
        157, 166
    style, 245
Capella, Martianus, 48
Carnegie Clubs, 55
Carnegie, Dale, 55
Carrol, Wallace, 176
Carter, Jimmy, x, 6, 27, 51, 61, 95, 141,
    144–46, 157, 160, 164, 171, 173–
    74, 183, 184–85, 196, 204, 210–13,
    217, 241, 244

Carter's use of narrative, 138–39
Carter Mondale, 27
Cary, Mary, 74
Casey, William, 230
Casserly, John, 225
Castiglione, Baldassare, 71
Castro, Fidel, 219
Cataline, vii
Cather, Willa, 18
Catt, Carrie Chapman, 110–11
CBS, 7, 52, 60
Chamberlain, Neville, 101–103
Channing, Edward, 78
Chanson de Geste, 147
Chatham, Earl of (William Pitt), 19–20
Chaucer, 18
Chautauqua circuit, 36–37
Checkers Speech, 44, 62, 207
Chisholm, Shirley, 7
Churchill, Winston, ix–x, 5, 20, 29, 50,
    90, 177, 204, 217, 227, 239, 253
Cicero, vii, x, 5, 16–22, 24, 25, 45–47,
    51, 55, 204
Civil Rights Act, 58, 59, 138
Civil Rights Movement, 57
Civil War, 11, 17, 56
Claudius, 205
Clay, Henry, 5, 20, 209
Cleburn, General Pat, 138
Cleveland, Grover, 45
Coates, Wilmer/Wilma, 174–75
Coherence, 22, 153
Cohn, Roy, 64–66
"On Conciliation", 44, 49–50, 65
Confucius, 39
Connally, John, 157
Connor, Bull, 59, 60
Constitution, 24, 54
Contest speaking, 15
Contras, 30, 200
Conventions, 7, 9, 27, 61, 160, 168, 207,
    212
Conversation, 10, 45, 50, 53, 55–57,
    63–65, 66, 162, 165–200
Cooke, Cardinal Terrence, 191
Coolidge, Calvin, 53
Cooper, Gary, 135, 139
Corax, 47, 51
Corcoran, Thomas, 209
Corey, Herbert, 227
Cormier, Frank, 174, 183
Critias, 24
Cronkite, Walter, 158
Cuban Missile Crisis, 44
Cuomo, Mario, vii, ix

Dante, 18, 57
Darrow, Clarence, 32–42
Dartmouth College, 28
Darwin, Charles, 68
Davies, Eleanor, 74
De Oratore, 21, 55
De augmentia, 56
Deaver, Michael, 219
Debate, 7, 9, 10, 15, 22, 23, 50, 51, 239
Declaration of Independence, 24, 68
DeForest, Lee, 42
Degas, Edgar, 237
DeGaul, Charles, 90, 184
Delivery. *See* Canons of rhetoric
Demagoguery, 47
Democrats for Nixon, 195
Demosthenes, x, 3, 14, 19, 20, 24, 25, 29, 66, 204
Denton, Jeremiah, 121, 162
Descartes, Rene, 78, 80, 152, 245
Dewey, Thomas, 179
Dickens, Charles, ix
Dispositio. See Canons of rhetoric
Disraeli, Benjamin, ix
Dolan, Anthony, 232–33
Dole, Robert, 7
Dostoevsky, Feodor, 18
Douglass, Frederick, ix, 11, 210
Dulles, John Foster, 234
Dramatizing, 14, 60
Ducking stool, 67
Dunkings, 67

Eastwood, Clint, 134
Edmund Pettus Bridge, the, 59
Effeminate style, 67–89
Eisenhower, Dwight D., 10, 14, 100, 185, 188, 206–10, 218, 239
Eisenhower, Mrs. Dwight "Mamie", 185
Electricity, 45, 51–53, 55
Eliot, Charles W., 104
Elizabeth I, 76–77
Elks Club, 206
Elliott, Ben, 228
Elocutio, *See* Canons
Eloquence, old, 45–51
Eloquence, new, 51–66
Emerson, Ralph Waldo, 51, 52, 237
Emotions, 46
Enthymeme, 18, 217
Eunoia, 240
Epideictic rhetoric, 84, 118–64
Ethos, 65, 240
Euripides, 25, 71

Eve, 73, 155, 168, 207
Ewald, William, 210, 227
Example. *See* Figures of speech
Extempore, 17

Fairlie, Henry, 194
Fala, 44, 62
Fallows, James, 213, 226
Falstaff, 20
Farewells, 212
Federalist Papers, 48, 236
Fenelon, Abbe François de Salignac de La Mothe, 56, 68
Ferraro, Geraldine, 86–88, 112
Fiery oratory, 48, 56
Figures of diction, 80
Figures of speech, 5, 30, 48, 56, 61, 153, 162, 212
  antithesis, 5
  apostrophe, 30
  example, 5–10, 16, 21, 24, 30, 48, 52–53, 56, 153, 205, 207–8
  hyperbole, 14, 164
  interrogation, 30–31
  litotes, 30
  metaphor, 45–47
  paralipsis, 30
  synecdoche, 91–117
Figures of thought, 80
Fineman, Howard, 234
Fire metaphor, 45–47, 54
Fireside chat, 14, 43, 51, 55–56, 167
Fisher, Fred, 63–65
Fishwives. *See* Labels used against female speakers
Flaxman, John, 57
Flemming, Sir John, 42
Ford, Gerald, 6, 7, 61, 143–44, 146, 220, 225, 244
Ford/Carter debate, 112
Forman, George, 161
Foster, Stephens, 110
Fourth of July address, 15, 16
Frost, Robert, 235
Frye, Northrop, 19
Fuller, Margaret, 73, 76

Gadhafi, Moammar, 219
Gag, 67
Galbraith, John Kenneth, 209
Galileo, 248

Gandhi, ix, 109, 174
Gandy, Evelyn, 85
Garrison, William Lloyd, 110
Genesis, 41
Genius, 3
Genre, 33, 36
George Washington University's Media Analysis Project, 9
Gergen, David, 219
Gettysburg Address, 4, 24, 44, 93–94, 166, 231
Gilman, Charlotte Perkins, 72
Gipp, George, 161
Gipper, 161
Gladstone, William, ix
Glenn, John, 236
Goldwater, Barry, 10, 14, 113, 223
Gorbachev, Mikhail, 196, 219
Gordon, John Brown, 148–50
Gossip's bridle, 67
Gouvian, Saint-Cyr, Marshal, 221
Graduate Record Exam, 19
Grant, General Ulysses S., 196
Grayson, Mel, 219
Great Society, 50
Greco-Roman rhetoric, 49, 240
Greek rhetoric, 5, 11, 16, 17, 19–21, 47, 48
Greeley, Horace, iii
Greenfield, Meg, 157
Greves, Frank, 114
Grimke sisters, ix
Guazzo, Steven, 83
Guglielma of Milan, 74
Guttenberg, 27

Haiman, Franklyn, 234
Hale & Dorr, 64, 165, 167
Hale, Clara, 124–26, 133, 164
Halifax, Viscount (Edward Frederick Lindley Wood), 101
Hamilton, Alexander, 28, 51, 204–6
Hamilton, John, 28
Hamlet, 20
Hannibal, 28
Harding, Warren G., 95, 99, 210–12
Harlow, Bryce, 226
Harper, Robert Goodloe, 49
Harpies. See Labels used against female speakers
Harridans. See Labels used against female speakers
Harrison, William Henry, 208

Hart, Roderick, xi, 169, 221
Hart, Gary, viii–ix, 248–49
Hartman, Robert, 220
Harvard University, 17, 25, 63
Hawthorne, Nathaniel, 18
Hayne, Robert Young, 96
Hechler, Ken, 175
Henn, Lisa Zanetta, 243
Henry V, 20
Henry VIII, 194
Henry, Patrick, 90
Heretics. See Labels
Hippocrates, 72
Hitler, Adolf, 241
Hollander, Jacob, 212
Holmes, Oliver Wendell, 46
Holy Writ, 28
Homer, 25
Hoover, Herbert, 53, 95, 108
Hope, Bob, 156
Hoplite franchise, 47
Hortensia, 77
House of Burgesses, 239
House of Commons, 4
House of Representatives, 4, 7, 14, 24, 28–30, 54, 60, 61, 63, 67, 161–62, 164, 213
Howe, Julia Ward, 45
Howe, Louis, 204, 209
Hughes, Emmet John, 209, 218, 227–28, 232–33
Hughes, Langston, 101, 108
Hume, David, 55
Humphrey, Hubert, 7, 9, 173–4, 212, 222, 224–25, 229, 239–40
Humphreys, David, 223
Hutchinson, Anne, 74
Hyland, John F., 210
Hyperbole. See Figures of speech

Ickes, Harold, 210, 216
Inaugural address, 44, 61, 156, 165–67, 201, 204, 208–12
Inclinations, 46
Institutes of Oratory, 17
Intensity, 56
Interrogation. See Figures of speech
Intimacy, 61, 66
Inventio. See Canons of rhetoric
Isocrates, 5, 16, 19, 20

Jackson, Andrew, 16, 206
Jackson, Graham Washington, 133

Jackson, Jesse, 90, 114, 179–80
Jackson's Nullification Proclamation, 206
James, John W., 186
James, William, 55
Jay, John, 205
Jebb, R. C., 205
Jefferson, Thomas, 16, 29, 48, 61, 92,
   95, 97, 103–4, 108, 157, 212, 231–
   32, 234, 238–39, 246
Jefferson-Jackson day, 16
Johnson, David, 125
Johnson, Haynes, 146
Johnson, Lyndon B., 44, 50, 60, 115,
   139, 141–45, 153–62, 164, 173,
   223–24, 182–86, 189, 191, 194, 208
Johnson's use of narratives, 137–38
Johnson, Mrs. Lyndon B. "Lady Bird",
   186
Jonson, Ben, 71
Jordan, 51, 204
Jordan, Barbara, 88, 114, 239
Jordan, Hamilton, 51, 204
Joshua, 36
Judgment, 5, 21, 29, 50, 59, 162
Judgment at Nuremberg, 59
Juvenal, 77

Kahler, Erlich, 62
Kalb, Marvin, 86
Kant, Immanuel, 240
Kaye, Michael, 85
Kelly, Abby, 71
Kennedy, Edward, 61, 171, 226, 228,
   232–33, 236
Kennedy, George, 26
Kennedy, John F., ix, 7, 29, 43, 44, 50,
   59, 92, 95–97, 100, 102–3, 115–16,
   157, 176–78, 183–84, 188, 190–94,
   208, 223, 237, 229, 232–33, 235,
   239
Kennedy, John John, 44
Kennedy, Mrs. John F. "Jackie", 184
Kennedy, Robert, 145, 190, 222–24
Kennedy-Nixon campaign, 10, 50
Kerr, Walter, 253
Kerry, John, 239
Keynote address, 7
Khrushchev, Nikita, 217
King, Martin Luther, 90–91, 145, 190,
   232
Kinnock, Neil, 221–22
Kirkpatrick, Jeane, 87
Koch, Adrienne, 216

Labels used against female speakers
   fishwives, 68
   harpies, 68
   harridans, 68
   heresiarchs, 75
   heretics, 70, 73–75
   hysterics, 70, 72–73
   magpie, 68
   nag, 67–68
   raucous, 68
   scold, 67–68
   shrew, 68
   termagant, 68
   virago, 68
   whore, 69–71
   witch, 69–70, 75–76
Laela, 77
Lafayette, Marie Joseph, 209
Landon, Alf, 195
Lansing, Robert, 209
Laskey, Eliza, 71
Lectures on Rhetoric and Belles Lettres,
   53
LeHand, Missy, 216
Lincoln, Abraham, ix, 11, 20, 24, 29, 43,
   44, 46, 56, 61, 93–95, 108, 170–72,
   204, 208–9, 213, 231, 246
Lincoln Memorial, 44
Lindsay, John, 226
Lippmann, Walter, 206
Litotes. See Figures of speech
Livingston, Edward, 206
Lodge, Henry Cabot, 99
Logos, 240–41
Longworth, Alice Roosevelt, 179
Lord Belhaven, 28
Lubin, Dr. Isadore, 211
Lucian, 19
Lushwell, Rodney Ranquist, iii
Lysias, 20, 24, 26, 205

MacArthur, General Douglas, 91
Macaulay, Thomas Babington, 20, 54
MacNeil-Lehrer News Hour, 253
Madison Avenue, 29
Madison, James, 48, 104, 205
Magee, John Gillespie, 133
Magna Carta, 17
Magpies. See Labels used against female
   speakers
Mahdi, 55
Male discourse, 123
Mantra, 109

Marconi, Guglielmo, 42
Marmontel, François, 237
Marshall, George, 239, 242, 246
Mason, George, 92
Mason, John, 79
Matthews, Christopher, 123
May, Ernest, 205
McAuliffe, Christa, 128
McCann, Kevin, 226
McCarthy, Eugene, 7, 173
McCarthy, Joseph, 7, 9, 29, 63–66
McDonald, David, 177
McFarlane, Robert, 234
McGovern, George, 7, 116, 212
McKay, Douglas, 210
McLuhan, Marshal, 81
Medieval period, 48
Melville, 18
Memorable phrase, 90–117
Memorable picture, 90–117
Memory. See Canons of rhetoric
Menander, 25
Mencken, H. L., 32, 211
Michelson, Charles, 209
Mikulski, Barbara, 89
Mill, John Stuart, 73
Miller, Henry, 216
Milton, 5, 25
Mitchell, Dr. S. Wier, 72
Moley, Raymond, 204
Mondale, Walter, 10, 22, 27, 61, 190
Mondale-Reagan campaign, 10
Monroe Doctrine, 104–6
Monroe, James, 105–7
Moos, Malcolm, 209
Morrow, Lance, ix
Moses, 94, 205, 230
Motives, 46
Moyers, Bill, 208, 253
Mudd, Roger, xi, 14, 235–36
Munch, Edvard, 237
Munich Pact, 101
Murrow, Edward, R., 28, 29
Muskie, Edmund, 152, 226
My Lai Massacre, 155

Nag. See Labels used against female
     speakers
Narcissism, 156
Narrative, 13, 22, 62, 153, 156, 159
National Endowment for the Humani-
     ties, 18
National Journal, 213

Nemesis, 45
Nero, 205
New England's First Fruits, 17
New York Times, 6, 251
Newman, Edwin, 23
Newman, John Henry, 250
News, 5–7, 9, 10, 13, 14, 26, 43, 51, 57,
     60, 61, 65, 207, 214
Newspapers, 6, 10, 26, 29, 43, 209
Nguyen, Jean, 123–24, 161, 163
Nielsen, 6
Nixon, Pat, 63
Nixon, Richard M., 10, 50, 51, 62, 63,
     96, 102–3, 113, 116, 160–62, 164,
     171, 175–79, 184, 186–88, 191,
     198, 200, 207, 208, 212, 217, 224–
     25, 230, 241
     Nixon's use of narrative, 137
Noonan, Peggy, 129, 152, 162, 167, 209,
     228, 233–34, 242
North, Oliver, 29, 62, 230

O'Connor, John J., 253
O'Neill, Thomas "Tip", 123–24
Olympus, 56
Omaha Beach, 162
Ong, Walter, 54
Orality, 21
Orator, 3–5, 15–17, 21, 24, 25, 28, 30,
     46, 48, 52, 55
Orators and Oratory, 55
Oratory, 4–6, 11, 17, 19, 25, 29, 30, 43,
     48, 53–56
Ortega y Gasset, 62
Osborne, John, 228

Packard, Mrs. E. P. W., 74
Painting of thought, 56
Paine, Thomas, 248
Paine-Weber, 248
Paralipsis. See Figures of speech
Parker, Theodore, 94
Parliament, 28
Pascal, Blaise, 56, 152
Passion, 46–47, 209
Pathos, 240–41
Pericles, 5, 24, 43, 146
Pershing, "Black Jack" John J., 209
Petticoat Junction, 10
Peyton Place, 10, 14
Phaedrus, 26, 205
Philip of Macedon, 25

Phillips, Wendell, 22, 110
Phronesis, 240
Picture, rhetoric as, 14, 43–44, 53, 56, 58, 154–55, 165
Pillory, 67
Pitt, William, 19, 54
Plato, 18, 20, 26, 205
Plutarch, 3
Poetry, 5, 17, 19–24, 28
Pointe du Hoc, 162–64, 228, 242–43
Polemic, 47, 160
Political speechmaking, 212
Pond, James Burton, 6
Pope Boniface VIII, 74
Pope John Paul II, 27, 115, 205
Pope Julius II, 205
Pope Pius XII, 141
Premises, grounding, 98–100
Presidential candidates, 9, 206, 207, 212
Preston, William, 209
Price, Raymond, 225
Prometheus, 45
Psychological Operations in Guerrilla Warfare, 30
Public address, 6, 15, 45, 55, 56
Publius, 48

Quaker preachers, 75
Quintilian, 17, 18, 20, 22, 25, 30, 48, 51

Radio speeches, 7, 9, 10, 14, 26, 45, 53, 55, 61, 157
Rapin, Rene, 17–18
Raucous women. *See* Labels used against female speakers
Reagan, Nancy, 44, 62, 188
Reagan, Ronald, ix, 5, 6, 10, 13, 14, 22, 27, 29, 50–52, 57, 60–62, 88–89, 109, 112–13, 118–64, 165–200, 208, 218, 220, 228, 236, 241–54
Reagan's self-disclosure, 182–200
Reagan's stylistic consistency, 175–82
Reagan-Mondale debate, 22, 112
Reformation, 17
Renaissance, 20
Reporters, 6, 9, 30, 60, 112, 160, 206–7, 210, 211, 252–53
Rhetoric, of battle, 45, 47
Rhetoric, of fire, 47
Rhetorica ad Herennium, 22
Rice, Donna, viii–ix
Richards, I. A., 50

Rockne, Knute, 165
Roman rhetoric, 5, 11, 16, 19, 21, 30, 48, 49, 53–54, 205, 208
Roman and Medieval rhetorical training, 48
Roman figures of speech, 30
Roman model, 19
Roman oratory, 5
Romney, George, 113
Roosevelt, Franklin Delano, ix–x, 44, 50, 55, 62, 90, 95, 102–3, 107–8, 167–70, 183, 185, 191–92, 195, 201–4, 208, 210, 246
Roosevelt, Theodore, vii, 96, 98–99
Roseberg, Earl of (Archibald Philip Primrose), 7
Rosenman, Samuel, 201, 204, 209
Rovere, Richard, 223
Royal Society, 80

Sadat, Anwar, 61, 217
Safire, William, 14, 225, 230–31
Salcido, Jose, 140–41
Salinger, Pierre, 184
Satyrus, 3
Schlesinger, Arthur Jr., 96
Schroeder, Patricia, 69
Schwellenbach, Lewis B., 211
Scold. *See* Labels used against female speakers
Scopes trial, 31–42
Scopes, John Thomas, 32
Self-disclosive rhetoric, 44, 61–65
Self-effacing rhetoric, 160, 164
Self-indulgent rhetoric, 160
Self-revelation, 165–200
Senate, 14, 29, 210
Seneca, 205
Sennett, Richard, 62
Sentia, Maesia, 69
Sevareid, Eric, 206
Seward, William, 209
Shakespeare, William, 20, 29, 157
Shales, Tom, 253
Shelley, Norman, 227
Sheridan, Thomas Brinsley, 53
Shorey, Paul, 19, 20
Shrews. *See* Labels used against female speakers
Shrum, Robert, 226–27, 232–33
Simonides, 21, 22
Sir Gilbert, 53
Skutnik, Leonard, 121–25

Slogan, 29, 168
Slush fund, 63
Smitherman, Joseph, 59
Song of Roland, 147
Sophocles, 25
Sorensen, Theodore, 102, 208, 213, 223–24, 229, 233–34
Speechwriter, 14, 27, 154, 201, 204, 205, 208, 210, 212, 213
Spencer, Herbert, 53
Spot, 4, 7, 10, 14, 57
Sprat, Thomas, 80
Squier, Robert, 85, 173
St. Clair, Jim, 63, 64
Stahl, Lesley, 60
Stanton, Elizabeth Cady, ix, 110
State of the Union address, 153, 165–66, 168, 190, 212
Steiner, George, 45
Stevenson, Adlai, 7, 206–8
Stockman, David, 218
Stoics, 20
Stone, Lucy, 69
Storytelling, 165
Style, 3, 17, 19–21, 24, 45, 46, 53–56, 67, 157, 160, 205, 211
Sumner, Charles, 5, 6, 56
Symbols, 22, 44
System of Oratory, 25

Tacitus, ix, 45
Talon, Omer, 80
Tanya, 116
Tayacan, 30
Television, 6, 9, 10, 13–14, 20, 26–27, 29, 43–45, 50, 53, 55, 57, 59–60, 62–64, 154, 167, 207
Terence, 25
Termagants, 68
Text, 9, 26, 27, 65, 204, 208, 210, 211
Thatcher, Margaret, 91
The Modern Language Association, 18
Theuth, 26
Thucydides, 5, 24, 157
Tisias, 47, 51
Tomlinson, Kenneth Y., 156
Tone, 28, 46, 54, 56, 65, 160, 164
Tongues of fire, 45
Tower Commission Report, 198–99, 245
Trapuel, Anne, 74
Treptow, Martin, 126, 154–55
Trivium, 16
Trojan, 45

Trujillo, Sgt. Stephen, 121–23, 164
Truman, Harry S., 100, 172–75, 181–82, 184–85
Truth, 29, 46, 65, 154, 156, 206
Tully, Grace, 216
Turnus, 45
Twain, Mark, 244

Ussher, Bishop James, 37

Valenti, Jack, 183
Valerius Maximus, 69
Vandenberg, Arthur, 107
Verbal distillation, 66
Veto messages, 212
Vietnam war rhetoric, 11, 15, 60, 155–67
Viragos. *See* Labels used against female speakers
Virgil, 19, 25
Visual dramatization, 13, 27, 44, 56, 59–61, 66, 167, 168
Volstead Act, 109
Voltaire, 231
Voting Rights Act, 60

Wallace, George, 60, 61
Ward, John, 25
Washington, George, 4, 9, 24, 29, 61, 94, 99, 104–7, 160, 200, 205, 206, 209, 223, 249
Washington's farewell address, 24, 107
Webster, Daniel, ix, 5, 20, 24, 28, 47, 53–55, 94, 96, 231, 233, 208
Weinraub, Bernard, 235
Welch, Joseph, 63–66, 239
Wells, H. G., 99–100
White, John, 221
Whiting, John, 75
Whitman, Walt, 18, 216
Whores. *See* Labels used against female speakers
Wigglesworth, Michael, 25
Wilson, John, 73
Wilson, Woodrow, 32, 42, 46, 53, 95, 98, 100–107, 116, 208, 212, 232, 246
Wilson's "neutrality of thought" proclamation, 208

Winans, James, 54
Winter, William, 85
Winthrop, Jonathon, 72
Women's style, 54, 59, 67–89
Wooten, James, 173

Writing, 16, 19, 22, 23, 26, 55, 156, 201,
    205, 208, 210, 212, 213

Zanatta, Peter Robert, 243

Printed in the United States
120247LV00001B/142-147/A

9 780195 063172